THE FALL OF THE ANCIENT MAYA

DAVID WEBSTER

THE FALL OF THE ANCIENT MAYA

Solving the Mystery of the Maya Collapse

With 84 illustrations

To my wife Susan Toby Evans, who first suggested that I do this book, and who offered advice and encouragement throughout the writing of it.

First published in hardcover in the United States of America in 2002 by Thames & Hudson Inc., 500 Fifth Avenue, New York, New York 10110

thamesandhudsonusa.com

Library of Congress Catalog Card Number 2001094765
ISBN 0-500-05113-5

Printed and bound in Slovenia by Mladinska Knjiga Tiskarna

CONTENTS

PROLOGUE

"SAY, WHAT HAPPENED TO ALL THOSE MAYA, ANYWAY?" No words are more calculated to strike dismay in the hearts of Maya archaeologists. I hear them frequently, usually just after I settle down in my airplane seat en route to Mexico, Honduras, or Guatemala. Soon the usual pleasantries are exchanged with my fellow passengers, and inevitably someone asks me where I am going and why. During my incautious younger years I innocently responded that I was heading off to excavate at some ancient Maya center. Then, with utter predictability, came the dreaded question. Nowadays, older and wiser, I usually mutter something vague about "business" and then bury my nose in the airline magazine.

Why this reaction, especially from someone who has spent a professional lifetime trying to reconstruct what the ancient Maya were like and what ultimately happened to them? Certainly the question itself is a sensible one, and the people who ask it are genuinely interested in the answer. Perhaps, as tourists, they have visited Uxmal or Chichen Itza, or if more intrepid, Tikal, Calakmul, or Copan, all great centers of ancient Maya civilization. They know something about the Maya and they want to know more. In particular, they want an expert's opinion about what they believe to be one of the world's great archaeological mysteries, variously and confusingly attributed to disease, famine, droughts, earthquakes, volcanic eruptions, invasions, internal wars, peasant revolts, collapse of trade routes, cultural fatigue, and ecological catastrophe.

One answer, of course, is frustration. Like most professors, I can hold forth at mind-numbing length about my own subject, but even a couple of hours on an airplane is not enough time to try to tell someone what happened to the Maya, not because we know so little, but because we know so much and have so many opinions and interpretations. Moreover, the presumed demise of Maya civilization is not what most people imagine it to be – they would be surprised, no doubt, to hear that many of my colleagues don't even like to use the words "Maya collapse."

A related problem is that public perception of what the ancient Maya were like and their eventual fate is so different from the professional one, and this divergence is partly the fault of archaeologists themselves. Like our colleagues everywhere, we Mayanists love to bask in the limelight, and for better or worse, the flamboyant archaeological record we deal with gives us plenty of opportunity to do so. Scarcely a month goes by without news of the discovery of some new tomb, palace or set of inscriptions appearing in newspapers or magazines. The Discovery and History television channels routinely feature images of the glories of ancient Maya civilization, and I recently watched a television commercial earnestly enjoining me to visit Maya archaeological sites before 21 December 2012, when the narrator assured me that, according to the Maya Long Count calendar, the world would end (although it is by no means certain that the Maya believed this).

Many things Maya have thus entered our collective consciousness and Mayanists themselves sometimes fall under the spell of the interpretations they package for the public. In September 2000 one of my colleagues drew international attention to himself by claiming to have discovered a Classic Maya palace of unprecedented size. This "find" was featured on the front page of the *New York Times* and even in the sober *Chronicle of Higher Education.* Archaeologists, myself included, were amused by these self-promoting antics, because the Maya ruins in question had been found many years ago, partly mapped in the 1960s, and a detailed plan of this particular palace (not clearly the largest known) was published in 1978.

Such media hype is possible because the Maya have left us one of the most impressive archaeological records of any ancient people, replete with huge buildings, carved and painted monuments, and rich tombs. And most of these things lie on or near the surface, easily accessible both to archaeologists and, unfortunately, to looters too. How many Maya sites are there? No one really knows, but in 1938 a noted archaeologist put the estimate at 800, and he was counting only places of respectable size.[1] Today's total is considerably higher, not including the innumerable house platforms and other modest buildings that cover the surrounding landscapes.

Why many of these places were abandoned is indeed an intriguing historical issue. The rest of this book is in effect the archaeologist's revenge – what I would say if I had the leisure to fix my hapless interlocutor with my ancient mariner eye and subject him or her to a 100,000-word lecture about what happened to all those Maya, complete with pictures.

The first section of the book provides an introduction to Maya civilization, which was essentially unknown prior to the mid-19th century when a handful of early gentlemen-travelers and explorers brought it to the attention of the wider world and virtually created the several meanings of the word "Maya" as we use them today. Just why the ancient Maya exercise such a powerful hold on our imaginations is partly due, as we shall see, to this process of discovery. I also provide a short overview of the environments in which Maya civilization developed, a chronological timeline, and a brief introduction to the collapse.

But what is a civilization? How do the Maya relate to this grand and problematical sociocultural concept? And what does it mean to say that civilizations, Maya or otherwise, collapse? These questions are addressed in Chapter 3. Most people are unaware that complex and vigorous Maya societies that we could reasonably call "civilized" survived until the Spaniards first arrived in Yucatan early in the 16th century, and even long afterwards. I describe them in some detail because they form one of our principal windows into the Precolumbian Maya past and set the stage for a detailed discussion of the Classic Maya (AD 250–800) – the victims of the famous collapse. In some respects this is the most important part of the book, because it reviews what we know today about the Classic Maya, as well as what we do not know, using evidence from archaeology, inscriptions, and art. In essence it tries to answer the question "What collapsed?"

Even the earliest European explorers and colonists of Yucatan knew that ruins abounded, and they speculated about their origins and meaning. Subsequent perceptions of the collapse built on these early ideas, and have changed and shifted through time. Readers will discover that there were many "mini-collapses" throughout Maya history and prehistory, which was filled with discord, abandonments, and migrations. I next review a wide variety of proposed causes of the collapse and critically evaluate each one, given what we presently know about the nature of Maya society and culture history. Several case studies follow, chosen to capture the range of fates that are currently documented for specific sites and regions, and also to show the varied kinds of evidence that archaeologists have to use to make sense of what happened. Next we closely examine the fate of the Copan kingdom, which was so influential in forming our original conceptions of the catastrophe that overcame the Classic Maya. At Copan, more than anywhere else in the Maya Lowlands, we have an extremely rich record of what happened, some of which derives from my own research there. Finally I provide my personal overview of the Classic Maya collapse, building on all the information of the preceding chapters.

Before getting on with our story a word of caution is in order. "What happened to the ancient Maya?" is a big historical question, on the same order, say, as "What caused World War II?," or "Why did the Soviet Union collapse?" Neither of the latter two questions can be answered simply or to everyone's satisfaction even though many of us actually lived through these changes and we have abundant historical information about what happened in each case. Outbreak of a major world conflict or the disintegration of a gigantic sociopolitical system are processes far too complicated to be reduced to a few simple causes, and they resist our human yearnings for nice, neat, straightforward explanations. Trying to explain the Maya collapse using only archaeological remains, supplemented by very limited written records of an ancient people outside our own cultural tradition, is infinitely more difficult. Nevertheless, archaeologists, along with epigraphers, art historians, geographers, botanists, paleoclimatologists, and a host of other specialists, have made considerable headway in understanding this great historical puzzle.

As we shall see in the following chapters, Maya scholars agree about many things but vociferously disagree about others. Most such disagreements are honorable ones. Sometimes they concern issues about which we have little or no good information from art, inscriptions, or archaeological remains, so a wide range of interpretation is not only possible but desirable. Sometimes disagreement reflects training – epigraphers, art historians, field archaeologists, and laboratory specialists all tend to have different perspectives. Finally, we are to some degree like the proverbial blind persons each feeling one part of the elephant – we imagine the ancient Maya primarily through the things, places, and methods central to our own research, experience, and temperaments. Because how we try to explain the Maya collapse depends upon how we conceive of Maya culture and society, these differences of opinion are important. In the chapters that follow I refer to many controversies and summarize different points of view, but I also plainly emphasize which positions I prefer and unabashedly champion my own interpretations and prejudices. My account of the Maya collapse is thus necessarily a personal one, predicated on what I think the Classic Maya were like. Because understanding the collapse is still very much a work in progress, the subtitle of my book is "Solving the Mystery of the Maya Collapse."

My own biases and preoccupations will become evident soon enough, but it is only fair to make several things clear from the outset. First, unlike many Mayanists who spend most of their careers exploring the royal/elite manifestations of Maya culture, I can usually be found slogging about rural landscapes trying to locate the household remains of Maya farmers, and then later digging these up to find out how ordinary people lived and how to reconstruct and understand Maya settlement, demography, and agricultural systems. Perhaps more than some of my colleagues I have a "bottom-up" as opposed to "top-down" perspective. Second, many scholars believe that the Maya must be understood in their own terms. I was professionally raised as a good comparative anthropologist and am convinced that reference to the wider human experience is a vital resource in any archaeological reconstruction.[2] Readers will consequently encounter many comparative asides to other ancient civilizations and cultures, both in Mesoamerica and the wider world, which I hope will be instructive. Third, I am a bit of a skeptic about how unique or accomplished or numerous the ancient Maya were, a stance that does not always endear me to my colleagues. Finally, I cannot read Maya inscriptions (in fact only a handful of people in the world can really do this well, although dabblers and dilettantes abound), so I defer to the experts when it comes to the complex issues of textual interpretation.

Thanks to comparatively recent epigraphic insights, as the following chapters will show, the Classic Maya have emerged into the penumbra of history. We know the names of hundreds of kings, queens, and lesser notables, the wars, accessions, religious rituals, and other events in which they participated, and the dates on which these events occurred. Much of Classic Maya history has recently been admirably summarized by Simon Martin and Nikolai Grube in their invaluable book *Chronicle of the Maya Kings and Queens* (2000), on which I depend for much of the historical framework presented below.

Author's Note

Just how to spell various native names and other terms is an extremely vexing issue, especially for a non-linguist. There is as yet no standard orthography for the multitude of Maya words used in this book, nor is it clear to me exactly who the authorities are who institute orthographic changes with breathtaking frequency. I have therefore somewhat arbitrarily adopted the following policy, in consultation with my editors. Place names are given their most common and traditional spellings in the interest of confusing the reader as little as possible. For example, Copan is preferred over Kopan, and Calakmul over Kalakmul. Where foreign words of any derivation appear for the first time I give them in italics, and thereafter in roman letters. A special problem exists with the names of Maya rulers. Anyone reading even the recent literature will encounter a bewildering variety of designations or names for the same king. Least confusingly, some are simply identified by their order of succession, as in Ruler 1, 2, etc. Before glyphs could be read phonetically, some kings were also given nicknames based on the pictorial elements of their "name" glyphs or loose translations of what the glyphs were thought to mean, such as "18 Rabbit" of Copan. Increasingly, epigraphers provide their favorite phonetic spellings of the presumed Maya pronunciation of the names, using the English alphabet, but as yet there is no overall agreement even on this level. I accordingly use the most recent authoritative document I know of – presently Simon Martin and Nikolai Grube's *Chronicle of the Maya Kings and Queens* (2000). Where dynastic lists are given, such as that for Copan in Chapter 5, I provide most or all of the many name and title variants that have been previously used. To further simplify matters the editors and I agreed that none of the diacritical marks used in Spanish should be included in the text – apologies to Spanish readers.

Archaeologists almost invariably use the metric system, and metric figures are standard in most publications. Because the English reading public is not necessarily familiar with such measures, in the text I give metric figures first followed by their equivalents in miles, acres, etc.

– 1 –
NEW DAWN

As was his habit, the great K'uhul Ajaw ("holy lord") Yax Pasaj Chan Yoaat intently watched the eastern horizon for the first faint light of his namesake, the rising sun. Despite the fact that it annoyed his councilors and courtiers (or perhaps because it did so), he enjoyed climbing alone each morning to this lofty perch on the flat plaster roof of the great building named Pat Chan. There he could luxuriate in the cool hour before dawn, watch the mist rise from the river, and consider all the things that he had to do, undistracted by the bustle of his own household. Most of all he liked the way the light gradually crept along the hills and fields, bringing a new day to the kingdom founded so long before by his revered predecessor, K'inich Ajaw Yax K'uk' Mo'. Soon he began to hear the familiar morning sounds as people stirred in the houses crowding the valley floor and the nearby hillsides. On the gentle breeze floated the faint murmur of voices, the bark of dogs, and the pungent smell of wood smoke as cooking fires were rekindled.

Yax Pasaj found this personal morning ritual immensely reassuring because what he saw each day was so predictable. Of course it could not be otherwise, because order and balance in all things flowed from his own vital essence as ruler, from the ceremonies that he carried out, and from the powers of his ancestors and predecessors sleeping in their tombs all about him. Yax K'uk' Mo' himself lay close by, deep beneath a towering pyramid temple that the king's masons were even now completing. This building, along with the one on which he sat, was one of the many ambitious construction projects in which Yax Pasaj took great pride. Soon he would hear the chink of tools as the royal sculptors worked on his own tomb, just across the plaza, and see the long lines of carriers bringing stones from the quarries to the north. As always, the day would bring him many royal cares and decisions, and he envied the great ones in the Underworld, who were so potent when conjured up by the living, yet so untroubled in the afterlife by the day-to-day burdens of kingship. Oh well, he might join them soon enough – he was after all almost 50 years old.

With an effort the king turned his mind back to more practical matters.

Runners had arrived yesterday, bringing news of the approach of an entourage of visitors from the distant kingdom of B'aakal, many weeks away to the northwest where his aged mother, Lady Chak Nik Ye' Xook, had been born. Among them was an illustrious maternal relative, and Yax Pasaj sincerely hoped that this guest could divert the old lady, whose domineering ways did not always sit well with her son. He himself looked forward to hearing news of the great events of that far-off land, with its many kings constantly embroiled in diplomacy, political intrigue, and outright wars. Stories of battles and conquests appealed to Yax Pasaj. Sometimes he envisioned himself as a great warrior, and regretted that his own quiet, rather out-of-the-way kingdom had no powerful enemies to subdue on its borders. He always looked forward to those occasions when he could don his ritual military regalia, symbolic of his larger role of pacifier of the forces of chaos, and he had instructed his artists to portray him garbed and dancing as a powerful cosmic warrior on the walls of his mortuary temple (Fig. 1).

Welcome and exciting as such visitors were, they always presented difficulties. The great plazas containing the stelae and altars of earlier rulers had to be tidied up and lavishly decorated, and the ball courts made ready for play (Plate 1). It would never do to put any but the best face forward to foreigners. Women complained because of the great quantities of maize that they had to grind, and the endless jars of maize beer they had to brew. Emissaries had been sent to the fringes of the kingdom, two or three days walk away, to obtain deer, which were increasingly scarce, for the great feasts. While Yax Pasaj himself was seldom harassed by such petty concerns, he had to deal with the fretting of his royal officials and courtiers. His advisors had been interminably discussing the protocol essential to a successful visit, and busy sorting out and repairing the appropriate royal paraphernalia, long stored away unused in the palace. At least, Yax Pasaj reflected, there was an interval of comparative calm left to him, because the reception of the guests had been scheduled for a propitious day chosen by the wise men who consulted the ancient, sacred books. When that day came, however, the king knew that as royal host all his carefully honed skills of diplomacy and decorum would be required. Not only the guests, but almost all his own people, many thousands of them, would assemble in the enormous public spaces of his royal court, and all eyes would be upon him.

By now the sun was up, and as always the king took pleasure in the vista before him. As far as he could see the hillsides were covered with the houses, orchards, and fields of his subjects (Plates 9–10). Powerful as Yax K'uk' Mo' and his other royal predecessors had been, surely the kingdom had never

1 *Yax Pasaj is portrayed in warrior garb on the walls of Copan Structure 18, his probable funerary temple. Whether the king ever fought any real wars is uncertain.*

before been so populous or so widely respected. And as he surveyed the brilliant green of new vegetation sprouting up after the long dry season, he hoped it would be prosperous this year too. All of the necessary ceremonies had been carried out and all the prognostications were favorable, but sometimes the gods and ancestors were fickle, withholding the life-bringing rain. Yax Pasaj tried to ignore the oldest farmers of his kingdom, who claimed that when they were young the crops were better and people less often hungry. After all, it was the nature of old men to grumble that everything was better in their youth. Yax Pasaj sometimes yielded to such thoughts himself, but knew that they were merely the illusions of age, and that in the long run everything, good and bad, repeated itself endlessly.

On the valley floor below him, arrayed along a broad causeway extending out from the royal compound, the king could see the imposing residences of his great nobles and courtiers, most only a few minutes walk away. Some of these grandees were his own close relatives, while others were unrelated leaders of the powerful families that had dominated the valley as long as anyone could remember. No doubt they too were preoccupied with the impending festivities, in which they themselves would take prominent roles. Clearly visible now near the end of the causeway in the curve of the river were the red-painted buildings comprising the sprawling compound of Mak-Chanal, who bore the exalted title of *aj k'uhuun*, one of the high officials of the land. It was a grand place – perhaps too grand. Many people were eager to seek the patronage of such a powerful noble, whose fortunes were clearly on the rise. Only a few years before Yax Pasaj himself had graciously officiated at the dedication of Mak-Chanal's elaborate new house, which was embellished with façade sculpture and a throne as finely carved and painted as any in his own royal residence. In return for the demonstration of royal favor, Mak-Chanal had acknowledged himself as the king's man. High-born individuals coveted marks of distinction and the privileged attachments to the royal court that they conveyed. One had to do such things to honor prominent people, and after all Mak-Chanal's father had been a loyal servant of earlier kings. But one day the ambitious *aj k'uhuun* might go too far. It was rumored that he coveted a bride from the king's own house. He was a man to be watched.

But Yax Pasaj shrugged off all these cares. As always the ascent of the new dawn sun filled him with confidence, so obviously was it a harbinger of his own unchallenged efficacy. Did not his own name mean New Dawn Sky Lightning God? Was he not the sun to his people, far above the petty concerns and jealousies of ordinary folk? Then he heard the shrill cries of his youngest daughter, sent by his women to summon him to the morning meal, and sighing, rose to meet the new day.

I made up this little vignette of Maya life as it might have been in the late 8th century AD, but it is based on real places and real people. Yax Pasaj actually existed. He was the ruler of Copan, one of the most famous of all Classic Maya kingdoms, situated in a verdant mountain valley in what is today western Honduras (Fig. 2). Copan is a traditional toponym in this region, and was also the name of an Indian leader who led a gallant but futile campaign against the Spaniards in 1530. At least since that time the same name has been attached to the great ruins we now know to be the court center of Yax Pasaj and his dynasty. Exactly what the ancient Maya called their royal capital or their kingdom is uncertain, but to judge from surviving texts it was probably something like Ox Witik.

The little morning scene I concocted would have taken place in the late spring of AD 785, during the 22nd year of Yax Pasaj's reign when he was probably about 40–50 years old, a considerable age for his time (he lived, in fact, for at least another 25 years, dying sometime after AD 810). No foreign visit of the kind I imagined is recorded in the many inscriptions at Copan, but great lords commonly traveled from one center to another. We know that Yax Pasaj's mother Lady Chak Nik Ye' Xook was a woman from the distant center of B'aakal (or "Bone") about 450 airline km (281 miles) away to the northwest, so lengthy journeys of this sort surely took place. Today we call this much visited site Palenque. A sculptured panel from Yax Pasaj's own funerary temple shows motifs similar to those found on the sarcophagus of Palenque's famous ruler of a century earlier, K'inich Janaab' Pakal I (Plate 16).

2 *Map of the Highland and Lowland Maya regions of Mesoamerica with sites mentioned in the text. (Inset) Map of Mesoamerica showing the locations of non-Maya sites that have implications for our understanding of Maya culture and history.*

Yax Pasaj was a great builder during the first half of his reign, and tourists who visit Copan today can admire the remains of his royal projects, particularly Structures 11 and 16, the huge temple-pyramids he erected over the buildings of his predecessors. Structure 11 was one of Yax Pasaj's first great projects and was probably completed in AD 776. We know that stairways led to the roof of its summit temple, so the king might well have climbed there for his morning reveries. The Maya regarded such great buildings as living things, and gave them names. According to some epigraphers Structure 11 really was named "Pat Chan," which translates as "Underside of the Sky" or "Constructed Sky."[1] Sitting atop this carved model of the sky that he himself had planned and built, Yax Pasaj had reason to feel on top of his world.

Deep beneath Structure 16, just a short distance to the northeast, is a tomb which is probably that of Yax K'uk' Mo', whose name means "Great Sun First Quetzal Macaw." Yax K'uk' Mo' had intimate connections with the distant metropolis of Teotihuacan in Central Mexico, and might even have come from that far off place.[2] He was much celebrated on the carved monuments of his successors as the founder of the Copan dynasty, although there are hints of earlier kings or notable people, and his reign ushered in almost exactly 400 years of subsequent growth and decline.

Yax Pasaj was the 16th successor in Copan's royal line, having assumed the throne and the royal titles in AD 763. Though his reign was a long one, he might well have had good reason to feel misgivings about his political position. Not only was his mother a foreigner, but his father was probably not the 15th king, K'ak' Yipyaj Chan K'awiil ("K'awiil Who Fills the Sky with Fire"). Perhaps to impress visitors and his own lords alike, in AD 776 he dedicated Altar Q, one of the most important monuments ever made by the ancient Maya (at least from our perspective), because of the dynastic information it contains (Plate 2). Around the four sides of the rectangular stone monolith are depicted all the rulers of Copan in the order of their succession, each sitting on his own name glyph. The front shows Yax Pasaj himself facing the founding ancestor of the dynasty, and accepting from him a baton or scepter of rule. Yax Pasaj's accession date is carved between them, a clear assertion of his royal legitimacy. The king had his artisans carefully position Altar Q at the foot of the great stairway ascending the temple that covered Yax K'uk' Mo's tomb, where a replica of it may still be seen today.

One can no longer climb to Yax Pasaj's morning perch because the roof of Structure 11, as archaeologists prosaically designate this building, long ago collapsed and has never been reconstructed. From any similarly lofty position, however, and especially on a foggy morning, the valley still appears

3, 4 Mak-Chanal sat in state on this 6-m (19.7-ft) long throne in the central room of his palatial residence, the House of the Bacabs. The inscription gives his title and name, and the date on which the throne was dedicated. King Yax Pasaj apparently presided over the dedication ceremony in person. (Below) Mosaic façade sculpture in the form of scribal figures flanked the main doorway of the House of the Bacabs.

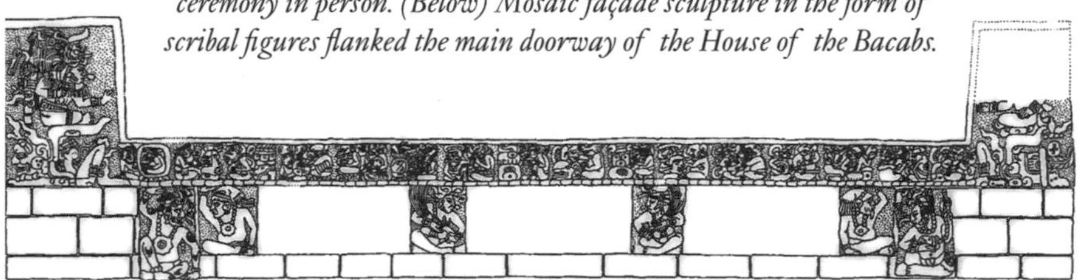

much as it did in the late 8th century. Looking to the north one can see Copan's Great Plaza, where many carved images of kings still stand, and the imposing Ball Court. Yax Pasaj's fictional visitors would have been feted in these great public spaces, which could easily have accommodated as well the whole population of the Copan kingdom. Fronting on the Ball Court Plaza is Temple 26, with its Hieroglyphic Stairway (Plate 3), another grandiose monument celebrating the dynasty. To the south, attached to the looming mass of the Acropolis, was the actual residence of the king, where he slept and ate surrounded by his family and retainers.

On the old river terrace extending to the east for about 800 m (0.5 miles) is an enormous residential zone dominated by the remains of the households of Copan's nobles. And in the far distance are the many restored courtyards and buildings of Mak-Chanal's great compound, where in 1981 my students and I excavated the elaborate hieroglyphic throne dedicated by Yax Pasaj on 10 July AD 781 (Figs 3 and 5). For Mak-Chanal was also a real person whose aj k'uhuun title might mean something like "Keeper of the Sacred Books," or more simply, "Scribe." In the most general terms, the title seems to refer to an important official who in some sense "provides" for or "provisions" his king and polity.[3] Near-life-sized sculpted figures on the façade of the "House of the Bacabs," which contained the bench, show a gorgeously dressed figure holding the scribal tools of brush and inkpot. These figures might represent Mak-Chanal himself (Fig. 4).

My story is set at Copan because it is the Classic Maya center that I know best, having put in many field seasons there between 1980 and 1997. My colleagues, however, could tell similar stories about the Maya of Palenque, Tikal, Calakmul, Caracol, Dos Pilas, Piedras Negras, Yaxchilan, or Quirigua. All these great royal capitals, along with many others, thrived in the 8th century AD (Fig. 2). All probably then seemed to their respective rulers to be vigorous places, with long, distinguished histories and with bright futures. All of them, in fact, would be largely abandoned within a century. In some regions the surrounding rural populations disappeared at about the same time, while in others the populations dwindled away much more slowly.

As we shall see, our conceptions of the Maya collapse have been painstakingly built up by finding out what happened to specific capitals, dynasties, polities, and populations, and we know much more about some than others. As it happens, Copan has been unusually important in developing our current conceptions of Maya civilization because of the abundance of its inscriptions and wide-ranging scope of the archaeological work done there. Nowhere else do we have such a comprehensive picture of the demise of a Classic Maya regional polity. Yax Pasaj and his kingdom will appear many times in the following pages. For now, we need only note that K'uhul Ajaw Yax Pasaj Chan Yoaat was the last in the long line of Copan's kings. Today you can still see his proud warrior image on the temple atop his looted tomb, but all of his efforts to preserve the well-being of his kingdom ultimately proved futile.

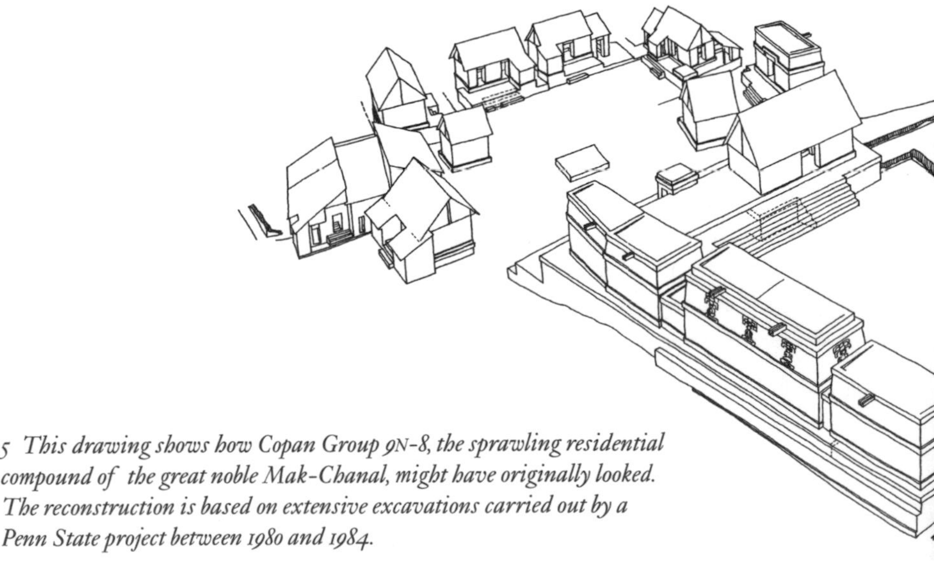

5 This drawing shows how Copan Group 9N-8, the sprawling residential compound of the great noble Mak-Chanal, might have originally looked. The reconstruction is based on extensive excavations carried out by a Penn State project between 1980 and 1984.

Inventing Maya Civilization

A thousand years after the dynastic collapse at Copan – in late November 1839, to be exact – two Europeans squatted in front of a rectangular stone altar. They could see it clearly for the first time, lit by the dappled sunlight filtering through the forest canopy that their workmen had thinned with machetes and axes. With their fingers they traced the 16 figures carved in low relief around the sides of the stone block, and brushed the leaves from the hieroglyphs that covered its surface. Although they could not read the glyphs, they surmised that the monument depicted a conference of some sort, and that the writing recorded "some event in the history of the people who once inhabited the city." The "city," of course, was Copan, and the monument was Altar Q. Both, along with the very idea of Maya civilization, were about to be brought to the attention of the wider world for the first time.

Neither of the two travelers was a likely Maya explorer.[4] John Lloyd Stephens, the shorter, red-bearded one, was the 34-year-old scion of a prosperous New Jersey family transplanted to New York City. After training for the law, Stephens succumbed to wanderlust and in 1824 he traveled through the then raw western frontier of the United States. A decade later, following a short and unsatisfying stint of lawyering, he embarked, as so many privileged young men of his time did, on a tour of Europe that included not only the well-worn circuit of England, France, Italy, Germany, and Austria, but also Poland, Russia, Greece, and

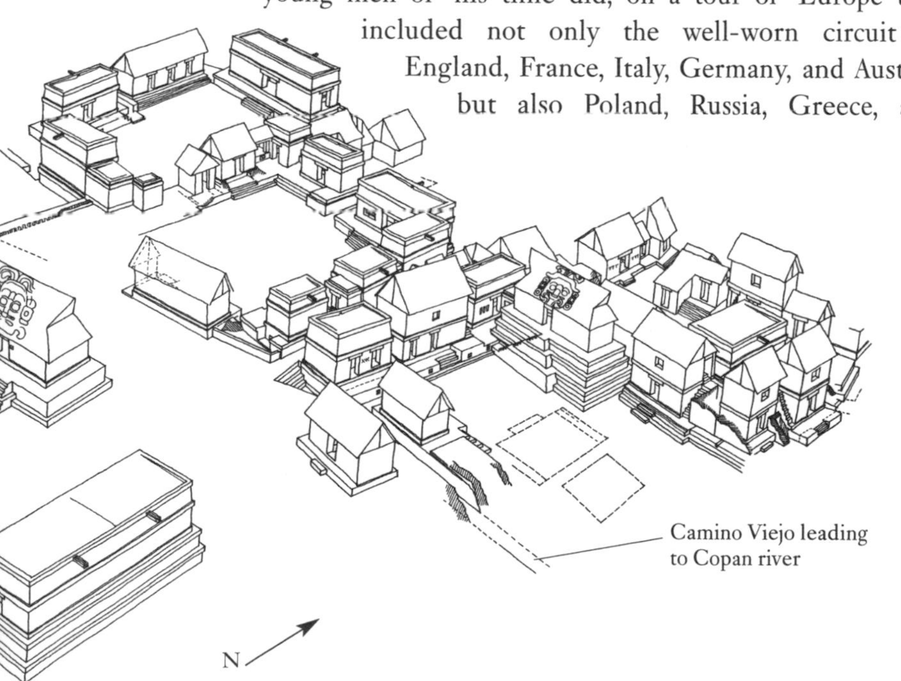

Turkey. Stephens was particularly captivated by the exotic sights and cultures of the eastern Mediterranean and by the many Greek and Roman ruins that every educated tourist visited in those days.

In November 1835, unable at short notice to book transatlantic passage home to New York, Stephens went instead to Egypt. There he met Mehemet Ali, the wily old despot who, with ruthless cunning and violence, had consolidated power over the Nile valley, Syria, and the Sudan in the aftermath of Napoleon's failed invasion a generation before. Armed with the amiable pasha's firman, Stephens sailed up the Nile for three months, absorbing a landscape of antiquities unmatched anywhere in the world. Hearing of even more fabled ruins in the deserts of northern Arabia, he disguised himself as an Arab and guided by local Bedouin made a dangerous journey to Petra, the long-abandoned, rock-carved capital of the ancient Nabataeans that had been rediscovered in 1812 and since visited by only a handful of intrepid Europeans.

Stephens returned to New York via London with no particular ambitions and facing the unpalatable prospect of resuming his legal career. Fortunately, those friends who heard his stories urged him to write a book describing his adventures. The result was *Incidents of Travel in Egypt and Arabia Petraea*, published in 1837, which was unexpectedly a wild success both in the United States and Europe. Encouraged by critical reviews and enriched to the tune of $15,000 (immense royalties for an American author of the time), Stephens immediately churned out a second well-received volume describing his European travels, and by 1838 he was a literary sensation at a time when the United States had practically no writers of reputation, and certainly none who made a decent living with their pens.

The Englishman Frederick Catherwood was the more experienced of the two Maya explorers. Six years older than Stephens, he had been apprenticed as an architect and draftsman. Fascinated by lectures he heard on archaeology, Catherwood left England for Greece in 1823 and spent most of the next decade traveling and drawing in the Near East. Among other occupations he served as architectural advisor to Mehemet Ali, measuring and repairing many of the great buildings of Cairo. Stephens providentially met Catherwood in London as he was returning from his own travels, and later again in New York, where Catherwood had established himself as an architect and also operated *The Splendid Panorama of Jerusalem*, a commercial venture centered around a giant painting of the kind so popular in pre-photography days. There a partnership fateful for the emergence of Maya archaeology was born.

Neither Stephens nor Catherwood knew anything about the Maya in 1838, nor, for all practical purposes, did anyone else. Many early Spanish accounts that were later to be so informative about New World peoples still moldered in archives and private collections in Mexico or Europe. During three centuries of colonial rule, moreover, Spanish authorities in the New World exhibited very little interest in antiquities or ruins, which were often mined for building materials or for gold. There were of course exceptions. Soldiers, priests, and officials sometimes wrote descriptions of ancient monuments or cities, often on their own initiative, and some tried to save works of Pre-columbian art from destruction. Very occasionally the Spanish crown or an energetic viceroy dispatched an expedition to investigate a particularly interesting ruin and bring back relics and drawings. By and large, however, there was no sustained study of ancient things or development of systematic archaeology. Such ruined cities and works of art that did attract scholarly attention were typically attributed to antediluvian peoples or to ancient Egyptians. Foreigners with an interest in antiquities were not encouraged to travel through Spanish dominions.

All this was rapidly changing even as Stephens and Catherwood first encountered each other in London, in large part thanks to Napoleon Bonaparte. Although his conquest of Egypt in 1798 ended in military fiasco, Napoleon's artists and natural scientists returned to France loaded down with the first abundant documentation of an ancient non-European civilization. A European craze for all things Egyptian broke out, intensified by the decipherment of hieroglyphics in 1822. Archaeology was suddenly fashionable. Napoleon's depredations in Spain and his manipulation of the Spanish throne, moreover, weakened the ties between Spain and her colonial possessions. After several earlier insurrections, Mexico finally declared independence in 1821. Two years later the ramshackle Confederation of Central American Republics was formed, comprising Guatemala, Honduras, El Salvador, Costa Rica, and Nicaragua. Suddenly foreigners were welcome in the former Spanish possessions, trade flourished, and reports and publications of mysterious lost "Mexican" cities began to circulate in Europe and the United States. These included a brief description of the picturesque ruins of Uxmal in 1838 by Jean Frédéric Waldeck, and another in 1836 of an even more remote and mysterious place called Copan, by Colonel Juan Galindo. Among those who heard these rumors were Stephens and Catherwood, who were already familiar with the stirring accounts of the Spanish conquest by the soldier-writers Hernan Cortes and Bernal Diaz. What better opportunity could two prosperous, experienced, and footloose gentlemen-travelers wish for? All of the ruins they had visited in Europe and the Near East were known to history, and had been visited and described by many others before them. Mexico and Central America promised wholly new discoveries, not to mention financial profit.

History provided the opportunity, but as it turned out politics provided the means. Stephens had long been an outspoken supporter of Andrew Jackson and later of his protégé, Martin Van Buren, who became president in 1837. As a reward for this political support, Van Buren appointed Stephens his minister to the Confederation of Central American Republics. The forests, minerals, and agricultural resources of America Central, as it was then called, had attractive commercial potential and the region also offered feasible overland routes between the Atlantic and Pacific, and even perhaps scope for a canal. Unfortunately, this whole amorphous political entity was then in a condition of almost total chaos and virtually cut off from the outside world. Officially, Stephens was charged with ascertaining the whereabouts and status of the Confederation's government and with retrieving consular documents from Guatemala City. Unofficially, it was tacitly assumed by Stephens and Van Buren that his appointment was diplomatic cover for the archaeological explorations that he and Catherwood proposed to undertake.

When the little two-man expedition set sail for Belize City in early October 1839, New World prehistory in general, not just that of Latin America, was essentially a blank. Ignorance, of course, never discourages speculation, and the origins of New World peoples were variously ascribed to migrations of Phoenicians, Carthaginians, Scandinavians, Chinese, Africans, or denizens of lost continents, among others, with the most reputable authorities favoring the Lost Tribes of Israel. Fiercely debated as these alternatives were, on one point there was almost universal agreement – New World people were rude and barbarous, and if indeed they had accomplished anything of note it derived from the influences of Old World civilizations. William Robertson, author of the hugely influential *History of America* (1792), wrote that "Neither the Mexicans nor Peruvians [were] entitled to rank with those nations which merit the name of civilized," and he dismissed glowing descriptions of huge cities, spacious palaces, and imposing temples by the earliest Spanish explorers and conquerors as "highly embellished."[5] Certainly no one at the time believed that great civilizations had independently emerged in the New World. There was no concept of Maya civilization at all, and even the word Maya was seldom heard.

Standing in the overgrown ruins of Copan, Stephens and Catherwood were about to change all this. After a long and arduous overland trek, during which they were arrested and released by partisans of one of the several contending Central American supremos, they finally arrived in the Copan valley about six weeks after their departure from New York, "...with the hope rather than the expectation, of finding wonders."[6] Both men were familiar with earlier sketchy accounts of Copan, including Galindo's – but neither was prepared for what he saw.

> The city was desolate. No remnant of this race hangs round the ruins, with traditions handed down from father to son and from generation to generation. It lay before us like a shattered bark in the midst of the ocean, her masts gone, her name effaced, her crew perished, and none to tell whence she came, to whom she belonged, how long on her voyage, or what caused her destruction ... all was mystery, impenetrable mystery, and every circumstance increased it.[7]

Although the masonry buildings were so deteriorated and covered with vegetation that it was hard to form any clear idea of their original design, Catherwood's architect's eye immediately recognized that they compared favorably in scale and quality of construction with the great temples or tombs of Greece, Egypt, and the Near East. He also realized that the difficulty he experienced in first trying to draw the images carved on the great stone columns, or stelae, using his camera lucida (a prism that appears to project an image onto paper) was due to the fact that the designs were utterly unfamiliar to him and unrelated to those of the Old World civilizations he knew about. So distinctive were these monuments that the mere sight of them

> put to rest once and forever all uncertainty in our minds as to the character of American antiquities, and gave us the assurance that the objects we were in search of were not only interesting as the remains of an unknown people, but were works of art as well, proving, like newly discovered historical records, that the people who once occupied the American continent were not savages.[8]

Drenched with rain, plagued by *garrapatas* (tiny ticks that dig into one's flesh by the hundreds), and combating mosquitoes by puffing clouds of smoke from cigars made from the tobacco that then (as opposed to ruins) constituted the valley's main claim to fame, the two men cut survey lines linking the monuments and buildings and made the first map of Copan. Everything they saw convinced them that these were the remains of a people unknown to history, and who yet recorded history in their own right. For everywhere there were hieroglyphs and these, more than any other discovery, seized Stephens's imagination. He assumed, rightly as it turned out, that the glyphs on the monuments recorded the names and titles of real people and that the inscriptions told the story of the great events of the kingdom. Nothing frustrated him more than being unable to read them, but he had no doubt about the sophistication of the ancient inhabitants:

architecture, sculpture, and painting, all the arts which embellish life, had flourished in this overgrown forest; orators, warriors, and statesmen, beauty, ambition, and glory had lived and passed away, and none knew that such things had been, or could tell of their past existence.[9]

Stephens's reaction to what he saw reflects the sensibilities of his times. The art historian Esther Pasztory points out that as the practice of evaluating art through its religious connotations declined in 18th-century Europe, objects came to be appreciated for their own aesthetic qualities.[10] Just as the excellence of individual artists was measured by their creations, so too did larger artistic traditions reflect the genius of a people. By the early 19th century many archaeologists and historians such as William Robertson ranked cultures according to their aesthetic accomplishments, which in turn reflected their moral and intellectual capacities. Faced with the architecture, art, and inscriptions of Copan, Stephens did the same, exclaiming that: "America, say historians, was peopled by savages; but savages never reared these structures, savages never carved these stones..."[11] Although he knew nothing of the institutions or organization of the long-lost people of Copan, he assumed that these must have been very complex, comparable to those of the historical civilizations of the Old World.

Copan also evoked in Stephens the romantic effusions so typical of early-19th-century writers:

In Egypt the colossal skeletons of gigantic temples stand in unwatered sands in the nakedness of desolation; but here an immense forest shrouds the ruins, hiding them from sight, heightening the impression of moral effect, and giving an intensity and almost wildness to the interest.[12]

Moral musings were subordinated to a hard-headed commercial sense as he and Catherwood swung in their hammocks each evening, discussing the possibility of acquiring the monuments and bringing them back to the United States, where they would be exhibited for profit and eventually form the core of a new museum. Ruins were a glut on the market in 1839, and Stephens eventually acquired Copan for a mere 50 dollars (bemoaning afterwards that he could have had it for even less). Nothing ever came of this investment, however, and after three weeks Stephens left Catherwood behind to finish his drawings, and regretfully set off to Guatemala City to pursue his diplomatic duties, which as it turned out he discharged very conscientiously.

Neither Stephens nor Catherwood ever visited Copan again, nor did any professional archaeologists until more than 40 years later. Instead, after a side trip to the great ruins of Palenque, they returned to New York where Stephens rapidly wrote his immediately and hugely successful *Incidents of Travel in Central America*, profusely illustrated by Catherwood. Gratifingly celebrated and enriched as New World antiquarians, in 1841–42 they made another rigorous journey throughout the northern parts of the Yucatan Peninsula that resulted in the 1843 *Incidents of Travel in Yucatán.* Both books are still in print.

Altogether Stephens and Catherwood visited 44 archaeological sites and made hundreds of drawings and daguerreotype images. In the process, as Stephens's biographer Victor von Hagen asserts, they literally invented the idea of Maya civilization. During their travels they saw that the styles of the buildings and monuments at all the sites they visited were variations on a single great cultural theme, and more particularly that everywhere the glyphs were the same.[13] When they later saw a copy of the Dresden Codex, a screenfold book of then unknown origin in a German collection, they realized that the painted hieroglyphs were identical to those carved on the monuments that Catherwood had drawn. Plainly the same impressive ancient culture had thrived over a huge region of tropical America.

Equally important, and much more controversial at the time, was Stephens's assertion that this civilization was independent from those of the Old World:

> The works of these people, as revealed by the ruins, are different than the works of any other known people; they are of a new order, and entirely and absolutely anomalous: They stand alone ... unless I am wrong, we have a conclusion far more interesting and wonderful than that of connecting the builders of these [Maya] cities with the Egyptians or any other people. It is the spectacle of a people skilled in architecture, sculpture, and possessing the culture and refinement attendant upon these, not derived from the Old World, but originating and growing here without models or masters, having distinct, separate, and indigenous existence; like the plants and fruits of the soil, indigenous.[14]

It was no longer necessary to conjure up ancient Egyptians or Lost Tribes of Israel to account for all these ancient wonders. Instead, Stephens proclaimed, "Opposed as is my idea to all previous speculations, I am inclined to think that they were constructed by the races who occupied the country at the time of the invasion by the Spaniards, or of some not very distant progenitors."[15] Here he unambiguously identifies a new civilization. Although he knew the native language spoken in Yucatan was called Maya, only later did scholars begin to use the label "Maya civilization."

Most important of all from the perspective of this book, Stephens and Catherwood also invented the very idea of the Maya collapse. The abandoned centers of Copan, Uxmal, and Palenque impressed upon Stephens the melancholy "moral lesson" of the frailty of human endeavor. Nothing affected him more than that all this ancient greatness should have come to nothing and be utterly forgotten.

> Here were the remains of a cultivated, polished, and peculiar people, who had passed through all the stages incident to the rise and fall of nations; reached their golden age, and perished.... We went up to their desolate temples and fallen altars; and wherever we moved we saw the evidence of their taste, their skill in arts.... In the midst of desolation and ruin we look back to the past, cleared away the gloomy forest, and fancied every building perfect, with its terraces and pyramids, its sculptured and painted ornament, grand, lofty, and imposing.... We called back into life the strange people who gazed in sadness from the walls; pictured them, in fanciful costumes and adorned with plumes of feathers, ascending the terraces of the palace and the steps leading to the temples.... In the romance of the world's history nothing ever impressed me more forcibly than the spectacle of this once great and lovely city, overturned, desolate, and lost.... overgrown with trees for miles around, and without even a name to distinguish it.[16]

People who visit Copan or Palenque today often feel something of this same emotion, and still wonder what happened to the Maya. One might even say that the invention of the idea of the collapse was the single most important factor in creating Maya archaeology and sustaining it as a vital enterprise for over 150 years.

– 2 –

THE MAYA MYSTIQUE

IN GEORGE LUCAS'S MOVIE *Star Wars*, the heroic rebel forces attack from a secret base hidden deep in tropical forest and camouflaged by the towering ruins of ancient buildings. Images of both the forest setting and the temples in fact derive from the great Classic Maya center of Tikal in northern Guatemala. All of us, like Stephens and Catherwood, have been at least subliminally affected by such images, as well as by other kinds of information concerning the Maya that is routinely purveyed by various forms of popular culture. The Maya are not simply some run-of-the mill, dry-as-dust people who lived long ago and who are mainly of interest to archaeologists. Rather we have collectively appropriated them, as we have done with certain other ancient civilizations (most notably ancient Egypt) for our larger cultural uses. In the Maya of our imaginations are reflected many of our own hopes, fears, and fascinations.[1] We expect things Maya to be beautiful, exotic, and dramatic, and especially mysterious, and of course the concept of the catastrophic collapse of Maya civilization fits the bill perfectly.

It is this mind-set that Gordon Willey, the dean of Maya archaeologists, once labeled the "mystique" of the Maya, and I can provide an excellent example of it from my own experience. In 1970 I was excavating the huge system of ditches, causeways, and embankments surrounding the Maya center of Becan, smack in the middle of the Yucatan Peninsula in the Mexican state of Campeche. These earthworks had been discovered many years before, but exactly what they represented was unclear. We now know that they are one of the largest and earliest fortifications found anywhere in Mesoamerica, probably dating to the very end of the Preclassic period, around AD 250 or a little before.

Becan in those days was quite an isolated place and we seldom had visitors. One day, however, a small plane landed on our primitive airstrip cut out of the forest, first having prudently buzzed it several times to scare away browsing pigs and deer. The pilot turned out to be an enthusiastic amateur student of the ancient Maya who knew that a project supported by the National Geographic Society was working in the area. We showed this gentleman around our various excavations, and he was greatly impressed by Becan's towering buildings and ornate mosaic façade sculpture. When I took him on a tour of the defensive system, however, he became increasingly disgruntled, and even visibly agitated. Finally he asked me if I was really certain that these were fortifications. When I told him all the compelling reasons for thinking so, he exclaimed "Goddammit, somewhere there has to have been a peaceful civilization!"

Our visitor had internalized, and obviously highly valued, what had long been one of our fondest collective beliefs concerning the Classic Maya – that somehow, isolated deep in their tropical forest homeland, they had escaped the violence and conflict that characterized all other historically documented civilizations. Such a "peaceful Maya" perspective was especially seductive for many people in 1970, right in the middle of the Vietnam war.

For reasons that we will explore later, by the early 1940s the Classic Maya had become a kind of intellectual Shangri-La for our wishful thinking about the past and about the human condition. As the archaeologist George Stuart once put it, "The Maya began to take on a non-human aspect. Here was the strangest race of people that ever lived ... gentle astronomers forever gazing towards the sky, and never doing anything that other people did."[2] Somehow they had avoided or rejected the incessant warfare and military expansion that later characterized the Aztecs and Incas, and lived harmoniously together. They were ruled by benevolent astronomer-priests and unafflicted by invidious social divisions. Religious devotion, not the ambitions and demands of kings, motivated the Maya to build temples and ball courts at dozens of great centers. And these were not cities like the Aztec and Inca capitals, but instead vacant ritual places, temple centers visited by most people only for the elaborate ceremonies that celebrated the gods of the Maya cosmos. Around these centers prosperous farmers somehow supported themselves for centuries without harming their fragile tropical environment. It is this charming picture of a benign, accomplished, and peaceful civilization that our visitor found so attractive and that was, and remains, so widely shared.[3]

Even by 1970, of course, it was clear that very little if any of this arcadian perspective was true. Subsequent research has definitively put to rest the "peaceful Maya," "vacant ceremonial center," and "priest-peasant" theories. Nevertheless, a lot of nonsense is still written about the Maya because this mystique has such a powerful hold on our collective imaginations. Take, for example, an article in one of the very airline magazines in which I some years ago sought refuge from the questions of fellow passengers. It breathlessly informed me that the ancient Maya built palaces with 100 or more rooms while Europeans still lived in mud huts. Well sure, plenty of Europeans lived in mud huts (or similarly ramshackle dwellings) in the 8th or 9th centuries AD, but so too did most Maya people at the same time. And Minoans, Greeks, Romans, and Etruscans, among others, occupied impressive palaces long before the Maya did. The same article ended by evoking the magic of enigmatic Maya ruins, and the imponderable mystery of what happened to the civilization that built them.

The Attractions of the Maya

Why do people care what happened to the Maya in the first place? Why are the Maya so fascinating? While writing this chapter I was invited by a colleague to address a class he was teaching on public conceptions of archaeology, in which the Maya figure so prominently. When I raised the question of why the Maya were so often labeled "mysterious," whereas the Romans or Greeks were not, the students replied that the Maya were "exotic," or "foreign" because they were not connected developmentally to the general tradition of Western civilization with which most members of the class identified. Of course this is only a partial explanation, because we rarely hear the equally exotic Aztecs or Incas called mysterious. The reason instead has much more to do with the perpetuation of the Maya mystique. Only a few students, it turned out, had much grasp of the very recent decipherments or archaeological discoveries that have yielded such detailed information about ancient Maya history and culture. To them, the Maya were still largely prehistoric and hence inherently mysterious, like the Etruscans, whose texts we still cannot read.

Among Precolumbian New World peoples there are three high-profile societies that everyone has heard something about – the Aztecs, the Incas, and the Maya. All represent native American civilizations that produced great centers with monumental buildings, impressive art, and (at least the Aztec and Maya) their own written records. Of these three civilizations, the Maya have most strongly captured our imaginations.

The Aztecs of highland Mexico and the Incas of the Central Andes were both what one might call "upstart" peoples, whose respective empires emerged less than a century before the arrival of Europeans. Although the Aztecs were literate, very little of what they wrote prior to 1519 survives. The Incas certainly kept complex records using knotted cords (*kipus*), but had no system of writing. Much of what we know about the Aztecs and Incas consequently derives from documents and ethnohistoric accounts of 16th- and

17th-century writers. Aztec scribes continued to make pictorial documents in the Precolumbian tradition for about two generations after the Spanish conquest. Some documents were even commissioned by Spanish officials and accompanied by Spanish glosses. Other accounts record the testimony of indigenous informants who were participants in their respective New World cultures. Still others come from Spanish soldiers, priests, and officials, as well as native individuals educated after 1519 who described the conquest or perpetuated Precolumbian traditions in the books, wills, petitions, and other documents they wrote using the European alphabet.

All such accounts are of variable reliability and incompletely understood, and certainly there are many details of Aztec and Inca culture that remain unclear and controversial. If we take all these literary sources together, however, and supplement them with archaeological evidence, our information about these two great Precolumbian civilizations is very rich. Both are in effect historically documented cultures. What eventually happened to them, however dramatic, is also ultimately prosaic – they were conquered by foreigners. In short, very little about the Aztecs or Incas is fundamentally mysterious.

The Maya, however, are something very different – especially the Maya who lived between about AD 250 and 800 in the southern and eastern parts of the larger culture area called Mesoamerica. These people created the impressive civilization that Stephens and Catherwood discovered, and most people today know several things about them: they built big buildings, they were accomplished astronomers and mathematicians, they were impressively literate, and most importantly, their civilization suddenly "collapsed." Because the ancient Maya are so remote from us in time, we have no accounts of them comparable to those available for the Aztecs and the Incas. Much about them remains unknown, although we understand a great deal more now than we did just a few years ago. The greatest mystery of all is the apparent catastrophe that overtook many Maya centers between about AD 750 and 900. In the popular imagination these places were suddenly and completely abandoned. Architects and sculptors laid aside their tools, kings and nobles left their palaces, and farmers stopped tending their fields. Somehow this apocalyptic conception fascinates us far more than episodes of gradual decline or sudden conquest documented for other cultures.

Since Stephens's and Catherwood's time the idea of the Maya collapse has been fed by the romantic image of lost and abandoned cities enshrouded in tropical forest, still awaiting discovery – an image that still has a powerful psychological allure for many people. When I first began doing Maya archaeology in the late 1960s such places still existed. If not quite lost in the ultimate sense of the word, there were plenty of great sites that had been visited only by wandering chicleros (men who harvested the sap of a tropical forest tree) and a handful of archaeologists, who recorded (and sometimes carried off) their carved monuments and made rough maps of their temples, ball courts, and palaces, thus continuing the tradition of exploration that began more than a century before. Those days are now mainly gone, as is much of the forest. Sites that I saw untouched by the spade are today excavated, restored, and visited on a daily basis by people staying in the adjacent Club Med. Even so, some of the most famous centers remain incompletely cleared and mapped. Archaeologists are still charting and testing the peripheries of Palenque, possibly the most celebrated and frequently visited of all Maya capitals.

Fortunately a few really backwoods places still exist. While writing this book I spent part of each spring at Piedras Negras, a huge concentration of temples and palaces perched high on a limestone escarpment overlooking the Usumacinta river in northwestern Guatemala (Fig. 6). Working at a place like Piedras Negras is difficult, to say the least, and even dangerous. The heat can be stifling, the food is terrible, it is hours to the nearest doctor or hospital, and the most common topic of conversation is the first cold beer or margarita one will drink when the seemingly interminable field season is finally over. But there are compensations that make it all worthwhile. The lush tropical forest is virtually untouched since the Maya left it more than a thousand years ago. We see jaguar prints on the paths around our camp on the way to work in the morning, and we can walk for miles without encountering anyone not attached to our own project. Remains of hundreds of masonry buildings, almost invisible in the dense vegetation, dot the hills and ridges. Most of these sites are habitations of ancient Maya common people, but some were the impressive establishments of lords subject to the powerful kings of Piedras Negras. Excavating in such remote places can be extremely seductive, alone except for one's workmen, the solitude broken only by the occasional chatter of monkeys high in the trees overhead. Few Maya archaeologists are immune to the attractions of this kind of work and they communicate its romance to the wider public in many ways.

Paradoxically, Maya centers are also very accessible to anyone with an urge to visit them. Most of the Aztec capital of Tenochtitlan is now destroyed or buried under modern Mexico City, and the Inca capital of Cuzco is smothered by Colonial and later buildings. Other Inca ruins such as Machu Picchu are spectacular, but highland Peru is pretty far away for most people to travel. A short plane ride from Miami or Houston, however, or a cruise ship from Galveston, now takes tourists within easy driving distance of

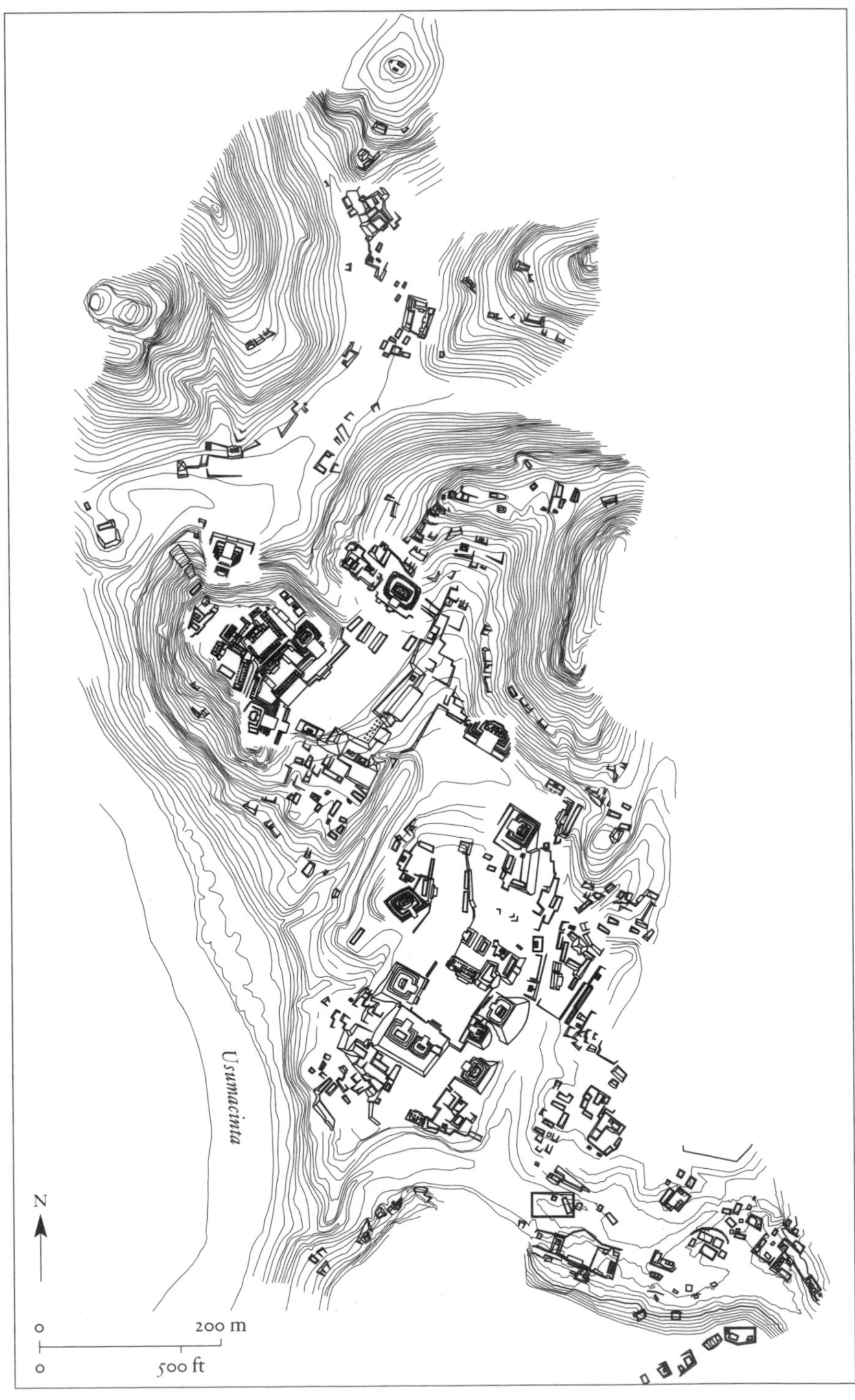
Usumacinta
N
0
200 m
0
500 ft

scores of Maya archaeological sites that have been cleared, mapped, and reconstructed. In the 1950s, a century after Stephens and Catherwood slung their hammocks in its ruined palaces, few people except an occasional archaeologist visited the walled center of Tulum, set amid the spectacular limestone cliffs and white sand beaches of the east coast of Yucatan. Now thousands of tourists crowd Tulum each day. Copan Ruinas had six houses when Stephens and Catherwood arrived in 1839, and was still a sleepy Honduran town only connected to the outside world by sometimes impassable dirt roads when I first worked there in 1980. Now it is a bustling place with fine hotels and excellent restaurants serving the tourists who arrive by the busload to visit the nearby ruins.

And the trip to one of these great centers certainly repays the effort. Ornate temples, some in excess of 60 m (200 ft) high, surround spacious plazas filled with carved stelae and altars. Deep inside some of these huge buildings are the tombs of kings including Copan's founder K'inich Ajaw Yax K'uk' Mo', and, most celebrated of all, that of K'inich Janaab' Pakal, the great 7th-century lord of Palenque. One can wander through the rooms of the royal palaces where Maya kings lived, and see the ball courts where they played a game that was sometimes just a stimulating sport, and sometimes something far more exotic and sinister. So impressive are these central places that archaeologists have been unduly preoccupied with them, creating a "big-site" bias that, as we shall see later, still inhibits our understanding of the Maya in important ways.

Then there is the art. All civilizations are associated with great and distinctive traditions of art, which as we saw by the 19th century had become an index of cultural advancement. Stephens and Catherwood showed that the Maya are no exception. Ancient artists created world-class sculpture, as exemplified by the sarcophagus lid of K'inich Janaab' Pakal (Fig. 7), and by countless other carved stelae, altars, and building façades. From tombs and caches come beautiful polychrome vessels and delicate figurines of gods, humans, and animals, along with jade masks, carved shells, and effigy flints. No one could ever mistake these wonderful objects as other than Maya in origin. They are prominently displayed in museums, and unfortunately also coveted by unscrupulous collectors, patrons of the looters who plunder so many archaeological sites.

6 Plan of Piedras Negras, Guatemala. Many important sculptures and inscriptions were found here in the 1930s, and a recent project carried out between 1997 and 2000 has revealed much new information concerning this medium-sized Maya center on the Usumacinta river.

7 *Sarcophagus lid of K'inich Janaab' Pakal I, 7th-century ruler of Palenque. Excavations in the early 1950s showed for the first time that pyramids sometimes covered the tombs of dynastic rulers.*

Finally there are the inscriptions that so fascinated Stephens and that constitute a unique bridge between past and present. Inscriptions, we now know, fall according to our perception into two great classes (although these were probably inseparable to the Maya themselves). One set records a system of mathematical notations and concepts, including the idea of "zero" or "place," that was used to record several complex calendars and to astronomical observations that traced the cycles of the sun, moon, Venus, and other heavenly bodies. Scholars have been able to read these mathematical symbols and calendrical glyphs since early in the 20th century (although the exact correlation with the Gregorian calendar remained controversial until much later). The most distinctive of the several Maya calendars is called the Long Count, which essentially measures the number of elapsed days since a beginning date, just as the Western calendar does. Because the Maya were the only Precolumbian Mesoamerican people who recorded comprehensible dates over hundreds of years, information preserved on Classic Maya monuments for a long time provided the central chronological framework for all of Mesoamerica, until radiocarbon dating and other chronometric methods finally allowed the construction of independent regional sequences.

Even more important from our perspective, Maya scribes, alone among New World peoples, developed a system of hieroglyphic writing that, by the 7th or 8th century AD, could accurately replicate almost any verbal utterance they cared to make. Maya inscriptions constitute the earliest corpus of intelligible texts found anywhere in Mesoamerica. Inscriptions were written on bark paper in screenfold books called codices, and also carved and painted on stone monuments, ceramic vessels, bones, and many other objects. Fortunately for us, both dates and inscriptions were combined in single texts, creating a chronicle of dated events that constitutes a kind of history, just as Stephens surmised.

Epigraphers can now decipher hieroglyphs quite well, with the result that the ancient Maya are no longer anonymous from our perspective. Today we can read the names of rulers and other prominent people, as well as their titles and offices, and details of their births, deaths, wars, gods, and rituals. There are toponyms for particular centers and for other places on the Maya landscape. Because dates can now be correlated with our own calendar, all this information is firmly anchored in time. Just as important, both the content and linguistic structure of ancient texts reveal much about Maya mental sensibilities, cognition, and world-view. Although we have no eyewitness accounts of the ancient Maya as we do for the Aztecs and Incas, in a sense we have something better – messages encoded directly by them, unsullied and undistorted by the vagaries of some interface with expanding 16th-century Old World cultures.

Archaeologists still routinely uncover such messages in unexpected places. I arrived at Piedras Negras in April 2000 just in time to find my colleagues pondering a newly discovered panel carved of fine limestone (Plate 20). Measuring almost 1.5 m (5 ft) on a side and weighing about 3000 pounds, it had fallen from a prominent position on a temple high above. Glyphs on the panel revealed that it was commissioned by Piedras Negras's 3rd ruler in AD 706 to celebrate events (particularly military exploits) in the life of his father, the 2nd king. This individual, one Itsamk'anahk II, came to the throne as a boy of 12 and thereafter enjoyed an immensely long and prestigious reign. Just a year earlier excavators investigating two peripheral structures at nearby Palenque unearthed an inscribed throne and panel dating to the 8th-century reign of the king K'inich Akhal Mo' Naab' III. Close by they found a richly painted tomb, still to be opened, that might contain the remains of Pakal's grandmother, a great lady who ruled the kingdom in her own right. Inscriptions such as these now provide us almost with an embarrassment of riches, and have begun to drive the archaeological enterprise in a manner scarcely imaginable 20 years ago.

No wonder, then, that the Maya fascinate us as few other ancient civilizations do. So intellectually and aesthetically accomplished were the Maya of our imaginations that they were long ago heralded as "the Greeks of the New

World," and the "Mother Culture" of Mesoamerica – the clever people who devised the first calendars, invented the first writing systems, the concept of zero, and raised the first monumental buildings. And they did all this with only a very rudimentary technology. But although their civilization endured for centuries, all this sophistication could not ultimately save the Maya from a mysterious, sudden, and dramatic fate. At least so goes the popular story.

Who are the Maya?

What does the word Maya mean? We must consider this question in some detail because there are more meanings than most people realize, and because it provides us with the opportunity to establish some essential background and introduce some issues we will discuss later. Perhaps the best way to start out is to emphasize that although it is tempting to think of Maya as a general label, Precolumbian Maya people probably never thought of themselves collectively as an ethnic group in the modern sense, nor, until very recently, did their descendants. Sixteenth-century Spaniards sometimes referred to "Maya Indians," but in the copious Colonial-era documents written in native languages indigenous scribes very seldom used the term Maya for self-description, and possibly even regarded it as derogatory. Although the word is certainly of New World origin, in virtually all of its specific uses – linguistic, geographical, and cultural – outsiders have in fact created the modern meanings of Maya.

Most fundamentally Maya (or Mayan) is a linguistic term that refers to a set of approximately 31 closely related languages and dialects, many of which are still widely spoken in southern and eastern Mesoamerica (Figs 8 and 9). Taken together, these comprise what linguists call the Macro-Mayan language family. Beginning in the 16th century, the Spaniards in Yucatan used the label Maya for the language spoken by the Indians there, as apparently did the natives themselves.

According to the historical linguist Joseph Greenberg, all Mayan tongues derive from a very ancient group of ancestral languages spoken by the earliest migrants into the New World. Greenberg calls these languages, along with their descendants, Amerind. Although Greenberg's classification is controversial, the southerly distribution of Maya languages and their complex internal diversity suggest that they do have very deep roots in southern and eastern Mesoamerica. Linguists offer various reconstructions of the origins and geographical spread of Mayan languages themselves, but two things are clear. First, these languages are quite different from those spoken in most

8 *This map shows the huge area where Mayan languages were spoken in the past or are still spoken today. They dominate eastern and southern Mesoamerica.*

neighboring regions of Mesoamerica. Second, the major Mayan language groups resemble one another closely, differing among themselves about as much as European Romance languages do. Such similarity argues for a common origin in fairly recent times and/or a high degree of interaction.

Roughly 5,000,000 people still speak one or another form of Mayan language (no one knows the exact number). All surviving languages of the Macro-Mayan family, except for an isolated enclave of Huastec (or Wastek), are distributed throughout a solid block of territory that includes the southeastern highlands of Mexico (especially the modern state of Chiapas), the adjacent highlands of Guatemala further to the southeast, and the mountains of western Honduras and El Salvador. Maya speakers also live in the low-lying northern parts of the Yucatan Peninsula that comprise the modern Mexican states of Yucatan, Campeche, and Quintana Roo. Between lie the extensive tropical lowlands of Guatemala, sparsely populated only a few decades ago but now being rapidly colonized by migrants from many places. Prior to AD 800 this region was the heartland of Maya civilization, which also extended throughout the territory of modern Belize.

Because Mayan speakers have long occupied this vast region of Mesoamerica, which altogether measures about 324,000 sq. km (126,360 sq. miles), the word Maya also has a geographical meaning that is essentially coextensive with the linguistic distribution. Although the Maya homeland as a whole lies in the tropics, it exhibits great variation in topography, climate,

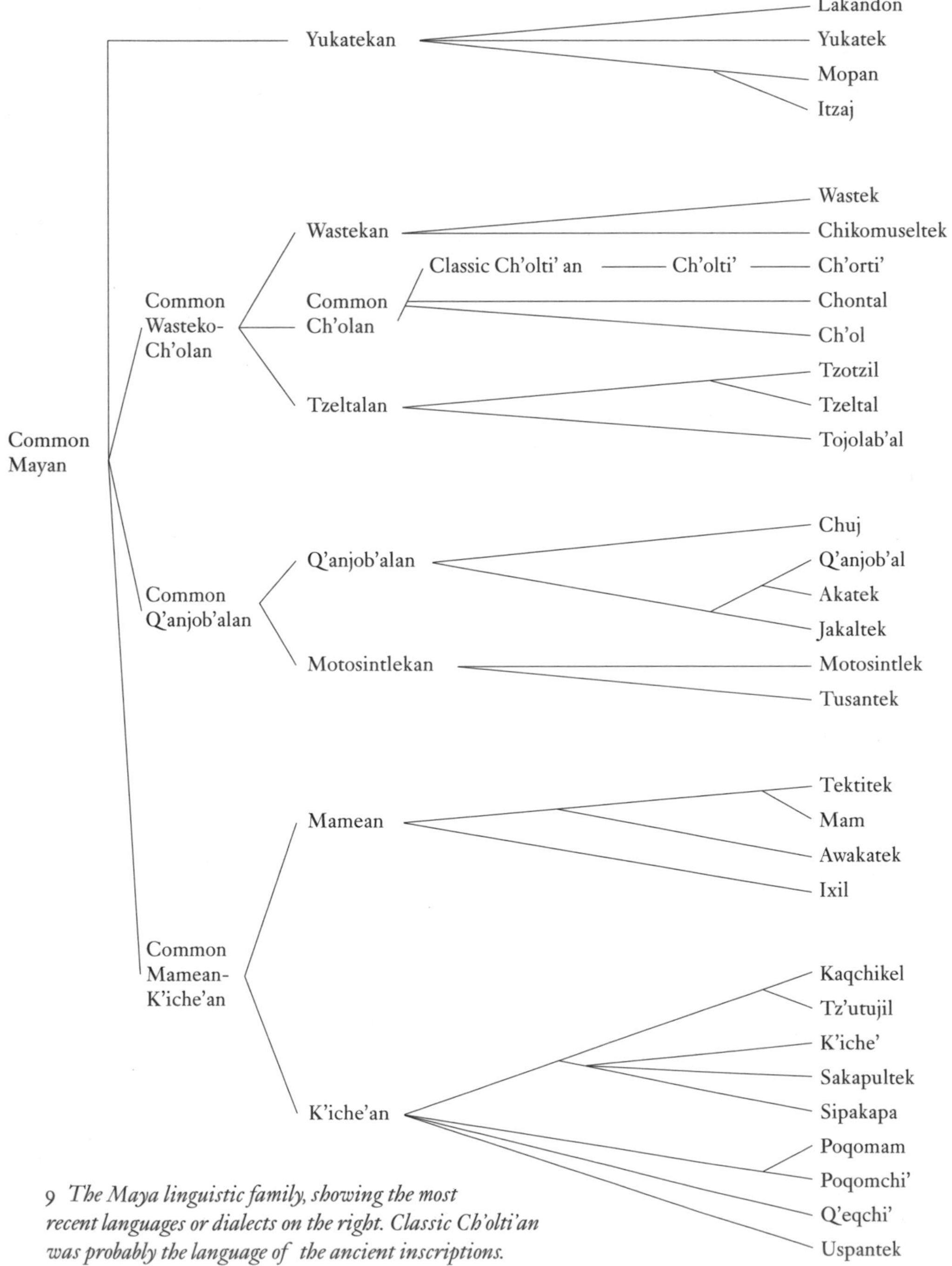

9 *The Maya linguistic family, showing the most recent languages or dialects on the right. Classic Ch'olti'an was probably the language of the ancient inscriptions.*

and vegetation. The most fundamental distinction is between the Highland regions in the south and the Lowlands to the north. Today the Maya Highlands, at elevations over 1000 m (3290 ft), have some of the densest populations of Native Americans found anywhere in the New World, many of whom still live in very traditional communities. Although reconstructions of linguistic origins are problematical, most Mayanists believe that these Highland zones were the original homeland of the ancestral proto-Mayan language because of the great linguistic diversity historically found there. Separation of the main Mayan language branches probably took place between about 2000 BC and AD 100, as populations migrated into the northern Lowlands or otherwise diverged from one another.

Lowland regions are geographically far more extensive, totaling around 250,000 sq. km (97,500 sq. miles). For comparison, this is about the same size as the United Kingdom or the U.S. state of Colorado. Because of its lower elevation, this zone is typically hotter and more humid than the Highlands. There are comparatively few large rivers on the vast limestone shelf of the Yucatan Peninsula (especially in the north) because the porous bedrock promotes underground drainage. Even here, though, there is great variation. Around Piedras Negras the countryside is dominated by steep hills and ridges covered with high tropical forest nourished by 2500 mm (98 in) of annual rainfall. In contrast, rainfall in northern Yucatan, an extremely flat limestone plain, varies between about 450 mm and 1000 mm (18–40 in) of rain, and supports only scrubby vegetation that mostly loses its leaves in the dry season.

Contrary to popular opinion, there is no true "rain forest" even in the heart of the Maya Lowlands, but rather several seasonal tropical forest communities with many deciduous or semideciduous species. While stripping ancient architecture during the height of the dry season at Piedras Negras, I have often cursed the falling leaves that must be raked away every couple of days so that photographs can be taken. And despite the primordial impression given by the lofty canopy, the forests that exist today are hardly natural, but rather artifacts of thousands of years of human interference.

Rainfall, mainly transported by easterly winds, is strongly seasonal over the whole Lowlands, although here again there is a lot of variation. In Yucatan the rains begin in May or June, and then taper off in October, allowing only one crop. Around Piedras Negras some rain usually falls in every month, so "dry season" is a relative concept. At Copan, on the southeastern margins of the Maya region, rain declines in December and January and by late April the landscape is parched, hot, and dusty. People and animals eagerly await the onset of the summer rains in mid-May that inaugurate another agricultural season and an almost miraculous burst of new vegetation.

Where rainfall is high enough and falls at the right time, more than one crop of maize or beans can be grown, but the main wet season crop is everywhere the most crucial. Unfortunately, rains can be very unpredictable, especially in the drier north, so uncontrollable risk to farmers' crops is high. The dramatic dry season-wet season transformation profoundly influenced the Maya worldview, in which death and regeneration were major themes. Even today farmers carry out ceremonies, such as the chac-chac rituals of Yucatan, to ensure the all-important rainfall.

Many kinds of evidence indicate that in the past there were significant shifts of climate, and particularly fluctuations in temperature and rainfall, that affected the development of Maya civilization. Some archaeologists believe, for example, that early in the Classic period (see below) the climate was comparatively warm and dry, making the northern part of the Yucatan Peninsula less hospitable than the wetter south. Similarly, cool and moist conditions might have predominated during the great burst of population and cultural creativity during the 7th and 8th centuries.[4] Although we do not yet understand these changes in detail, such fluctuations have recently been championed by paleoclimatologists and some archaeologists as prime causes of the Classic collapse.

Many geographers and anthropologists have pointed out the seeming incongruity of the development of Classic Maya civilization in this humid tropical Lowland setting, a kind of environment widely believed to be too limited in agricultural potential to support dense populations. Some even concluded that the "advanced" components of Classic culture must have developed elsewhere and been introduced into the tropical Lowlands. We now know that this was not the case, but the Maya did face many environmental challenges and limitations, and as we shall see later, severe problems stemming from land use seriously affected some ancient kingdoms.

A third meaning of the word Maya refers to the cultural tradition, developed over thousands of years, that is broadly characteristic of Maya speakers. This tradition includes not just language, but all aspects of generally shared culture, or what we might call "folkways": basic ways of farming, cooking and eating, building structures, reckoning kin relationships, apportioning and inheriting resources, defining and regulating gender and sexuality, attitudes toward death, wealth, and rank, and many other very fundamental aspects of life.[5] Of course, at no time in the past were such folkways absolutely uniform across hundreds of thousands of sq. km. As one would expect in a geographical region so extensive and diverse, over many centuries local Maya populations and polities developed not only their own languages and dialects, but also different architectural, ceramic, and artistic styles, writing conventions, and subsistence practices. Nor were these folkways immune from change through time – in fact quite the contrary, because they formed a critical adaptive interface with the larger natural and social environments. Still, change was often slow enough to preserve broad cultural identity. Many Maya folkways, such as reverence for ancestors and belief in various kinds of souls, are of very ancient origin and still thrive today.

Archaeologists have devised the following general chronological framework for this long Maya tradition, and we will refer to substantial parts of it in later chapters.[6] Most important are the Early and Late Classic periods, when ancient Maya culture reached its maturity. While these time periods allow us to break up Maya history conveniently from our point of view, they do not imply any sharp discontinuities in culture change, or that all sub-regions developed in some kind of overall, lock-step fashion. Nor, of course, were any of these chronological thresholds perceptible to the ancient Maya themselves, with two probable exceptions – the Terminal Classic period from about AD 800 to 1000 when the Maya collapse occurred, and the early 16th century, when the Spaniards arrived.

Paleoindian Period	before 7000 BC
Archaic Period	7000–2500 BC
Early Preclassic Period	2500–1000 BC
Middle Preclassic Period	1000–400 BC
Late Preclassic Period	400 BC – AD 250
Early Classic Period	AD 250–600
Late Classic Period	AD 600–800
Terminal Classic Period	AD 800–1000
Early Postclassic Period	AD 1000–1250
Late Postclassic Period	AD 1250–1519

Exactly when we can identify the first Mayan speakers is uncertain, but there are signs of Paleoindian activity in the region perhaps as early as 9000–8000 BC, judging from distinctive fluted stone points characteristic of terminal Pleistocene hunter-gatherers that have been found in Belize and in the Guatemalan highlands. The environment then was distinctly cooler and dryer than today, and had more xerophytic vegetation. Beginning about 7000 BC conditions became warmer and more humid, and the tropical broadleaf forest of recent times established itself. Artifacts found in Belize suggest that

Archaic peoples continued this general hunter-gatherer way of life, although some finds are controversial and accurate dating is difficult.

Early farmers are somewhat better documented. The two basic agricultural staples of the Maya diet have historically been maize and beans. Wild ancestors of both these crops were native to temperate and subtropical regions of highland Mesoamerica. Both crops, along with many others, were probably domesticated before 5000 BC, but only spread widely after about 3000 BC. Indirect evidence of preceramic human horticultural activity in the Maya Lowlands, in the form of fossil pollen (including that of maize and manioc) and other indicators of environmental disturbance, dates back to 2500 BC or before.[7] Pioneering farmers cleared upland forests for their shifting gardens, and also made drained fields along the moist margins of wetlands at surprisingly early times to plant auxiliary crops. More direct archaeological indications of these farmers such as pottery, permanent houses, and other accouterments of settled life only appear much later, around 1400–1200 BC. These are the remains of small agricultural communities established along rivers or swamp margins, and they yield early pottery that has strong stylistic connections to that found in the highlands of southeastern Mexico and western Guatemala. Although there is no way short of inscriptions to reconstruct language from archaeological remains, it is probable that these farmers spoke some early variant of Mayan.

Prior to about 650 BC we can detect no signs of particular social or political complexity in the archaeological remains of these early settlers, although obsidian and other objects imported from Highlands to Lowlands show that scattered populations were by no means isolated from one another. During the next two centuries a few communities in the central Maya Lowlands and Belize began to build masonry civic structures 10–14 m (33–46 ft) high, some with stucco masks and other decorative elements that have a generic resemblance to those found at later Classic period sites. About the same time even bigger structures were erected in the valleys of El Salvador. Boulder sculptures there, and also along the Pacific coast of Guatemala and Mexico, show sophisticated symbolic motifs that possibly reflect influences from the Olmec culture of the Mexican Gulf Coast. At various highland centers elaborate burials, large buildings, stone stelae, and what might be early glyphs and numerals all appear by about 400 BC. Some archaeologists believe that the basic ideological and iconographic conventions of kingship originated in highland centers such as Kaminaljuyu (where Guatemala City is now located).

Once thought to have been a time of simple farming villages, we now know that the Late Preclassic period brought spectacular changes. Similar pottery styles spread throughout much of the Lowlands and populations (almost certainly Mayan speakers by this time) increased dramatically. The scale, design, and construction methods of Late Preclassic public buildings prefigure those of later Classic times, as do façade decorations, which depict early versions of religious and royal symbols once thought diagnostic of Classic Maya society. Also evident in both Lowlands and Highlands are increased trade, rich burials, human sacrifice (probably associated with war), fortifications, stone monuments depicting humans in elaborate costumes, and, most significantly, evidence for the use of early hieroglyphs and perhaps calendrical inscriptions. Extensive modifications of the landscape in the form of canals and reservoirs appeared by about AD 1. In fact, most of the important elements of Maya civilization emerged during Late Preclassic times, although many were subsequently reworked and given a later, distinctive Classic stamp.

If we had to identify a single region where these definitive Lowland Maya features first crystallized in durable form, it would be the northern Peten area of Guatemala, adjacent parts of southern Campeche just across the Mexican border to the north, and in the river valleys of Belize to the east. Here were situated the great innovative centers of Mirador, Nakbe, Calakmul, Tikal, Uaxactun, Yaxha, and Cerros. By AD 100 the fundamental building blocks of complex Maya culture were firmly in place, and the stage was set for the extraordinary Classic florescence of the next seven centuries.

Inscriptions indicate that by AD 200, or perhaps a bit earlier, the first known dynasties of Maya kings were established at a few great Lowland centers such as Tikal, so it is convenient to begin the Classic period at AD 250. Thereafter royal lines proliferated as new centers were founded, and traditions of elite culture in the form of architecture, art, iconography, and writing spread widely at the same time. Rulers increasingly celebrated their distinguished descent and their participation in ritual and war on the inscribed monuments they commissioned. Nor were Maya kingdoms isolated in their tropical forests. Trade, with all of its attendant political and cultural influences, linked them with other polities as far away as the Basin of Mexico, 1000 km (625 miles) to the northwest, then dominated by the huge metropolis of Teotihuacan. Because even the earliest inscriptions are written in Mayan, we can identify Mayan speakers with certainty for the first time, even though their Preclassic predecessors almost certainly spoke one or another Mayan language as well.

The Late Classic period between AD 600 and 800 marks the mature phase of Maya civilization in the Lowlands. Populations reached unparalleled size, peaking in most areas in the 8th century. Between 40 and 50 centers boasted distinctive emblem glyphs that formed parts of the titles of their kings, some of whom could trace their lines of succession back through 30 or more generations. A broadly similar elite tradition of art, Long Count dates, inscriptions, and architecture achieved its widest distribution, so much so that archaeologists once spoke of the period from about AD 730 to 790 as the "period of uniformity."

This brings us to the final meaning of the word Maya – essentially the one invented by Stephens and Catherwood. To most people the label connotes not the basic cultural tradition or folkways of Maya speakers in general, but rather the impressive architectural, artistic, and intellectual achievements of the Classic Lowland Maya, which collectively are manifestations of an elite subtradition. Only Maya people of elite or royal rank really understood the conventions of writing, the reckoning of time, the complex canons of sculpture and painting, or the structure of the cosmos and the nature of the gods, and although everyone had ancestors, the ancestors of kings and nobles were by far the most powerful. Many very basic folkway elements survive in Maya daily life today, but this elite sub-tradition, which we will examine in more detail later, does not.

We now recognize that there never was sufficient internal cultural homogeneity to warrant use of the label "period of uniformity." Not all regions or polities of the Maya Lowlands bought into this whole package of elite culture, and even where they did, no king or polity ever established political unity over all the others. Although warfare is detectable as early as Preclassic times, after AD 550 there is increasingly abundant evidence from the inscriptions of the shifting alliances and interminable wars among many of these kingdoms. Nevertheless, as Stephens and Catherwood intuitively realized (especially with regard to the hieroglyphs), there was enough shared elite culture, especially in the southern Maya Lowlands, to identify the florescence of a great world civilization between AD 250 and 800.

The Problem: The Collapse of the Classic Maya

Developments of the 8th century bring us to the main theme of this book, and a thumbnail sketch of what we will discuss in greater detail later on. Beginning shortly after AD 750 some Classic centers and polities began to show signs of severe trouble, as reflected in the cessation of dated monuments, abandonment of elite building projects, and changes in ceramic inventories. These symptoms are first evident on the western margins of the

Lowlands. The last date recorded at the previously vigorous center of Palenque is AD 790, and over the next 150 years many dynasties failed, including Palenque's. Some centers were abruptly abandoned as kings lost their power and the supporting populations disappeared as well. Elsewhere the decline was more gradual, and lesser nobles and some of the supporting population persisted for a time. The last gasps of the old tradition occurred during the Terminal Classic period, and by AD 1000 many great Classic centers, if not entirely abandoned, were no longer occupied by kings and nobles, nor surrounded by large and prosperous populations of rural farmers. What makes this collapse especially puzzling is its apparent abruptness at some centers and the fact that some of the most impressive sculptures and buildings were erected on the very eve of the catastrophe.

Disruption of this impressive Classic Maya elite tradition, along with the polities and populations that expressed it, is what most people think of as the Maya collapse. More specifically, there was a dramatic political, cultural, and demographic failure that took place over about 150–200 years. As we shall see later, however, this was not the first cultural crisis experienced by the ancient Maya and it was primarily a phenomenon of the southern Lowlands. Even there it did not affect all Maya kingdoms and regions in the same way, nor did it destroy Maya civilization, which continued on until the Spaniards arrived. Still, something dramatic certainly happened to the Classic Lowland Maya beginning in the 8th and 9th centuries, and explaining this crisis has fascinated and challenged archaeologists since Stephens so evocatively captured its drama in words and pictures over a century and a half ago.

As recently as the early 1980s the collapse interval formed a kind of conceptual threshold between prehistory and history, between the Maya we knew ethnographically or could reasonably reconstruct from various kinds of historical records, and those Classic Maya who wrote, but whose writings remained opaque to us. Exactly what collapsed, and how and why it did so, are the basic themes of this book, and fortunately we know much more today than we did just a short time ago, not least because we can make much greater sense of the inscriptions.

This brief overview of Maya culture history is enough for now. In later chapters we will discuss many of these developments in greater detail, particularly those of the Late Classic period. One important conclusion from even this short survey, however, is that Maya civilization, though never isolated from wider influences, is of New World origin and developed gradually in southern and eastern Mesoamerica. It was not, as some scholars thought only a short time ago, introduced from outside, although it was stimulated by profound influences from Central Mexico. We also now know that however tempting it once was to trace all important Mesoamerican innovations back to a Maya "Mother Culture," monumental architecture and sculpture, rich burials, and almost certainly calendars and writing in fact all emerged earlier elsewhere. The Maya were simply one regional variant of a more general Mesoamerican pattern of civilization, although they certainly developed and refined many important aspects of it to levels of unparalleled sophistication.

Archaeologists, epigraphers, art historians, geographers, and other students of the ancient Maya are themselves ambivalent about the Maya mystique. Many were first attracted to the Maya because of it and prefer to emphasize the uniqueness of the Maya cultural tradition. Others, myself included, are of a more comparative temperament, and instead try to evaluate the ancient Maya in light of ancient civilizations in general. Whichever view we take, it is nonetheless true that the Maya mystique has been a good thing for archaeologists. Those explorers who followed Stephens and Catherwood often portrayed themselves in romantic ways (Fig. 10), and we are still consciously or unconsciously adept at perpetuating the Maya mystique because it keeps the Maya before the public in ways both profitable and congenial to us. After all, someone has to pay for my airline seat, and for the research that it transports me to. And after all, despite all that we now know about the ancient Maya, there is still plenty of mystery to keep us busy.

10 *Beginning in 1858 the French explorer Desiré Charnay took celebrated photographs of Maya ruins such as Palenque and Uxmal. Here he is shown in full period adventurer garb in his book* Les Anciennes Villes de Nouveau Mond.

– 3 –

CIVILIZATION AND THE MAYA

ONE RETORT I MIGHT MAKE to the question of why Maya civilization collapsed is that it didn't. Because this assertion appears to fly in the face of widely cherished views about what happened to the Maya, it leads us to the three themes of this chapter: one, a brief overview of what the Spaniards found when they first began to explore the Maya regions of Mesoamerica in the early 16th century (a topic we will take up again in greater detail in the following chapter); two, an analysis of what we mean by the concept of civilization, and three, what it means to say that civilizations "collapse." All this is a lot to cover, but essential to the presentation that follows.

Europeans Meet the Maya

Europeans first encountered the Maya and the larger world of Mesoamerican civilization during several expeditions at the beginning of the 16th century.[1] Christopher Columbus made his fourth and final voyage of discovery to the New World between 1502 and 1504. After several years of disappointed retirement in Spain, during which he saw others capitalize on his earlier ventures, Columbus at last persuaded Queen Isabella to fund one more expedition to what he still imagined to be the eastern extremities of Asia. In May 1502 he proudly sailed with a fleet of four caravels outfitted at the Queen's expense, no doubt immensely gratified that her instructions honored him as "Admiral of the Islands and Tierra Firma that are in the Ocean Sea on the Side of the Indies." Unfortunately this grandiloquent title did not impress his powerful enemies in the Caribbean, where he was denied entrance to the harbor of Santo Domingo by its Spanish governor. Undeterred, Columbus sailed away to the south and east and followed the coastline of what we today call Central America from Honduras to Panama, recording what he saw and searching for a passage that might lead him further west to Indochina or India.

On 30 July 1502, the little Spanish fleet met a native seagoing vessel off the coast of Guanaja, one of the Bay Islands of Honduras. Unfortunately the original account of this meeting is now lost, but two later versions survive. One is a second-hand account of the fourth voyage by the Italian chronicler Peter Martyr, who "debriefed" many early explorers. The second was written down many years later by Columbus's son Ferdinand, an eyewitness, whose following reminiscences are mixed with insights from his later experiences in various parts of New Spain:

there came at that time a canoe as great as a galley, eight feet wide, all of a single trunk.... Amidships it had a canopy of palm leaves, like that of gondolas in Venice, which protected what was underneath in such a manner that neither wind or waves could wet anything within. Under this canopy were the children, women, and all the baggage and merchandise. The crew of the canoe, although they were twenty-five, did not have the spirit to defend themselves against the batels [a kind of small Spanish vessel] sent in pursuit. The canoe thus taken by us without a fight was brought to the ships where the Admiral gave many thanks to God, seeing that in one moment, without effort or danger to his own men, he had been provided with a sample of all the things of that land. He then ordered that there should be taken from the canoe whatever appeared to be most attractive and valuable, such as cloths and sleeveless shirts of cotton that had been worked and dyed in different colors and designs, also pantaloons of the same workmanship, with which they cover their private parts, also cloth in which the Indian women of the canoe were dressed ... also long swords of wood with a groove along each edge, wherein stone knives were set by means of fiber and pitch, cutting like steel when used on naked people; also hatchets to cut wood, like those of stone used by other Indians, save that these were of good copper, of which metal they also had bells and crucibles for smelting. For food they carried roots and grain such as they eat in Española, and a certain wine made of maize, like the beer of England, and they had many of those kernels which serve as money in New Spain, which it appeared that they valued highly.[2]

At the time, of course, Columbus did not realize that this was one of the first European encounters with people from the mainland civilization of Mesoamerica (he guessed that he was off the coast of Indochina). Although we cannot be absolutely sure that the occupants of this vessel were Maya speakers, it is a very strong possibility, especially because he understood them to say that they came from a land called Maia. In any case, they were certainly traders coming from the west where a vigorous maritime commerce extended all around the coast of the Yucatan Peninsula.

Ethnic or cultural affiliations aside, it is clear to us in hindsight (as indeed it was to Ferdinand Columbus) that this merchant vessel carried valuable products, some of which originated in regions as far away as the Mexican highlands. The "swords" were cutting weapons of the kind called *macuahuitl* by the Aztecs, probably edged with obsidian blades from volcanic deposits in the Basin of Mexico. Copper must also have originated at a considerable distance because it is not found in Yucatan. Elaborate cloth was a common tribute and trade item throughout Mesoamerica, and the "kernels" were cacao (chocolate) beans used to make a costly drink much enjoyed by wealthy and powerful people and also as a kind of special-purpose currency for economic exchange. The geographer Carl Sauer surmised that the crucibles might have been used for melting gold, a product of the interior of Honduras. We do not know exactly who the women and children were. Some of them might have been family members of the male crew, although there was also a widespread traffic in human slaves at the time. Finally, the master of the vessel seems to have been a principal merchant who was probably the patron or manager of the trading venture. This individual was one of a general class of such merchants who traveled widely across Mesoamerica both on land and water, and who were later to prove invaluable as guides and informants for the Spanish because of their geographical and political knowledge.

Had Columbus reversed course and sailed west back along the track of this native canoe he would have struck the Yucatan coast, the main homeland of the 16th-century Lowland Maya (he had heard rumors of the mainland of Mesoamerica on his earlier second voyage). Instead he continued south and east, leaving that discovery to others, although at the time he and his crew seem to have recognized that the canoe, its occupants, and its contents all suggested the existence of complex societies very different from those known in the Antilles. By the early 16th century the word Maya was used as a geographical referent for parts of Central America and Yucatan by scholars in Europe and began to appear in various spellings on early maps (Fig 11). This paralleled the native usage, for in Columbus's time Maia or Maya seems to have been a generic term describing the whole northern part of the Yucatan Peninsula.

As it turned out, it was many years before the Spanish turned their attention from the Caribbean world and Panama to the mainland of Mesoamerica. In fact, the first certain contact we know of was accidental, although in the long run it had momentous consequences. In 1511 a handful of men and women from a Spanish shipwreck were washed ashore somewhere along the northeast coast of Yucatan, a land locally called Maya. According to later and probably sensationalized stories, these unfortunate castaways were captured by an evil local chief. Some of them were sacrificed and eaten, while others died of disease and overwork. A few Spaniards escaped and found refuge with lords hostile to their original captor, and two of these men, Jeronimo de Aguilar and Gonzalo Guerrero, somehow survived. Both were enslaved, and Aguilar spent the next seven years as a lowly servant attached to the household of a lord named Taxmar, drawing water, working in the fields, and carrying heavy loads on trading expeditions. Guerrero, so the story goes, was made of sterner stuff. He went south to the province of Chetumal where he entered the service of Nachan Can, the most powerful chief of the region, renounced Christianity, got himself tattooed all over, married a woman of high rank (in one account Nachan Can's daughter), and rose to the position of local war leader, in which capacity he was eventually killed campaigning against his fellow Spaniards. Whether this dramatic account of Guerrero's career is true or not, it was Aguilar who eventually played an important part in subsequent Spanish contacts with the Maya. A legacy of this early incidental contact might well have been a great plague, possibly smallpox, that swept Yucatan in about 1515–16, and was described in later Maya writings.

11 *Early map by Alonso de Santa Cruz (1545) showing forms of the words "Maya" and "Yucatan" (with the original 16th-century epigraphy slightly changed for clarity).*

Aguilar had to languish in captivity for a long time because the Spaniards did not begin purposeful reconnaissance of the Mesoamerican mainland until some years later, when rumors and stories seem to have been circulating about hitherto unknown but impressive kingdoms and towns. Peter Martyr recounts that a group of native refugees who landed in Darien (Panama) claimed to have come from "...a country where the people, living in a state of society under organized laws, used [books]. They had palaces, magnificent temples built of stone, public squares, and streets laid out for commercial purposes."[3]

In 1517 an ill-prepared expedition of erstwhile colonists from Cuba under the command of Francisco Hernandez de Cordoba skirted the coast of Yucatan, which they believed to be an island, from its northeast tip all the way to the town of Champoton on the west. Along the way they spotted impressive towns, one of which appeared so large that they nicknamed it "Grand Cairo." Going ashore at various places Cordoba's men skirmished with the inhabitants, saw elaborately carved stone buildings with "idols" in them, found a few tantalizing objects of gold, and took two natives captive, naming them Julian and Melchior. Attempts to communicate with the local Maya through signs elicited the response "yucatan," a term of uncertain meaning which thereafter became another geographic label. Most impressive were the two towns of Campeche and Champoton they saw on the west coast, each presided over by powerful lords. At Campeche, said to have had 3000 houses, the lord initially welcomed the Spaniards when they came ashore for water, but the landing party hastily withdrew after a large force of heavily armed warriors quickly assembled. Farther down the coast near Champoton, an equally impressive town apparently fortified with stockades, the ruler refused from the first to trade or to allow Cordoba to victual his ships. When an armed party went ashore to get water a fierce battle erupted in which many Spaniards were killed or captured and others wounded, including Cordoba himself, who ordered a retreat to Cuba where he shortly died of his injuries.

Although Cordoba's expedition ended disastrously it does provide us with some excellent eyewitness accounts of the first contacts with the Maya. Bernal Diaz del Castillo, that durable war-horse who much later wrote a stirring narrative of the conquest of New Spain, sailed with Cordoba as a young man and remembered that at Campeche

> They led us to some very large buildings of fine masonry which were the prayer-houses of their idols, the walls of which were painted with the figures of great serpents and evil-looking gods. In the middle was something like an altar, covered with clotted blood, and on the other side of the idols were symbols like crosses, and

all were colored. We stood astonished, never having seen or heard of such things before.[4]

In their report to Diego de Velasquez, the Governor of Cuba, the survivors of the expedition emphasized exactly this latter point – the land of Yucatan was unlike any in the Antilles. There was a densely populated countryside where farmers grew maize as the principal crop, and large towns with houses and temples of stone, all presided over by local lords and priests who could quickly summon up formidable numbers of warriors. Workmanship of many objects removed from the temples was superior to that hitherto encountered in the New World, and some Spaniards speculated that they were made by descendants of Jews exiled by Roman emperors in the 1st century AD.[5] Nor were the Spaniards the only ones to gather intelligence from the Cordoba voyage. News of European ships and the battle at Champoton eventually reached Motecezuma, ruler of the Aztec empire, far away in his lofty mountain capital of Tenochtitlan in Central Mexico.

Galvanized by the discoveries of the Cordoba adventure, Velasquez, along with other Spaniards whose desire for gold and Indian labor could no longer be satisfied in the Antilles, quickly organized a much better-equipped expedition that set sail in 1518, commanded by Juan de Grijalva and accompanied again by the intrepid Bernal Diaz. Making landfall on the southern end of the previously unknown Cozumel Island, just off the east coast of Yucatan, they met a Jamaican woman who was the last member of the crew of a fishing canoe that had been blown ashore two years before. She reported that all of the men, including her husband, had been sacrificed, but she had survived and learned to speak Maya. The ever opportunistic Spaniards added her to their little contingent of interpreters and sailed on along the coast of the mainland, where they saw towns so impressive "that the city of Seville could not look larger or better."[6] When they arrived in the vicinity of Champoton they fought another fierce, punitive engagement with the Maya and finally drove them from the town.

Continuing south and west, the fleet entered the Laguna de Terminos and eventually explored several major rivers further along the Mexican Gulf Coast. One of these, called Tabasco by the locals, they renamed the Grijalva in honor of their commander. In this region they found that the Maya, forewarned of their approach, had prepared fortifications and ambushes (Diaz claimed that 24,000 men from several provinces had responded to the muster – surely an exaggeration). Fortunately Grijalva used the interpreters Julian and Melchior to defuse the potential confrontation, and a lively trade in trinkets and food took place. Seeing that Bernal Diaz and the other Spaniards were excited by a few pieces of gold jewelry they had been given, the Maya assured them that although they had little such stuff themselves there was plenty to the northwest, in which direction they pointed, exclaiming "Mexico, Mexico." If their intention was to get rid of the troublesome Spaniards, they succeeded. The expedition continued west and eventually landed on the coastal fringes of the Aztec empire, where they found emissaries of Motecezuma sent especially to look for them. Here too they acquired gold, and shortly thereafter returned to Cuba.

Grijalva's successful reconnaissance caused a frenzy of preparation in Cuba, where Governor Velasquez and others hurried to launch a well-armed trading expedition thinly disguised as a colonizing effort and schemed among themselves to decide who should lead it and how the profits should be disposed. Command eventually fell to Hernan Cortes, who outmaneuvered other candidates and who quickly sailed with a partially prepared fleet to other Caribbean ports, fearing that the intense political jealousies of rival factions in Cuba would cause Velasquez to recall him. Debriefed by Grijalva in Trinidad, Cortes collected more ships, men, horses, and arms at various places, and laid on provisions of cassava bread, salt pork, maize, and hay. Fully equipped at last, and carrying 16 horses and 508 soldiers (including the ubiquitous Bernal Diaz), his fleet of 11 ships departed for Cozumel Island on 10 February 1519, the first stage in a great saga of adventure and conquest that led, just two and a half years later, to the downfall of the Aztec empire. What concerns us here, however, is part of this dramatic story that few people know – Cortes's encounters with the Maya.

Far from being the rapacious conqueror of popular imagination, Cortes could be subtle and accommodating when occasion demanded. He and his men ingratiated themselves with the inhabitants of Cozumel and learned through the interpreter Melchior that two "castillans," as the Maya called them, were somewhere on the mainland a few days' travel away. Indian messengers with letters and glass beads (for purposes of ransom) were sent off to find these Castilians, who of course were Aguilar and Guerrero, and to encourage them to join Cortes, for whom they would be invaluable sources of information about Yucatan if they could escape their captors. Aguilar was overjoyed to buy his freedom from his demanding chief and hurried off to a nearby town to persuade Guerrero to do the same. Content in the midst of his family, however, Guerrero demurred, and Aguilar, after being berated by Guerrero's wife for foolishly trying to lure her husband away, hastily departed by canoe for Cozumel. As he stumbled ashore on the beach he looked to the astonished Spaniards exactly like a Maya, but soon identified himself and told his dramatic story. From this point on, Cortes possessed excellent intelligence concerning the nature of Maya society. Just as important, Aguilar proved an able interpreter, doubly useful since Julian had died and Melchior soon defected from the Spaniards and rejoined his own people.

Cortes was obviously impressed by the Maya he encountered along the coast. In the first of five "letters" directed to his sovereign Charles V back in Spain – intensely political reports intended to justify his actions, secure his privileges, and promote his reputation – he remarked that

> There are some large towns and well laid out. The houses in those parts where there is stone are of masonry and mortar and the rooms are small and low in the Moorish fashion. In those parts where there is no stone they make their houses of adobes, which are whitewashed and the roofs covered with straw. There are houses belonging to certain men of rank which are very cool and have many rooms, for we have seen as many as five courtyards in a single house, and the rooms around them well laid out, each man having a private room. Inside there are also wells and water tanks and rooms for slaves and servants of which they have many. Each of these chieftains has in front of the entrance to his house a very large courtyard and some two or three of them [houses] raised very high with steps up to them and all very well built. Likewise they have their shrines and temples with raised walks which run all around the outside and are very wide: there they keep the idols which they worship, some of stone, some of clay and wood, which they honor and serve with such customs and so many ceremonies that many sheets of paper would not suffice to give Your Royal Highnesses a true and detailed account of them all. And the temples where they are kept are the largest and the finest built of all the buildings found in the towns; and they are much adorned with rich hanging cloths and featherwork and other fineries.[7]

In Tabasco, where Grijalva had been well received the previous year, Cortes found thousands of Maya warriors assembled under the chiefs of eight provinces at a place called Cintla. According to Bernal Diaz

> All the men wore great feather crests, they carried drums and trumpets, their faces were painted black and white, they were armed with large bows and arrows, spears and shields, swords like our two-handed swords, and slings and stones and fire-hardened darts, and all wore quilted cotton armor.[8]

Several fierce battles were fought with these Tabascan hosts before their commanders finally made a truce, bringing to the Spanish camp presents of food, gold, and 20 female slaves. One of these women, Malinali, was originally of high rank and understood both Mayan and the Aztec language Nahuatl. She was rechristened Dona Marina by the Spaniards, and in combination with Aguilar gave Cortes the final crucial link in his chain of communication.

Cortes's 1519 voyage also provided Europeans with firm indications of Maya literacy. Members of the expedition later told Peter Martyr that they saw many books in buildings on Cozumel Island, and the Spaniards observed that Maya military commanders in Tabasco kept track of their various contingents using written records. One of the four Precolumbian Maya books that can still be read, called the Madrid Codex, surfaced in Spain near the end of the 19th century, where according to some accounts it had been in the possession of Cortes's family some three centuries earlier. It probably originated somewhere around Champoton and might very well have been collected, along with other objects, by Cortes himself and sent back to Spain. Another book, the Grolier Codex, is written in a Mexicanized Maya style and was apparently found much more recently (its origins are a bit of a mystery) near the parts of Tabasco where Cortes's fleet landed. Descriptions of Maya books, along with two real Aztec ones, eventually were taken to Spain in December of 1519 by Cortes's agent Francisco de Montejo, who later conquered Yucatan. Undecipherable though they were, these books astounded Peter Martyr and other scholars at the Spanish court much more than the marvelous objects of gold, silver, precious stones, feathers, and cotton that accompanied them.

From Tabasco Cortes set off for his fateful encounter with Motecezuma and so we will leave him for the moment, although he will appear again later as he makes the first epic European journey though the heartland of ancient Maya civilization.

These and other Spanish accounts of the early 16th century show that very complex societies then existed in the northern Yucatan Peninsula and adjacent parts of the Gulf Coast. Dense populations of farmers grew maize and a wide variety of other crops on well-tended landscapes. Priests officiated in lofty, brightly painted temples filled with carved images of gods and the bones of prominent ancestors. These temples, along with elaborate residences, fronted on spacious plazas that defined the centers of towns with thousands of well-built houses and inhabitants. Powerful men ruled these towns and some, called by the Spaniards *calachuni*, held sway over outlying territories as well. When necessary calachuni could quickly summon up thousands of disciplined warriors to confront each other or the Spaniards. Nobles and rulers were supported by the taxes and labor of farmers. Lords and other rich men also owned slaves and engaged in long-distance trade in cacao, jade, cotton, copper, gold, honey, salt, and many other valuable commodities. Wise men painted inscriptions in books, and reckoned time using complex calendars. And all the way from Cozumel Island to Tabasco people spoke one or another Mayan language.

It seems reasonable from all this to conclude that a vigorous Maya civilization was thriving over a huge part of eastern Mesoamerica when the first Spanish explorers arrived. But of course it all depends on what we mean by "civilization."

What is Civilization?

"It is a long way from savagery to civilization."[9] With these stirring words John Wesley Powell, one-armed Civil War hero, explorer of the Grand Canyon, and founder of the Bureau of American Ethnology, began his presidential address to the Anthropological Society of Washington in 1885. In those days no one doubted that civilization referred to the most progressive stage of human accomplishment in the long evolution of social, political, and economic institutions, technology, arts, literature, morals, and intellectual attainments of all kinds. This sweeping concept was much in vogue in the late 19th century and in one form or another continues to be so today. Type the word civilization into the search program of any library computer catalog and dozens of book titles will appear on the screen, many of them of very recent date. So common is the term that most people probably assume that it has been with us for a long time, that its meaning is perfectly clear, and that historians and anthropologists universally find it useful. None of this is true.

Consider a couple of recent uses in the *New York Times Book Review*, which I dutifully read each Sunday morning. The first states that civilization "...is a time-honored term for cultures that grow enough food to support specialized non-farmers in cities." Though admirable for its conciseness, this definition casually excludes societies such as early Egypt or the Maya themselves who never developed cities as we understand them (just wait: I defend the essential "non-urbanness" of the Maya in Chapter 5). Another problem is that civilization has taken on so many different colloquial meanings. In a second *Times* review I read that a French anthropologist went to study the civilization of the Trobriand Islanders (isolated horticulturists and fishing people in the western Pacific), and just a few sentences later that one of his reasons for doing so was to get away from civilization. In the first usage civilization simply means any peoples' particular culture, and one might thus legitimately speak of the civilization of a society of hunter-gatherers or simple farming people. In the second, civilization refers to a general type of society very different from that of the Trobriands. We also use the term for very broad traditions of culture, as in "Western civilization," then go right on to talk more specifically about Greek or Roman civilizations nested within this larger framework. All this is confusing to say the least, and we must step back in time to sort out a useful definition and understand how it has emerged.

When Columbus first set sail in 1492 he sought a route to China and Japan, the great kingdoms of eastern Asia. Based on accounts of Marco Polo and other travelers, he expected to encounter densely settled agricultural landscapes, populous cities, great kings and lords served by literate officials, skilled artisans, wealthy merchants, and bustling markets – in short, societies not too different from the European and North African ones he knew about, and that we today would call civilizations. The islands of the West Indies that Columbus and later explorers first found and colonized were certainly populated, but displayed little of this hoped-for wealth and complexity. By the early 16th century, as we already saw, the Spaniards discovered much more impressive societies on the mainland of Mesoamerica, including the Maya Lowlands. No Spaniard of that time, however, could ever have used the word civilization to describe them.

Take as an example Hernan Cortes's own account of the people he observed on his march through Mexico toward the Aztec capital, Tenochtitlan, shortly after his encounters with the Maya in Tabasco. According to recent English translations of his second letter to Charles V, Cortes called these people "civilized," but in the original Spanish he used instead terms like *gente de razón* – literally "people of reason." By this he meant that the societies he saw had classes of cultivated people comparable to those of contemporary Europe – wealthy, hereditary lords who lived in cities, who possessed refined manners and exhibited considerable intellectual and aesthetic attainments, who were supported by the taxes and labor of well-behaved peasants, and who dominated complex and well-organized polities with specialized political, religious, and economic institutions, including markets and far-flung foreign trade.[10] In other words, these Mesoamericans had the kinds of hierarchical, rational, well-ordered, urban-centered societies that Cortes knew from Europe, the Near East, and North Africa, and that Columbus had originally expected to find in Asia. Cortes certainly made value judgments about the people he saw in terms of their comparative sophistication and worth. Mexicans and Lowland Maya impressed him and his fellow Spaniards far more than the Indians of the Caribbean. But he did not and could not use the word civilization, as we might today, as a label to contrast some general kinds of societies with others.

Neither Cortes nor Columbus, of course, knew much about the many diverse cultures inhabiting the New World in the 15th or 16th centuries. Later explorers, merchants, and colonists documented an enormous variety of societies not only in the New World, but throughout Asia, Africa, Australia, and the Pacific as well. Social theorists were thus challenged to develop vocabularies and classificatory schemes to make sense of an ever-increasing sample of non-European societies ranging from small bands of hunter-gatherers to huge states and empires. The concept of civilization as Powell understood it was a product of this enterprise, but it took a long time to emerge.

It always pays to consult an authoritative source, so I turned to a crumbling original copy of Samuel Johnson's 1755 dictionary in the Rare Books Room of my university library. There I found an entry for "civilisation," but it referred to a narrow legal procedure, nothing like our modern meaning. Other more pertinent entries included "civilize," "civilizer," and "civility." Definitions for all these words had one thing in common – they contrasted "barbarity," "savagery," or "brutality" on the one hand, with the "state of being civilized," or rationally governed, on the other. As early as Roman times the distinction was made between the city-dweller, civil and urbane in manner, as opposed to the rustic bumpkins unfortunate enough to live elsewhere. And in the mid-18th century Voltaire wrote a celebrated poem (Le Mondain) about all those wonderful refinements – art, literature, manners, wine, fine cuisine, elegant clothes – that made life so enjoyable for the civilized elements of society.

According to the great French historian Fernand Braudel, not until 1752 was civilization first used by Europeans in something like its modern sense of a general type of society in contrast to others.[11] By the first decades of the 19th century it had also acquired a more particular meaning, as in Roman civilization, or Chinese civilization, but even as late as the 1840s many authors virtually ignored it. One has to search diligently to find the word in John Lloyd Stephens's voluminous travel writings, which were written about the time my own great-grandparents were born.

It is fair to say that when most people today hear the word civilization they think of three things. First, like Cortes and Columbus, they envision societies that are large in scale, that have complex organization and orderly government, and that are distinguished by impressive intellectual and aesthetic achievements. Second, they literally think of impressive things – famous cities, monumental buildings, tombs, paintings, sculptures, written inscriptions and literary compositions, and technological innovations. Third, they make a kind of evolutionary judgment: that civilizations did not always exist but instead developed slowly out of simpler societies in various parts of the world, and that this process is one of cultural improvement. It is this last concept of cultural evolution in particular that emerged in the last half of the 19th century and that became intimately bound up with ideas of teleological culture change, progress, and moral superiority.[12]

A few years before Stephens and Catherwood set out for Copan another famous traveler, Charles Darwin, sailed along the southern Chilean coast in H.M.S. *Beagle*. Glimpsing from his ship a small band of indigenous foraging people, he remarked that

> The sight of a naked savage in his native land is an event which can never be forgotten. The astonishment which I felt on first seeing a party of Fuegans on a wild and broken shore will never be forgotten by me, for the reflection immediately rushed into my mind: such were our ancestors. These men were absolutely naked and bedaubed with paint; their long hair was tangled; their mouths frothed with excitement; and their expression was wild, startled, and distrustful. They possessed hardly any arts, and like wild animals, lived on what they could catch; they had no government, and were merciless to everyone not of their own small tribe.[13]

Darwin does not use the word civilization here, but his patronizing reaction to these "savages" was widely shared by his mid-19th century contemporaries. By far the most revealing part of this passage, though, is the remark "such were our ancestors." Darwin almost reflexively makes an evolutionary assumption: European societies of his own time had gradually emerged out of a similar primitive human condition. For Darwin this idea certainly implied progress, in contrast with an older Judeo-Christian tradition that explained varying degrees of social and cultural conditions in terms of inevitable degeneration, or devolution.

By Powell's day this idea of progressive evolution was firmly entrenched. As he himself proclaimed a bit further along in his stirring 1885 peroration:

> The evolution of man is the evolution of the humanities, by which he has become the master of the powers of the universe, by which he has made life beautiful with aesthetic art, by which he has established justice, by which he has established means of communication, so that mind speaks to mind even across the seas; by which his philosophy is the truth of the universe.

Heady stuff indeed! And of course Powell's audience no doubt believed that all these achievements were most conspicuously embodied in the larger Euro-American culture to which they themselves belonged. Like Darwin, they imagined that their own civilization had evolved gradually out of earlier, more primitive stages, that this progression could be measured by anthropologists, archaeologists, and historians, and that it was truly progressive. Lewis Henry Morgan for example, one of the founders of American anthropology, assigned particular cultures to various stages of "savagery," "barbarism," or "civilization" according to such criteria as their subsistence patterns, attitudes toward property, and whether or not they possessed the bow and arrow, pottery, or phonetic writing, all of which in turn reflected various mental capacities. Writing weighed particularly heavily in such assessments of cultural attainment, an attitude that is still expressed today. As one scholar of written records bluntly put it, "Writing exists only in a civilization, and a civilization cannot exist without writing."[14]

Given all this, it should be clear why many historians and social scientists today find the term civilization objectionable. Not only has there long been widespread disillusionment with the sturdy 19th-century faith in human progress, but critics object that the idea of civilization shared by Powell and most (but not all) of his contemporaries was at best ethnocentric and paternalistic and at worst outright racist. "Advances" such as writing are today regarded by some social critics as instruments of oppression. And because innovation and progress were seen as both inevitable and highly desirable (at least for some of the human species), the label civilization trumpeted the moral, institutional, intellectual, and technological superiority of the very peoples who invented it in the first place and made it the capstone of all-embracing evolutionary schemes. It thus represented an ideological justification for colonial expansion, oppression, and exploitation. In post-modern terminology, all this is part of a bankrupt, ethnocentric "meta-narrative" of Western society that is useless for comparative purposes. We must instead evaluate each human culture in its own terms, so this line of thought goes, not according to some abstract and ultimately invidious yardstick of general evolutionary accomplishment.

Value judgments and political correctness aside, many anthropologists pointed out that evolutionary schemes like Morgan's were hopelessly muddled and arbitrary anyway. The Incas, who dominated the largest Pre-columbian empire the New World had ever seen, lacked writing (although they did keep records using the kipu). Impressive Polynesian societies made no pottery, and hunting-gathering people on the Northwest Coast of North America lived political and social lives far more complex than those of many farmers. It was simply impossible to force all this cultural variety into neat evolutionary pigeonholes. And as we now know, people who never attained "civilization" in anything like the manner envisioned by the 19th century evolutionists certainly were not changeless, but developed in their own distinctive ways. The Fuegians Darwin saw might have possessed no government in the European sense, but they certainly had intricate and effective means of regulating their social and political lives. In short there is nothing teleological about cultural evolution, no universal inevitability in the emergence of civilizations or any other particular kind of social order, and nothing that distinguishes one culture as creatively or morally superior to others.

There is much to be said for these critiques. Certainly some early evolutionists expressed themselves in racist ways (or ways that we now find useful to interpret as racist), and unsavory individuals and political factions certainly used ideas derived from 19th-century cultural evolution for self-serving, and sometimes extremely destructive purposes. And no doubt each of us, like the French anthropologist who journeyed to the Trobriands, has sometimes felt the urge to get away from our own modern version of civilization. Considering the complex origins of the word, its multiple, subjective, and sometimes objectionable meanings, its capacity for abuse, and the impossibility of classifying cultures in one seamless continuum, we might be better off without it, and indeed without the whole related notion of cultural evolution. Unfortunately we do not have this option. As the library catalog exercise shows, civilization is so entrenched in our literature and discourse that if we jettisoned the term we would simply have to invent another one to use in its place.

Nor, contrary to what many people believe, are what we may broadly call evolutionary sensibilities unique products of Western thought. According to the chronicler Diego Duran, the civilized Aztecs viewed the foraging Chichimecs who lived on their northern borders much the same way Darwin saw the Fuegians:

> They were wild and rustic ... they lived among the peaks and in the harshest places of the mountain, where they led a bestial existence, with no propriety or human organization. They hunted food like beasts of the same mountain and went naked all day without any covering on their private parts. They hunted all day for rabbits, deer, hares, weasels, moles, wildcats, birds, snakes, lizards, mice, and they also collected locusts, worms, herbs, and roots, on which they lived. Their whole life was reduced to this, hunting for these things.[15]

Pictorial manuscripts created by various Aztec groups to document their own histories show their Chichimec ancestors gradually being transformed into more cultured, "civilized" beings. Associated myths of world origin envision the Aztec gods as creating a successive series of more sophisticated humans, each subsisting on superior foods, beginning with acorns and culminating with maize. Nor are such sensibilities confined to Mesoamerica. Ancient Chinese myths postulated a series of ancestral heroes who successively invented the accouterments of civilization. Apparently many peoples who live in hierarchical, literate, urban-centered societies commonly assume a continuum of culture change from simple to complex, and are quite capable of the invidious comparison.

Most important of all, more than a century of archaeological research in many parts of the world has documented something very much like the cultural evolution envisioned by Powell, Morgan, and their contemporaries. In the Near East, Egypt, China, the Indian subcontinent, Mesoamerica, and the Central Andes, what we can reasonably call civilizations all emerged independently and gradually out of much simpler, kin-based, hunting-gathering and village horticultural societies. Seen in the long career of the human species, here was a new kind of human condition, one that manifestly needs to be examined and if possible explained. Cultural evolution, like biological evolution, is a fact, however it happens, whether we like it or not, and despite whatever lessons we wish to draw from it.

The trick, it seems, is to say exactly what we mean when we use the term civilization in a comparative evolutionary sense, and a modern consensus has emerged among anthropologists and archaeologists, who define civilization in a technical way different from most of its colloquial usages. Central to this consensus was V. Gordon Childe, an Anglo-Australian archaeologist who was one of the most influential evolutionary thinkers of the mid-20th century. For Childe civilization and cities were virtually synonymous – a view that the 16th-century Spaniards would probably have shared. In an immensely influential article called *The Urban Revolution* (1950), Childe presented a sort of checklist for the definition of urban civilization that featured a mix of institutional and economic criteria on the one hand (e.g., urban settlements, social stratification, production of food surpluses, foreign trade, complex occupational specialization), and more specific cultural attainments (e.g., monumental architecture, representational art, writing) on the other.[16] Although notions of progress were still central to Childe's thought, his formulation lacked the pejorative moral and racist dimensions inherent in some earlier definitions of civilization.

Few people today would champion Childe's strict trait-list approach because it has some of the same defects as Morgan's. As I have said, not all ancient civilizations had writing or cities (as Childe envisioned them), and there was no automatic, lock-step emergence of all of Childe's criteria through time. But in a more general way his discussion still anticipates the core of our current conception of civilization, in that any ancient culture that exhibited some effective mix of the features he identified would likely be called one. Each anthropologist or archaeologist would no doubt give a slightly different definition, but most would be along the following lines:

A civilization is a territorially expansive and distinctive Great Tradition that retains its cultural identity over hundreds or thousands of years, the specific state-type polities that carry this tradition, and the processes by which it has originated, maintained itself, and spread.

Let us examine the nuts and bolts of this definition, beginning with the concept of the state, bearing in mind that our main concern is pre-modern, agrarian (i.e., non-industrial) civilizations, and especially those that arose earliest in their respective regions of the world.

The Ancient State

Although the state itself takes a variety of forms, thus raising other definitional issues, we generally understand it to be a kind of hierarchical political order. Marked political centralization in ancient states was commonly focused on hereditary rulers and associated titled courtiers or bureaucrats occupying formal offices of government or positions of high social rank. These privileged people dominated power relations. The relationship between political status and kinship was reduced in such states as compared with other kinds of political systems. Closely associated with the political structure of ancient agrarian states was a social order characterized by well-developed stratification – i.e., domination by a small segment of people who enjoyed high social rank, privileged access to economic resources, and who were supported by taxes and labor extracted from a class of farmers. As a general rule of thumb anthropologists and archaeologists estimate that the farming segments of most such societies comprised 70 percent or more of the total population. Even today some modern countries that are incompletely industrialized retain similar high ratios: 64 percent of China's people were still farmers in AD 2000 (as compared to between one and two percent in the United States).[17] The reason for this disparity is that with simple technology and heavy reliance on human labor in ancient times, each household of producers could only generate sufficient surpluses to support a very small number of non-farmers. Later on we will see that this rule has important implications for understanding the Classic Maya collapse. Where stratification was especially well developed and members of strata had shared self-interests, we can properly speak of social classes.

Other common (but far from universal) features of early states included complex occupational specialization, widespread trade, market exchange, concentration of physical coercion in the form of professional armies or police forces, judicial institutions and legal codes, and organized state religions. These institutions and their associated ideologies served to bolster the central apparatus of government and the highly differentiated social order. Most states were composed of many communities, one or more of which was a true urban center or political capital. Although kinship remained important for some purposes, it was ineffective in integrating diverse social, political and economic groups and communities, hence the increased importance of new kinds of non-kin institutions that regulated human affairs. So defined, ancient states were usually both demographically and territorially larger than non-state societies. Columbus expected to find Asian states on his westward voyages.

All classifications, of course, suppress variety, and not every ancient state exhibited all these organizational characteristics to the same degree. Some, like Egypt, had extensive territories dominated by a single ruler, while others, such as Sumer and the Maya, developed a pattern of many small, autonomous polities. Markets were well developed among the Aztecs, whereas the Incas stressed centrally controlled redistribution of goods. Urbanization was more pronounced in the Indus valley than in Shang-dynasty China. Some early states had rigidly defined elite classes, while others had a meritocratic dimension that allowed even humble people to achieve high office and prestige. Such differences make each ancient state somewhat distinctive in institutional terms. Nevertheless, all of them broadly shared many of the listed features, and especially one or another form of social class structure and effective political centralization. It was these general similarities between Old and New World states that Cortes intuitively recognized on his initial journey through Mexico.

If we adopt these organizational criteria for our definition of civilization, then clearly we would not apply the term to hunter-gatherers like the Fuegians Darwin saw or the Trobriand Islanders, distinctive, interesting, and even admirable as these peoples might be. Because states develop out of simpler political forms, however, there are many societies, especially those known mainly through archaeology, that are difficult to classify, as we shall see later.

But civilizations are much more than political entities. On my bookshelves are many volumes with titles like *The Lost Kingdoms of the Maya*, *Atlas of*

Ancient Egypt, or *China's Buried Kingdoms*. These books are filled with pictures and descriptions of temples, palaces, elaborate tombs, beautifully carved or painted inscriptions, sculptured monuments, and wonderfully crafted objects made of pottery, precious metals, jade, ivory, or rare woods – durable, material manifestations of ancient cultural complexity, technological skill and aesthetic sensibility. What is significant about all these things, apart from their scale and quality, is that they are so different from one civilization to another. No one would mistake an Egyptian temple for a Chinese one, or confuse the cuneiform scripts of Sumer with Maya hieroglyphs. It is the idiosyncratic forms of such elements and the ways that they are combined that give each particular civilization its qualitative dimensions – what we might call its "style." Stephens and Catherwood were struck by the uniqueness of Copan's artifacts in 1839, and by the larger pan-Maya patterns (particularly the use of the same hieroglyphs) that they later detected at Palenque, Uxmal, and other long-abandoned centers.

More important is that such objects collectively represent just the material façade of the institutional, aesthetic, intellectual, ideological, philosophical, and technological attainments of all these cultures – the very things that 19th-century evolutionists felt most clearly confirmed superiority and progress. Such objects were highly valued and deeply imbued with meanings for the people who produced and used them. In their original settings some people understood the details of these meanings better than others, and derived advantages from such knowledge. But they conveyed broader cultural signals as well. When we look at the jade mask of a buried Maya ruler or a Chinese bronze ritual vessel most of the original detailed meaning is lost to us, but these objects are so sophisticated and powerful that they still command our admiration.

And of course many other impressive and important things were not preserved or were expressed behaviorally – modes of speech, manners, and rules of decorum and comportment were originally just as essential to the operation of ancient complex societies. Despite our current rejection of pejorative cultural comparisons, it is only fair to say that we are still most likely to label as civilizations those complex societies that manifest such qualitative elements in complex, durable, and grandiose ways. Along with the more intangible cultural attainments they reflect, these things collectively comprise what we call Great Traditions, which were heavily associated with the elites of ancient civilizations. Although jade, writing, bronze, or any number of other things might be available to everyone, elites refined the patterns of their use into forms that emphasized social distinctions.

Complex societies, of course, have no monopoly on aesthetic or symbolic excellence. Ethnographic art departments of major museums are filled with beautiful carvings, weavings, weapons, and even buildings made by people such as the Kwakiutl of the Northwest Coast, the Maori of New Zealand, the Dogon of West Africa, and the Asmat of New Guinea. All these objects are just as culturally distinctive, aesthetically sophisticated, and laden with meaning as any associated with Egypt, China, or the Maya. Moreover, some traditions of so-called "primitive art" were remarkably durable – in fact the earliest one known to us, cave art produced by Upper Paleolithic hunter-gatherers, exhibits considerable continuity over more than 20,000 years. What distinguishes these traditions from the Great Traditions of ancient civilizations (apart from some obvious differences such as the lack of writing) is that they were produced by non-state societies, and hence carried different kinds of meanings. To put it another way, they did different kinds of "work" in their respective cultural settings, and were reproduced differently through time.

Great Tradition elements in early civilizations were Janus-like, conveying two fundamental and conceptually opposable sets of messages. One set symbolized the superiority, exclusivity, and dominance of high-ranking individuals or groups, and the institutions and ideologies with which they were most closely identified. Sometimes these messages were very immediate, personal, and fleeting, situationally conveyed between individuals in a particular social context by a gesture, a posture, or a word. Only narrative art or inscriptions preserve fragments of this rich tradition of elite behavior (Plate 23). Other messages were embodied in more durable forms, such as the huge royal pyramids of Egypt or the great images of kings that Stephens and Catherwood found in the ruins of Copan. Such monuments were made (in part) to impress a wider audience – other elite people, commoners, and perhaps ancestors or gods. None of these things, of course, was made to impress us, but they retain the powerful capacity to do so.

A second set of messages served to cloak and justify social, political, and economic inequality with images, symbols, and rituals that asserted collectivity and universal values. For example, royal art and architecture of Old Kingdom Egypt projected the political dominance of the ruler, but also the inevitability and rightness of his rule and its role in maintaining the cosmic and social well-being essential to all Egyptians. Such monuments created social spaces encoded with meaning, within which individuals were enculturated, consciously or otherwise, to the broader traditions and postulates of their societies, and they consequently facilitated the reproduction of hierarchical social relations and world views through time. Great Traditions of civilizations are thus part of a different kind of cultural package than those of more egalitarian societies because they are inextricably linked with the political and social forms of the state, with social inequality, and are often most obtrusive at the urban or courtly centers where state institutions and facilities are concentrated.

Many Great Tradition elements were effective precisely because they had their origins in the folkways of the simpler societies out of which states evolved. As we shall see later, for example, Maya kings seem to have built their royal personae partly on the foundations of very ancient shamanistic beliefs and practices. Some elements were borrowed from other cultures, as the Maya probably borrowed from the Preclassic Olmec of the Mexican Gulf Coast, and still others represent innovations made for specific purposes. Whatever their origins, when particular state-type societies manifest grandiose and distinctive Great Tradition patterns over large geographical regions and long periods of time, we are likely to call them civilizations. In Mesoamerica and elsewhere the widespread sharing of such patterns is primarily due to contacts among elites.

Those ancient civilizations that emerged first and independently of one another in Mesoamerica, the Central Andes, Egypt, Sumer, China, and the Indus valley are sometimes called primary civilizations, and they most intrigue both the general public and archaeologists. Part of their allure is that in their earliest stages they are from our perspective prehistoric cultures, like the Indus valley (whose script we cannot read), or only quasi-historical in the sense that the earliest comprehensible written records are very limited and reveal much less than we would like to know. The origins of primary civilizations thus retain an aura of mystery and romance.

Some of their associated Great Traditions were comparatively short-lived. The Indus valley civilization flourished on the western Indian subcontinent between 2600 and 1900 BC, then declined, leaving few obvious connections with later historically documented cultures. In fact archaeologists discovered the Indus valley tradition only in the 1920s. In China, by contrast, many Great Tradition elements including a sophisticated writing system have been passed down in surprising continuity for more than 3000 years. Of course very few states survive for even hundreds of years, much less thousands, nor is any Great Tradition generally expressed by a single political entity at any given time (although this was the case for long periods in China and Egypt). More common is the pattern found in Mesopotamia or Mesoamerica, where multiple regional states, themselves ethnically and linguistically diverse, shared basically the same Great Traditions.

Because civilizations are so dynamic, in any broad historical tradition there are typically periods of little change punctuated by episodes of extraordinary innovation and expansion. Innovations often emanate from cities, which is one reason why Childe and others conflated urbanism and civilization. Great Traditions and their associated political and social institutions are disseminated by trade, cultural prestige, or by political domination or conquest, as among the Incas and Aztecs. Within any particular civilization, moreover, regional polities develop their own variants of a more far-flung Great Tradition. Kingdoms coalesce, expand, and fall apart. Successive polities adjust their political institutions to new circumstances and rework their Great Tradition elements accordingly. Because they are so dynamic civilizations have, for better or worse, tended to dominate, destroy, or absorb other kinds of societies. Whether or not we choose to regard them as desirable, progressive, or humane social forms, civilizations are unquestionably highly competitive, influential, and expansionistic in political, economic, and cultural terms.

Amidst all this dynamism the great early civilizations retained for centuries or millennia their own distinctive core cultural identities, which is the fundamental reason why they still impress us today. Association with these traditions can still confer prestige, construct cultural identity, and legitimize power. Shortly before his downfall the Shah of Iran sponsored a gigantic celebration of 2500 years of Persian civilization (never mind that his own dynastic roots extended only as far back as his usurper father), while in Iraq Saddam Hussein has his name impressed on the mud bricks used to reconstruct ancient ziggurats, in emulation of the kings who originally built them thousands of years ago. Both of these examples remind us that the human individuals and factions who socially reproduce Great Traditions and their political forms are themselves opportunistic agents, using culture for their own purposes.

Neither state-type political institutions nor impressive Great Traditions necessarily connote, of course, superiority or progress – often quite the contrary. Ancient agrarian civilizations such as Egypt or China were in many respects very conservative societies. Many of the Great Tradition elements that so impress us were created by or for elite people who most benefited from a strongly hierarchical political and economic status quo. Life for ordinary people was typically short, difficult, more often than not unhealthy, and devoid of much economic or social mobility. Ancient states were characterized by strong, permanent, social inequalities and precious little social justice in any sense that we understand it today. Many Great Tradition elements and the ideologies behind them symbolized and reinforced these invidious relationships and the world views that gave them legitimacy. Images of collectivity cloaked privilege and exclusion, and the perspective they provide about any early civilization is largely a top-down one. In short, it is difficult to make the case that most people were better off than their ancestors in the simpler, more egalitarian societies from which civilizations emerged in the first place, nor is this observation relevant to a modern understanding of cultural evolution.

Still, ancient civilizations were culturally very distinctive and impressive in scale and organization. Our concern today is not to draw moral lessons from them as our intellectual forebears did, but rather to understand why these kinds of societies, so unusual in the long evolutionary career of the human species, emerged in the first place, how they functioned, and most importantly why some of them, including the Classic Maya, collapsed.

Explicit and succinct as our definition of civilization is, it still leaves us with one archaeological problem – it is much easier to recover durable Great Tradition elements than it is to reconstruct patterns of political or social organization. In fact much of the history of archaeology consists of efforts to fill museums or private collections with just such glamorous stuff, or to reconstruct ancient sites to attract tourists. But in the absence of very detailed and comprehensible written records how can we be sure that a particular ancient culture was institutionally complex enough for us to call it a civilization, even if its architecture, art, and intellectual accomplishments are extremely impressive?

Sometimes surviving Great Tradition elements, such as those of Old Kingdom Egypt, are so sophisticated, abundant, obtrusive, and massive that they themselves convinced scholars, even before hieroglyphs could be read, that Egypt was a civilization in every sense of the word. By contrast, the Indus valley culture has left us far fewer impressive remains, so its organizational features are much debated and its complexity is largely inferred from its huge urban centers. The Preclassic Olmec of the Mexican Gulf Coast had an extremely sophisticated and flamboyant tradition of architecture and sculpture. Was it a civilization? Many archaeologists think so, but many others, myself included, believe that Olmec polities were institutionally too simple to warrant the label. And what about the Mississippian peoples of the eastern and central United States, who built monumental temple complexes at centers such as Cahokia, Moundville, and Etowah, but who left little preservable art and had, apparently, no writing? Our definition thus creates a certain indeterminacy for many ancient cultures, and as we shall see later this issue has important implications for the Maya. That we cannot always agree on whether a particular ancient society merits the label "civilization" in part reflects our complex and often inadequate terminology and also the quality of our archaeological information. Nevertheless, one measure of the value of a concept is not so much that it has a succinct, highly consensual meaning, but rather that it makes us think. In this sense, civilization has been, and will remain, both a highly useful and challenging concept.

We have taken a long conceptual digression since we left Cortes in Tabasco, preparing for his fateful advance on the Aztec empire. Presumably we can agree for now that something reasonably like a civilization existed in the 16th-century Maya Lowlands, an assertion that I will develop in greater detail shortly. This brings us to the final issue of this chapter: what do we mean when we say that civilizations collapse?

The Collapse of Civilizations

Curiously, as Joseph Tainter pointed out some years ago in his excellent book *The Collapse of Complex Societies* (1988), archaeologists have very seldom concerned themselves with how societies collapse from a broadly comparative perspective. I say curiously because after all it is the job of archaeologists to grub about amongst the remains of ancient cultures, whether civilizations or not, that are defunct – that almost by definition "failed" in some sense of the word. Sometimes failure is dramatic and complete. For example the Tasmanians, foraging people who for thousands of years occupied the large island off the southeastern coast of Australia, were destroyed both as a population and as a culture by European colonists in the 18th and 19th centuries. For more complex societies this kind of collapse is exceptional, in part because human behavior is so flexible and capable of such rapid change, and because large populations are less vulnerable to such extinction (there were only about 4000 Tasmanians). More typically, humans change their customs, technologies, institutions, and beliefs to accommodate new circumstances, and in the process leave behind a cast-off and outmoded husk of recoverable materials that forms the archaeological record.

If we apply the idea of collapse to civilizations as we have defined them, we obviously must distinguish between two levels of phenomena – what happens to individual state-type polities and their populations on the one hand, and to their associated Great Traditions on the other. We must, in other words, separate the process into its institutional and cultural manifestations. Take a familiar example. When we say that western Roman civilization "collapsed" what we really mean is that the centralized Roman state broke up, its characteristic institutions were destroyed or fundamentally altered, its economy was severely disrupted, and its Great Tradition elements were lost, dramatically changed, or absorbed into other cultures.

When Samuel Johnson noted in his dictionary that individual states could rise from "barbarity" to "civility," and then fall again, Rome was probably the foremost example in his mind. Yet the city of Rome was never abandoned, the core population of northern Italy never disappeared, and the Latin language slowly evolved into modern Italian (among others). Just as important, elements of the Roman Great Tradition, including architecture and art, legal and social concepts, military organization, royal titles, and written history, philosophy, and literature, to name just a few, all survived in one form or another. To put all this another way, the specific, integrated civilizational "package" of western Roman political and social institutions and their Great Tradition elements was so disrupted that it no longer makes sense for us, from our historical vantage point, to talk about Roman civilization after the 5th century AD. On the other hand, a larger cultural entity we call Western civilization inherited a complex legacy from Rome that has proved very durable. This is a far cry from the kind of extinction visited on the Tasmanians and much more like what happened to the Maya.

Turning to China, the situation is more complicated. For long intervals during its extraordinary history China was unified under strong dynasties, and at other times it broke up into a patchwork of smaller independent states, often in intense competition with one another. Mongols, Tibetans, Manchus, and other foreign invaders variously established their dominance over the ethnic Chinese. But even during periods of political fragmentation each state shared similar patterns of organization and culture, and foreign conquerors famously absorbed Chinese ways as well. Language, folkways, and many Great Tradition elements survived all this political flux. Changing as required to meet new circumstances, Chinese statecraft and elite culture preserved a remarkable identity down to the present. The leaders who unleashed the dramatic and violent Cultural Revolution of the 1960s recognized the great cultural weight of the past, and revealingly their attempt to disconnect Communist Chinese society from its deep historical roots was an abject failure. We obviously cannot talk of the collapse of China in the same sense as we do that of Rome.

Whatever the causes of social, political, and economic crises, repeated cycles of collapse and recovery show Chinese civilization to be very resilient, both politically and institutionally. This capacity for recovery is itself something that needs to be explained just as much as collapse does. In his book

Dynamics of Apocalypse, John Lowe pointed out that sociocultural systems, unlike organisms, do not "die," but adapt to stresses by restructuring themselves.[18] One of the puzzles of the Classic Maya collapse, as we shall see later, is lack of recovery in many parts of the Lowlands between the 9th century and the arrival of the Spaniards.

Tainter himself preferred to focus on the institutional dimensions of collapse, which he saw primarily as a political process. Here, slightly paraphrased and reordered, are the elements he believed signaled political breakdown:[19]

- Less stratification and social differentiation
- Less political centralization, less top-down control and management of economy and political groups, and diminished coordination and organization among groups or factions of all kinds
- Simpler patterns of occupational specialization and economic production
- Demographically and territorially smaller political units
- Less regimentation of and control over the behavior of individuals and groups
- Decreased and more circumscribed exchanges of information and resources among individuals and groups, and between centers and peripheries
- Diminished production of Great Tradition components, such as monumental architecture, art, and inscriptions.

To these we might add overall population decline, abandonment of settlements (and most particularly cities or royal centers), invasions by foreigners, and diminished confidence in or even rejection of collectively held postulates and values concerning religion and political ideology. We can use this list as a sort of recipe for assessing the collapse of civilizations, remembering that some parts of it are easier to detect archaeologically or historically than others. Much of it would certainly apply to the "collapse" of the western Roman civilization, and parts of it, as we shall see, are pertinent to the Classic Maya.

Tainter stressed political processes because he was concerned not just with civilizations, but with other kinds of complex societies as well. Among his case studies, for example, was the 13th-century abandonment of the great Puebloan centers of the southwestern United States. The problem is a bit more complicated for us because we are interested in the collapse of particular kinds of complex societies that are not defined strictly in political terms. Tainter agrees that architecture, art, and literary achievements are the elements that define the concept of civilization, but he calls these things merely the 'epiphenomena' of social and political complexity. I see them instead as precisely the elements that transcend the political fortunes of particular states, that facilitate the appearance of new polities, and that allow us to identify the imposing and durable traditions of culture we call civilizations over large regions of the world.

Like civilization itself, collapse can obviously mean a lot of things. Tainter's attempt to find common processes and regularities in the collapse of complex societies is in the best spirit of comparative anthropology and archaeology. As he himself realized, however, we have to elicit such generalities from individual cases, and the Maya present us with one of the most spectacular on record. We now turn to an assessment of Mesoamerican and Maya civilization, and a more detailed examination of what Europeans encountered in the 16th century.

– 4 –

MESOAMERICAN CIVILIZATION AND THE MAYA

WHERE DO THE MAYA FIT INTO our concept of civilization? First, on the most inclusive level, all of the elements of the definition developed in Chapter 3 apply broadly to Mesoamerica as a whole, one of the six large regions of the world where primary civilizations are known to have emerged. Because the New World was isolated for so long from Europe, Asia, or Africa, it served as a kind of great evolutionary laboratory, as Stephens realized even in 1839. But the roots of this perception lay even deeper in the past. Remember that although the Spaniards had no broad evolutionary perspective, Cortes was struck by the familiarity of much of what he saw, particularly the ways in which societies were organized and governed. Kings, nobles, cities, merchants, markets, skilled artisans, tax-paying peasants, scribes, books, state religions – all these made sense to him, and had the word civilization been in his vocabulary he might well have used it to describe 16th-century Mesoamerica. That all this complexity developed independently convinces many anthropologists today that there are regular, recurrent processes of cultural evolution.

But on the other hand, the Spaniards were perplexed and shocked by many things they encountered among these *gentes de razon.* How could people who worshiped idols and a pantheon of savage gods live such orderly and disciplined lives? How was it possible for people to be so clever, refined, and aesthetically sophisticated, yet at the same time so depraved that they practiced human sacrifice and cannibalism? Early missionaries, even those who intimately knew and admired Indian ways, characterized them as "captives of Lucifer."[1] Unlike Stephens and Catherwood, they could not easily disentangle the aesthetic appreciation of architecture and art from (to them) its heathen ideological and moral implications. More practically, how did markets and trade thrive without the use of coinage, or some universal system of weights and measures? Why was the technology of Mesoamerican peoples so primitive by European standards? The Aztecs, Maya, and their neighbors knew nothing of the true arch or other sophisticated architectural elements, and they had no iron or steel tools, making do instead with implements of stone, wood, bone, fiber, and clay.[2] They lacked functional wheels for transport (although there were wheeled figurines), sails for their vessels, or any other complicated machines such as pulleys that could increase the efficiency of human or animal muscles. Nor were there large domestic animals to carry loads, to pull plows or vehicles, or to harness to mills. As we shall see later, such energetic and technological simplicity had major effects on Mesoamerican polities, settlements, and economic and political institutions. For now, we need only note that this "paleotechnic" material culture and energy regime made Mesoamerica seem highly unique to the Spaniards. Developments in Mesoamerica do show, however, that extremely complex cultures can evolve in the absence of much technological change, an idea that is very counterintuitive to us because our lives are so affected by rapid and powerful innovations.

Unlike ancient Egypt, Mesoamerican civilization was never politically unified, even by the warlike and expansionistic Aztecs, and it was certainly far from ethnically homogeneous – at the time of the Spanish conquest something on the order of 260 separate languages and major dialects were spoken there (some 80 are still spoken today). In part because the landscape is so spatially extensive, so compartmentalized by rugged terrain, and so ecologically diverse, many distinctive complex societies developed after about 2000 BC. All of them had roots in earlier foraging and farming cultures and so they collectively inherited some common folkways. From this original common stock, as well as later innovations, the impressive Mesoamerican Great Tradition was gradually assembled.

Just how far back in time we can identify something we could reasonably call a civilization has no firm answer. Some archaeologists believe that Mesoamerica's oldest "Mother Civilization" was that of the Gulf Coast Olmec, whose great centers of San Lorenzo and La Venta thrived during the Early and Middle Preclassic periods, or roughly between 1200 and 400 BC. Monumental temple-pyramids and stone sculpture, incised and polished objects of jade, reverence for jaguars, raptorial birds, serpents, and crocodiles, glyph-like symbols, and possibly calendrical notations, all appeared early in the Olmec heartland. Nor was all this emergent complexity confined to the Gulf Coast. Other impressive Early and Middle Preclassic cultures existed in the Mexican highlands, on the Pacific coast of Mexico and Guatemala, and elsewhere. Mesoamerican civilization, both in its institutional and qualitative dimensions, thus seems to have had multiple roots by Classic period times.

There were, however, several regions where political and cultural developments were particularly precocious and sustained. Chief among these were the Basin of Mexico, the valley of Oaxaca, and the Maya Lowlands and Highlands. We can thus properly speak of several Mesoamerican regional sub-traditions that interacted and shared information with one another, just as Greek or Roman civilizations were expressions of a larger European tradition of culture.

Archaeologists do agree that states with urban centers formed at least by about 500–300 BC in the valley of Oaxaca and shortly thereafter in the Basin of Mexico. Many regional states subsequently appeared throughout Mesoamerica, sharing in varying degrees and somewhat different forms an overarching Great Tradition defined by distinctive patterns of art, architecture, writing, calendrics, technologies, and world views. This tradition eventually encompassed about 900,000 sq. km (350,000 sq. miles) and endured, with many changes and regional variants, until the Spanish conquest. Seen in this perspective, the Maya and Aztecs who Cortes observed in 1519 were only the latest manifestations of a much older and deeper Mesoamerican pattern.

The Classic Maya have long been a kind of "wild card" among ancient world civilizations, and even within Mesoamerica. Some archaeologists and historians rank them as the equals of the great early cultures of Egypt, Mesopotamia, China, the Indus valley, and the Central Andes. Others entirely omit the Maya from comparative overviews of the world's first archaic states. Such divergence of opinion is partly due to the fact that the tropical Lowland Maya environment was long envisioned as too homogeneous, fragile, and otherwise inhospitable to allow the local development of complex societies and to sustain them for centuries. As recently as the 1960s, in fact, the Maya were rather dismissively regarded by some archaeologists as a "secondary" civilization, transplanted from elsewhere and doomed to eventual failure.

Similarly, the urban status of Maya centers has long been debated, as has the complexity of their economic and political institutions. Before hieroglyphic inscriptions could be adequately read, it was commonly assumed that the Classic Maya had a very unique organizational structure and thus could not easily be compared with other ancient states. Now that the Preclassic archaeological record has been fleshed out we know that the first idea is incorrect, and we long ago abandoned the "vacant ceremonial center" and "priest-peasant" models of Maya society. Even with all the new insights from the inscriptions, however, details of ancient Maya social and political organization are hotly debated, so this issue still lingers. And the Maya variety of

Mesoamerican civilization seems curiously non-dynamic when compared to the expansive vigor of the Aztecs and earlier highland Mexican powers. Right until the Spaniards arrived Maya civilization remained coextensive with the distribution of Maya speakers.

On the other hand, no one doubts that the Classic Maya left behind one of the most flamboyant, exotic, and well-preserved archaeological records in the world. If impressive buildings, great art, rich tombs, and writing are our yardsticks, then the Maya were unquestionably civilized. Major elements of the distinctive Classic-period elite subculture, or the Classic Maya Great Tradition as we can now call it, include

- monumental masonry temples, palaces, sweat baths, tombs, and other buildings that share similar architectural features (e.g., pyramidal forms and the use of the corbel vault, lime plaster and cement)
- stone altars, stelae, lintels, benches, and building façades carved and painted with images of kings, elite people, gods, and ancestors as well as dates and inscriptions
- a shared set of stylistic artistic conventions that, though expressed differently through time and space, are distinctively Maya in character
- writing in the form of glyphs that stand for both whole words and for sounds
- bar and dot numerals that express a vigesimal system of counting
- screenfold books made of bark paper
- calendars that emphasize recurrent cycles, including a 260-day ritual calendar and a 365-day solar calendar
- a Long Count calendar based on the linear passage of days from a beginning point far in the past
- observation of the cycles of the sun, moon, Venus, and other astronomical bodies, and calculation of their patterns of commensuration
- reverence for blue-green stones, including forms of jade
- ball games played on special masonry courts
- a set of deities associated with the forces of nature and the structure of the cosmos who must be propitiated and sustained with offerings of many kinds
- use of chocolate (cacao) as an elite drink, as tribute, and possibly as special-purpose currency
- belief in multiple creations of the world
- belief in a multi-layered heaven and underworld
- reverence for ancestors and deification of them
- shamanism
- complex notions of the death and resurrection of plants, animals, and people

• belief in the existence of soul elements that could be detached from the body and in spiritual companions, often in the form of animals, that are associated with individual humans

• belief in prophecy, divination, and oracles

• belief in the efficacy of sacred or semi-divine kings

• artistic themes and rituals that emphasize death, mutilation, and sacrifice.

Stephens and Catherwood formed their original conception of a great New World civilization only on the basis of the first elements of this list – art, architecture, and writing. We now know that some of these features, such as the logosyllabic form of writing, represent specifically Maya innovations. Others, such as the Long Count calendar, might have been invented in other parts of Mesoamerica, but were perfected and used most effectively in the Maya Lowlands. The 260- and 365-day calendars, the ball game, reverence for blue-green stones, the uses of cacao, and concepts of multiple world creations, by contrast, were developed elsewhere and widely shared among Mesoamerican peoples. But even these common elements acquired their own distinctive Maya stamp, and taken together they constitute the unique "package" of the Maya Great Tradition. This tradition, most widely and exuberantly expressed during the 8th century AD, is what principally attracts us today and forms the core of our concept of Maya civilization, just as it did for Stephens and Catherwood. In the rest of this chapter we consider to what degree it was still present when the Spaniards arrived on the scene.

The Maya of the Conquest

We already reviewed the earliest, incidental contacts between Spaniards and Lowland Maya. Now we must examine what the early 16th-century Maya were like in more detail for three reasons. First, they have long been a rich source of ideas used to reconstruct the Classic Maya, who were after all in some ways their biological and cultural forebears. All archaeologists, whether they acknowledge it or not, rely on their knowledge of historically or ethnographically documented cultures to flesh out their conceptions of ancient peoples. Many of my colleagues believe strongly in what anthropologists call the direct historical approach – i.e., the idea that comparisons can most usefully be drawn between ancient cultures and their descendants in a direct historical line. Some even argue that broader comparative perspectives are improper. While I personally think the latter viewpoint is unnecessarily limited, there is no doubt that many continuities existed between the Classic Maya and the Maya of the conquest, just as there were, say, between the

England of Chaucer and of Queen Victoria. For example, much of what we know about ancient Maya deities, astronomy, and rituals derives from information in three of the surviving Postclassic screenfold books.

Because we have so much historical information about the 16th-century Maya, they also serve as a convenient reminder of the corresponding deficiencies of the archaeological record. Whether or not particular elements of late Maya society and culture were direct survivals of more ancient ones, we can at least appreciate them as parts of living human systems, so they serve as useful springboards for some of the issues raised in the next chapter.

Finally, I want to correct an impression that is widely held by the public (and, I have discovered, even by some of my anthropological colleagues): that the Classic collapse reduced the Maya in general, where they survived at all, to the level of simple farming villagers. To the contrary, a vigorous tradition of Maya civilization still thrived when the Spaniards landed in Yucatan. In fact, although most people don't know it, the last independent Maya kingdom survived deep in the forests of Guatemala until the end of the 17th century.

So what were these latter-day Maya like? We have three main sources of information about them, apart from archaeology itself: four surviving Maya books, accounts written by Spaniards during and after the conquest, and post-conquest documents written by literate Maya people, some of which preserve vestiges of earlier oral traditions or lost Precolumbian writings. Both of the latter sources are subject to errors and biases. Even the most sophisticated Spanish observers misunderstood much of what they saw, and their writings are full of omissions and distortions. Maya scribes and officials often wrote in traditional formulaic and esoteric ways that are difficult for us to understand today (as in the several prophetic Books of Chilam Balam composed long after the conquest). Even such prosaic documents as wills and testaments, which native officials wrote in the vernacular, must be carefully interpreted because they were often formulated at least in part to further Maya ends vis-à-vis their colonial overlords. Nevertheless, used carefully, documents flesh out a complex picture of late Maya societies that can help us understand their Classic-period forebears. One of the earliest such accounts brings us back to Cortes.

In 1521 Hernan Cortes and his companions, along with thousands of Indian allies, stood amid the smoking ruins of the Aztec capital, Tenochtitlan. After two years of marching, fighting, and political intrigue, all serious resistance was crushed and the last emperor, Cuauhtemoc, had been captured. From Indian informants the Spaniards quickly acquired some idea of the vast extent and riches of the empire that they had so improbably seized, and

Cortes dispatched his most trusted commanders to bring other parts of Mesoamerica under Spanish control, including regions far beyond the bounds of earlier Aztec conquests. Reports eventually reached him in 1524 that one of these captains, Cristobal de Olid, had rebelled against his authority in far-off Honduras. Determined to chastise Olid personally, Cortes traveled to Espiritu Santo, a Spanish outpost on the Isthmus of Tehuantepec, where he organized an expedition of about 230 Spaniards, of whom 93 were mounted. This tiny European force was augmented by more than 3000 Indian allies, led by their own native commanders, who hauled artillery, munitions, and food, and tended a caravan of 150 pack horses and a herd of pigs. The invaluable Dona Marina came along as interpreter, and so did the incredibly durable Bernal Diaz.

Because such a force could not easily be transported by sea, Cortes instead decided to march overland to Honduras, believing that en route he could gather important information about unknown lands and begin the process of pacifying them. The ex-emperor Cuauhtemoc and other highly ranked Aztec lords were carried along as hostages against political unrest back in Central Mexico. During his arduous six-month journey through uncharted territory, which Cortes recorded in his fifth letter to Charles V, he and his Spanish soldiers became the first Europeans to pass through the heartland of Classic Maya civilization. What they saw, and more importantly what they did not see, heavily conditions our conceptions of the Classic Maya collapse.[3]

After laboriously slogging through the swamps and across the rivers of Tabasco, in late February 1525 Cortes and his men reached a town called Itzam K'anak on the middle reaches of the Rio Candelario. Itzam K'anak was a substantial place with many large buildings and the capital of the Chontal Maya province called Akalan, famous for its merchants who knew the trade routes across the Yucatan Peninsula. Akalan's ruler, Pax B'olon, was forewarned of the approach of the Spaniards by Indians fleeing their villages and welcomed Cortes as a friend. Over the next two weeks the expedition rested at Itzam K'anak while Pax B'olon's people stockpiled provisions for the next stage of the march. During this interlude a rumor reached Cortes that his Mexican contingent, supported by inhabitants of the town, planned a revolt under the instigation of Cuauhtemoc. According to one account of this incident the plot was betrayed to the Spaniards by Pax B'olon himself. In any case, Cuauhtemoc and another Indian lord were promptly executed, and so ended the dynasty that created Mesoamerica's greatest empire.

Armed with a map and led by two Akalan merchants as guides, Cortes left Itzam K'anak on 15 March and his column progressed rapidly along what was obviously a well-defined track through forests and savannas. Along the way the Spaniards encountered towns and villages, some of them elaborately fortified, from which the inhabitants had fled. Enough Indians were coaxed back from their hiding places to provide provisions and directions, and the Spaniards moved on until they saw in the distance a great expanse of shimmering blue water (known today as Lake Peten Itza) where they had been told was the town of a powerful lord named Canek. Canek himself soon met them on the lake shore, where he was promptly subjected to a long religious harangue and to Cortes's pronouncement that King Charles V was the overlord of the whole world. Canek replied politely that this universal sovereign had not previously come to his attention, but that he had indeed heard of Maya battles with foreigners on the coast of Tabasco five or six years before – which of course were those of Cortes's own 1519 expedition.

After an exchange of gifts, Cortes and a small bodyguard went by canoe with Canek to his island capital of Nojpeten at the western end of the lake, leaving the rest of the army to march around by land to the southern shore. Cortes stayed only briefly at Nojpeten (or Tayasal as Bernal Diaz called it), and when he departed he left six men behind, as well as a sick horse, which Canek promised to care for. Subsequent Spanish legends claimed that the Itza, as Canek and his subjects were called, still worshiped an effigy of this horse and treasured some of its bones as relics almost two centuries later.

The rest of the journey was a nightmare struggle through a wilderness of forest and rugged mountains. Torrential rains swelled the rivers the Spaniards had to cross, and they were frequently lost in a landscape with almost no population. Most of the horses died, and the exhausted army suffered from starvation and fevers. Eventually the remnants of the expedition, by now numbering only several hundred in all, reached the shores of Lake Isabal in April 1525. There they finally met the Spaniards they had marched 500 miles to find, only to learn that Olid's insurrection had been put down by loyal officers long before. Cortes wisely chose to return to Mexico by sea.

Several important things are clear from what Cortes saw on his epic traverse of the central Maya Lowlands. First, he visited two considerable polities populated by speakers of two different Maya languages. Canek's realm, the more important of these for our purposes, was located around the great lake system of Guatemala's northeastern Peten region. Canek (we now know his proper title and dynastic name to have been Ajaw Kan Ek') was the principal lord of a loosely articulated Itza polity that included much of the territory around the lake and extended as far as southern Belize. Ajaw Kan Ek' dominated the core of this realm, while more distant towns and regions were ruled by other nominally subordinate lords, some of whom were members of his own family. War was more or less ongoing. Enemies of the Itza included the Kejaches, through whose territory northwest of the lake Cortes had traveled, and where he saw both fortified and recently destroyed towns. Ajaw Kan Ek' had his house, or palace, at a town the Spaniards referred to as Tayasal, which probably had only 2000 inhabitants or so in Cortes's time.

Despite its apparent isolation, the Itza polity was in regular touch with Tabasco over the Akalan trade routes, and also with southern Belize (where Ajaw Kan Ek' possessed cacao plantations) and places even farther east. Although population was heavily concentrated around the lakes, there were outlying towns as well, especially along the merchant roads. Cortes of course had no way of knowing the total population of the central Peten region through which he traveled, but a reasonable estimate would be 25,000–30,000 people for the early 16th century, given what we know from later times.

Equally important is what Cortes did not see or report. Even though he and his men traveled through the old heartland of Classic Maya civilization, they saw no really impressive, thriving centers apart from Itzam K'anak, and certainly none comparable to the Classic centers that we will review later. They saw no major ruins either, although they passed within a few km of Tikal and other long-abandoned Classic centers. Ajaw Kan Ek's own capital was so small that neither Cortes nor Bernal Diaz felt obliged to comment much on it, nor on the king's royal residence either. Such neglect contrasts sharply with their admiring descriptions of the towns, cities, and palaces they encountered elsewhere in Mesoamerica. Even though the Spaniards must have passed within a few miles of Palenque, Tikal, and other Classic period sites, they seem to have heard no rumors of these ruins. And finally, although the landscape was by no means deserted, the population that Cortes saw was a far cry from the hundreds of thousands or even millions of people that had inhabited it 700 years before. Forest had reclaimed the great Maya centers themselves, and also much of the carefully cleared and tended agricultural landscape that had supported them. Not only had Classic Maya civilization collapsed, but it had also failed to recover in any impressive way.

Here we leave Ajaw Kan Ek's kingdom for the present, although we will return to the dramatic story of its conquest at the end of this chapter. More important now are the Maya of northern Yucatan, about whom we have far more information for the 16th century.

Yucatan in the 16th Century

After the fall of the Aztec capital Tenochtitlan, the Spaniards turned their attention once again to Yucatan, which they already knew to be a populous region, and hopefully one of considerable wealth. Royal permission was required to undertake new conquests, however, and ultimately the choice fell on Francisco de Montejo, a trusted lieutenant of Cortes. Montejo had missed out on the conquest of Mexico because he had been sent back to Spain in 1519 to represent Cortes's interests in the interminable legal wrangles at the royal court in Valladolid. There Montejo, a man of some influence who also married a rich widow from Seville, eventually got himself confirmed Adelantado, a hereditary title conferring the right to conquer and colonize new lands in the king's name (but at his own expense). In December 1527 he sailed for Yucatan with a small fleet, partly funded by his wife's personal fortune, hoping to emulate Cortes's brilliant feat. Unfortunately the warlike northern Maya proved to be both more impoverished from the Spanish perspective than the Aztecs and much more difficult to subdue, partly because they had no central capital or ruler and also because many Spanish soldiers soon defected for richer pickings in Peru, where Francisco Pizarro was plundering the almost unimaginable wealth of the Incas. Nearly two decades of campaigning, the last phases directed by Montejo's son and nephew, were needed to finally bring the northern Maya Lowlands under Spanish control in 1546. What we know about the nature of northern Maya society at the time of the conquest and the latter half of the 16th century has greatly influenced our reconstructions of the Classic Maya, and consequently our ideas about the collapse.

By far the single most important written account of the 16th century is Fray Diego de Landa's *Relación de las Cosas de Yucatan*, which summarizes Maya life and history, as well as details of the Spanish conquest. This important document, which has survived in incomplete and garbled form, languished in Spanish colonial archives until 20 years after Stephens and Catherwood visited Copan. Ironically, we have Landa to thank for almost single-handedly eliminating most of the then extant Precolumbian Maya books, and he destroyed some of its great buildings as well.

Born in Spain about the time that Cortes set off on his march to Honduras, Landa went to Yucatan as a Franciscan missionary in 1549, only a few years after the Montejos finally prevailed. There he learned to speak Yucatec Mayan, studied Maya religion and customs, and expressed considerable concern over the cruelties that Spaniards inflicted on the native population, although he also appears to have been obsessed and repelled by idolatry.

Landa soon assumed the high religious office of provincial, and one of his early projects in 1553 was to partly level an enormous pyramid temple at the site of Izamal, about 56 km (35 miles) southeast of the colonial capital of Merida, to serve as the foundation for a church and convent.

One of Landa's duties was also to investigate, using corporal means if necessary, any signs of apostasy among the newly (and often nominally) converted Maya. Hearing rumors of idolatrous behavior at the town of Mani, seat of the Xiu, one of the most famous preconquest Maya families, he arrested, punished, and tortured scores of native leaders and schoolmasters. According to later and rather garbled accounts, his most notorious act occurred sometime around 1562 (the exact date is uncertain), when he and his assistants burned all of the native Maya manuscripts, or codices, that they could find. While Landa did not succeed in destroying all Maya books (later clerics knew of surviving codices and sometimes studied them), he certainly did irreparable damage to one of the world's rich literary traditions. Landa's precipitous and high-handed actions incurred the displeasure of his superiors and he was subjected to a long trial in Spain. As part of his defense he wrote the *Relación* in about 1566, relying on his own knowledge and on information from three highly-ranked Maya informants. Finally vindicated, he was elected Bishop of Yucatan in 1572 and returned to New Spain, where he lived out the last six years of his life.[4] The following overview of contact-period Maya society is based on Landa, along with many other sources, and is enlivened by quotations from his *Relación*.[5]

At the time of the conquest the densest Maya populations were found in the northern part of the Yucatan Peninsula, along its east and west coasts, and around Lake Peten Itza (Fig. 12). No trustworthy census figures exist for that time; estimates range from 2.3 million to as low as 600,000 people for this region as a whole. I personally prefer the lower estimates and believe that a range of 600,000–800,000 is reasonable. Some zones were more heavily populated than others, but even in Mani, one of the largest and most prosperous of the 16th-century polities, overall population density was probably well below 20 people per sq. km (52 per sq. mile). The relevance of this figure for our understanding of the Classic Maya will become apparent later.

Agricultural production is basic to any agrarian economy, and the 16th-century Maya grew a variety of subsistence and other crops. By far the most important of these was maize, which along with beans probably contributed at least 60 percent to the diet of the average individual. Other staples were squash, sweet potatoes, and manioc, and lesser crops included tomatoes, chile peppers, tobacco, cocoa (chocolate), and dozens of others. Some crops, espe-

12 *According to the ethnohistorian Ralph Roys, northern Yucatan was divided up into 16 "provinces" at the time of Spanish contact. Some of these might have been politically centralized, but others consisted of looser confederations of small polities led by local rulers called batabs.*

cially fruits, were planted in houselot gardens or special plots of land in towns, while others were cultivated in *milpas* (an Aztec word for cornfield) at some distance from the principal residences of the farmers; as recently as the 1930s it was common for rural people to walk distances of 8 km (5 miles) or more to cultivate the most productive soils.

> The lands today are common property, and so he who first occupies them becomes the possessor of them. They sow in a great number of places, so that if one part fails, another may supply its place. In cultivating the land they do nothing except collect together the refuse and burn it in order to sow it afterwards.[6]

Landa and other early writers do not describe farming practices in detail, but passages like the above, supplemented by more recent ethnographic information, have led many Mayanists to identify communal ownership of land and swidden (sometimes called slash and burn) production as basic to the 16th-century economy. Swidden agriculturists in the Maya Lowlands today cut down the vegetation on small plots of land (typically several acres in size), and then burn the dry detritus just before the rains come. Such burning has both good and bad consequences. Debris that would interfere with cultivation is eliminated, weeds, insects, and other pests are killed, and the resulting layer of ash provides some fertilizer. On the other hand, thin humus levels of the fragile tropical soils are damaged and many nutrients are lost as gases. Several plant species are typically grown together in the burned-off fields, and even the comparatively thin, stony soils of Yucatan provide good crops for one to several years. When yields begin to decline and labor inputs (especially for weeding) rise, fields are abandoned, ideally for as long as 15 to 20 years, by which time forest has grown up again and the soil has recovered much of its fertility. To the 16th-century Spaniards this seemed like a wasteful system because so much land was uncultivated in any given year. To them the forest was a wilderness to be reclaimed and made productive. To the Maya the forest, or *k'ax*, was an integral segment of their agrarian resources that was essentially in fallow, and the repository of valuable plant and animal products.

Extensive agriculture of the kind Landa described requires surprisingly little labor to get a good crop, and can be carried out by the members of a domestic household using only simple tools. It is well-suited to a system in which individual farmers "owned" the standing crops in their fields and the resulting harvests, but have only usufruct rights to the land itself, with overall possession in the hands of some larger collective.

Some Mayanists believe instead that in the early 16th century land was owned by individual families or other social groups and that it was used much more intensively than suggested by the milpa model. If such ownership, along with the associated micromanagement of the landscape that it implies, was an essential feature of contact-period agriculture, it would have important implications for the political economy of the Classic Maya. Debate on this issue continues, but the population densities cited above are certainly consistent with swidden production. Despite these low densities and the high productivity of maize under optimal circumstances, droughts, plagues of locusts, and other agricultural catastrophes often resulted in food shortages and famines. One such drought occurred in 1535, midway through the conquest, and rainmaking rituals of various kinds to avert such disasters were (and are) well established in Yucatan.

No matter who owned the fields or exactly how they were cultivated, one cannot overestimate the significance of maize for the 16th-century Maya, both in dietary and cultural terms. As one Colonial official put it:

> If one looks closely he will find that everything [these Indians] did and talked about had to do with maize; in truth, they fell little short of making a god of it. And so much is the delight and gratification they got and still get out of their corn fields, that because of them they forget wife and children and every other pleasure, as if their corn fields were their final goal and ultimate pleasure.[7]

Actually, they did make a god of it. And as we shall see later, the necessity – one might even say the compulsion – to make maize robbed the descendants of the 16th-century Maya of an all-important military victory.

Like all Mesoamericans the Maya were poorly provided with domestic animals. Households raised dogs, turkeys, ducks, and a form of stingless bee that produced abundant honey. Because so much of the landscape was uncultivated, however, a wide variety of animals, most importantly deer, could be hunted or gathered for animal protein, and tame deer (sometimes nursed by Maya women) and other wild animals were regularly kept in houselots. Fish supplemented the diets of those who lived close to rivers, lakes, or the sea, but many Maya communities were effectively land-locked.

The first Spanish explorers were much impressed with the towns they saw in Yucatan. In a celebrated passage, Landa characterized Maya settlements this way:

> Before the Spaniards had conquered that country the natives lived together in towns in a very civilized fashion.... Their dwelling place was as follows: in the middle of the town were the temples with their beautiful plazas, and all around the temples stood the houses of the lords and the priests, and then (those of) the most important people. Thus came the houses of the richest, and of those who were held in the highest estimation nearest to these, and at the outskirts of the town were the houses of the lower class.[8]

Unfortunately the early Spaniards tended to use words rather loosely, so a term like "pueblo," for example, might refer to an actual settlement such as a village, a town, or even a city, as well as to various larger political, ethnic, or territorial collectivities. It is thus difficult to form any concrete idea from statements like Landa's of how highly nucleated these towns actually were, a problem made more acute by the relocation of many Maya into new settlements after the conquest. A few Postclassic Maya communities such as Mayapan (abandoned about AD 1450) certainly consisted of large zones of densely packed houses delineated by formal walls (Fig. 13), but these were exceptional places. Most "towns" probably consisted instead of a nucleus of civic structures, plazas, and residences of wealthy and elite people, much as Landa describes, surrounded by concentric zones of less dense habitations interspersed with cultivated land extending out for many km. Supporting this interpretation is an account of one of Montejo's columns, said to have marched without stopping from noon until early evening from the edge of the "town" of Chauaca to the precincts of its cacique, or chief, at the center. Because the Spaniards must have covered at least 10–12 km (6.25–7.5 miles),

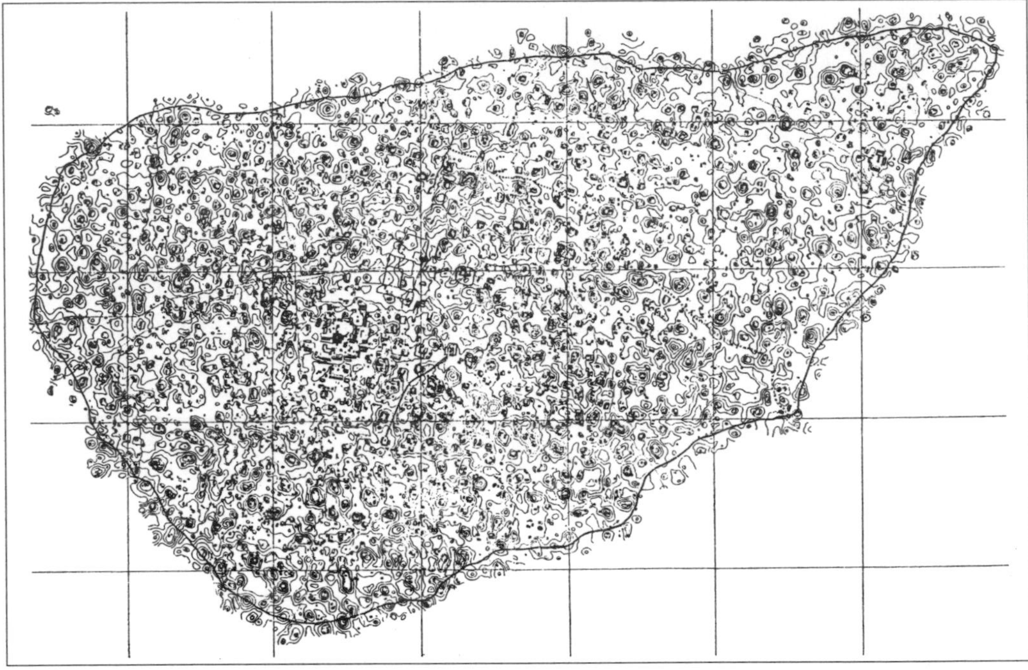

13 *Map of Mayapan (each grid square is 500 m on a side). Note the very dense concentrations of residential architecture within the wall that give this site an urban appearance.*

this so-called town was more likely a whole political district, including the principal settlement and its rural hinterland.

Houses of lords and priests probably resembled the palatial, multi-structure compounds described earlier by Cortes, and some late examples have been excavated (Fig. 14). Such compounds consisted largely of masonry structures that were smoothly plastered and painted and contained many kinds of facilities, including wells, storerooms, and shrines where skulls or other remains of important ancestors were kept. Rear segments of residences were private family spaces while front rooms were used to receive guests, to transact business, and to settle disputes. Gifts and tribute were brought to the adjacent courtyards for redistribution. Households of elite people were probably quite large, consisting of the lord's family as well as various retainers and slaves. Their complex economic affairs were managed by an official called a *caluac*, who served the resident noble. When lords left their residences they were often accompanied by sizable retinues. Presumably the captive Spaniard Aguilar served just such a household.

Maya commoners, in contrast, lived in small houses constructed of stone,

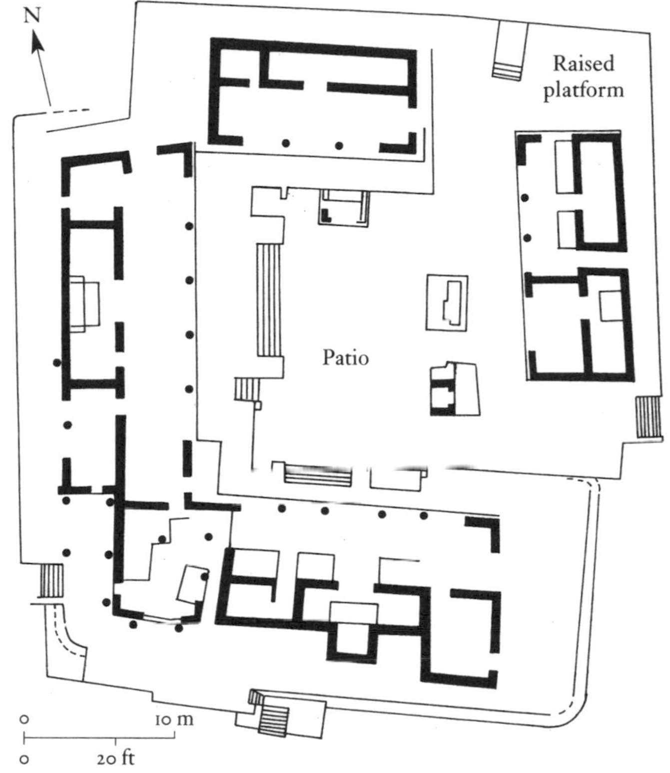

14 *Plan of one of the elite residences excavated at Mayapan by Carnegie Institution archaeologists in the 1950s. Its pattern of many large buildings grouped around a patio recalls both Spanish descriptions of 16th-century palatial houses, and those of the Classic Maya, such as the compound of Mak-Chanal at Copan.*

poles, and thatch, much as traditional families do today in northern Yucatan. Houses, along with detached kitchens, shrines, and storerooms, all sometimes surrounded by a garden and houselot wall, were the most conspicuous settlement features on the Maya landscape. Many compounds of this kind housed extended or joint families.

The issue of settlements leads us to the question of how communities or political units were organized. One line of evidence comes from postconquest legal documents written in Maya by native notaries or scribes. Several recent groundbreaking studies by ethnohistorians Matthew Restall, Philip Thompson, and Sergio Quezada provide the basis for the following overview.[9]

According to Restall, who has interpreted native documents in his book *The Maya World*, each postconquest Maya person was born into an indigenous community called the *cah*, which was fundamental to both social identity and economic well-being. Restall argues that the cah combined political, territorial, and social dimensions and was the "sole central and indisputable unit of Maya sociopolitics." Essentially each cah consisted of a named unit of people centered on a particular nucleated town, which held land and other resources in common and had its own governing body. In some cases particularly large Precolumbian centers such as T'ho (a community now buried or destroyed by Merida, the colonial capital of Yucatan) might have been subdivided into quarters or wards, each representing the political core of a separate cah. All *cahnal*, as members were called, had common interests and were frequently in conflict with other *cahob* (the suffix *-ob* indicates the plural form). Within the cah individual nuclear families possessed houses and private land, and could also claim access to common land in the larger cah territorial holdings. Spatial delimitation of the polity was not strictly territorial in the modern sense, but rather extended to the most distant plots of land (themselves often carefully marked) habitually cultivated by members of the cah, land being the principal resource.

Cah members who shared the same patronym conceived themselves to be related and acted as a kind of localized lineage, called a *chibal* by Restall or a *cuchteel* by Quezada. Landa observed that people

> make much of knowing the origin of their lineages ... and they boast much about one of their lineage who has distinguished himself ... [they] consider all those of the same name to be related and treat them as such. Thus when anyone goes to a part of the country where he is unknown and in need, he makes known his name, and anyone of the same name receives him and treats him with good will and kindness. Thus no man or woman marries another of the same name, because they regard this as a great infamy.[10]

Members of the same chibal lived close to one another, helped one another at farming tasks, and acted collectively as a faction to defend their interests within the cah, led by a lineage head or prominent man (*ah kul*). In any particular cah or region some chibalob were richer and more prestigious than others. Because marriage was almost unknown between chibal members, people tried to find spouses in chibalob of similar or greater status. One's social identity thus depended not only on membership in a particular cah, but also on the chibal to which one belonged and the local rank of that chibal, some of which were recognized as noble.

Principal leader of the colonial cah was the *batab* (pl. = *batabob*), a title that means something like "headman." Batabob were always nobles, but did not automatically inherit their positions. Rather their eligibility for office was determined by a complex mix of considerations, including class, chibal affiliation, wealth, political experience, and relationship to the previous batab. Factions developed around ambitious men seeking the batabship. Once in office the batab governed with the help of a town council, as well as lesser officers. Together they settled internal cah disputes, collected tribute and taxes, mobilized the population for labor service and religious festivals, and represented cah in its interactions with the wider colonial world. Thompson's studies have shown how surprisingly durable the title and role of the batab was – originating in Precolumbian times, it still designated elite Maya community leaders well into the 18th century.

Restall believes that the cah was also a very traditional form of organization that functioned in much the same manner before the Spaniards arrived – the basic political building block of preconquest society. The pre-Spanish cah or batabil (batabship) of course, would have been an independent unit not subjected to a foreign colonial administration, and its territorial core was usually the Maya elite center as described by Landa, not one of the highly nucleated towns later created by the Spaniards (although some large pre-Spanish towns certainly existed, such as Champoton). It was probably one of these little batabil that Montejo's forces traversed.

The reconstructions of Restall and his colleagues refine, and in some ways take issue, with an older one by the ethnohistorian Ralph Roys.[11] Roys identified 16 political units in northern Yucatan at the time of the conquest. Like Restall, Thompson, and Quezada, he thought that the basic units were batabil, composed of the central place of the batab-governor and the land and smaller settlements and farmsteads in the immediately surrounding countryside. But he also believed that aggregations of batabil formed several different kinds of larger "provinces." The simplest and most fragile provinces consisted of loose aggregations of batabil whose leaders were unrelated to one another (i.e., did not share the same patronym) and who cooperated only on the basis of mutual self-interest, not lineage solidarity. Somewhat more stable provinces were formed by a politically cohesive set of local batabil whose noble leaders mostly came from the same lineage. When collective action was necessary these little polities banded together against common enemies, although they also fought among themselves. Finally, the most complex provinces were ruled by very powerful leaders boasting the native title *halach uinic* ("true man"). Each halach uinic was a sort of glorified batab, who ruled his own local batabship but had also extended his sway over others as well, adopting the exalted title *ajaw* which set him above lesser rulers as a kind of petty king. The *holcacab* or head town of the halach uinic served as a regional capital, giving its name to the polity as a whole. Subordinate batabob lacked the independent political initiative of those in the two less centralized kinds of provinces. Probably the best known such centralized province was

Mani, covering about 10,000 sq. km (3860 sq. miles), and ruled from the holcacab of the same name by a halach uinic of the Xiu family.

Restall's work helps us to understand better the internal character of the earlier Precolumbian batabil, but he thinks there is very scant evidence for the multi-cah provinces identified by Roys. He notes that the Maya word *cuchcabal*, sometimes translated as "province" or "jurisdiction," has the general sense of "sub-unit" and can have many specific meanings. Restall in particular thinks that the halach uinic title was an honorific situationally conferred on the particularly respected or powerful batab of a dominant cah, and he doubts that one cah and its leader could consistently control others. Quezada and Thompson lean toward the more centralized interpretation, and think that halach uinicob sometimes dominated not only other batabships, but also little local units that did not fall under the jurisdiction of a batab, administered by an officer of commoner rank called an *ah holpop*. To the extent that provinces existed, their boundaries, like those of the constituent batabil, were fluid and frequently contested.

It remains to be seen if future research can reconcile these somewhat divergent views, but clearly the halach uinicob encountered by the Spaniards were very powerful leaders. Whether they could meddle with impunity in the affairs of their constituent batabs or impose batabs of their own choosing on local communities is unclear, but they certainly mobilized support from many batabil, exerted influence over very large territories, and were treated with special deference. Fortunately we are on somewhat firmer ground with regard to more general aspects of rank and social organization.

Sixteenth-century Maya society was strongly hierarchical. At its apex were people collectively called *almehenob*. *Almehen* (the singular form) is usually translated as "noble," but in Maya it literally means "child of a woman" (*ah*) and "child of a man" (*mehen*). Together they indicated that a person had inherited two distinguished names – the patronyms of both the father's and the mother's lineages. Of these, the father's was most important and provided the chibal identification. Specific combinations of names conferred social prominence, similar to the contemporary Spanish usage of *hidalgo* ("son of something") or to a member of the English knighthood or rural squirarchy. Although identification with the father's family line was emphasized, nobles in particular cultivated their distinguished maternal connections.

Nobles were themselves ranked into several subgroups: great dynastic patrilineages that enjoyed the widest political jurisdictions, lesser noble families with more local influence, and what were in effect petty elites or gentry. Only for the most distinguished ruling families (whose male heads were called by the Spaniards *señores naturales*) did chibal identity matter much beyond the territorial limits of the cah itself. Nobles took special care to preserve detailed knowledge of their descent lines, aided by priests who probably kept genealogical records in books. Some illustrious men appear to have had more than one wife or concubine, although the accounts are contradictory on this point.

As in 16th-century Europe, especially prominent families had illustrious names, including the Xiu, the Cocom, the Pech, the Chel, and the Capul. These grandees were most concerned with proper reckoning of descent, and the passage of offices, titles, and privilege down in the male line. Possible hieroglyphic expressions for several distinguished patronyms have been identified at the sites of Uxmal and Chichen Itza, where they were recorded hundreds of years earlier. Noble members of these kin groups dominated affairs in specific communities or regions, and some of them, most notably the Cocom of Sotuta and the Xiu of Mani, were traditional enemies. Both these family names had very old pedigrees and associations. Ethnohistoric accounts attribute the 8th-century founding of Uxmal, a major center (and now favorite tourist attraction) in the Puuc hill country, to an individual named Ah Kuy Tok Tutil Xiu. Descendants of this illustrious ruler illustrated the genealogical history of their house in Colonial times (Fig. 15), and the eminent Mayanist Sylvanus Morley fondly remembered being the guest, in 1940, of Don Nemesio Xiu, a humble farmer who was also the direct descendant in the 38th generation from Ah Kuy Tok Tutil Xiu.

People of high noble rank claimed descent from distinguished foreigners (Nahuatl-speaking "Mexicans" from the west). Prominent people also set themselves apart by displays of status symbols, esoteric knowledge, and elite decorum, and were hedged about with a special etiquette. Halach uinicob, for example, were often carried in palanquins and accompanied by impressive entourages.

Nobles were also rich, and to be rich meant to own or otherwise control land, labor, and articles of commerce. In fact, the single most important correlate of noble status was exemption from tribute, or more accurately, the fact that one was supported by the goods and services of lesser folk. Nobles' compounds were built and maintained by commoners, whose households or towns also paid taxes in the form of maize, beans, chile, salt, fowl, dried fish, cotton cloth, turkeys, honey, precious stones, and occasionally slaves. Lords owned parcels of especially productive lands, such as cacao orchards, some of which were located at great distances from their residences. Slaves cultivated these lands and also served as load-bearers, for many Maya lords were also

15 *This drawing illustrating the genealogy of the Xiu family was made in about 1557 by a Maya noble. Although he used European conventions, the image strongly reflects the Maya emphasis on elite family connections, a tradition that long predated the arrival of the Spaniards.*

great merchants involved in long-distance trade. Quite possibly the canoe encountered by Columbus was part of one of these elite trading ventures, and its paddlers might well have been slaves.

Supporting all this complexity, and of course much lower in rank, were the commoners, whom the Spaniards labeled by the Nahuatl term *macehual* in their documents, but who seem to have been indigenously called by several terms (as recorded in Colonial Spanish dictionaries) including a *col cab*, *hembal uinicob*, *membe uinicob*, and *yalba uinicob*. These variously have the sense of peasant maize farmers, or "inferior" or "lower" men, and thus served to contrast commoner with noble status. Contact-period census figures are scarce, but these people, along with other basic producers such as fishermen, probably comprised 70–90 percent of the population. This estimate is not only based on the general rule of thumb for ancient agrarian states, but is also supported by more recent census information. As late as 1794, for example, the proportion of Maya Indian farmers (or tribute-payers) to non-Indian consumers in Yucatan varied between about 71 and 94 percent.[12]

Exactly how Maya commoners related socially to nobles at the time of European contact is unclear. Despite their strong sense of inherited privilege and their obvious ability to extract goods and services from commoners, there were gradations of status between the two groups. Members of both sometimes shared the same patronym, and some commoners were rich men, prominent in the affairs of their communities.

Lowest in rank, and probably never very numerous, were the people whom the Spaniards called "slaves" (*esclavos*), but who are probably better thought of as economically and socially debased or indentured commoners who were literally possessed by rich masters. Landa claimed that slavery of this kind was introduced only late in the Postclassic period by one of the great lords of Mayapan. Very few *pentacob*, as these individuals were called, were born into slavery. Most seem to have been acquired as war captives, but others were debtors and criminals. Apparently children could be sold into bondage by their parents, and some slaves were later redeemed by their families. Slaves could be bought and sold, were widely traded, and constituted an important kind of wealth. Although some were sacrificed, most were probably attached to the households of nobles, for whom they did menial or specialized work. If the stories about the captured Spaniard Guerrero are trustworthy, talented slaves could rise to privileged positions as important retainers of specific lords, much as Greek slaves did in ancient Roman households.

Contact-period Maya society was obviously well-stratified, not only in social terms, but also politically and economically. Roys used the word "caste" to describe the relationships among nobles, commoners, and "slaves" but I think it implies too strong a distinction. "Class" seems more accurate, with the proviso that class boundaries were somewhat fluid, depending on birth, wealth, marriage, and the fortunes of war. At any rate, nobles were responsible for civic order.

> The lords governed the town, settling disputes, ordering and settling the affairs of their republics, all of which they did by the hands of leading men, who were very well obeyed and highly esteemed, especially the rich, whom they visited, and they held court in their houses, where they settled their affairs and business, usually at night.[13]

Our understanding of exactly how polities were governed is sketchy, but batabs were aided by many subordinates. Landa's comment indicates that rich members of the community wielded much influence, and batabs had associated officers of several kinds who bore specific titles, although exactly how they were recruited or what they did is not always clear. These included *ah k'in* (priest), *ah kulel* (deputy), *ah can* (speaker), *holpop* (head of the mat), and *ah cuch cab* (a man who represented some kind of community subdivision). As we shall see shortly, there were also specialized military titles. Restall thinks that only the batab office was restricted to nobles, but people of high rank might have dominated the others as well. If halach uinicob were as powerful as Roys thought, they and their deputies would have formed another level of administration concerned with appointing the subsidiary batabob and retaining their allegiance and cooperation. In any case, the governmental structure of 16th-century Maya polities was probably very simple and nonbureaucratic by our standards, and no doubt there was a good deal of variation from one polity to another as well. Certainly there was abundant conflict.

From their earliest contacts the Maya impressed the Spaniards as fierce and accomplished warriors. Even allowing for the exaggeration of enemy numbers by Cortes, Bernal Diaz, and others who fought them, it is clear that hundreds or even thousands of warriors were quickly mustered, which in turn shows that most able-bodied men were prepared to fight and that they probably kept their own weapons in their houses. Towns or other central places were sometimes permanently fortified, and the Maya were also adept at throwing up temporary defenses of earth and timber.

Although batabs went into battle there were also special war-chiefs, or *nacoms*, associated with the more important towns who provided the most experienced and effective military leadership. Nacoms were elected for three years. When hostilities began nacoms enlisted bands of accomplished local warriors, called *holcans*, who possessed their own arms and who sometimes proved as troublesome to the towns they putatively served as to their enemies. Bernal Diaz reported that during battles in Tabasco the Indians cried out to each other to kill or capture the Spanish "*calachuni.*" That these Maya applied the title halach uinic to Cortes suggests that even the greatest of their own lords ventured onto the battlefield along with their batabs and nacoms, and that killing or capturing an enemy halach uinic could ensure victory.

As in most ancient agrarian societies, some battles were highly choreographed and ritualized, as were other phases of the warfare process. Nacoms were supposed to withdraw from normal life and remain celibate during their tenure. During an important yearly ceremony called Pacum Chac the nacom was carried to a temple, where he was treated almost as a living idol; offerings were made to him while a war dance was performed. War captives were often sacrificed, and body parts kept as trophies. Whether a successful warrior of common origins could rise in rank as among the Aztecs is unknown, but men who killed or captured important enemies were certainly honored and feasted.

Wars were fought for land, for slaves, to avenge insults and punish theft, and to control trade routes and the sources of various valued products, particularly salt, which was extracted from lagoons on the northern shore of the peninsula. Agricultural crises seem to have provoked conflict, for during droughts

there would be a great want of water, and many hot suns, which would dry up the fields of maize, from which would follow a great famine, and from the famine thefts, and from the thefts slaves and selling those who stole. And from this would follow discords, and wars between themselves and with other towns.[14]

Although wars among separate towns (or cahob?) were most frequent, as this passage from Landa suggests there were also internecine conflicts over succession, property, or insults between factions of the same community or polity. As in highland Mexico some Maya lords, notably the Xiu ruler of Mani, threw in their lot with the Spaniards, hoping that these powerful foreign allies would help them overcome their traditional foes. In addition to conventional battles, Maya lords were not above trickery, sometimes luring their enemies within reach with protestations of friendship and then massacring them. A famous incident of this kind occurred during the 1535 drought when a party of Xiu, promised safe passage by their Cocom enemies to the sacred *cenote* (a kind of natural well) at Chichen Itza, where they wished to sacrifice slaves, were all treacherously killed. The Xiu/Spanish alliance was partly motivated by the Xiu lineage's desire to avenge this incident.

Religion

The Spaniards were both fascinated and horrified by Maya religious beliefs and practices, and left us so much detailed information that I can only briefly summarize it here. Landa reported that

They had a very great number of idols and of temples, which were magnificent in their own fashion. And besides the community temples, the lords, priests, and the leading men have oratories and idols in their houses, where they made their prayers and offerings in private.[15]

Both community and private rituals revolved around the stone, wood, or clay images (idols) that the Spaniards found so offensive. Images, along with books, other religious paraphernalia, and possibly the bones of particularly revered leaders, were kept in temple rooms atop high pyramidal substructures, and also in private shrine rooms in the house compounds of important people. As in highland Mexico, human sacrifices and blood offerings were made in the temples. Both humble people and great lords made pilgrimages to distant places, such as shrines along the east coast of Yucatan, Cozumel Island, and the great well at Chichen Itza, where they made sacrifices of many kinds.

The Maya worshiped many gods, most of which were personified forces of nature or otherwise identified with them. Ancestors were also venerated, particularly those of nobles, and the distinction between ancestors and gods was not always sharply defined. Much ritual concern focused on those deities associated with sun, wind, rain, and other forces essential to agricultural fertility. Priests were intermediaries with the gods, and are often described in early 16th-century accounts:

> The office of the priest was to discuss and to teach their sciences, to make known their needs and the remedies for them, to preach and to publish the festival days, to offer sacrifices, and to administer their sacraments.[16]

We do not know how priests were recruited, but because they had to master a good deal of esoteric knowledge and played such a prominent part in community life they were probably men from important families. Like nobles, they were supported by gifts and offerings. Among their duties was to make and use books:

> Their books were written on a large sheet doubled in folds, which was enclosed entirely between two boards, which they decorated, and they wrote on both sides in columns following the order of the folds. And they made this paper from the roots of a tree and gave it a white gloss upon which it was easy to write.[17]

Some nobles possessed books, and a few even learned to read them (for which they were greatly respected), but it was mainly priests who were literate. The few books that have survived are sacred almanacs filled with depictions of gods, astronomical and religious information, and used as instruments of prophecy. If Landa and his fellow clerics had not destroyed so many others we might have historical and genealogical records as well.

Inscriptions include much calendrical lore. Maya concepts of time were very different from our own and emphasized cycles in which events in a sense recapitulated themselves. Scrutiny of past events, along with calendrical and astronomical concordances, provided prognostications of what would happen in the future. Although the Classic Maya Long Count calendar had been largely abandoned by the 10th century, the northern Maya continued to use a related cycle they called *u kahlay katunab*, or the "Count of the K'atuns."

16 *This sketch of the K'atun Wheel was made by Bishop Landa. The Count of the K'atuns was still used by Maya scribes and priests even after the Spanish conquest.*

A *k'atun* was a period of 7200 days, or about 19.7 of our solar years (Fig. 16). Each k'atun was itself subdivided into 20 units (*tuns*) consisting of 360 days, an interval 5.24 days short of a solar year. Thirteen k'atuns followed one another in succession and then the cycle started over again, defining a total period (called a *may*) of somewhat more than 256 true solar years. Events were thus fixed within these 256-year cycles, extremely significant blocks of time something like our own centuries except that they did not progress in a linear fashion (i.e., each cycle did not have its own successive numerical designation). This meant that each named day in the k'atun count reappeared, or "came around" again, every 256 years. What happened at specific times during one k'atun cycle, it was believed, could be used to predict, or prophesy, what would happen during the recurrence of that k'atun. As Grant Jones puts it

The past … occurs in the future in somewhat predictable forms – with differing details but with thematic regularities that reoccur. The writing and recitation of k'atun histories, therefore, were acts of prophesy making, because what had occurred once could be expected to occur in some form thirteen k'atuns, or 256 years, later, and yet again in future appearances of the k'atun, ad infinitum. The k'atun historian was a prophet-priest who potentially wielded immense political influence and power, for he could rewrite the past in order to prewrite the future. What prophets chose to report about previous eras, that is, could be used by political decision makers (who were often priests themselves) to plan and justify their future actions. Prophetic history was a dynamic, ever-changing accounting of time and events that, far from freezing the past as "fact," could always be used to reinterpret and rewrite the past for the convenience of the present.[18]

In the 16th century Maya priests were able to track a sequence of these k'atun cycles, with associated events, extending back over more than 1000 years to the beginning of the 5th century AD. Some recurring k'atun endings (particularly "8 Ahau") were consistently associated with famines or other catastrophes that had supposedly happened in the past, and might happen in the future. Concordances among dates in the k'atun count (called by archaeologists the Short Count), the Julian calendar used by Landa, and our own Gregorian calendar eventually yielded the key to understanding the earlier Classic period Long Count.

Shamans, or sorcerers as the Spaniards called them, provided many services, the most important of which was curing. Although the office of native priest was suppressed very shortly after the conquest, shamans survived and still carry out their traditional roles in both the Maya Highlands and Lowlands. Those found today in Yucatan are called *H-men*, and they combine the roles of shaman and priest. They officiate at community rituals, and also use divination and other ceremonies to detect the causes of disease or misfortune, which are often ascribed to defective or absent soul elements and related to various kinds of spiritual pollution or defilement. Oracles in many forms conveyed information from gods and ancestors.

Sixteenth-century Maya religion is finally distinctive for something that it lacked: a tradition of divine or semi-divine kings who were personally responsible for the balance of the cosmos in general and for the well-being of their polities and subjects in particular. As we shall see later, kingship of this kind was essential to the Classic Maya, and its absence has important implications for the Classic collapse.

The Last Maya Kingdom

Early on the morning of 13 March 1697, a small Spanish rowing vessel carrying 108 soldiers smashed through a screen of enemy canoes and approached the island town of Nojpeten, which was defended by a swarm of Indians behind makeshift fortifications. Martin de Ursua y Arizmendi, commander of this Spanish force, later reported that his men held their own fire until they received a volley of enemy arrows, to which they responded with the discharge of a cannon and then stormed ashore. By 8 am all the surviving Maya defenders had fled and the town was firmly in Spanish hands.

So ended the last New World kingdom ruled by a native dynasty – the very same Itza kingdom that Cortes had visited on the shores of the great lakes of northern Guatemala 172 years earlier. Few people today realize that this last outpost of Maya civilization survived so long, although the dramatic story of its fall to Spanish invaders has been recounted many times, most recently and comprehensively by Grant Jones in his book *The Conquest of the Last Maya Kingdom.* Like the northern Maya, the Itza provide particularly important insights into what the Classic Maya might have been like, especially because they lived on the same landscape abandoned by their forebears centuries earlier.

It is tempting to imagine the Itza and their neighbors as an isolated Maya population that somehow survived for centuries deep in the Peten forests, descendants of the people who had built and then abandoned nearby Classic centers such as Tikal. According to their own accounts, however, most were relative newcomers. The Itza, along with three other local groups, the Kowojs, Kejaches, and Mopans, spoke Yucatecan Mayan dialects. Prominent nobles of the Itza and the Kowoj, who dominated the two core provinces of the region, claimed to have been mid-15th-century migrants from northern Yucatan – respectively from Chichen Itza and Mayapan – refugees from unsettled times associated with the breakup of the northern confederations centered on these two great sites. Their enemies the Kejaches, along with the little-known Mopans, might well have lived in the Peten forests much longer.

To the southwest of the lakes lived more remote people called Lacondones. Long celebrated by anthropologists as exemplars of traditional Maya lifeways, the ethnohistoric Lacandon Maya in fact were fairly recent (16th century?) Yucatecan migrants to the region, where Cholan languages had earlier been spoken. Historically documented movements of the Itza, Lacandones, and Kowoj have important implications for the Classic Maya collapse, because they provide some intimations of how extensive the spatial dislocation of whole social groups could be under stressful conditions.

Throughout the long colonial period before Ursua's campaign, the Spaniards and the unconquered Itza were well aware of each other and interacted in many ways. Spanish efforts to establish outposts in Belize in the last half of the 16th century caused disruption of Indian communities there, and many native people fled into the interior, some as far as Itza territory which was about 12 days' travel distant. Other Maya escaped into the forests from

Yucatan or Tabasco as conditions on the *encomiendas* of the conquerors (estates to which Indians were assigned as laborers) worsened in the early 17th century. Efforts to recapture or control these fugitives were ineffective and the refugees stirred up endless trouble on the colonial frontiers. Some groups also engaged in a lively illicit trade involving many products, effectively circumventing Spanish taxation. Colonial authorities assumed, probably correctly, that the Itza were heavily implicated in all this political and economic turmoil. Certainly the Itza used their warriors to control territories and populations on their borders as buffers against attack by the Spaniards or other traditional enemies. Even worse, the pagan Itza subverted the process of Christian conversion by preserving the old habits of idolatry and sacrifice and luring their Maya brethren away from the Church.

Spanish civil and ecclesiastical authorities were predictably concerned with suppressing the Itza, and individual priests, soldiers, and officials in Yucatan and highland Guatemala saw the opportunity for personal glory in this effort. For decades various ill-organized attempts met with little success. Finally, in 1617–18 two audacious Spanish friars managed to make their way to the Itza capital, which they reported had 200 houses. There they made a good impression on the ruler and according to one account destroyed an idol in the form of the horse left at Nojpeten by Cortes almost a century before. More important, they brought a delegation of 150 Itza, including some prominent men, all the way back to Merida. Two follow-up visits included unsuccessful negotiations aimed at converting the Itza to Christianity and placing them under at least nominal Spanish control. Thereafter relationships deteriorated badly, with frequent attacks and massacres by both the Itza or their rebel proxies on the one hand, and the Spaniards on the other. Ursua's campaign finally put an end to all this trouble, not by establishing immediate and firm Spanish control over the region (a process that took much longer), but rather by smashing the old Itza power and drastically reducing the region's population.

Although we have no written accounts of the Itza comparable to those available for northern Yucatan, Grant Jones's research, along with that of earlier writers, provides the basis for the following summary.

In 1695, just two years before the conquest, the Franciscan friar Avendano y Loyola interviewed the Itza king and his chiefs, and from what they told him he estimated the population in their lake domain at around 24,000 people.[19] Jones thinks there were as many as 60,000 people in the whole lakes region in 1697, with the various groups distributed in roughly the same way they were in Cortes's time (Fig. 17). The Itza were concentrated at the western end of Lake Peten Itza, and they probably controlled the region to the east as well. Kowojs

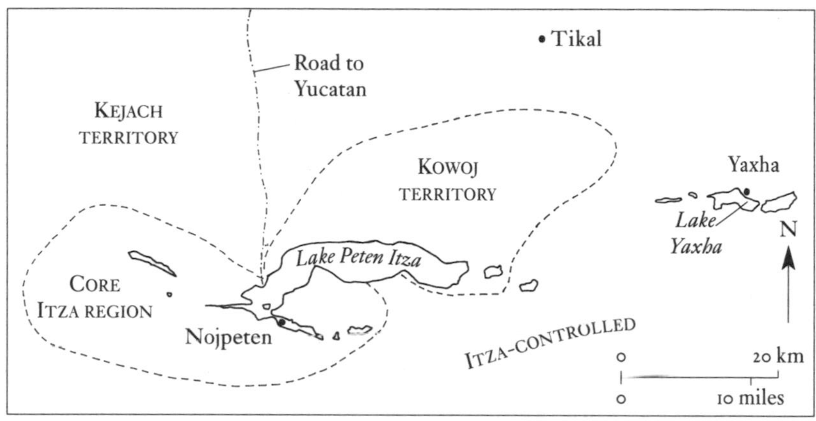

17 *The Itza region in the late 17th century. During his 1524–25 journey the little army of Cortes probably approached along the road shown leading to the north. Note the presence of celebrated Classic centers such as Tikal and Yaxha close to the Itza heartland.*

occupied the lake shore and mainland on the north and northeast. The hostile Kejaches lived to the north and northwest of the lake, along the route of the Spanish advance, and Mopans were dispersed over a wide area to the east, even as far as Belize. About 40–50 towns, ranging in population from a few hundred to 2000 people, were controlled by the Itza. Many were located on bodies of water and were either fortified or situated in defensible positions. Some towns were of greater importance than others, especially those where elite lineages had their principal residences. Many families probably lived outside of towns in smaller dispersed farmsteads.

Basic subsistence practices and crops resembled those of the northern Maya, although the landscape was more heavily forested and rainfall much higher. Commercial crops included cotton, cochineal, and indigo. Canoe traffic on the lakes enabled people to move between their settlements and fields and also facilitated communication between towns. The lakes themselves provided lacustrine products of many kinds, and hunting was an important adjunct to farming.

The Itza called their territory Suyua Peten Itza, and their capital, Nojpeten ("big" or "great island" in Maya), was situated on a steep island attached to the mainland by a causeway at the western extremity of Lake Peten Itza. Today the modern town of Flores sits atop the Itza settlement. Some Mayanists envision the overall polity as a loose confederation of semi-independent ruling lineages and their constituent territories. Jones believes instead that Nojpeten constituted the symbolic center (and 5th "direction") of a larger polity that was conceived of in quadripartite terms – a well centralized kingdom or mini-empire built up by conquest and dominated by the Itza royal lineage(s), with subsidiary rulers integrated through marriage alliances and inclusion in a great governing council. Whichever interpretation we prefer, there are obvious echoes of the Yucatecan halach uinic, who also bore the ajaw title, and his subordinated batabs. In 1697 there seem to have been about 22 titled Itza persons of special prominence, four of whom (apart from the king) bore the title Ajaw B'atab' and four others simply B'atab'. Like their northern cousins, Itza elite people put great store on both their paternal and maternal lineage connections. Although there was a strong emphasis on descent through the father's line, royal women played potent political roles.

In Jones's view the Itza kings, whose dynastic title/name was Ajaw Kan Ek' (Lord Serpent Star), were clearly more powerful than the other leaders. The incumbent Ajaw Kan Ek' in 1697 was assisted by a co-ruler called the AjK'in Kan Ek', who was his own cousin and who discharged the duties of chief priest, a kind of dual leadership that puzzled the Spaniards greatly and that apparently was duplicated in each of the four political segments. Rulers of all ranks seem to have had ritual, administrative, and military duties and were aided by a council of lesser notables who might have represented individual towns. Despite the putative ascendancy of the Itza royal family, Jones notes that the supreme ruler had to answer to his "court," and that there were many destabilizing forces in Itza society. To the extent that centralized rule existed, it depended on the fine balancing of dynastic and lineage politics. Rather than territorial units, it is probably better to think of Itza polities in terms of webs of political relationships among powerful people that could be very durable, but that could also shift suddenly and unexpectedly.

In support of this perspective was the fact that at the time of Ursua's incursion there was considerable internal factionalism and outright conflict, to some degree clearly stimulated by the pressures of the invasion. The Kojows were the chief rivals of the Itza. Their province was named for their own ruling lineage, but its political geography is poorly known. The Spanish priests who visited Nojpeten two years before Ursua's final assault saw many structures on the island that had been burned down about three months earlier in an internecine Kojow raid, and during their stay the perpetrator of the attack brazenly strolled through the capital with an entourage of warriors in full war regalia, apparently immune from any retaliation by the Ajaw Kan Ek' and his people.

Details of Itza social organization remain unclear. In northern Yucatan many basic patterns of life survived relatively intact even after 1546, including native structures of ranking and privilege, and the accounts of Landa and other chroniclers were greatly enriched by such survivals. Unfortunately the conquest of the Itza spawned no Landa, and even had a similarly talented observer emerged he would have found it difficult to record comparable information for the Itza. Extreme social disruption resulted from the conquest itself, from subsequent conflicts for supremacy among still-independent Itza factions, and by dramatic and rapid population loss (which Jones estimates at 50 percent by 1701). Whether the Itza had any social group resembling the cah is uncertain (although Restall thinks this is very likely), as are details of the ways in which commoners related to lords or whether slaves were an important social component as they were in Yucatan.

Nor do we have a good picture of the Itza capital, because the remains of Nojpeten lie today under the modern Guatemalan town of Flores. As many as 5000 people might have been concentrated there to resist the Spanish assault, but the population was probably somewhat smaller under more ordinary circumstances. Eyewitness descriptions of Nojpeten are very sketchy, and one can interpret them as describing either a town in the normal sense of the word or alternatively an elite residential and ritual enclave (I prefer the latter perspective).

The little hilly island, which is somewhat less than one sq. km (247 acres) in area, was certainly crowded with buildings – in 1525 Bernal Diaz remarked on the dazzling white appearance of the town when seen from a distance because of its many plaster walls. Crowning the hill at the center of the community was an imposing temple, the largest on the island, presided over by the AjK'in Kan Ek'. It measured about 17 m (56 ft) at the base and apparently was a standard masonry pyramid rising in several terraces to a richly sculptured holy-of-holies on the summit. Perhaps this building was a conscious model of the so-called Castillo at Mayapan, the northern center to which so many noble Itzas traced their ancestry. Anywhere from nine to 21 other temples of various sizes were also built on the hillsides of the island. Descriptions vary, but some of them apparently had masonry floors and wall bases, benches, and superstructures mainly made of perishable materials. Interior rooms held ritual paraphernalia and provided private spaces for priests.

Jones believes that Nojpeten was divided symbolically into four quarters by major intersecting streets and that each of the senior titled notables of the kingdom maintained a residence in the appropriate segment. These were not simple houses, but rather elaborate compounds with dormitories, kitchens, oratories, and storage facilities, all possibly contained within enclosure walls. If this reconstruction is correct, these residences, along with the temples, would have dominated the town, with a fringe of surrounding commoner houses all along the low shoreline. The royal residence of the Ajaw Kan Ek' was still located where Cortes saw it, about 40 paces from the shore near the eastern landing stage of the island. In front of the palace proper was a spacious courtyard in which stood a carved stone monument. Guests were received in an antechamber of the palace containing a great stone "table" (possibly a raised altar) surrounded by "seats" (raised benches?) for 12 "priests." Jones speculates that this hall functioned as a *popol na* – a kind of council house common at Maya centers. There are no good descriptions of the private domestic facilities of the Ajaw Kan Ek' and his household, but the upper parts of the palace were built of poles and thatch. Its precincts apparently were not off-limits to the general public, because Spanish visitors were exasperated by the many people who crowded into its rooms to gawk at them. Like Cortes, Ursua and his men do not seem to have been overly impressed by the splendor of the palace, which was probably just a somewhat more elaborate version of other Nojpeten elite residences, although large enough so that the Spaniards later used it as a barracks.

As in northern Yucatan both temples and houses contained sacred images and there were clearly specialized priests, although high-ranking nobles in general seem to have been involved in rituals. Ceremonies included the sacrifice of animals, and the Spaniards also claimed that the Itza sacrificed and ate human victims. Other accounts suggest that the high priest AjK'in Kan Ek' was a kind of shaman, who after his capture was possessed by spirits and flew into trances during which he exercised supernatural powers such as conjuring up fierce storms. Of course the Spaniards were titillated by such stories, and used them for their own propagandistic purposes, but given what we know about the Maya elsewhere we cannot discount Maya claims to such powers.

The Itza possessed prophetic books that must have closely resembled the codices of the northern Maya and were based on the same k'atun cycle. Unfortunately none has survived. A few of the Franciscan priests who visited Nojpeten had seen similar books in Yucatan and knew something of their contents. Much has been made in the literature of putative native prophecies foretelling that the Itza of Peten should pass under the rule of foreigners during a baleful k'atun named 8 Ajaw, which just happened to begin in the fateful year 1697, almost exactly 256 years from the fall of Chichen Itza according to indigenous Maya chronicles. Even if these stories are true, the Maya were by no means slaves to their own prophecies but rather used them opportunistically for their own purposes and, as we shall see later, discounted them when convenient. Jones believes that the Franciscans, who possessed their own millennial proclivities, were probably as much the sources of these predictions as the Itza, in effect attempting to capitalize politically and spiritually by using a native belief system against the Indians.

❦ ❦ ❦

Taken together, the Maya of northern Yucatan and the Itza provide a useful baseline from which to consider two issues. First, can we reasonably apply the label civilization to what the Spaniards found in the Maya Lowlands in the early 16th century? Apparently so. Both the northern Maya and the Itza had large polities, well-defined social classes, and some degree of centralized rulership. Commoners and "slaves" supported nobles and kings, who were hedged about with special etiquette and privileges and who claimed distinguished descent that separated them from ordinary people. Both built imposing temples and elite residences, made and kept books of various kinds, and manipulated mathematical and calendrical systems of considerable sophistication. Wealth differentials were marked, and widespread trade sponsored by nobles extended to regions far beyond the Maya Lowlands proper.

To the first Spaniards who saw all this first hand, the Maya seemed very impressive compared to other New World peoples they knew. Of course these 16th-century soldiers and explorers had no inkling of earlier Classic civilization. Better informed Mayanists later came to see Postclassic society and culture in Yucatan as "decadent" or, as one of my students recently put it in an exam "past their prime." In particular, the prevalence of warfare was for many archaeologists a symptom of the degeneracy of late Maya culture, as compared to their purportedly peaceful and high-minded Classic predecessors. Judgments like these, of course, probably reveal more about our own cultural preferences than anything about the Maya themselves. Readers accustomed to the idea that some sort of complete catastrophe overtook Classic Maya civilization in the 8th or 9th century will probably be surprised at the survival of so much complexity, which complicates a nice, neat story. Rather than collapsing in some total sense, Maya civilization showed surprising endurance even though its main geographical locus shifted dramatically.

The second question is even more important. Can we use what we know about the conquest-era Maya to help understand their Classic forebears? Even the rich Classic archaeological, epigraphic, and artistic evidence we possess fails to provide answers to all our questions, and so for generations many archaeologists have projected patterns known for the 16th century or later back into the past. Such use of ethnohistoric analogy reminds us that important elements in our definition of civilization are durability and identity, both in terms of sociopolitical organization and Great Traditions.

That there is considerable continuity is unquestioned. Both the ancient and the historical Maya, for example, used the ajaw title. Both sets of cultures had rulers, nobles, and commoners. Both made similar astronomical observations, used the same vigesimal system of arithmetic, reckoned time with closely related calendars, and worshiped many of the same deities. Both wrote the same basic hieroglyphic texts in screen-fold books, and had broadly similar traditions of art and architecture. Wishful thinking to the contrary, warfare on a considerable scale was at all times present. Most or all of these continuities (and many more could be listed) are presumed to exist because they were inherited by the 16th century Maya from their Classic predecessors.

On the other hand, many dimensions of Maya culture and society as the Spaniards knew them had changed profoundly during the centuries since Classic times. Neither Cortes nor any other European explorers saw centers remotely comparable in size and splendor to Tikal, Calakmul, or Copan. Classic art and architecture, with few exceptions (and always keeping the vagaries of preservation in mind), is much richer and more accomplished than what the Spaniards reported or that archaeologists have documented for the 16th century. The Long Count calendar, that superb Classic Maya intellectual achievement, had long been abandoned. Divine kingship, the central institution of the ancient Maya, is only faintly reflected in the ajaws and halach uinics of the chronicles, and we have no impressive royal tombs for any late Maya rulers. Were the "slaves" that are so conspicuous in the 16th-century records even present in Classic times? We have no idea.

We must also bear in mind that civilization was by no means uniform among the Classic Maya themselves. For example, Maya societies of the northern Lowlands were rather different from those of the south. Their environments were different, they expressed their own regional variant of the Maya Great Tradition, and they did not experience the dramatic political collapse and depopulation of their southern cousins. It is these societies that were directly ancestral to the ones the Spaniards encountered. Remember too that even the Itza traced their origins back to these northern Maya.

In short, the Maya of the conquest preserved a kind of watered-down version of the great Classic tradition of civilization, to which they added their own distinctive regional innovations. While we obviously must use as much information from that time as possible to form ideas about the Classic Maya, we must do so with extreme care. We now turn to an overview of Classic civilization to understand what, in fact, collapsed.

– 5 –

THE CLASSIC MAYA, OR WHAT COLLAPSED?

WE ALL KNOW WHAT HAPPENS in the aftermath of an airliner crash in which all the passengers and crew perish. Experts retrieve and study as much of the wreckage as possible and look for signs of failure in any of the essential systems of the aircraft. They also try to recover the data recorders ("black boxes") that preserve detailed information about the functioning of these systems prior to the crash, as well as the final conversations of the pilots. These experts are in somewhat the same position as archaeologists studying the Maya collapse, in the sense that they did not personally witness the original catastrophe and cannot interview the participants. Instead they must reconstruct what happened by analyzing a huge mass of inert bits and pieces, themselves highly damaged and incomplete, that no longer constitutes a functioning airplane. All these fragments are the equivalents of the abandoned buildings, broken pottery, tombs, refuse, and all the other stuff that makes up the archaeological record.

Our aeronautical experts do, however, have two huge advantages over the archaeologist. First, their job is to reconstruct what was essentially one event at a specific time and place involving a single machine. Far more important, and assuming that the disaster was caused by system failure (as opposed to human error or an extraneous factor such as a collision or a terrorist's bomb) they have design specifications for the intact airplane – they already know all about the things that might have failed.

Archaeologists investigating the Maya collapse must instead try to explain not just a single recent event, but an ancient process of decline that took place over more than a century, and that involved many polities and hundreds of thousands or even millions of people who were culturally very different from us. Moreover, we obviously lack specifications – cultural "blueprints" – for the ancient Classic Maya. Our job is thus a twofold one: first we must reconstruct what the Maya were like, and then try to explain what happened to them. This task of reconstruction is difficult enough by itself, but is made more so because from the time of Stephens and Catherwood our efforts have been influenced by the one big "fact" of Classic Maya civilization – its mysterious demise – much as observations of subatomic particles by physicists are distorted by their own instruments.

On the principle that we cannot meaningfully comprehend the collapse without understanding the societies, political systems, and populations involved, this chapter addresses two issues. First, what do we know, or think we know, about the Classic Maya? Second, and just as important, what do we not know that might be pertinent to figuring out what happened to them? Our main concern is the central and southern Maya Lowlands on the eve of the collapse in the 8th century AD, a period archaeologists have traditionally regarded as the most mature phase of Maya civilization. Classic inscriptions are the closest approximation we have of the black boxes from the crashed airliner and have become central to our interpretations, so they provide a logical starting point.

Inscriptions, History, and the Classic Maya

Early Spanish explorers were fascinated by the New World books they encountered, which more than anything else signaled to them the sophistication of Mesoamerican cultures. Although the first books they saw were Maya, the first literary tradition with which they became familiar was that of the Aztecs. Palaces in Central Mexico housed libraries, and the manuscripts they contained, mainly in the form of screen-fold books made of fig-bark paper or deer skin, recorded several kinds of information. Early in the 17th century the chronicler Alva Ixtlilxochitl, a descendant of the royal house of Texcoco (one of the three allied capitals that dominated the Aztec empire), reported that his ancestors

> had writers for each genre: some who handled the Annals, putting in order the things that happened each year, by day, month, and hour. Others were in charge of genealogies and ancestors of persons of lineage ... some of them took care of painting the limits, boundaries, and boundary lines of the cities, provinces, towns, and places, and of the lots and distributions of lands.... Others of the books of laws, rites, and ceremonies that they practiced as infidels; and the priests of the temple of their idolatry ... and of the feasts of their false gods and calendars. And finally it was the responsibility of the philosophers and sages who were among them to paint all the sciences that they knew and attained and to teach from memory the songs that [preserved] their sciences and histories.[1]

Although they destroyed plenty of Aztec books, especially those dealing with religious matters, the Spaniards recognized the obvious utility of some of these genres and in fact native scribes, often influenced by European conventions, openly used the indigenous pictorial writing tradition for two or three generations after the conquest, sometimes recopying and thus preserving ancient accounts. Native documents were introduced into law courts as evidence, and some, such as the celebrated Codex Mendoza, were produced under the patronage of Spanish officials. Conspicuous among surviving or recopied manuscripts were those dealing with the histories of the various Aztec polities (*altepeme*; singular = *altepetl*) and their ruling dynasties, so these traditions were never completely lost.

Nor were the Aztecs the only Mesoamerican writers of history. Screenfold books painted by ancient Mixtec speakers, who lived in and around Mexico's valley of Oaxaca, preserve Mesoamerica's longest historical narratives reaching back to the mid-10th century. Genealogical relations among 25 generations of Mixtec kings, queens, and nobles were recorded, as were their mythological origins, marriages, alliances, wars, and intrigues.

Unfortunately, thanks to the depredations of Bishop Landa and others, Maya books did not fare so well, and we do not know whether they contained historical information comparable to that compiled by the Aztecs or Mixtecs. Not only was there wholesale destruction of books and suppression of the hieroglyphic literary tradition (all but dead in Yucatan by the late 16th century), but the four surviving Maya codices were all probably painted just prior to the conquest (one might even have been made after the Spaniards arrived). Although these books and other postconquest manuscripts created by Maya scribes retain vestiges of historical information, none is very helpful in understanding most aspects of Classic Maya life and society.

When Stephens and Catherwood contemplated the hieroglyphs on Copan's Altar Q, almost nothing was known about Classic Maya writing at all, and certainly not its content. Reasoning from what he knew about other ancient civilizations, Stephens assumed that the glyphs recorded history, by which he meant the names and titles of kings and other important people, significant events in their lives or kingdoms, and the dates on which those events took place. Other scholars concurred, but decades of effort produced no decipherments, mainly because the nature of the script was misunderstood.[2]

Only one part of the inscriptions yielded easily to decipherment – dates expressed in several different but related calendars. Two of these, called respectively the Tzolkin and the Haab, recorded relatively short cycles of 260 days and 365 days. Together they meshed to form a longer Calendar Round cycle of 52 years. More important was the Long Count, which presented a linear reckoning of time calculated from a beginning point. We will discuss this calendar in more detail in Chapter 6. For now, the important point is that early on it was evident that the Classic Maya were extremely interested both in temporal cycles and in specific chronological milestones. These provided archaeologists with an invaluable time frame, but also suggested that the still unreadable parts of the inscriptions mainly conveyed esoteric ritual and astronomical information in a script not easily reduced to one or another spoken Maya language.[3]

By the mid-1940s the opinion of Harvard archaeologist Sylvanus G. Morley, then the most prominent Mayanist of all, was widely shared:

> The Maya inscriptions treat primarily of chronology, astronomy – perhaps one might better say astrology – and religious matters. They are in no sense records of personal glorification and self-laudation, like the inscriptions of Egypt, Assyria, and Babylon. They tell no story of kingly conquests, recount no deeds of imperial achievement; they neither praise nor exalt, glorify nor aggrandize, indeed they are so utterly impersonal, so completely nonindividualistic, that it is even probable that the name-glyphs of specific men and women were never recorded upon the Maya monuments.[4]

The old and now discredited "priest-peasant," "vacant ceremonial center," and "peaceful Maya" perspectives derived heavily from this supposed esoteric content of the then-unreadable inscriptions.

Beginning about 1960, and especially since 1980, an avalanche of decipherments has emerged, principally because of the belated recognition of the heavily logosyllabic character of ancient Maya writing (i.e., glyphs record whole words or other meaningful parts of speech, or syllables), which allows it to be directly related to daughter languages recorded in Colonial times or still spoken today. Also apparent now is the extremely close relationship between art and writing; for example, what appear to be elaborate costume elements worn by rulers often have phonetic meanings. Stephens's assumptions about the content of inscriptions turn out to be true, and texts now yield detailed insights about the Classic Maya that would have astounded Morley. But did the Classic Maya write history?

We can safely assume that all ancient peoples had historical traditions, in the broad sense that they possessed stories, poems, myths, and other traditional accounts concerning what happened in the past. These were usually passed down orally or in the form of performances that have left no detectable traces in the archaeological record. Some of my colleagues bristle when such peoples are called "prehistoric" or "ahistoric" because they think these labels are belittling. What these words really mean, at least to me, is simply that from our perspective there is no intelligible, detailed information in the form of inscriptions or other kinds of texts that helps us understand a particular ancient culture. Fortunately this is no longer an issue for the ancient Maya.

Quite possibly scribes at Copan, Tikal, and scores of other Classic centers wrote long, formal, historical annals and detailed genealogies in their books just as the Aztecs and Mixtecs did, but if so, these have not survived. Instead we have many shorter, more durable inscriptions carved on stone, wood, or bone, or painted on ceramic vessels, building façades, stairways, and roofs, and on the walls of rooms, tombs, and caves. By one recent estimate there are at least 15,000 such inscriptions, most of them dating between AD 600 and 900, and particularly to the 8th century. Inscriptions are usually combined with architectural settings, artistic images, and mathematical/calendrical symbols that together form more complex, integrated texts that focus on specific events in war, ritual, or courtly life, individual life experiences such as birth or death, the ownership of things, and sometimes the names or functions of objects. A few texts, such as the Bonampak murals, convey true narratives – sequences of real events in their proper order (Plate 21).

Whatever their content, we can assemble textual information into something like ancient Maya history, particularly when we have good information about where it came from. A stela or a painted vessel bearing a text is of course meaningful in itself, but it is also an artifact, and like all artifacts is best understood in its larger archaeological context. Tatiana Proskouriakoff, the pioneer epigrapher who first intuited the general character of the inscriptions at Piedras Negras, did so as much on the basis of their contexts as their glyphs. Unfortunately many inscribed objects have been looted and so lack this critical dimension of meaning.

Maya texts resemble the black boxes of our crashed airliner in that they effectively preserve information, but they are different in one fundamental respect – they were not meant for us. Exactly who their messages were meant for depends on the specific text in question. Carved stelae and altars placed in spacious open courtyards were obviously positioned to be seen by the general populace of a Maya kingdom, as were inscriptions on the exteriors of surrounding buildings. Inscriptions inside temples or palaces had a more restricted audience, and some texts engraved or painted on the walls of tombs or mortuary objects were seemingly directed at the gods or ancestors. Texts, and the objects on which they were placed, were themselves imbued with power, quite apart from the specific messages they conveyed.

Even a visible text was not equally meaningful to everyone. Given the highly pictorial nature of the script no doubt even humble Maya people could pick out a glyph here or a numeral there (I function just about on this peasant level of perception myself). Monumental sets of glyphs emblazoned on some buildings probably were as recognizable to Maya peasants as were coats of arms to their medieval European counterparts. And Maya commoners could also recognize images of gods, kings (Plate 18), or nobles, and the significance of some of the stylized postures these beings assumed and the costumes they wore, much as illiterate European peasants could recognize statues of saints on the sculpted façades of great medieval cathedrals. Only an extremely small proportion of the population, say 10 percent or less, was probably literate in any effective sense. Most literate individuals were nobles, along, perhaps, with a few educated artisans who carved or painted monuments. Because many texts were probably read aloud in public performances, however, their content was accessible to people of all ranks.

Some dates and inscriptions clearly refer to mythological events thousands or even millions of years in the past or future. Most, though, present information that from our perspective appears inherently historical. For example, names and titles of kings are often attached to numbers that give their order in dynastic succession; thus an individual named Waxaklajuun Ub'aah K'awiil is recorded as the 13th ruler of Copan. Even more telling is Altar Q itself. Once thought to show a "congress of astronomers," we now know that it represents a dynastic monument depicting and naming each Copan king in his proper order. When accompanied by dates, such texts allow us to place people and events in time, not only in a relative sense, but often very accurately in terms of our Gregorian calendar.

The important thing to remember, though, is that such texts were not intended as historical accounts, but rather situated specific events, often of a highly esoteric nature, within the framework of intervals of time significant to the Maya. Texts were, in other words, primarily dedicatory or commemorative in character and served to associate specific objects, events, and individuals with calendrical milestones in a sacred timescape. What makes them seem historical are the attached references to people, places, and events in the narrative that culminates in the dedication event for the monument itself, which is usually the focus of the inscription. Almost all art and inscriptions are "formal" in the sense that they were commissioned by kings or other noble people, usually for important ritual or political purposes. Entirely lacking (except possibly as graffiti sometimes found scratched on walls, Fig. 18) are the more spontaneous and mundane documents – wills, testaments, court records, inventories, menus, or laundry lists – that historians today find so useful in filling in the details of "official" history elsewhere in the world.

Most inscriptions are very short. Some, found both on portable artifacts as well as monumental carvings and buildings, are labels or captions that name an object, tell who made or possessed it, or what its function was. An inscription on a polychrome vase, for example, might label it as a vessel for drinking chocolate, and also identify its owner. Only a few texts such as the Hieroglyphic Stairway at Copan (with more than 2000 glyphs) are long enough to be effective narratives, and most texts concern themselves with very local and parochial matters. No matter what their content, texts had an independent ritual and esoteric dimension and were never purely utilitarian, as most of our own writing is. Despite these limitations, and whatever they might have meant to the Maya themselves, texts do convey to us many kinds of information, most importantly events in the lives of rulers and other nobles, including birth, accession, death, wars, religious and political rituals, and royal visits and family relations. These events, along with specific names, titles, and dates, enable us now to do two things we could not do several decades ago – assemble an historical framework and gain insights into the ways in which Classic Maya people thought about the world.

In addition to direct records or assertions of events, we can sometimes read between the lines to infer less obtrusive, but sometimes dramatic stories. For example on 15 January AD 378 a celebrated personage named Siyaj K'ak' arrived at the great center of Tikal and inaugurated a new dynastic line.[5] He seems to have had strong connections to the great central Mexican metropolis of Teotihuacan, and perhaps even came from there. On the very day of his arrival the incumbent Tikal king Chak Tok Ich'aak was involved in a

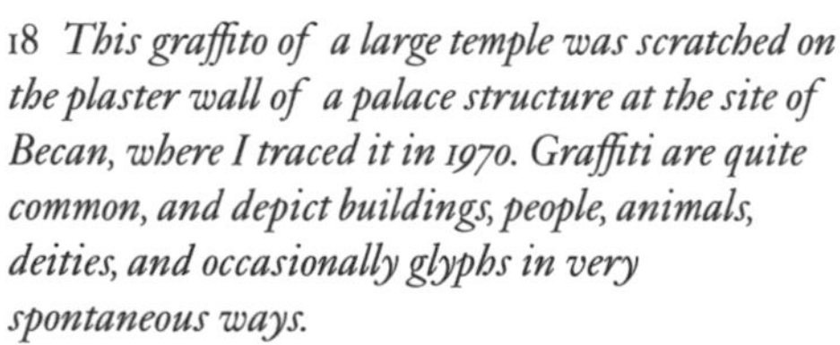

18 *This graffito of a large temple was scratched on the plaster wall of a palace structure at the site of Becan, where I traced it in 1970. Graffiti are quite common, and depict buildings, people, animals, deities, and occasionally glyphs in very spontaneous ways.*

"water-entering" event that might refer to his death, and we hear no more about him. Although the texts do not unequivocally reveal what all this means, one can well suspect some kind of political skullduggery.

So have the Classic Maya emerged into the full light of history? One way to think about this question is to imagine looking at something through a window that is very dirty in some places, and crystal clear in others. Where readable ancient texts have been recovered, they provide us with incredibly nuanced and detailed perspectives concerning some aspects of Classic Maya life, thought, and society pertinent to understanding the collapse. On other subjects they are entirely mute. There is also considerable geographical spottiness in their distribution. Inscriptions are few and far between at centers north of Calakmul, for example, although there were many vigorous northern Classic polities. Even in the heartland of Maya civilization the extremely imposing center of Yaxha, just 30 km (19 miles) southeast of Tikal, has produced very few inscriptions compared to its more famous neighbor. Some of this variability reflects the intensity of archaeological testing (as in the Tikal/Yaxha case), and in others different elite sensibilities with regard to the uses and display of texts. Nevertheless, taken in conjunction with other kinds of archaeological evidence, the available corpus of texts has revolutionized our understanding of Classic society.

Before turning to a more detailed overview of the ancient Maya one word of caution is necessary. There was enormous variation not only in texts, but in most other things Maya, especially during the crucial 8th century AD. Centers and their associated polities developed in locally distinctive environments, had different histories, different territorial and demographic scales, and no doubt were internally organized in distinctive ways. Lowland Maya people spoke several vernacular languages and dialects and used different kinds of tools and pottery from one region to another. Even the widely disseminated and cosmopolitan elements of the Classic Maya Great Tradition had many regional variants. No one would mistake a Palenque temple for one built at Tikal, or the sculptural style of monuments at Quirigua for that at Caracol. Questions such as "how was the office of king passed from one generation to another?" or "how were Maya kingdoms governed?" are thus most appropriately answered on a case by case basis. Such an approach is beyond the scope of this chapter or indeed this book, but I will do my best to make useful generalizations while still smuggling in references to many of these differences. We will start with the major political and social components of Maya society, and then consider larger questions of religion, centers and political systems, government, and economics.

Kings, Lords, and the Humble Maya

Our view of the Classic Maya is predominantly a "top-down" one. Archaeologists were at first understandably attracted to the ruins of the largest and most elaborate Maya royal centers and to this day most research still is focused on them. Equally important is that texts (which of course are most numerous at such places) were produced or commissioned by people of very high rank (usually rulers) and they express most clearly the actions and sensibilities of royal or elite people, whose names and titles we know.[6] The single most commonly occurring glyphic expression, in fact, is *ajaw*, usually translated as "lord," but literally meaning "he who proclaims, or shouts" (revealingly, the Aztec title usually translated as king – *tlatoani* – has a very similar meaning: "he who speaks," or "great speaker"). We already saw that this durable honorific was still used by some Contact-period rulers, but it obviously has extremely ancient origins.

Kings

Classic Maya kings were very different from their 16th-century counterparts despite the continuity in the ajaw title. Most conspicuously, as Stephen Houston and David Stuart have pointed out, they were sacred kings, personal embodiments of moral gravity for their people while they lived, and sometimes apotheosized as gods when they died. Classic polities seem heavily focused on the bloodlines that dominated the royal office, a pattern not so heavily emphasized in Postclassic or Contact-period times. Individual dynasties traced their origins to mythic rulers who lived thousands of years in the past, or to sets of gods who were in some sense their progenitors. At Piedras Negras, for example, one monument celebrates a founder who lived in 4691 BC, a time when there were not even farming communities, much less kingdoms, in the Maya Lowlands.[7] What we think of as 'standard' royal monuments, in which art, dates, and inscriptions are all combined on stelae, appear to be erected only after about AD 250.

Upon ascending their thrones Classic rulers affixed names such as K'uhul Ajaw ("holy lord"), or K'inich Ajaw ("sun-faced lord") to their ajaw title (royal women used a *k'uhul ixik* title, meaning "holy woman"). Such grandiose appellations, which often include directional affixes, emphasized the sacred qualities of rulers, personally linked them to particular deities, and pointedly distinguished kings from lesser people of ajaw status and from one another. Kings and other royal family members at Piedras Negras, for example, often used the distinctive title K'inil Ajaw (Sun Lord), as well as the name "Water Turtle" (*ahk*) which linked them to the aged earth deity represented as God N in much later Maya books. Sometimes these royal names and titles changed during the history of a local ruling line, hinting at different styles or ranks of rulership, or prestigious accomplishments. A ruler of Yaxchilan gloried in the title "He of Twenty Captives."

Particular kings, dynasties, and kingdoms were associated with sets of patron deities chosen from the wider Maya pantheon. These gods were sometimes presented as supernatural "ancestors" who had lived in some previous creation thousands of years before. Rulers adorned themselves with god symbols and even impersonated gods during rituals. Inside the great temples or god-houses were images believed to be periodically inhabited by gods, as well as god-bundles containing supernaturally charged objects. Some of these temples were mortuary monuments covering the elaborate tombs of deceased kings (Plate 17). Palaces contained ornate thrones on which kings are shown sitting in royal majesty, receiving the attentions of their courtiers. All of these precious things were in some sense "owned" by their royal patrons and closely bound up with effective rulership. Capturing, destroying or defiling the spiritually potent places or sacred objects of an enemy ruler was a major symbolic goal of Late Classic war.

Because of their close association with the sun and other gods, and also with powerful royal ancestors, kings were thought to be personally responsible through their deportment and ritual activity (especially sacrifices) for the well-being of their realms, of their subjects, and of the cosmos in general. Some Mayanists envision them as great shamans, magical people who claimed the ability to enter the supernatural world and communicate with powerful supernatural beings, often aided in these efforts by their ancestors or their personal *wayob* (spiritual companions or co-essences). Supernatural efficacy also attached to rulers and other ancestors who were to our way of thinking "dead," but whom the Maya revered as still-powerful forces. Many inscriptions record the re-entry of tombs and the rituals that took place in them, which included mysterious manipulations of skeletal remains, referred to by such terms as "bone-slicing" (Plate 14).

We know that in later Mesoamerican societies people of high rank were thought to be imbued with souls more powerful or exalted than those possessed by lesser people, and Classic Maya royal presentations seem to indicate similar attitudes. Kings were conceived as ethereal, flowery, fragrant beings who influenced events effortlessly through their moral personae and personal demeanor. In the inscriptions rulers generally refer to themselves in the third person and do not overtly claim to do things. Instead they participate passively in actions, in the sense that their very presence activates events.

1 Ball courts were among the most conspicuous features of Classic Maya royal centers. This one at Copan is the second largest known. The game was played widely in Mesoamerica for both ritual and recreational purposes.

2 Copan's Altar Q depicts 16 successive rulers carved around the four sides of the monument. On this side the 16th king Yax Pasaj Chan Yoaat (middle right) accepts a scepter from the long-dead dynastic founder K'inich Ajaw Yax K'uk' Mo'.

3 Copan's Temple of the Hieroglyphic Stairway contains the longest-known Classic Maya inscription. Built in the 8th century, it celebrates the kingdom's dynastic history and leads to a summit temple sacred to K'inich Ajaw Yax K'uk' Mo'.

4 (*opposite, above*) Not only Maya kings possessed wonderful sculpture. This throne-like bench, carved with images of the sun, moon, and Venus forming a sky band was found in a noble's residence about 820 m (half a mile) from the Temple of the Hieroglyphic Stairway.

5 (*right*) Life-sized statues of Copan's rulers were originally set at intervals on the Hieroglyphic Stairway. This one, dressed as a warrior, was reconstructed from the fallen debris of the stairway.

6 (*below*) Bacabs were gods who held up the four corners of the Maya world. Here the carving of a bacab, shown characteristically as an old man, forms the support for a throne found in the residence of another great Copan noble, Mak-Chanal.

7 (*left*) King Waxaklajuun Ub'aah K'awiil was one of the great builders of Copan. He raised many stelae depicting himself in ritual garb, like this one in Copan's Great Plaza. His death at the hands of enemies in AD 738 cut short his impressive royal career.

8 (*below*) Copan's greatest lords lived in sprawling compounds with many rooms arranged around courtyards. This partly reconstructed set of buildings included a workshop where fine objects were crafted from imported marine shell.

9 (*opposite, above*) Most common Maya people were farmers who lived outside the great court centers. Stone foundation walls like these are all that remain of a modest Copan residential structure originally built of highly perishable materials.

10 (*opposite, below*) Today some Copan houses are still built in traditional ways. This one has a stone foundation supporting walls of saplings covered with mud plaster. Palm thatch forms the roof. Cylindrical objects hanging below the eaves are bee hives.

11 (*opposite, above*) Aerial view of Tikal, one of the greatest Classic Maya centers. The temples and palace in the foreground were completed in the 8th century AD. High tropical forest now covers most of Tikal's epicenter, where hundreds of masonry buildings extend over several square kilometers.

12 (*opposite, below*) Tikal's Central Acropolis was the main residence of the king and royal family, and also served political and administrative functions. From modest beginnings in the 3rd century AD it expanded into a vast compound of linked courtyards surrounded by hundreds of rooms.

13 (*right*) This mosaic vessel, made with many small pieces of green jade, bears the name of Tikal's great ruler Jasaw Chan K'awiil, who came to power in AD 682. The carved effigy on the lid probably represents the king himself, who was eventually buried, along with the vessel, beneath Temple I.

14 (*below*) Ancient Maya lords sometimes opened tombs and manipulated the remains of long-dead people, particularly relatives or ancestors. Tikal Altar 5 shows two nobles, one probably Jasaw Chan K'awiil himself, carrying out a ritual featuring the bones of an important woman whose identity remains unclear.

15 One of the most famous of all Maya buildings, Tikal's Temple I was completed sometime around AD 740–750. It covers the tomb of Jasaw Chan K'awiil, whose son and successor possibly finished the building and dedicated it on his father's behalf.

For example, a royal inscription would not normally say "I captured eight captives," but rather "he is the captor of eight captives." In effect kings were regarded almost as objects, the personified political and ideological fetishes of their people. They styled themselves in agrarian tropes as beneficent husbandmen or cultivators of their realms, much as Christ is metaphorically portrayed in Christian imagery as the shepherd of his flock. As we shall see later, they also presented themselves as fierce warriors, and Maya royal rhetoric became more aggressive and assertive through time.

Rulership (*ajawlel*) thus had a pronounced theocratic dimension reflecting a basic postulate of Classic Maya culture: the moral, political, and natural orders were one. I hasten to add that this is not a reversion to the old "priest-peasant" or "theocratic" model of Maya leadership, but reflects a conception fundamental to political ideology in virtually all ancient civilizations.

Although we are not concerned here with the origins of kingship, new evidence shows that several dynasties had very direct early relationships with Teotihuacan. A generation after Siyaj K'ak' established himself at Tikal, K'inich Yax K'uk' Mo', the dynastic founder of Copan, surrounded himself with Teotihuacan imagery; his very name recalls combinations of motifs found on wall murals at Teotihuacan itself. Some archaeologists even surmise that the decline of Teotihuacan is implicated in the Classic Maya collapse, although as we shall see later the chronology does not support this view.

The conquest-period Maya made much of lineage and descent and a handful of great families constituted potent political factions. This brings us to the issues of royal succession and kinship in Classic times. At centers where texts are abundant and reasonably clear, archaeologists have documented long dynastic sequences. Copan's Altar Q is unusual in its condensed and explicit presentation of 16 successive rulers on a single monument, and the dynastic list derived from it and other monuments, as well as associated archaeological research, is shown in the table overleaf.

A much longer king-list has been patched together from multiple texts at Tikal, where a line of at least 34 rulers (with some breaks and dynastic shifts) extended back to the end of the first century AD. Comparably long series are reconstructed for a few other centers such as Naranjo and Altar de Sacrificios, but most sequences are much shorter and all of them have ambiguities (most importantly, there might have been Late Preclassic rulers whose names were not recorded). The actions and reputations of specific kings were known and inscribed far beyond the boundaries of their own realms, so dynasties and events are reconstructed not simply from texts at a specific capital, but from a much wider network of references.

The Copan Dynastic Sequence[8]

SUCCESSION ORDER	NAMES, TITLES, AND VARIANTS Most recent accepted names/titles in **bold**	IMPORTANT DATES OR ESTIMATED REIGNS (all AD)
Ruler 1 (founder)	**K'inich Yax K'uk' Mo'** "Green-Sun First Quetzal Macaw" "Blue Quetzal Macaw" "Sun-eyed Green Quetzal Macaw"	Accession in 426 while en route to Copan; death probably about 437.
Ruler 2	**K'inich Popol Hol** "Mat Head"	Accession *c.* 437; death date unknown.
Ruler 3	Name unknown	Accession and death dates unknown, but last half of 5th century.
Ruler 4	**Ku Ix**	Accession and death dates unknown.
Ruler 5	Name uncertain; possibly **Yu-? [ku?]-a**	Short reign at end of 5th century.
Ruler 6	Name uncertain; possibly **Muyal?-Jol?**	Short reign at end of 5th century.
Ruler 7	**Waterlily Jaguar** "B'alam-?-Na" "Jaguar Sun God"	Accession about 504–544.
Ruler 8	**"Head-on-Earth"**	Short reign in mid-6th century.
Ruler 9	**Sak-lu**	Accession 551; death probably 553.
Ruler 10	**Moon Jaguar** "Tzik B'alam" "Cleft-Moon Leaf-Jaguar"	Accession 553; death 578.

SUCCESSION ORDER	NAMES, TITLES, AND VARIANTS Most recent accepted names/titles in **bold**	IMPORTANT DATES OR ESTIMATED REIGNS (all AD)
Ruler 11	**Butz' Chan** "Fire-drinking? Sky Lightning God" "Smoke Snake" "Smoke Sky"	Birth 553; accession 578; death 628.
Ruler 12	**K'ak'-u-?' Ha'?-K'awiil** "Fire-drinking? Water K'awiil" "Smoke Imix God K" "Smoke Jaguar"	Accession 628, death 695.
Ruler 13	**Waxaklajuun Ub'aah K'awiil** "18 Rabbit" XVIII-Jog	Accession 695; death 738.
Ruler 14	**K'a' Joplaj Chan K'awiil** "Smoke Monkey"	Accession 738; death 749.
Ruler 15	**K'ak' Yipyaj Chan K'awiil** "Smoke Shell" "Smoke Squirrel" "Smoke Caracol"	Accession 749; death *c.* 763.
Ruler 16	**Yax Pasaj Chan Yoaat** "First Dawned Sky Lightning God" "Yax Pasah" "Yax Pac" "New Dawn" "Madrugada" "First Dawn" "Yax Sun-at-Horizon"	Accession 763; death unknown, but sometime after 810.
Ruler (?) 17 or unsuccessful pretender(?)	**Ukit Took'** "Patron? of Flint"	Active sometime around 822.

Although the English term "dynasty" suggests descent of a title or office in a single family line, it can have other implications, even among kingdoms sharing the same broad political ideology. Rene Viel, for example, thinks that iconographic and other evidence at Copan shows that several royal lineages shared (and competed over) the office of king, so rulers were not necessarily descended from their immediate predecessor.[9] During Early Classic times at Tikal there is clear evidence that kings had fathers who were not former rulers in the local dynasty. Specific dynasties ruled one site or region, or sometimes several.

Occasionally, as at Palenque, royal ancestors or relatives are clearly identified and their relationships noted. Elsewhere the inscriptions practically ignore kin connections. Where dynastic information is sufficiently detailed we can detect a preference for succession from father to son in the male line, but without rigid primogeniture (the title *ch'ok ajaw* – "young" or "unripe lord" – signifies an heir-apparent). Maya royal families evidently had flexible strategies for passing on rulership. For example the rulers of Piedras Negras seem at first to have passed the office from father to son, and then switched for unknown reasons to fraternal succession during the last reigns.[10]

Patterns like this probably reflect in part the status of the mothers of various claimants. Maya kings sought prestigious spouses for themselves and their sons, and the wives thus recruited might actually outrank their husbands (marriage of a superior woman to a male of lesser status is called hypogamy). No doubt nobles tried also to marry their daughters into more exalted royal lines (hypergamy). Royal women consequently figured prominently in attempts to restrict or maintain access to the office of king, especially when appropriate male heirs did not exist or were too young, as when Ruler 2 at Piedras Negras ascended his throne at the tender age of 12 years. Some grand women ruled kingdoms. The most famous was the Lady Yohl Ik'nal (Heart of the Wind Place), who dominated affairs at Palenque between AD 583 and 604 and was the grandmother of the great ruler Pakal. At Yaxchilan some of the finest sculptures feature another exalted lady, K'ab'al Xook, to whom a major temple seems to have been dedicated during her lifetime.

Interpolity marriages such as that of the father of Copan ruler Yax Pasaj to another grand woman from Palenque (see Chapter 1) were common, reflecting the desire for alliances with other royal families and the desire to reconcile old antagonisms. Some alliances triggered the resurgence of a local dynasty, as at Naranjo, which was reinvigorated after a series of earlier military defeats when a royal woman was imported from Dos Pilas, far away to the west. Aztec rulers often took more than one royal bride for political purposes, but whether the Classic Maya pursued this same strategy is unclear. Inscriptions at some centers associate two or more royal women with a single king, but we cannot tell whether this indicates polygyny or serial monogamy (there is, oddly, no known glyph for "marriage"; we infer this relationship when a man and woman are recorded as the father and mother of someone).[11] The most likely arrangement for both kings and other high elites was to have one principal wife at any given time, along with other consorts of lesser rank, with all of the consequent potential for succession disputes.

Behind all this matrimonial and political maneuvering lay the motivation to keep rulership, along with important economic and other perquisites such as titles and rituals, under the control of particular great families that probably in a loose sense approximated patrilineages, something like the dominant regional chibalob of the 16th-century Maya, or perhaps the noble "houses" of Europe (see below). Kings sometimes took the names of illustrious predecessors to reinforce their connections to a dynastic line. Unexpectedly, however, we have no direct inscriptional evidence for lineage organization, nor are well-ordered, lengthy genealogies a major concern of Maya texts (although they might have been recorded in books or preserved in oral traditions).

Attempts to retain political office were not always successful. Texts hint at dynastic conflicts, usurpations, foreign interference, and (very rarely) abdications. If the story of the "Mexican" usurper Siyaj K'ak' and his arrival at Tikal is properly interpreted, it suggests that he might have been abetted by powerful political allies at the Tikal court.[12] More direct and grisly signs of such power struggles come from destruction levels and other evidence of violence detected in excavations. Particularly suggestive are multiple burials of men, women, and children found at Tikal, Yaxuna, and elsewhere that are interpreted as the remains of royal/elite families deposed and massacred by enemies. A dramatic example is the "Skull Pit" at Colha, which yielded the decapitated heads of 20 adults and 10 children of both sexes.[13] Skulls had still-articulated vertebrae and the skin seems to have been flayed from the faces of some victims. Following this event the building in which the skulls were interred was destroyed, as apparently was much of the rest of Colha. While the Colha evidence might be attributed to external war, it is often difficult to distinguish between internecine mayhem and attacks by outsiders.

Given all this rivalry and political tension, as well as the fact that kings were directly or indirectly responsible for the creation of most texts, it is fair to ask how much the inscriptions reflect self-serving interests – in a word, political propaganda. Insofar as we are interested in Maya cognition this issue hardly matters, but if instead we use texts to reconstruct ancient events and organizational patterns it clearly does. Mayanists hold varied opinions about the "propaganda" question. Some think that opportunistic manipulation was minimal and mainly manifested itself in the glossing over or omission of defeats, usurpations, or other inconvenient information. Others believe that Maya kings (and some elites) deliberately and even cynically manipulated texts to accomplish their own ends, much as some modern politicians do.

Examples can be found to support either point of view. Dynastic claims of extremely ancient origins are common, and from our perspective quite unbelievable. The inglorious capture and sacrifice in AD 738 of Copan's ruler Waxaklajuun Ub'aah K'awiil is predictably not mentioned on the Hieroglyphic Stairway, which he began, and which was finished many years after this debacle. Instead, he is attributed a splendid warrior's death. Similarly Yax Pasaj, whose reign was almost certainly a troubled one, took great pains on Altar Q to show himself as the successor of a seamless line of rulers, with strong symbolic ties to the dynastic founder. A more active manipulation of information seems to lie behind the innovative sculptural programs initiated by Tikal's king Siyaj Chan K'awiil in the mid-5th century, in which war symbolism and linkages to Teotihuacan plausibly reflect dynastic conflict and usurpation. And of course archaeologists have long known that Maya kings destroyed, buried, or relocated many monuments of their predecessors. Such episodes were no doubt often motivated by reverence, but we cannot entirely rule out political opportunism.

As discussed previously, symbolic elements of the Great Traditions of early civilizations projected images of collectivity that masked invidious social and economic distinctions. My own opinion is that Maya kings were adept at such impression management, and especially during the critical 8th century actively used texts to bolster the general institution of rulership and to pursue their personal and factional ambitions. Outright lies were not necessarily part of this strategy, and self-serving manipulation of information might have been rationalized as legitimate and even beneficial to their subjects. Some non-royal lords were apparently similarly opportunistic. Ancient behavior of this kind points out the crucial issue of texts as artifacts – i.e., things to be interpreted in their wider archaeological contexts, which often yield independent checks on the reliability of the written record.

Ultimately the real issue is not truth or lies, but how reliable the texts are for the purposes to which we wish to put them. Ancient lies, evasions, omissions, exaggeration and editing are themselves informative about many things. What matters most is the quantity and quality of texts in a site or region, how well-preserved and readable they are, and the questions we ask of them.

By the mid-8th century there had been Maya kings for at least 600 years. Most Maya people could probably not conceive of any legitimate political system not dominated by a king, and to this extent the institution was unquestioned. Unfortunately we have no "bottom up" accounts that tell us how ordinary people viewed their kings. In some other ancient civilizations with strong sacred rulers, especially Egypt, we know that lesser people often expressed an earthy, almost skeptical attitude toward particular pharaohs. Political ideology and formal attributes of rulership aside, there were weak Maya kings and strong ones. Those who possessed unusual talent, intelligence, energy, longevity and charisma were successful, admired, and long remembered, and the fortunes of kingdoms rose and fell according to the capacities of their rulers. Just what kings did for their people we will consider shortly.

Kingship was paradoxically the central institution that served both to unite and to divide Maya civilization during the 8th century just before the Classic collapse. Many generations of intermarriages, alliances, and visitations among ruling families had helped to disseminate widely the basic elements of the elite Great Tradition, including literacy, architectural styles, artistic conventions, standards of courtly behavior, political ideology, royal symbolism, and burial practices. Participation in this common (although by no means uniform) tradition tied together the rulers and other great lords of many independent kingdoms, even those antagonistic to one another. Beneath this veneer of sameness seethed ancient animosities, jealousies, conflicting claims to titles, prestige, and resources, endless intrigue, and outright war. And in the end Maya kingship was afflicted by a fundamental paradox to which we shall return later – there were many local sacred or divine rulers, but all of them had universalist pretensions.

My discussion has necessarily focused more on kingship than on kings. But we must never forget that in ancient times each Maya ruler was a living, breathing presence and an individual personality to his (and occasionally her) subjects and contemporaries. Political fortunes and cultural vigor of kingdoms were strikingly correlated with the presence of accomplished rulers. The most powerful and durable of them (a surprising number lived into their eighties or even nineties), were in their day awesome figures whose deeds and reputations reverberated far beyond the limits of their own realms. For the Maya, in other words, kingship was intensely personalized and historically contingent. Native people in New Guinea liken the death of an illustrious man to the collapse of a giant forest tree – something immense, familiar, reassuring, and seemingly immortal is suddenly gone. One can only imagine that the ancient Maya felt much the same disorientation and loss when Pakal of

Palenque was finally laid to rest in his grand tomb beneath the Pyramid of the Inscriptions, or Copan's dynamic Waxaklajuun U'baah K'awiil was done to death by his enemies at Quirigua.

Lords

But there were other notable people besides kings. In February 1990 my students and I excavated the carved bench shown in Plate 4. It was found buried by debris in the collapsed summit room of a major palace structure at Copan. We were in the middle of shooting an episode for the *Out of the Past* television series and I had confidently assured the film makers that we would produce a bench on demand for their video crew, which was standing by expectantly at the cost of several thousand dollars per day. It showed up gratifyingly on schedule (unlike the rich burial that I also promised), largely because two other similar benches had previously been recovered at Copan and their whereabouts was becoming predictable. Carved on the bench is a skyband motif, an extremely exalted theme in Maya art usually associated with rulers, yet the building where it was found was almost a kilometer from the royal residence. We had found a similar bench, inscribed with a hieroglyphic text, just a few hundred meters to the south in the house of the great noble Mak-Chanal, ten years before.

Such monuments (which represent throne-like "seats of power"), the elaborate buildings in which they are found, along with rich burials, art, and inscriptions, all reveal that Classic Maya society included privileged people apart from kings who enjoyed unusual social prestige, great wealth, and high political rank. Although the terms gloss over distinctions no doubt important to the Maya themselves, we call these people collectively lords (used here to denote both men and women), nobles, or elites. Nobles formed the political connective tissues of Maya polities and understanding them is crucial to our conceptions of political and economic relations and how kingdoms collapsed. Research explicitly dedicated to the elite component of Maya polities is fairly recent, however, and what we know is still quite limited.

Representational art, particularly in the form of detailed scenes painted on polychrome vessels (Fig. 19), depicts nobles as the close associates of kings. They accompany rulers in battle and present to their overlords captives who they have "harvested" on the kings' behalf. Typically garbed in gorgeous costumes and fanciful headgear, nobles are shown in intimate attendance on rulers in palace rooms, where they engage in ceremonies and feasts, offer tribute, and receive presents. At Copan archaeologists have provisionally identified a men's house where young lords might have resided and been edu-

19 *Maya court scene on a polychrome vessel found at Aguateca. Such depictions are quite common, and provide a wealth of information about courts as central institutions of ancient Maya life.*

cated. Clearly nobles participated in and benefited from the widely shared Great Tradition of Classic Maya civilization. Like rulers, they impersonated gods during rituals. Some were ball players, and illustrious families might even have had their own ball courts. The grandest lords possessed impressive masonry houses and ritual buildings like the one where we found the Skyband Bench, and their façades were sometimes decorated with impressive sculpture. Remains of these elaborate households accord surprisingly well with Cortes's description of a 16th-century noble compound cited on p. 56. Burials and houses of nobles yield a wide range of costly, exotic materials or objects produced by skilled artisans.

We are fortunate to have such evidence because epigraphers have deciphered only a few terms that clearly refer to nobles. People other than kings certainly bore the ajaw title, although without the supplementary honorifics that denoted royal status. So far as we can tell only close male or female relatives of rulers were called ajaw. Another possibility is that any distinguished Classic Maya person who could document descent from former kings was an ajaw (much as the highest Aztec nobles with such descent were collectively called pipiltin). Sometimes ajaw is directly attached to what seem to be noble titles or offices, as in *b'aah ajaw* (Head Lord) or *yajaw k'ak'* (Lord of Fire).[14]

A second noble title that we already met at Copan, *aj k'uhuun*, was widely used throughout the Maya Lowlands. Glyph captions on ceramic vessels sometimes give both the personal names and the aj k'uhuun appellation for people shown in palace scenes, some of whom are royal spouses. It is often loosely translated as "courtier," but more specific translations offered are "He of the Holy Book" or "He of the Headband," and some epigraphers think it is a scribal title. All we can say for sure is that it refers to a close connection between a ruler and a titled person who is in some sense a provider or provisioner for the king and polity.

Better understood is the title *sajal*, most frequently encountered in the western Maya Lowlands and only sporadically elsewhere. It refers to an office of considerable importance, perhaps something like that of a subordinate governor of a dependent center. Often associated with sajal references is a glyph (*uchab'jiiy*) that seems to indicate the functions of overseer or guard. The title also has military overtones because sajals are depicted on war monuments as captives or captive-takers. Sajals of different ranks were "seated" or confirmed in office by kings who in some way "possessed" or "owned" them, although the nature of the relationship varied from kingdom to kingdom. Some sajals seem to have been seated shortly after royal accessions, suggesting that the office was an appointed or delegated one, but there are also hints that it was hereditary. Some monuments associate sajals with *bacabs*, Maya gods who held up the heavens, and the epigrapher David Stuart suggests that this convention metaphorically reflects the support that sajals provided to their rulers. Women could be sajals. At least one of them is recorded as the mother of a king, and a male sajal was a royal brother-in-law, so people of this rank occasionally married into royal families. Interestingly, both the titles sajal and aj k'uhuun are rare before AD 672 in the Maya Lowlands. Thereafter they increase rapidly in number even as overall regional populations rise, suggesting new levels of emergent political complexity in Late Classic times.[15]

High nobles at some centers sported motifs on the façades of their houses identifying them with particular skills or crafts, such as the scribe and sculptor imagery found at Copan. Perhaps these were their actual duties, but on the other hand they might only reflect honorific court epithets that conferred prestige but implied no specific work. Supporting the first interpretation is the recovery by Takeshi Inomata and his colleagues of scribal implements from burned buildings at Aguateca (about which more later). Specific titles or terms in the inscriptions refer to warriors who are important enough to be named as victims or captives, and these might also have been parts of the noble honorific repertoire. Just who the noble was who sat in such splendor on the Skyband Bench unfortunately remains unknown because there are no associated inscriptions, although he must have been of extremely exalted rank.

Inscriptions and art typically show that elites derived status symbols and titles from the munificence of rulers; such bias is expectable because most monuments were commissioned by kings, and naturally emphasize their roles as great benefactors. Nobles are most conspicuously identified by extravagant costumes, headgear, personal possessions, and propinquity to the ruler in war, ritual, and courtly activity. But as the historian Jaques Barzun has wryly noted, "It is an uncommon trait to be content with style and no substance."[16] Nobles were presumably also more fundamentally rich, in the sense that they had rights over the labor and products of commoners, and quite possibly in some sense "owned" valuable parts of their landscapes.

Unfortunately the texts tell us very little about the political economy, and such wealth is only indirectly signaled by the scale and sumptuousness of elite residences and tombs. An especially vexing question is the extent to which (or even if) kings manipulated food as a kind of political currency (what anthropologists call "staple financing"). Clearly prestige objects served such purposes ("wealth financing"), but even here we do not know much about how kings or their households were involved with the production or acquisition of such coveted materials or objects, or by what means they were exchanged.

On two other crucial issues we are almost completely ignorant: what were the origins of Classic Maya elites and how were they organized? Several main possibilities suggest themselves, none necessarily exclusive of the others. The first has already been raised: noble lineages might have consisted of people who could trace their descent back to one or another king – and if kings were polygynous, this kind of reckoning would potentially have produced a sizable elite component after only a few generations. On the other hand, elite families (although often intermarried with royal ones) might have had independent origins and possessed their own lengthy, exalted pedigrees. Just such families were powerful, for example, in early Japan. Finally, elite status might have been delegated by the king as it was in Old Kingdom Egypt. In the latter case highly-ranked Maya people would have had no legitimate independent authority or power of their own, and there would have been a meritocratic (as opposed to hereditary) dimension to elite recruitment and identification, as well as stronger centralization of political authority in royal hands. My own opinion is that noble status mainly derived from the first two principles. There was plainly a meritocratic element in Maya society, most clearly seen in the rewards given by kings to successful warriors, and no doubt some artisans of modest origins enjoyed high prestige. I doubt, however, that anything like the Egyptian pattern existed. Whatever their origins and relationships with kings, it is increasingly clear that Maya nobles, like great magnates anywhere, pursued their individual and familial interests, sometimes at the expense of their own rulers and polities.

The Humble Maya

Supporting all this complexity were the broad backs of Maya farmers, about whom we know solely from archaeological remains, some of which are remarkably complete. Late in the summer of AD 590, give or take a few years, the inhabitants of a sleepy little Maya community in the Zapotitan valley of El Salvador suddenly felt the ground shake and heard an ominous roaring sound. Peering anxiously from the doorways of their adobe and thatch houses, they saw fire and smoke on the near horizon, and swiftly took flight with whatever few possessions they could carry. Within a few hours their houses, courtyards, and fields were buried beneath 5 m (16.5 ft) of volcanic rock and ash, where they lay undisturbed for more than 1000 years.[17]

In 1978 Payson Sheets, an archaeologist from the University of Colorado at Boulder interested in the effects of volcanic activity on ancient landscapes, examined the remains of what appeared to be a collapsed house buried beneath volcanic debris. A bulldozer had accidentally uncovered these remains, and Sheets initially assumed that they were those of a recent house overwhelmed by a volcanic catastrophe. But closer inspection revealed no modern artifacts, and Sheets eventually realized that the little house was very ancient. As it turned out, he had discovered part of an entire farming community buried by an eruption that took place in the late 6th century AD, and his many subsequent years of research at Ceren, as the village is now called, provide the best glimpse of how ordinary Maya people lived (Ceren's remarkable remains are today preserved as a museum by the Salvadoran government).

I noted before the rule of thumb that in agrarian civilizations most people – 70 percent or more – were food producers. Because of their simple technology and lack of animal energy sources, the proportion of ancient Maya food producers was quite high – probably in the 80–90 percent range. Although there are no recorded censuses in the inscriptions (or indeed any other direct references to commoners), wherever we have adequate settlement information these estimates appear reliable in order-of-magnitude terms, as we shall see later at Copan.

In coastal regions and perhaps along a few large rivers, some families made a living by fishing or salt-making, but most commoners spent their lives as farmers, growing the same basic range of crops documented for Contact-period times and adjusting their lives to the great seasonal cycles of nature. Remains of their household structures, originally built of poles, mud plaster, and thatch, abound on the modern landscape, but very little is usually preserved apart from the foundation platforms of stones and earth, such as those that I excavated at Piedras Negras in 1999 (Figs. 20, 21). At Ceren, Sheets and his colleagues were able to reconstruct whole household compounds, including houses, kitchens, and storerooms, surrounded by gardens and small fields.

The Ceren community is a small dispersed village, but elsewhere Maya farmers more commonly lived in small house groups scattered widely over the landscape. Some such groups were suitable only for very small numbers of people – presumably nuclear families (married couples and their children). Others probably housed extended families composed of several generations of relatives. This settlement pattern of dispersed households presents a particular challenge for archaeologists investigating the collapse, because each represents a site that must be approached on its own. If instead most Maya people had lived at the big centers, or in large outlying towns, it would be easier to detect wholesale abandonment of large numbers of buildings. On the other hand, the ability to locate and map hundreds or even thousands of individual domestic structures enormously helps in making demographic estimates.

Excavations in and around houses generally (but not always) yield burials of men, women, and children. Pretty clearly many people were buried where they lived, but certainly not all of them. Most Maya were disposed of in ways we do not understand, and some archaeologists believe that house burials often featured individuals of special social significance to the household or other social group in terms of identity and resources.

Not all humble Maya were "rural" people, of course, and they probably had well-developed social distinctions among themselves. As the ethnographer Evan Vogt noted of modern villagers, "I have never encountered a more rank-conscious people than the contemporary Maya."[18] At some centers such as Copan many low-ranked people lived in the dense residential zones around the monumental cores. Some inhabitants of very large elite compounds were probably ordinary people attached in some fashion as retainers, dependents, or lesser relatives of the resident lords. Wherever they lived, they were mainstays of the political economy. Labor recruited from their households built temples and palaces. The crops they cultivated supported the households of kings and elites, where farmers undoubtedly also provided personal service on a regular basis. And in their little house compounds, where women's labor was particularly centered, they produced cloth, honey,

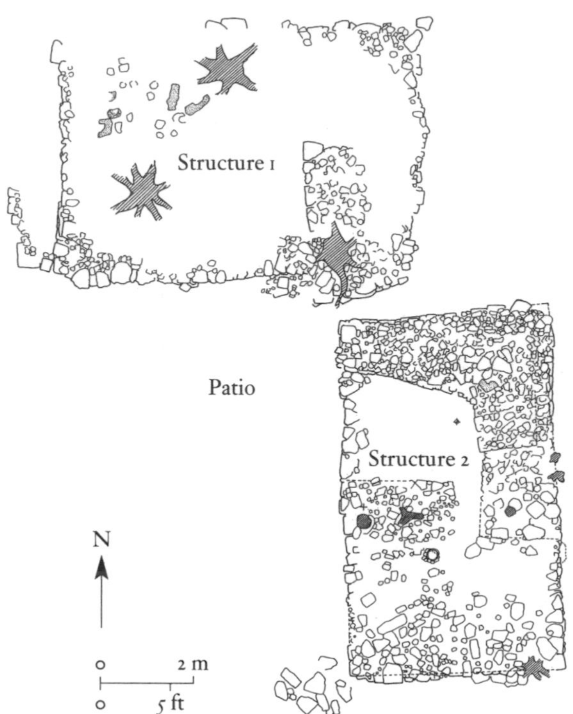

20 *This plan shows the foundations of two small residential structures excavated by the author near Piedras Negras, Guatemala, in 1999–2000. Until recently archaeologists usually ignored unimpressive remains like these. Houses, kitchens, and storage buildings that originally stood on them were the household facilities of Maya commoners, who constituted the vast bulk of any kingdom's population during Classic times.*

and many other things for royal and elite consumption.

Evidence for all this activity is normally sparse. Finds at Ceren reveal how much is lost to us in the normal archaeological record. Sheets found scores of pottery vessels on the house floors, some containing stored food or even the remains of meals. Grinding stones for processing maize stood where they were being used when the eruption occurred. Obsidian blades were carefully stored in the thatch of the roofs, and even the species of plants being grown in the household gardens could be determined. Nowhere else do we have such a clear view of how most Maya people lived out their lives.

Despite their overwhelming numbers and fundamental importance to Classic Maya societies, ordinary people are anonymous in the texts. We do not know for certain the name of a single person of humble status or even any term that collectively designates commoners. There is no information in the inscriptions about how they organized themselves, nor does Maya art record the minutiae of the everyday lives of ordinary people, as Egyptian paintings and carvings depict farmers and artisans. Such anonymity raises one of the most important issues for understanding both the nature of Classic society and its ultimate collapse – how did the huge mass of ordinary people relate to kings and lords? Once again I think there are several likely possibilities.

21 *Heather Hurst painted this reconstruction of the buildings shown in Fig. 20 after observing the excavations. Such sets of household buildings typically include one or several structures, and were utilized by small family groups.*

Matthew Restall, whose work on the Colonial-period "world of the *cah*" we already reviewed, believes that lineage organization has very ancient roots among the Maya. Imagine that something like the Colonial *chibal* lineages operated in Late Classic times, but without the marked class differences between nobles and commoners. In such a model (Fig. 22) nobles are the most highly ranked family members in networks of kinspeople linked from highest to lowest, all of whom might share a common patronym. They are supported by their lesser kin and in turn represent their interests vis-à-vis other lineages and the king (who heads his own royal lineage). They also, however, share among themselves common elite sensibilities, exchange spouses with other privileged families and the royal line, serve at court, and jockey for royal favor and political advantage. Societies organized in this fashion are ethnographically known for Africa.

There are three important dimensions of this kind of social order (not to be confused with "feudal" models proposed for the Maya by some archaeologists). First, elite leaders have their own political constituencies and economic supporters. Such a pattern would explain many things – for example how they got the labor to build, maintain, and staff their elaborate

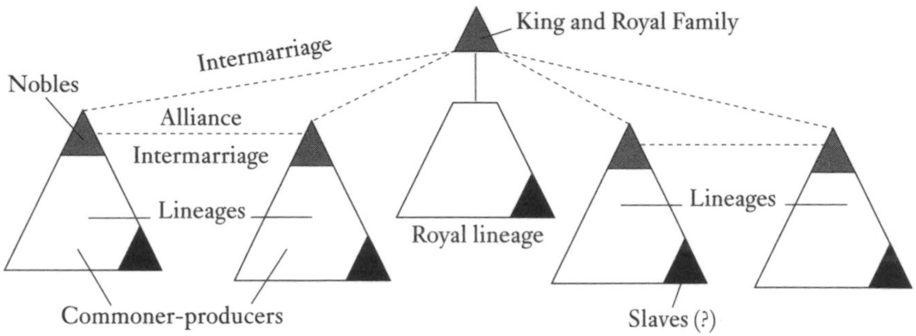

22 *Lineage model of Maya sociopolitical organization. Each large triangle represents a sizable kinship group that might include scores or even hundreds of people. Nobles occupy the top ranks, with commoners (and possibly slaves) ranked lower. Alliances and spouse exchanges link the lineage nobles with each other and with the royal family, which has its own set of lesser kinspeople.*

households. Second, common people were not politically marginalized, but had claims on their powerful relatives and on land and other resources that were held as common lineage property. Third, nobles occupied positions of privilege and opportunity, but also of considerable tension and ambiguity in which they had to balance their obligations to their kin-supporters with their increasingly pronounced noble identities and ambitions.

A second and somewhat simpler set of relationships is shown in Fig. 23. In this case the vast majority of humble people are separated from kings and nobles by a profound social gulf. Royal and elite families were organized into politically potent lineages, but commoners were excluded, organizationally atomized right down into small nuclear or extended families. Nobles claimed exclusive rights over the agricultural landscape and extracted labor and goods from farmers, but did not conceive of them as relatives in any meaningful sense. In this situation commoners are effectively peasants, marginalized

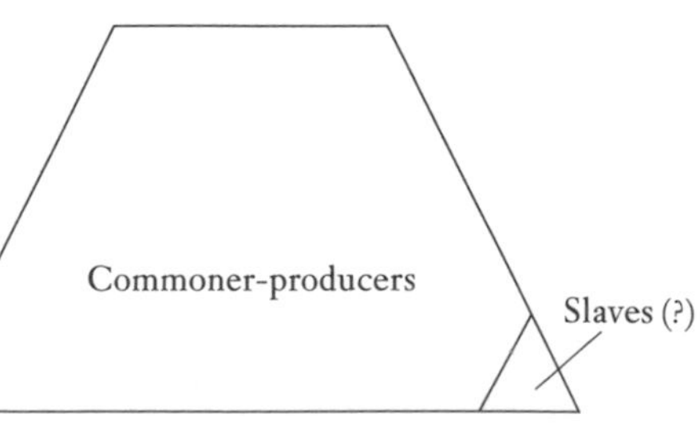

23 *A second model of Maya organization is more stratified in social, political, and economic terms. Here a pronounced social gulf separates kings and nobles from lesser people, who themselves have little independent political power or elite representation.*

or even excluded from political life. They have no automatic claims on lords or productive resources and no real ability to organize themselves politically to resist the demands of highly ranked people or represent their own interests. A system of social and political relationships very much like this operated in Hawaii just before Europeans arrived in the 18th century.

A third model (not exclusive of lineage organization) derives from what anthropologists call "house" societies.[19] Here "house" refers both to a residential place, and more importantly to a whole set of material and non-material resources – lands, titles, social privileges, and other kinds of cultural capital – that a core kin group of highly-ranked people in some sense possesses, and passes on across generations in a coherent manner. Houses in the latter sense often have distinguishing names. This concept of the corporate "estate" is historically familiar, because it describes how the noble "houses" of medieval Europe or Japan functioned. Among Aztec hereditary elites the *teccalli*, or noble house, was also a central organizing feature in the 16th century.

The main difference between the "house" and the lineage models is that all members of the "house" need not share a common ancestor, as in most lineages; "house" organization can situationally accommodate different kinds of kin. Moreover, house "members" can be attached in a variety of ways as non-related clients, tenants, or slaves, and they may adopt the house name (this makes the lack of references to lineages or lengthy genealogies in the inscriptions more comprehensible). For the principal proprietors of the house, the greatest benefit is the ability to attach laborers and political supporters. People affiliated with the house need not reside together, but for all of them it is a focus of identity and a source of rights to resources. "House" organization is consequently much more flexible and responsive to its fundamental purposes: the accumulation, retention, and transmission through time of the patrimony, or estate. Houses in the organizational sense endure much longer than families, and a symbolic focal point of house identity may be a real residence (or some other feature like a tomb). An advantage of the house model for archaeologists is thus that it might leave durable remains in the form of royal centers, or the palatial establishments of powerful nobles. The great residential compounds in the Copan urban core were plausibly the nuclei of noble houses.

What the house and lineage models share is the existence of corporate groups with their own interests and resources that they must protect and augment. The Contact-period Maya might have been developing in this direction. According to Philip Thompson, as late as the end of the 18th century native nobles in the Yucatecan town he studied asserted control by various means over a large percentage of the private land in the community. Moreover, the resident batab and town council also manipulated the disposition even of communal lands, further augmenting their economic dominance. Something very much like this pattern might well have characterized Copan and other Classic Maya polities.

There are other possible models, and elements of each of the ones discussed might have characterized one or another Maya political system during the 8th century. And of course these social arrangements are dynamic ones. Over time, a lineage-based system could have evolved into a more stratified or "house"-like one in a single polity. Schematic as they are, these divergent models force us to ponder what we do not know about Maya social and political organization and their very different implications for how Classic polities collapsed.

To summarize our discussion thus far, imagine yourself as an informed social scientist able to make a very brief tour through a Classic Maya kingdom. I think your first impression would be of two rather different categories of people (I hesitate to call them classes). The first consisted of masses of farmers who worked (and usually lived) on the agricultural landscape in modest households, producing most of what they themselves consumed. A much smaller segment of people would be removed from basic agrarian pursuits and supported by the surpluses generated by farmers. Most such people would appear wealthy and privileged. Conspicuous among them would be the ruler with his huge palace and court facilities, around which other powerful people congregated. Closer scrutiny, of course, would reveal a much more fine-grained and graduated set of relationships. Some nobles were more powerful, prestigious, and influential than others. Some farming families had more land than their neighbors, enjoyed special connections with nobles, and were rewarded, perhaps, for success in war or for their skills as artisans. This, for the present, is what seems reasonably certain.

In the preceding sections I have emphasized the "vertical," or hierarchical relationships among people of different ranks and status. Equally important are the more "horizontal" interactions among people on any given level, which might have been very fluid and opportunistic, and not tied specifically to formalities of rank. We can infer a fair amount about such interactions among royalty, but so far not much about how lesser nobles behaved in this regard (although the lineage/house models have some indirect implications). As for the commoners, we have practically no information at all. This is unfortunate, because we will see that the collapse did not everywhere affect people of different social ranks equally, and a powerful reason for this variation must be their internal organization, behavior, and adaptations.

Religion

Ancient Maya religion was so inseparably bound up with other aspects of life (I have already alluded to its connections with rulership and ancestors) that singling it out for discussion is somewhat artificial. Although inscriptions and art are replete with religious and ritual information, the Classic Maya left no books describing their religious ideas and practices in detail. Much of what we know is based on extrapolations from later Maya or other Mesoamerican religious traditions that are more fully documented. Because Maya religion is such an enormous subject I only briefly describe its major features here.

Like all Mesoamericans the Classic Maya were polytheists. They believed in a pantheon of gods, or perhaps more properly spiritual forces, that was heavily associated with natural phenomena such as earth, wind, water, rain, lightning, fire, and maize, and with human affairs – kingship, war, the activities of scribes, and farming. Some gods were vastly more important than others, especially the creator deities, those associated with the sun, the rain, the sky, maize, and the underworld. Often conceived in anthropogenic terms, gods could sometimes be well-intentioned and beneficent towards humans, and at other times hostile and harmful. Judging from the most complete religious narrative, the postconquest Quiche Maya book called the *Popol Vuh*, the gods themselves had very human attributes and even shortcomings. They could be deceitful, vengeful, and certainly might be mistaken and deceived.

Gods or spiritual forces could situationally inhabit images, or even human impersonators. This idea in turn reflects the associated notion that everything was in a sense inherently or potentially alive (a principle called animism). Even inanimate objects were enlivened, although some, like buildings, were created by humans and had to be infused with life or spirit through the proper rituals, particularly "fire-entering" events. Some kings such as Pakal of Palenque were evidently apotheosized as gods upon their deaths.

Although the basic gods were widely recognized by most Maya, they were by no means all worshiped everywhere. Instead, there appear to have been local cults that emphasized some subset of deities who were treated in ritually distinctive ways. Such "local" gods were patrons of particular polities and associated with specific dynastic lines or deities. They, or their physical manifestations, were in some sense possessed by rulers.

Deceased ancestors continued to play important roles in human affairs and were associated with various landscape features. Most ancestors were probably forgotten after four to six generations, relegated to a general realm of essentially anonymous spirits. As befits a hierarchical social order, however, the ancestors of prominent people were especially potent and significant.

The most important of them were long remembered and had to be carefully propitiated. They were not so much worshiped as recognized as still having powerful relevance for the political and ritual concerns of the living.

The Maya also shared the widespread Mesoamerican conviction that the gods had successively created and destroyed several previous versions of the world and its inhabitants. Metaphorically, these cosmogenic efforts were aimed at creating a milpa, or corn field, with humans as a kind of anthropomorphic maize whose role was to nourish the gods. Their last and most successful effort created the current world, dominated by humans. This cosmos was multi-layered, its principal elements consisting of heaven, earth (variously conceived as a rectangular house or maize field, a great crocodile, or as the back of a gigantic turtle), and the underworld. Colors and gods were associated with each cardinal direction (Plate 6), and in the center stood a great tree that connected heaven, earth, and underworld, as did sacred mountains and caves, both also associated with the ancestors.

Like the Aztecs, the Classic Maya probably thought that the current world was defective, and so continually threatened with disruption by the forces of chaos and darkness, and doomed to eventual destruction in its own turn. Humans, animals, plants, and even gods were subject to cycles of death and regeneration. It was the duty of humans to carry out rituals and make sacrifices to repay their debt to the gods and ancestors, to nourish them, and to avert chaos and disaster by ensuring balance and order in all things. The ultimate forces of disorder were essentially timeless and omnipresent, and so even the gods, who had their own fallibilities, could not control them either. In such a world, an orderly society could only exist and be maintained through work and effort, and by proper attention to the gods and ancestors. The properly ordered world or community was likened to the square maze field, and there was a strong contrast in the Maya mind between those aspects of the environment that had been "tamed" or "domesticated" through human effort, and the surrounding forest, which could be chaotic, unpredictable, and even sinister.[20]

Because sacred or divine kings had the most direct relations with gods and the most powerful ancestors, and hence extraordinary powers over the cosmos, they bore a special responsibility to guarantee, through their actions and persons, the well-being of their people and their kingdoms. Essential to this effort was divination and close attention to calendrical and astronomical cycles that monitored the state of the world. Despite their obsession with time, as elsewhere in Mesoamerica Maya people were pragmatically concerned with the day-to-day struggle to maintain prosperity and avert disaster.

Humans possessed complex soul elements, and if these became disordered, sickness or other misfortune might result. Shaman-diviners could diagnose the causes of illness and cure it through the proper ceremonies and offerings. At least some powerful humans had spiritual co-essences (*wayob*) that often took the form of impressive and even sinister animals such as jaguars. Souls of prominent people, particularly kings, were more potent, or "hotter," than those of lesser folk.

Although intensely disciplined people, the ancient Maya probably had no sense of sin as we know it. Bad behavior did not transgress a moral order, but instead consisted of intemperate acts that ignored one's ritual and ceremonial obligations, thus disturbing the all-important balance of things.

Last but not least, the Classic Maya shared with other Mesoamerican peoples the belief in a kind of mystical, utopian community that existed somewhere distant in time and space.[21] We know best how the Aztecs imagined this concept: a great metropolis inhabited by a multitude of happy, prosperous, and accomplished people, who lived together amicably under wise rulers. Called "Tollan" (the "Place of the Reeds") in Nahuatl, this marvelous place is usually identified archaeologically with Tula, a substantial pre-Aztec city to the northwest of the Basin of Mexico, and its inhabitants the Toltecs. Actually, there were probably several imagined "Tollans," because the idea appears to long predate Tula. In one sense all these splendid human-built places probably epitomized cosmic order, in opposition to the potential disorder of the natural world. Dynamic people such as the Aztecs believed it was their destiny to recreate new versions of Tollan in their own capital. For the Maya, who used the name Puh instead of Tollan, the concept might have referred to Teotihuacan. Whether real or imaginary, Tollan served not only as a model for human aspiration, but also as a place of origin, and of political legitimization for kings and elites.

Interestingly, Classic texts have yielded no unambiguous term that means "priest." Instead, kings and other high-ranking people carried out rituals and other spiritually charged activities. Some individuals associated with the title *ah k'in* (literally "Diviner," or "He of the Days") seem to have been especially knowledgeable about calendrical lore.

It is tempting to conclude that religion is one of the most distinctive or unique dimensions of any ancient agrarian civilization, and of course if we emphasize particular forms of rituals, symbols, iconography, and so forth, this is true. Some years ago Bruce Trigger, in his book *Early Civilizations: Ancient Egypt in Context*, concluded that beneath all this superficial variety lies a fundamental set of shared themes. These include animism, multiple gods or spiritual forces, leaders with divine or semi-divine powers, and the idea of a threatening world that could be manipulated by humans through ritual or sacrifice to ensure cosmic order, human fertility, and agricultural productivity. Classic Maya religion obviously fits nicely into this broad comparative perspective.

Centers and Courts

Virtually every reader of this book is a city person, and each of us has certainly grown up in social environments dominated by huge urban centers. We take such hypertrophied urbanization for granted, but most of us do not realize how recent it is. As late as AD 1900 there were only 16 cities in the entire world with populations in excess of 1,000,000 people (today there are over 400), and if we go back another century, only 17 cities in all of Europe had populations of over 100,000 people.[22]

No wonder that in the minds of V. Gordon Childe and other evolutionists the presence of urban centers was second only to writing as a hallmark of civilization. Many Mayanists, beginning at least with Stephens and Catherwood, routinely called places like Palenque or Copan cities. Others, puzzled by the evidently low concentrations of population at such places, the predominance of apparent ceremonial buildings, and the lack of neatly arranged streets and avenues in the western fashion, were uncomfortable with this label, an ambivalence that continues today. Consider this remark by Gordon Willey:

> the formal demographic requirements of urbanism, in the strictest sense, do not seem to be present in the Mayan lowlands in Classic times.... Yet lacking this, the Maya achieved city life in the broader sense, for many of the attributes of civilization ... are clearly present.[23]

Notice here the almost reflexive conflation of the concepts of civilization and city. Some of my colleagues, perhaps concerned that the Maya will somehow be devalued if their great centers are not called cities, continue to use the term, insisting that we should not impose our western concepts of urbanism on other cultures. Of course the Maya had cities, so the reasoning goes, albeit of their own distinctive kind.

There are two problems with this line of thought. First, our own urban concepts do not only conform to or derive from the European cultural experience. Columbus confidently expected to make landfall at the fabled cities of eastern Asia when he sailed westward in 1492, and they certainly existed even if he did not find them. Other Spaniards who shortly followed his lead knew and admired great cities such as Cairo, which they recognized were grander and more complex than any in Europe (remember that they christened one Maya town they saw "Grand Cairo"). More to the point, Cortes was extremely impressed with the urban character of the places he visited in Central Mexico.[24] Tenochtitlan, the Aztec metropolis that he finally conquered in 1521, compared favorably in scale and complexity to any European capital of its day except Paris and Constantinople. Cortes described these highland cities very differently than the Maya centers he saw during his travels and explorations (one might object that Classic centers were much larger, but see below). And this urban Mesoamerican tradition had very deep roots. In the 6th or 7th centuries AD only a handful of cities anywhere in the world were more impressive than Teotihuacan, located just 30 km (19 miles) northeast of modern Mexico City.

Recently I read a preliminary report about a small Maya center called Blue Creek, located in northern Belize. According to the author, Blue Creek was a "city" with a minimal area of 100–150 sq. km (40–60 sq. miles). Now this would make it some 10 to 15 times larger than imperial Rome in the 2nd century AD or the Aztec capital of Tenochtitlan in AD 1519, and roughly five to six times as large as Mesoamerica's best-preserved Classic city, Teotihuacan! Moreover, this "city" has only just come to our attention, having been invisible to generations of previous archaeologists who walked over the landscape. Something is seriously wrong with our comparative conceptions of ancient settlements when we play this fast and loose with nomenclature.

Some years ago my colleague William Sanders and I suggested that we call most Maya centers *regal-ritual cities*, a concept borrowed from the urban anthropologist Richard Fox. Our intention was to salvage the label city (thus pandering to the "city-envy" that afflicts many Mayanists) while still emphasizing how distinctive Maya centers really were. A plan of the central precincts of the most famous Classic Maya center, Tikal (Fig. 24), illustrates our basic perspective. Tikal has some of the largest buildings ever erected by the Maya, and if monumentality of architecture is one criterion of "cityness," then Tikal certainly qualifies (Plate 11). Notice, however, that the major architectural components at Tikal – temples, palaces, great plazas, and ball courts – are not densely packed together, but instead rather loosely distributed over an area of about 3–4 sq. km (1.16–1.54 sq. miles) and tied together by causeways. Much of the landscape between these concentrations of monumental buildings and ceremonial roads is either vacant or occupied by much smaller structures (Fig. 25). There is no highly nucleated zone of residential-

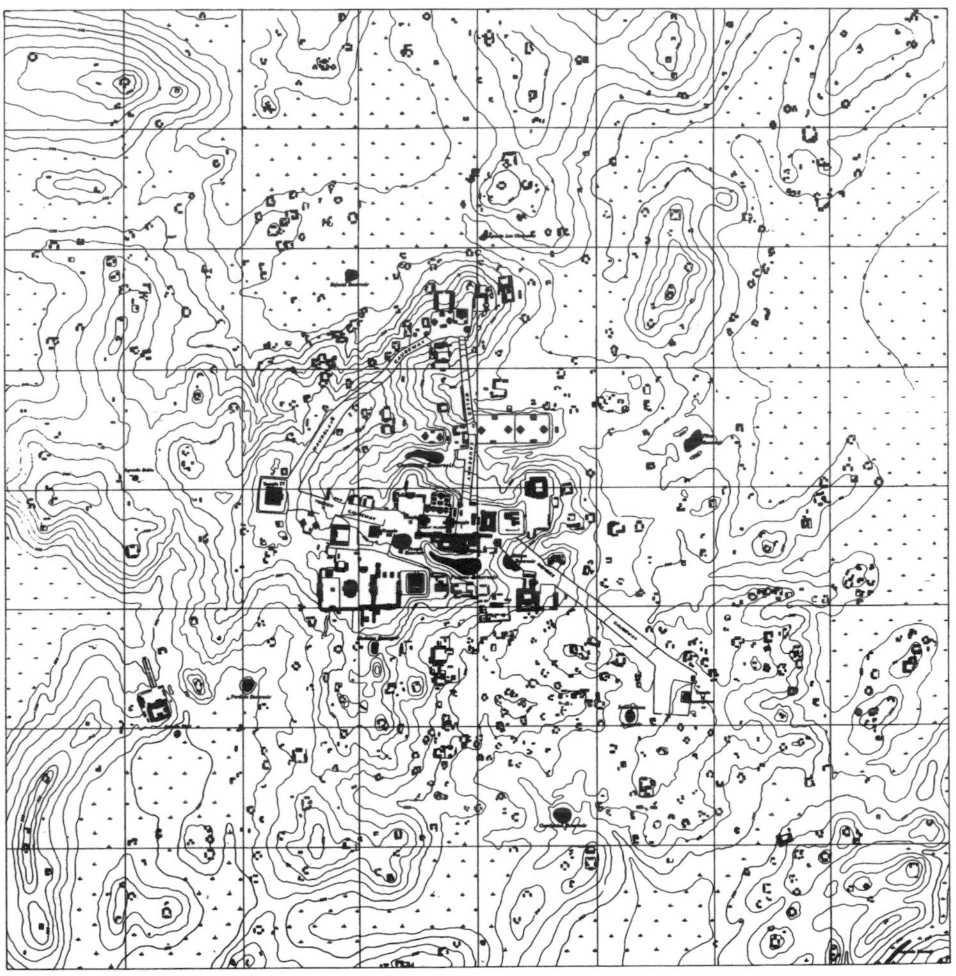

24 *The central 16 sq. km (6 sq. miles) of Tikal. Note the huge architectural complexes connected by causeways that comprise the site epicenter. Smaller house groups are situated on high ground around this core, and decrease in density with distance. Not shown is a system of earthworks found farther to the north and south. Each grid square is 500 m (1640 ft).*

scale architecture with perceptible boundaries. If you walked away from central Tikal in a straight line to the north you would first pass through a landscape where there were 100–200 structures per sq. km (259–518 per sq. mile), but if you continued on for about an hour settlement would be much less dense – around 31 structures per sq. km (80 per sq. mile) – and most outlying buildings would be smaller than those nearer the site core. Where settlement extends out in such a concentric fashion it is obviously very diffi-

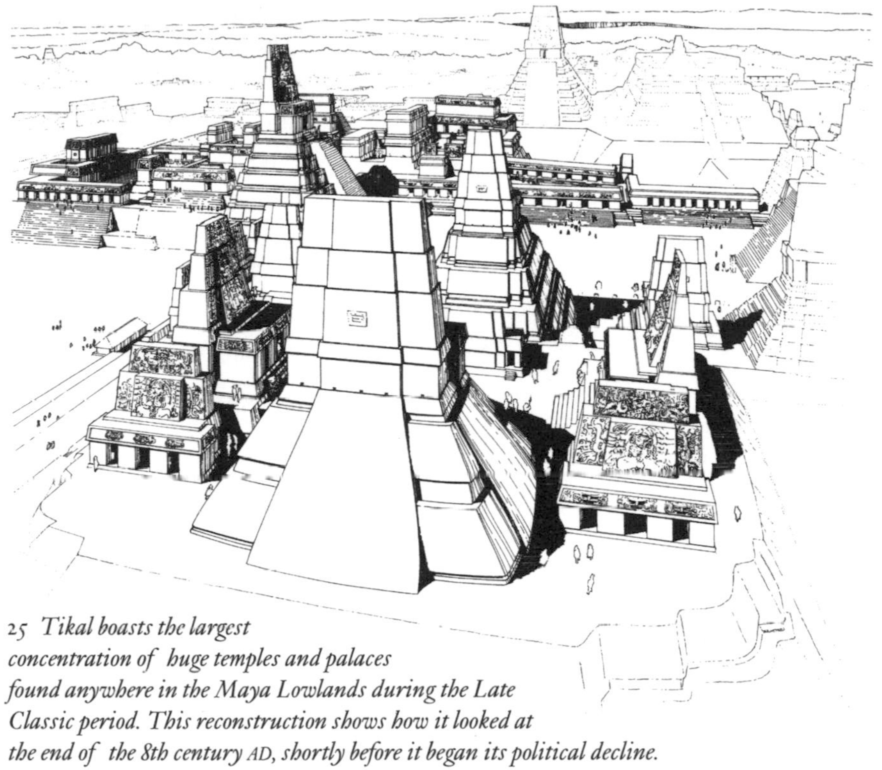

25 Tikal boasts the largest concentration of huge temples and palaces found anywhere in the Maya Lowlands during the Late Classic period. This reconstruction shows how it looked at the end of the 8th century AD, shortly before it began its political decline.

cult to detect community boundaries. Of course the monumental precincts at Tikal and elsewhere were the most obtrusive settlement features to early explorers such as Stephens and Catherwood, and to modern tourists as well, and are often labeled "epicenters" by Maya archaeologists to differentiate them from outlying settlement zones. Although some parts of Yucatan had similar settlement arrangements in the early 16th century, only one or two centers might have compared favorably with those of Classic times, and probably none approached Tikal in scale.

So far epigraphers have identified no Classic Maya word that refers in the abstract to cities or, for that matter, to whole kingdoms.[25] We know that some great centers had individual names, as in "Bone" for Palenque. References to such places, however, are inextricably bound to the titles and names of their rulers. And unlike in Europe and other Old World settings, there appear to have been no great central places where rulers or their dependent governors were not present. Palenque, Copan, or Tikal literally were "king-places."

Sanders and I argue that Tikal and other major Classic centers were essentially the gigantic household facilities of Maya kings (or in some cases sajals or other subsidiary nobles). Although the king and his family might have lived in only part of such a center (at Tikal the Central Acropolis is the main royal palace), the great buildings were all essential appurtenances of rulership. What we see on the Tikal map is the result of a thousand years of construction, much of which dates to the 8th century. Successive kings built new temples over old ones or razed ancient buildings to make way for their new projects. Old stelae and altars were destroyed or reverentially buried and replaced with others. Dead kings and their relatives were buried in specially prepared tombs that sanctified these royal places (the North Acropolis is Tikal's main necropolis), and these tombs remained central to ancestral ceremonies for many generations. Stelae, altars, buildings, and even tombs all displayed sculptured or painted images and texts that projected royal ideology and political authority. To surrounding populations, the dynastic place carried a heavy symbolic load, redolent of cosmic centrality and order.

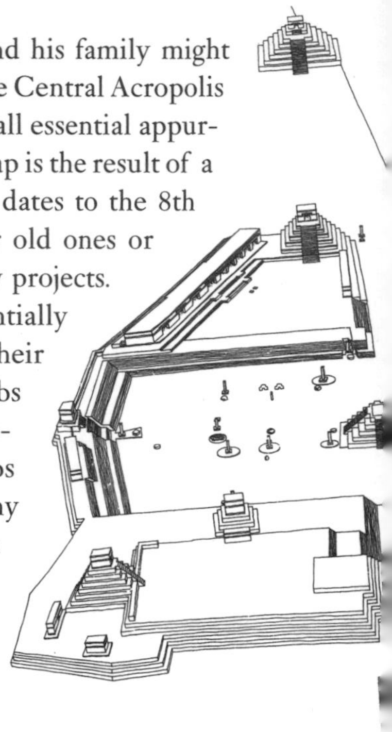

Tikal's rulers probably regarded all the major elements of this huge built environment as the core patrimony of their dynastic "house" (in both the residential and organizational senses), the durable symbols of their associations with the great people and events of the past, and also with the gods and the royal ancestors. Maya rulers, or at least the most successful of them, were strongly tied to such royal places. Centers were thus both residences and political capitals, but also obtrusive expressions of the cosmic order that kings professed to deliver to their kingdoms and subjects, and arenas for the expression of the high elite culture so essential to any tradition of civilization. Following up on this line of thought, we can also regard regal-ritual cities as great houses, and of Maya settlements collectively as a hierarchy of houses ranging from the tiny, perishable residences of farmers, through the elaborate compounds of nobles (foci of corporate "houses" in their own right), and culminating in the imposing royal centers.

Of course not all Maya centers are like Tikal, and anyone visiting several of them in the expectation of seeing some sort of shared general settlement plan or scale will be surprised. Newly completed maps of Palenque by Edward Barnhart reveal hundreds of closely packed small buildings extending to the west of the reconstructed archaeological zone visited by tourists.[26] Although chaotic in arrangement, this layout appears much more urban to

26 Reconstruction drawing of the Copan Main Group, the regal- ritual center of the Copan dynasty. The core residential facilities of Copan's kings during the last several reigns were in Group 10L-2, the set of small structures on the right.

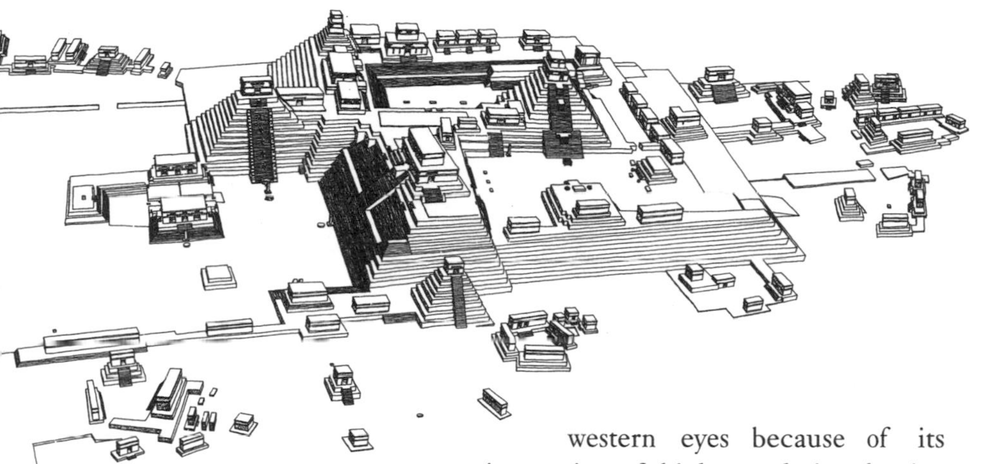

western eyes because of its impression of high population density. As presently known, Palenque is also much smaller than central Tikal – covering an area of about 1.2 sq. km (0.86 sq. miles). At Copan, the Main Group (the core of royal facilities) is even more compact – originally extending over about 0.15 sq. km (37 acres) before some of it was washed away by the river (Fig. 26). Flanking the royal compound on the valley floor were two great residential enclaves, dominated by elite compounds, where 12,000 people lived (although this is a maximum estimate). Most other Classic centers are also small (typically under 1 sq. km) and have more dispersed core populations than either Palenque or Copan. Despite all this variation, an important feature of the regal-ritual/royal household model is that Maya centers were essentially redundant in their basic functions.

In one respect I think Maya centers did probably resemble great cities elsewhere – they were in a continual state of decay and renewal. Anyone reading popular books about the Classic Maya has seen wonderful reconstruction paintings of Tikal, Palenque, or Copan, that depict beautifully maintained buildings, resplendent in their paint and plasterwork. Such reconstructions are quite deceiving. If we could visit such places in their heyday we would almost certainly see many great buildings standing derelict, others being actively used, and still others being built or renovated, much the same as in 16th-century Rome.

For Mesoamerican people everywhere the greatest centers, no matter what we choose to call them, were the places where kings and powerful nobles resided. Highland Mexican cities were royal places like Tikal or Copan, but they were also different in two important ways. Tenochtitlan and Teotihuacan each had populations of around 125,000 people clustered into areas of about 15 and 22 sq. km (5.9–8.6 sq. miles) respectively, so they were very large in area and had population densities in the 5000–9000 people per sq. km range (12,950–23,310 per sq. mile). Although such cities were places of extravagant courtly consumption, Cortes and other Spaniards were quick to note that they also had huge markets and well-developed commerce, evidenced by the many potters, stonemasons, carpenters, goldsmiths, and countless other specialists who lived in neighborhoods along the grid-like streets and canals. Many of their products were exchanged with other city dwellers at great state-regulated urban markets, to which thousands of rural people brought their own goods as well. Aztec merchants called pochteca led caravans of human porters throughout much of Mesoamerica, trading as they went. Nothing like these dense urban populations or highland economic institutions has been detected in the Classic Maya Lowlands.

Some Mayanists object that sheer scale is irrelevant to our assessments of urban status and complexity. But consider for a moment conditions in a huge Old World preindustrial city such as Cairo, which in Cortes's time had upwards of 500,000 inhabitants.[27] Individuals enjoyed considerable social anonymity amidst such multitudes, an experience we all have in modern cities, whereas virtually everyone habitually in and around a much smaller community such as Copan or Palenque probably knew most other people by sight, and something (perhaps too much) of their business. Social interactions were thus personalized to a degree impossible in a real metropolis. Similarly, the sheer aggregate numbers of inhabitants in Cairo and other Old World cities created levels of urban economic demand, consumption, and interdependence of exceptional complexity. And arts and intellectual pursuits tend to thrive where large numbers of practitioners communicate or dispute easily with one another. In all these ways and many more, scale does matter.

Sanders and I think that like Cairo, highland Mexican cities such as Tenochtitlan (and earlier, Teotihuacan) had a distinctive kind of urban ecology that required political control or economic influence over huge territories from which resources could be drawn – a pattern that did not develop in the Classic Maya Lowlands. If we extend the word city uncritically to all Mesoamerican centers, we unfortunately obscure these important kinds of variation. And as we shall see in the following chapters, the nature of Maya centers bears directly upon basic issues of the collapse. Although many of my colleagues will disagree with me, my conclusion is that had a Spaniard from early 16th-century Seville, a medieval Cairene merchant, or an Aztec noble from Tenochtitlan been able to visit several Classic Maya centers, they would all have found these places very different in character from their home communities, regardless of the terms they would have used to describe them. What they would have seen instead were court centers.

Classic Maya Courts

As we know from ancient Crete, Bronze Age Greece, and probably early Egypt, impressive central places commonly developed around royal households, and often functioned not only as residences but also as administrative, economic, military, and cultural centers. If Maya centers were primarily huge royal households, we can also think of them as courtly places where privileged people were in intimate, daily contact with rulers.[28] Judging from court societies elsewhere, such people included royal relatives, lesser nobles and their families, advisors and officials, guards and military personnel, visiting dignitaries and ambassadors, political prisoners and hostages, priests, scribes, scholars, physicians, entertainers, artists and artisans, and sundry other retainers, servants, dependents, guests, and general hangers-on. Many such individuals can in fact be identified in the court scenes shown on Classic Maya polychrome vessels and wall murals, and sometimes their names and titles are known. We already saw that great nobles attended kings, and works of art frequently depict them in court dress, hint at conventions of courtly protocol, and reveal many of the kinds of objects used in court settings. As befits a royal house, nobles and other courtiers were fed from the king's largess. The Bonampak murals which show scores of haughty people attended by dancers, standard bearers, and musicians, all involved in elaborate rituals, convey the richest narrative images.

Cross-culturally speaking, courts are peculiar institutions. Intensely person-centered, they are places where servants frequently have greater access to kings than powerful nobles, and where royal mistresses are as influential as high officials. Courts are essential to the effective administration of realms, yet at the same time are arenas of intense political competition and opportunism. While symbolically associated with particular places on the landscape, courts are often highly peripatetic, moving as the king moves. People at courts set standards of manners, etiquette, and taste that both separate them from ordinary people and inspire endless admiration and emulation. And more than any other institutions, courts were the principal vehicles that carried the Great Traditions of all ancient civilizations, the Classic Maya included. Literacy was the most standardized element shared among Maya court people, and new research by Stephen Houston, John

Robertson, and David Stuart suggests that a single prestige language was used everywhere in the inscriptions (much like Latin in medieval Europe or classical Arabic in the Middle East).[29] This language, which they call Classic Ch'olti'an, was once a living, vernacular tongue, perhaps during Late Preclassic times. It subsequently survived as a formal, "scribal" language, much as Sumerian did in the Near East long after its spoken forms had died out.

Shared linguistic and other conventions facilitated travel among Maya courts. Royal relatives visited one another, kings sent political emissaries to enemies or allies, and the devout made pilgrimages to shrines sacred to ancestors or gods. People carried back stories of the places they visited, and Maya kings doubtless took great pride, like rulers everywhere, in the splendor and reputations of their courts-cum-households, and competed with one another to raise the grandest buildings and finest monuments, host the most extravagant feasts, and carry out the most impressive rituals. By the 8th century such courtly status rivalry was intense, and as we shall see later contributed to conflict.

Some courts developed particularly fine traditions of painting or carving, and kings elsewhere probably sent their artisans to learn these skills. Similarly, the linguistic uniformity of the courtly script suggests the presence of a few great scribal schools. It appears increasingly probable that political hostages were required to live at the courts of some especially powerful rulers, a practice well developed among the Aztecs. Nor was courtly life only a royal prerogative. If, as seems likely, sajals often ruled subsidiary centers in the name of a dominant king, their households would have been mini-courts in their own right, duplicating on a smaller and subordinate level of settlement many of the functions of the king's court. And at Copan the lord who sat on the Skyband Bench, though no doubt in frequent attendance on the king, surely enjoyed the attentions of his own courtiers. Multiple courts within a polity facilitated government in many ways, but they were also potential places of internecine political rivalry.

In economic terms Maya courts were primarily consuming places, supported by the foodstuffs and labor of local farming families. From greater distances came feathers of exotic birds, jaguar pelts, jade, marine shells, cacao, and a host of other raw materials that flowed into the storerooms of kings and elites. Some products moved from one place to another as tribute, some as gifts, and some as trade, but all were probably monopolized to a high degree by elites. Most such items did not function as wealth in our terms, but rather as markers of social rank and power. To be sure, some things were also produced at courts. Royal artisans (*ah ts'ib* or *its'at*), some of whom were the sons of kings, carved stelae and altars or decorated polychrome vessels.

Women of rank wove the finest cotton mantles, and scribes painted books. All these things and many more funded the households of kings and elites, their ritual and political displays, and the great feasts at which gifts flowed freely among nobles. Much of this wealth was placed in their tombs when they died, and very little, so far as we can tell, ever worked its way back down to the majority of the population either through redistribution managed by elites or by some sort of market mechanism (markets have historically been much more weakly developed in the Maya Lowlands than in highland Mesoamerica, and there are few archaeological traces of them). In short, courts were places of conspicuous and even wasteful consumption that served, along with their elaborate architectural settings, to emphasize the primacy of rulers and those around them.

Sixteenth-century Maya kings and lords often possessed sources of wealth independent of the taxes they gathered from their followers. Some of them had plantations that grew cacao or other valuable crops, and others subsidized and took part in mercantile ventures. We do not know if such patterns have their roots in Classic times, nor whether Classic kings and lords possessed the "slaves" that were such valuable adjuncts to the political economy of the Contact period. Despite Landa's contention that this institution of social, political, and economic debasement was a late introduction in Yucatan, I suspect that something like it existed among the Classic Maya. If so, a term for it might lurk among the still-undeciphered glyphs.

Several regions of the ancient Old World, such as Bronze Age Greece and Crete, developed sophisticated, non-urban "palace economies" centered on royal courts similar in some respects to those of the Classic Maya, but also different in important ways. Massive ritual facilities were much less well developed, and there is also evidence for bulk storage of oil, wine, and other staple commodities, and for long-distance trade in such things, especially by sea. Kings and lords clearly administered local political economies to extract materials not only for their own elite households, but to fund far-flung commercial ventures. Only a feeble version of this pattern existed among the 16th-century Maya, and in my opinion it was also weakly developed in Classic times.

Government

Three decades ago, summarizing the then current information pertaining to the Classic collapse, Gordon Willey and Demitri Shimkin noted that Mayanists faced a big problem: how did various parts of the ancient sociocultural "system" relate to one another?[30] In particular, why did Maya commoners behave toward elites the way they did, and what did elites do in return? Understanding the governing institutions and roles of Maya kings and elites is obviously essential to our conceptions of the collapse of Classic kingdoms, and Willey and Shimkin identified administrative "overload" and "managerial failure" as major factors.

What then, if anything, did kings and elites do to ensure the smooth running of their realms? Were they in any sense hands-on managers of important affairs? Did something like an official bureaucracy exist in Classic times? Because issues of government are not directly addressed by the texts, we still lack satisfying answers to these questions. Powerful people, kings included, obviously organized and oversaw many activities. They mobilized labor to build and maintain temples, ball courts, causeways, and of course their own palatial residences. They ensured that farmers provided a constant flow of food and other materials to supply their large households, and somehow managed the production and circulation of some elite objects. Elaborate rituals and feasts required much planning and preparation, as did military campaigns and diplomatic initiatives. All this we can safely conclude, but exactly how they did these things remains unknown.

Presumably kings were not autocrats, but had to take into account the interests of lesser elite people, if not all of their subjects. We saw that among the 16th-century Maya there were numerous community officers and lineage leaders who settled disputes and generally kept order in towns ruled by batabob or halach uinicob. These individuals, along with other rich and influential men, were well respected and apparently obeyed. Some archaeologists, impressed by the apparent greater scale and complexity of Classic polities, believe there must have been much more well-developed hierarchies of officials or bureaucrats who were specialists in managing state affairs.[31] If so, they are not unambiguously named in the texts or clearly shown in Maya art, nor are they evident in the general archaeological record. Nor, in fact, is there any textual evidence that rulers were law-givers or had any formal role in settling disputes.

Pertinent to the issue of government is the small territorial and demographic scale of most local Classic polities. Imagine living in one of these kingdoms. From the king's seat it would take at most two or three days to walk to the borderlands of some neighboring ruler, although most people probably never had occasion to make such a journey. You lived out your entire life on a landscape occupied by a population equivalent to that of a mid-sized modern town, say in the range of 20,000 to 50,000 people. As in such towns everywhere you would be related to many of your neighbors, know many of them personally, and in any case you would recognize prominent individuals wherever they lived. Everyone would know something about everyone else's lives and reputations. Managing such intimate political systems is comparatively simple.

None of the activities of Maya kings and lords listed above, of course, was much concerned with the well-being of Maya commoners, except to the extent that war and diplomacy protected ordinary people from the aggression of other kingdoms, and that commoners believed in the efficacy of royal rituals. Many years ago William Rathje argued that certain resources such as salt, igneous rock for the *manos* and *metates* used to grind maize, and obsidian for cutting tools were all essential to ordinary households and had to be procured from great distances. Rathje's idea was that emergent Maya kings supervised the procurement of these and other materials, and used them to promote and maintain their own political ascendancy. Salt was certainly valuable and widely traded by the 16th-century Maya, but is hard to detect in the archaeological record for earlier times. I can attest from my own experience excavating many humble residences that the overwhelming majority of grinding implements were made from easily available local stone. Most such residences yield few traces of obsidian, and even where it is abundant, as at Copan, it continued to be widely traded even after kings and lords disappeared, so they don't appear necessary to its acquisition.

Some archaeologists have argued that Maya economies were heavily administered from the top by kings and their officials, notably in building and managing various kinds of essential infrastructural facilities, including the systems of agricultural terraces or drained fields found in some parts of the Maya Lowlands. These in turn produced the wealth that enriched regional Maya kingdoms, facilitated a brisk trade among them, and linked the whole Classic Maya Lowlands to larger Mesoamerican commercial networks.[32] We will return to this question later, but none of these constructions appear to me to require such elite management to build or maintain, nor is intensive commerce evident apart from elite items, and even these probably moved in small quantities most of the time.

Vernon Scarborough and his colleagues make another kind of managerial argument. They point out that despite the abundant annual rainfall in the central and southern Maya Lowlands there is a protracted dry season when little water is available on the surface in many regions, and of course during some years when rainfall is substandard. Scarborough believes that the great plastered plazas at Tikal and other centers were laid out to capture and divert rainwater into reservoirs, where it was stored and doled out during rainless months to the advantage of all, but particularly to the royal or elite hydraulic managers.[33] It remains to be seen whether such features are widespread, and of course they were not necessary at the many centers located on or near rivers or lakes.

Some of my colleagues believe that all aspects of commoner economic life were directly controlled by the aristocracy. If so it was not by necessity, for the simple reason that rural Maya people of the Colonial and modern periods for centuries have carried out their agrarian pursuits perfectly well without much (or any) intervention by elites. Most Maya farming families could probably manage their own household activities in the context of the peasant sector, and lords were probably most concerned with extracting labor and goods from them and maintaining social order. I suspect that nothing resembling a complex bureaucracy existed in ancient times, and that instead most tasks were assigned to royal relatives and to important people such as the *sajals*, *aj k'uhuuns*, and others who made up each royal court. To put this another way, each realm was administered as an extension of its royal household, with some tasks "farmed out" to nobles who had their own little courtly households. Affairs were probably handled very much on a case-by-case basis, with assignments going to the most able people around the king, regardless of their court titles. No doubt some tasks gravitated repeatedly to individuals who proved particularly capable of discharging them, so to some degree one could speak of specialized "officials." One hint at such flexible assignment of tasks comes from a carved panel at Tamarindito, recently analyzed by Hector Escobedo, that depicts an individual who was both a sculptor and a warrior. Similarly, at Palenque one lord held no fewer than three separate titles.

Scribes, of course, bore much of the administrative load. In some ancient societies scribal titles were both numerous and complemented in such a manner as to suggest bureaucratic functions. Thus Egypt had "document scribes," "scribes of the workshop," "field scribes," "treasury scribes" and a host of others.[34] Nothing like this is found in Maya inscriptions.

While the kind of system I propose might seem too informal to provide effective government, something very much like it worked well in early Egypt, which of course was a much larger and more complex political entity than any Maya kingdom. John Baines and Norman Yoffee conclude that only about 500 high officials ruled Old Kingdom Egypt, which had a population numbering somewhere between 1,000,000 and 2,000,000 people.[35] Most stable Maya polities by contrast had fewer people than the university at which I teach (which does, nevertheless, seem to require an astounding number of administrators).

Whether Maya polities had tight, centralized control emanating from the top, or looser, less bureaucratic forms of organization as I propose, is an important point. The first kind of system tends to be more fragile than the second, and more prone to total collapse. If Maya commoners could generally function independently of Maya elites in economic terms, we would expect more fragility at the top, and more durability at the bottom.

The Classic Political Landscape

By the 8th century the southern Maya Lowlands were densely packed with scores of large regal-ritual or court centers, and many more smaller ones. In some regions, especially around Tikal, these were sometimes so close to one another that on a clear day a king could see the temples of a neighboring center from atop his own, and of course much of the intervening landscape was densely settled by farmers. Even before hieroglyphs could be deciphered archaeologists realized that despite such proximity there was never any overall political unity in the Maya Lowlands. This view did not present much of a problem so long as Tikal, Palenque, or Copan were envisioned as largely vacant ceremonial places. Once it became apparent that they were instead political capitals ruled by dynasties of kings, the issue of just how the political landscape was constituted became much more complicated.

Beginning in the late 1950s epigraphers began to identify emblem glyphs in the texts. At first these were thought to refer directly to particular places or polities, and they eventually revealed complex patterns of wars, intermarriages, royal visits, and other interactions among elites. We now know that such glyphs always occur as parts of statements that include royal names and titles. Although not straightforward toponyms, they do convey the idea of a particular "holy lord" and the dynastic line and kingdom with which he was associated. Between 45 and 50 emblem glyphs are now known (Fig. 27), and their distribution is complicated. Some centers such as Tikal and Dos Pilas share the same one, suggesting a close historical association between their dynasties (Dos Pilas's royal line was probably a cadet branch of Tikal's). Others display multiple emblem glyphs, and for still others no such glyphs have been identified at all. Possession of an emblem glyph does not necessarily mean that a center is an independent political entity. Despite such uncertainties, emblem glyphs have proven invaluable in sorting out political relationships, especially because so far the texts have not yielded other terms

27 *Emblem glyphs associated with various Maya centers. These glyphs, always attached to the titles and names of rulers, were among the first clues that royal dynasties dominated Classic Maya polities.*

that more directly denote kingdoms or polities (although there are toponyms and words that seem to refer to land, and perhaps even to the property of rulers).

Mayanists agree that the Classic landscape was always politically fragmented and that most of the centers associated with emblem glyphs were capitals of independent kingdoms focused on a particular line of "holy lords." Along with their outlying attached populations, centers were the fundamental political units of Classic times, which are often called "city states." I dislike this label and prefer a more neutral term such as "polity" or "kingdom," although city-state does convey the general pattern of a central place and its rural hinterland. Just how big or how populous such polities were must be mainly inferred from archaeological data because no Maya ruler recorded the extent of his territories, the numbers of his subjects, or the locations of his kingdom's boundaries – at least in texts that have survived. Systems of ditches and embankments at Tikal, along with flanking swamps, define a region of about 120 sq. km (46.3 sq. miles). Similarly, in AD 652 Copan's dynamic 12th ruler, Smoke Imix, set up a series of seven stelae delimiting the most productive land in the valley (an area of roughly 25 to 30 sq. km (about

9.7–11.6 sq. miles) where most of his people then lived. While the political, economic, and cultural influence of both Tikal and Copan usually extended far more widely, these zones plausibly represent core hinterlands that were crucial to their respective dynasties.

One school of thought envisions the most stable Maya political units as small enough to walk across in two or three days – averaging perhaps several thousand square km in area. According to this minimalist view, the king of a particularly powerful polity such as Tikal might have had on the order of 50,000–60,000 subjects, while Yax Pasaj ruled only about 20,000–30,000 people in the Copan valley. Many other local kingdoms were much smaller. Political fragmentation has important implications for the Classic collapse. On the one hand, it fostered war and other forms of competition. On the other, historians have often singled out the rigidity of some highly centralized ancient political systems, such as Old Kingdom Egypt, and their consequent vulnerability to drought or other massive stresses. No such unity contributed to what happened to the 8th-century Maya.

Because our perspective on Maya political arrangements emphasizes the importance of large centers, especially those with their own emblem glyphs, archaeologists have usually worked out from center to periphery when analyzing Late Classic settlement patterns, which of course are valuable clues to political organization. Although the pattern of clearly defined regal-ritual capital with its local royal dynasty and surrounding hinterlands is the most common spatial expression of Maya political arrangements, there are some important exceptions. The polity of Pomona, long a mortal enemy of the kings of Piedras Negras, seems to have had no single capital, but instead consisted of several important confederated centers identified with the Pomona dynasty and its core territory. In some regions, moreover, there are few or no major sites and no apparent dominant dynasty. Instead many smaller groups of impressive structures lie scattered rather evenly over the landscape. This pattern is found in the Chenes-Rio Bec zone situated in the southern Mexican state of Campeche, just to the north of Calakmul. Recent regional surveys by the Guatemalan archaeologist Juan Pedro Laporte show much the same situation over large parts of the southeastern Peten, just west of Caracol.[36] Findings like these complicate the issue of Late Classic political structure. Obviously the Maya who lived in these small centers, which usually include palace structures and sometimes temples, ball courts, and carved monuments, were of higher status than the common farmers who lived all around them. But how they related to the ruling dynasties of places such as Caracol, Tikal, or Calakmul remains unknown.

How did Maya people define their kingdoms and identify with them? One insight derives from the basic unit of 16th-century Aztec society, the *altepetl* (literally "water-hill" in Nahuatl). Central to the indigenous altepetl concept was a long-established dynasty and a ruling king (or sometimes more than one), who people recognized as their "natural lord," or *señor natural*, as the Spaniards called him. Kings resided in elaborate palaces in capital towns or cities that combined the functions of ritual, political, and economic places (Plate 19). Around the royal facilities were the establishments of lesser hereditary noble houses as well. Altepetl territory – often very small – consisted of the landscape cultivated or otherwise used by the people traditionally attached to a particular line of natural lords, most of whom spoke a common language. There were several grades of commoners, or more properly subjects, who owed various levels of service to kings and lords. By 1519 there were no longer acknowledged kinship links between hereditary lords and commoners.

Shared by all these people was an origin or migration history that was preserved in books and that recounted how the ancestors of the kings, lords, and common people had arrived at their homeland and settled it. These historical accounts and documents in part functioned as claims to the altepetl resources and titles, and continued to do so long after the Spanish conquest. Although neighboring altepeme were usually almost indistinguishable from one another in language, religion, political organization, and material culture, each one constituted in a sense an ethnic as well as a political unit, tied together internally by the common heritage of its people and the mutual obligations recognized by kings and subjects. Most altepetl retained this identity even when conquered or otherwise absorbed by more powerful neighbors, and politically subject or "lesser" kings were still the social equals (and sometimes superiors) of their overlords. Because kings were linked by conquest, marriage, clientage, or alliance to other rulers beyond the altepetl limits, they had more cosmopolitan identities than their subjects. I think that in a general sense Classic Maya polities had somewhat similar features.

What did the political landscape look like from the perspective of a Maya king and his court? I doubt that any ruler thought of his personal realm as delimited by lines on a map, but rather in terms of where people lived (mainly farmers) who owed him some sort of allegiance or service, as in the altepetl. Rulers similarly had to take account of the great nobles in their domains, some of whom were probably their relatives. Expanding the territorial scale, any particular king also recognized a wider network of subordinate, allied, or at least friendly rulers whose great houses he, his courtiers, and his emissaries could visit without much risk, just like altepetl rulers, and upon whose help or neutrality he could rely upon in times of conflict. Small centers such as Uaxactun possibly were from very early times routinely under the influence or even control of their much larger and more powerful neighbors – in Uaxactun's case Tikal, located only 19 km (11.9 miles) to the south. And we know that by the 8th century some kings were associated with numerous subordinate sajals (as many as 14 had links with Yaxchilan's dynasty). But what about something more along Aztec lines, in which independent kings and kingdoms were subjugated by force or threat to others? This brings us to a much-debated subject – the question of larger Classic Maya regional political systems and their relationship to war and conquest.

Few themes are more obtrusive in Classic Maya inscriptions and art than war, and we saw earlier that the "peaceful Maya" theory has long been abandoned. War was most intense in the 7th and 8th centuries, and I defer more detailed discussion of it until later because conflict has so many implications for the collapse. Here our concern is the extent to which war contributed to the emergence of Classic political systems much larger than the local Maya polity.

Essential to Maya royal presentation was the depiction of the king as warrior (Fig. 28). Successful participation in war probably marked the coming of age of presumptive rulers as a prelude to ascending the throne. Kings took great pains to portray themselves as war leaders and to boast of their exploits, much like the coup-counting of Plains Indians in the western United States. They particularly celebrated themselves as personal captors of illustrious enemies, most of whom were speedily sacrificed. Sajals and other nobles are shown aiding the king in his battlefield exploits, presenting their own captives to him, and receiving rich rewards in return. Hieroglyphs associated with war monuments name the protagonists of such scenes, record specific kinds of war-related events, and show the emblem glyphs of the centers involved. One recent survey by Mark Child identified 107 war-related incidents involving 28 different centers, and surely this is just the tip of the iceberg.[37]

Some polities were traditional enemies for hundreds of years, and their kings had very long memories for political and military humiliations. A late monument raised by Ruler 7 at Piedras Negras, for example, celebrates the 8th-century defeat of Pomona. This victory is recorded as redressing a military reverse that occurred 237 years earlier, when the king of Pomona exacted tribute from the ruler of Piedras Negras. Ruler 7 did not have long to savor his dynastic revenge, because just a few years later he was crushed by forces from another long-time adversary, Yaxchilan, and his kingdom collapsed.

28 *Lintel 8 from Yaxchilan shows its 8th-century king Bird Jaguar (right) and an elite subordinate (left) seizing captives on the battlefield. These captives were themselves of high rank, as indicated by the name glyphs on their thighs (the one held by the king is called Jeweled Skull).*

Although there were many such local wars, the huge centers of Calakmul and Tikal, according to epigraphers Simon Martin and Nikolai Grube, were major antagonists in a series of long-term confrontations beginning in the 6th century. Martin and Grube think that through conquest, intimidation, and alliance Calakmul ("Snake Kingdom") and Tikal dominated many other local polities, creating "superstates," as they called them, whose influence extended over tens of thousands of square kilometers.[38] If polities of this size existed, they would have included hundreds of thousands of people (note, however, that even the largest proposed Maya "superstates" would have been about the size of a respectable northern Italian city-state of the early 15th century).

In retrospect, Simon Martin reflects that "superstate" was probably a poorly chosen word. It prompted some other Mayanists, and much of the popular press, to imagine effective central administration of multiple polities over huge territories. A more apt label might be "superpower," referring to a loose political system with several levels of rulers who do not share power equally. Again the Aztecs provide a handy analog. Wherever Cortes and his soldiers traveled, they discovered that people commonly identified not only their own local "señor natural," but also a distant and much more powerful ruler, by whom they meant Motecezuma, king of Tenochtitlan. Significantly, they tended to see this overlord as more exploitative and less legitimate than their local natural lord. As the Aztec empire expanded, new terminology was required to distinguish new ranks in the imperial hierarchy. This was accomplished by adding the affix "*hue*" (meaning "elder, revered") to the local title of *tlatoani*, or "señor natural." Thus a *huetlatoani* dominated several lesser kingdoms, and at the top were the great *huehuetlatoani* – the hegemons of Tenochtitlan and Texcoco who were masters of the whole "empire," which was really a kind of grand confederacy with effective bureaucratic administration only in its highland core region.

No one thinks that even the most powerful Maya rulers ever wielded comparable supreme power (though kings of Calakmul might have aspired to it), but textual information does support a more modest "superpower" structure based primarily on the expansion of elite networks in which there were greater and lesser kings – in fact this is what Martin and Grube originally envisioned. The well-documented wars among Tikal, Calakmul, and their proxies reflect vast geopolitical conflicts, not mere local squabbling. The strongest kings, such as those of both Tikal and Calakmul, adopted a special title, *kaloomte'* (formerly glossed as batab), that implies something like "high king," "overlord," "overking," or "paramount." Although we do not know exactly what kaloomte' denotes, like the more glorified Mexican titles it suggests far-flung royal influence and/or domination of small kings by big kings (or at least ambitious royal pretentions in this regard).

Conflicts were certainly widespread. Warriors linked to Calakmul attacked centers as distant as Palenque, 240 km (150 miles) to the west. Conquest glyphs proclaimed the victory of one center over another. Some defeated kings paid tribute to the victors, while others fled from their courts and sought refuge elsewhere. Some kings were "possessed" by others, according to glyphic expressions (*yajaw*), and on occasion a captured monarch was kept alive for years, presumably to serve his conqueror. Still other kings undertook royal rituals, including accessions, under the supervision of emissaries and sometimes royal visitors from afar (their roles signaled by the term uchab'jiiy – "he who supervises" – attached to their names). Sajals ruled centers under the control of distant dynastic masters. Whatever their ideological rhetoric, clearly not all kings were sovereigns. Personal ties between dominant and subordinate rulers even endured after death; in fact the most frequent statements of dependency link living lords to their deceased overlords.

Unfortunately, no Maya narratives tell us unambiguously what all this means. Did the rulers of Calakmul, Tikal, or Caracol create mini-empires enabling them to meddle in the dynastic affairs of their underlings, and impose upon them not only military and political allegiance, but also the obligation to pay tribute in labor and goods? Did subordinate rulers and peoples regard themselves as political vassals in new kinds of regional kingdoms that were administered in new ways from a few great capitals? Some Mayanists believe so. On the other hand, what we dimly see in the texts might reflect much looser, opportunistic coalitions of allies, in which even the most powerful partners could not easily control the others. Certainly some Maya kings subordinated weaker rulers, who for a time were their political dependents or clients, and we will examine one such regional polity in our later discussion of the Dos Pilas kingdom. Alternatively, weak polities might have actively sought alliances with powerful ones.

Arlen and Diane Chase propose regional polities intermediate in scale between city-states and "superpowers."[39] They argue that the optimal size of such a polity was about 60 km (37.5 miles) in radius (about a two-day walk) based on considerations of transport and military marching capacity, and data from known warfare incidents. They think that a single capital and dynasty could exercise effective economic and political control over such a territory – roughly 8000–11,000 sq. km (3000–4200 sq. miles) in extent. Hegemonies several times larger for strategic purposes and tribute situationally emerged, but were inherently unstable.

My own opinion (widely shared) is that although complex hierarchies of centers sometimes existed, none of the erstwhile hegemons was able to impose an effective central administration over a multi-center polity and dominate it for very long, even on the regional state scale. By the beginning of the 8th century, as we shall see, the Tikal-Calakmul standoff seems to have been resolved in Tikal's favor, but it left behind a legacy of antagonisms that perpetuated warfare and kept the Maya Lowlands politically fragmented on the eve of the collapse. Nevertheless, at all times there was sufficient interaction among Maya polities so that the whole Lowlands constituted a larger system of sorts, an important point to remember when we review ideas about the collapse.

How the Classic Maya Made a Living

In late May of 1848 General Sabastian Lopez de Llergo gazed out anxiously from a high tower atop the cathedral of San Ildefonso at Merida, the colonial capital founded by Francisco de Montejo to herald the successful conquest of Yucatan. To Llergo and the other frightened Mexican refugees holed up within the city's walls it seemed that after 300 years the Maya were about to take back their ancient homeland. Scattered Indian uprisings during the previous year had blossomed into a full-fledged rebellion. Insurgent bands burned many Yucatecan towns, ranchos, and haciendas, slaughtered the ladino and mestizo inhabitants they captured, defeated the government's soldiers and militia in the field, and finally obliged most of the survivors to barricade themselves in Merida, which seemed likely to be the last bastion of resistance. But then came a seemingly miraculous reprieve. Scouting columns sent out from Merida and the few other strong points still held by government forces reported that the Maya rebels had melted away, enabling the Mexicans to regain the military initiative.[40]

What saved Merida was an ancient imperative more powerful for agricultural people than any other – cultivating their fields. Despite the desperate entreaties of their batabs to press home an almost certain victory, the rank and file of the Maya armies knew that to stay and fight, and even to win, was ultimately futile if they and their families starved. At the end of May the clouds gathered, the weather turned warm and sultry, and hordes of ants suddenly swarmed, all harbingers of the onset of the summer rains. The son of one rebel leader later recalled that, "When my father's people saw all this they said to themselves and to their brothers 'Ehen! The time has come for us to make our planting, for if we do not we shall have no Grace of God to fill the bellies of our children ...'. Thus it can be clearly seen that Fate, and not white soldiers, kept my father's people from taking T'ho [the Maya name for Merida] and working their will upon it." As their ancestors had done for more than 4000 years, the Maya soldiers went home to plant maize. Although their initial offensive failed, their descendants resisted the Mexicans until 1911 in eastern Yucatan, a protracted conflict called the Caste War.

Nothing illustrates more dramatically that for the Maya, as for agrarian societies the world over, the most fundamental economic activity was wresting a living from the soil, a task that absorbed the bulk of the time, energy and skill expended by most people. Exactly how the Classic Maya made a living is so central to our concepts of the collapse that I purposefully left it to the end of our overview. Although 16th-century Maya farmers grew many field and orchard crops, by far the most important was maize. Maize was not just their basic dietary staple (with beans as a distant second), but also a magical plant, associated with the origins of both humans and the world itself – literally a gift of the gods. Close attention to the great god-driven seasonal cycles of nature revealed when the time was propitious for planting. Growing maize was far more than an economic necessity; it was also a recurrent, almost mystical act of consecration. Even today Maya subsistence farmers believe that a family that cannot produce its own maize supply is not quite respectable, and a poor farmer is seen as lacking energy, judgment, and motivation.

Unlike their counterparts in some other regions of the ancient world, most Maya farming households were probably able to rely on their own knowledge, skills, tools, and labor to carry on their productive activities, as many of their descendants still do today. Such traditional farmers usually develop conservative agricultural strategies that guarantee predictable returns for their families. Where management of crucial aspects of agriculture is in the hands of outsiders who have other economic motivations and less knowledge of local conditions, decisions about land use may have wasteful and destructive consequences. This is an important point, because as we shall see later one explanation for the Maya collapse is environmental degradation related to food production.

Even with simple tools and family labor, long-fallow swidden fields produced reliable crops as long as populations were small. Staples grown in outfields were widely supplemented by produce from "kitchen gardens" immediately around houses (these are used by the modern Maya and have been detected archaeologically at Ceren). As we saw earlier, overall population densities were under 20 people per sq. km (52 per sq. mile) in Yucatan when the Spaniards arrived. In fact, as late as 1940 there were still only about 416,000 people in all of Yucatan (today the capital, Merida, has roughly this many). Because shifting cultivation did minimal damage to the fragile tropical forest ecosystem it could be sustained over long intervals. Anyone visiting Uxmal, Becan, or other Maya tourist centers in late April or early May will still see the sky blackened by the immense pall of smoke produced by swidden farmers. Although two or more crops could be grown in some places, the main crop was always sown in May or June. If the gods sent the rains on time and the cornfields escaped damage by storms or insects, the Maya would prosper.

Did the Classic Maya have a similar agricultural economy? For many years most Mayanists simply assumed so. As early as the 1880s a few archaeologists became interested in the remains of small ancient houses, and remarked on their abundance around the monumental cores of Tikal and other places.

Generally, however, no one paid much attention to the landscape outside the great centers, or thought it necessary to investigate how many farmers lived on it and how they made a living. Then in 1921 an intimation that the Classic Maya were different cropped up from an unlikely source – one P. W. Schufeldt, an employee of the American Chicle Company, which then had a concession northwest of Tikal. From Schufeldt's camps hundreds of chicleros fanned out through the great forests between June and February each year to tap the sapote tree (*Achras zapota*), which exudes a latex-like sap called chicle used at that time to make chewing gum (hence the modern brand name Chiclets). Realizing how intimately these men knew the forest, Sylvanus Morley posted reward notices in chicle camps, saloons, and brothels, offering a $25.00 bounty for each large ruin they led him to, and $5.00 for each new inscription.

Schufeldt needed to feed his chicleros and their mules so he burned off hundreds of hectares of forest to plant maize (each man required a daily ration of one kilogram, or 2.2 lbs, and each mule twice as much). Cursory examination even of areas far from major Maya ruins revealed that "... these clearings, upon being burnt, showed every evidence that practically all the land had been occupied by small house-sites and land under cultivation." When Schufeldt pointed out the apparent demographic implications to Morley, who happened to be passing by, the archaeologist "... violently disagreed with me on this point. He told me he would not dare to return to Cambridge with any such theory."[41]

Shortly thereafter, in the 1930s, archaeologists began to carry out systematic surveys of the landscapes around major centers. Results supported Schufeldt's observations, and evidence from many subsequent survey projects tells the same story – ancient Maya house remains are extremely numerous, and by implication population densities were much higher, than those of the 16th century.

Just how many Classic Maya were there by the 8th century? Impressed by the apparent abundance and density of houses, in 1946 Morley ventured a seat-of-the-pants estimate of between 13.3 and 53.3 million for the whole Yucatan Peninsula (he favored the former figure). Another noted Mayanist, George Brainerd, did some crude calculations based on maize production and came up with a maximum figure of 5 million for the peninsula as a whole (we will see later why these estimates matter). I personally think even Morley's low estimate is ludicrously large, but in any case the critical population issue for us concerns those regions most affected by the collapse, the southern Lowlands. This area has not been completely surveyed, but it is clear that even in the 8th century its population had a "patchy" distribution, very dense in some places, with others virtually uninhabited. Using settlement data from a core region of some 22,712 sq. km (8835 sq. miles) that includes Tikal, Calakmul, and other large centers, geographers have recently advanced the figure of about 2.6–3.4 million for that zone alone.[42] Adding on another million or so to account for Belize, the western Maya Lowlands, and the southeastern frontier around Copan, we end up with a total in the 4–5 million range. I think we still overestimate ancient Maya populations, but even we cut these figures in half (which would get the total for the whole Lowlands pretty close to Brainerd's estimate), there were still plenty of Maya. As a recent demographic overview notes, "What differentiates ... the well-studied Peten region from most other early civilizations is the very large territory covered by high-density rural population."[43]

As we shall see later, some archaeologists who favor high populations believe that during the 8th century overall densities in some regions were in the range of 200–300 people per sq. km (518–777 per sq. mile).[44] Others opt for smaller estimates on the order of 100 people or so. Reconstructing ancient population size and density from settlement remains is notoriously difficult, but if even the lower figure of 100 per sq. km (259 per sq. mile) is accurate in order of magnitude terms, which seems likely, it much exceeds the capacity of long-fallow swidden cultivation. It was the very suggestion of such numbers that greatly perturbed Morley. This realization touched off a long-standing and heated debate – how did the Classic Maya support so many people, and what kinds of effects did Maya land-use have on their landscapes? These issues lie at the core of one of the major explanations for the Classic collapse, and I will consider them in detail later. Right now a couple of brief observations are sufficient.

To answer the first question, some archaeologists surmised that the ancient Maya depended heavily on staples such as manioc or sweet potatoes that have higher yields than maize and do not deplete soil nutrients so quickly, or on orchard crops such as ramon (*Brosimum alicastrum*) that are native tropical forest species. Dependence on such foods would contrast sharply with the practices of recent Maya villagers, whose measured caloric intake of maize is very high. Fortunately, new methods of light stable isotope analysis of bone samples from ancient Maya burials allow paleonutritionists to estimate the contribution of maize and other nutrients to the ancient diet. Results of such studies done on large skeletal samples suggest that maize contributed at least 50 percent (and usually considerably more) of the calories consumed by various Maya populations. One of the largest such studies, carried out by

David Reed on bone samples from 90 individuals from Copan, estimates that maize constituted about 62–78 percent of the daily caloric requirement, very close to that determined for Maya villagers in the 1930s by biomedical assays.[45] Apparently where the Maya diet is concerned the present is a reliable guide to the past.

As to the second question, archaeologists and geographers have long known that in some regions there were large systems of ancient agricultural terraces that might have allowed more intensive forms of cultivation without attendant erosion or other destructive processes. Even more significant to some are drained fields detected in swamps that have been compared (incorrectly) to the immensely productive *chinampas* built by the Aztecs on their lake bed to provision Tenochtitlan and other cities in Central Mexico. Later we will see that both these alternatives are problematical, and that there is plenty of evidence that the Maya radically and destructively altered their environments through burning, erosion, and deforestation.

Our greatest ignorance about Maya farmers concerns the ancient political economy. As the geographer B. L. Turner put it, we do not know "... the degree of control the elite exerted on the farming units, how decisions were made, how labor was organized, how production was distributed, the level of control of agricultural trade and the benefits derived from the farming units. Could Maya farmers trade or market surplus beyond that taken/given to the elite? Did farmers own their land or have inherited access to it? Were elite "taxes" fixed or not? Were cropping decisions controlled by communities? What did the farmer gain by supporting the elite, or did they gain?".[46] Perhaps the most important issue here is land-ownership. The anthropologist Robert Netting has long studied modern agrarian people who possess their own agricultural resources, whom he calls smallholders.[47] Such farmers are packed so densely on their landscapes that they cannot easily enlarge their holdings, which are also their homes. Instead they use simple technology and household labor to intensify their production in sustainable ways. Their motivation to do so heavily depends on the fact that they own their principal capital resource (land) and its products, and can make their own decisions about how to use them. Ancient Maya farmers might have had very different relations to land, and hence fewer incentives to husband their resources as carefully.

❧ ❧ ❧

Following up on our airliner analogy, it should be clear by now that our blueprints for ancient Maya society are still pretty incomplete. We discern the general "design" of Classic civilization much more clearly than we did a generation ago, and some of its constituent parts stand out in sharp relief. But despite the quasi-historical information from art and inscriptions, we still know very little about many aspects of Maya society fundamental to understanding the collapse. Each archaeologist has his or her own wish-list about what they would most like to know. My own would include answers to these questions:

1 What were the social and political relationships among Maya people of different ranks, both within and among particular polities?

2 How did Maya people (of any rank) assert claims to basic resources, especially land and labor, and transfer those claims through time?

3 Exactly what did Maya kings and lords do, if anything, to effectively govern or manage their kingdoms, subjects, subsistence economies, and agricultural landscapes? And lastly,

4 Did kings control essential flows of staple goods such as food? To what extent did they control the production, acquisition, and redistribution of prestige goods? To what extent did they manipulate either of these classes of goods as political currency?

Later on I hope to show why I think these issues are so important.

Something else should be clear as well. I remarked earlier that some archaeologists and anthropologists exclude the Classic Maya from their rosters of ancient civilizations. If we stick to the general definition of civilization developed in Chapter 3, the Maya really are a sort of wild card. Although their Great Tradition was extremely impressive and durable, it remains uncertain whether they were very state-like in terms of political organization. Falling back on more traditional evolutionary yardsticks such as Gordon Childe's, they had writing and monumental architecture, but court centers instead of true cities, comparatively little complex economic specialization, and quite possibly they lacked well-developed social classes (if we admit the possibility of the kin-based model). In short, the Maya are difficult to pigeonhole in terms of our present categories of cultural evolution, and this makes it more difficult to think about what might ultimately have happened to them. If our concern is only the reconstruction of the Classic Maya as a unique set of societies, then this issue of terminology is of course irrelevant. If, on the other hand, we try to understand them in a broader comparative perspective, as I believe we must, we have to face up to it because it colors our perceptions of the collapse.

Our overview of the Classic Maya reveals many continuities with the 16th-century Maya, but also some profound differences. Chief among the latter, in my opinion, is the distinctive institution of Classic Maya rulership, with its powerful, charismatic, and even quasi-supernatural rulers. Nothing like this existed in northern Yucatan when the Spaniards arrived, nor were there court centers comparable to Tikal, Palenque, or Copan, centuries old and rich in Great Tradition dynastic trappings.

Impressive as these Classic polities were, they also shared with the 16th-century Maya the characteristics of political fragmentation and, I believe, comparative economic self-suffiency, especially insofar as their all-important agrarian economies were concerned. Despite all the alliances, marriages, gift exchange, and other interactions that created and maintained a shared elite tradition, most kingdoms remained effectively or potentially independent segments in the wider context of Classic civilization. To put this in more evolutionary terms, each polity was adapted to the unique features of its natural and social environments.

These are important differences. As we shall see later, the Classic collapse in one sense manifests itself as the downfall of a distinctive form of ritual-political leadership. And the decentralized relations among Classic polities means that some sort of shock to a single, central authority or institution is out of the running as an explanation. Each Maya kingdom was instead buffered to a degree from what happened elsewhere. As will become apparent later, the collapse was in fact a protracted, patchwork process consistent with such segmentation.

To return to the simile with which we began this chapter, our overview of Classic society has focused on its dominant components, much as we could describe the parts of the crashed airliner. But remember that an airliner, when functioning properly, is a system in a comparatively "steady" state (apart from consumption of fuel, etc.). Maya civilization by contrast was in constant historical flux. The number of kingdoms and dynasties on the landscape multiplied, populations increased, warfare became more intense, and kingship took on new dimensions, to name just a few. Maya civilization, unlike our airliner, was never in any kind of stable equilibrium.

But we are getting ahead of our story. The premise of this chapter has been that we can't make much sense out of what happened to the ancient Maya unless we admit what we know and don't know about them. Equally true is that we can't develop explanations for the collapse without a firm grasp of the actual patterns of decline that set in during the 8th and early 9th centuries, an issue to which we now turn.

– 6 –

IMAGINING THE COLLAPSE

ANYONE READING THE LITERATURE on the Maya collapse will certainly be impressed, and probably somewhat bewildered, by the variety of explanations advanced over the years to account for it. One reason for this plethora of opinion is that the problem itself has shifted in time, chimera-like, in tandem with our ever-more mature reconstructions of the nature and culture history of Classic Maya society. Our principal concern in this chapter is identifying the pattern of the collapse – i.e., what needs to be explained – which we must obviously be clear about before we discuss proposed specific causes. I first trace basic perceptions of the collapse prior to World War II and then show, through a series of short case studies, that "mini-collapses" were commonplace throughout Maya history and prehistory, ending up with a brief overview of the patterns of the collapse as we understand them today.

Stephens and Catherwood's depictions of lost cities like Copan certainly triggered the first widespread perception that there was a big historical puzzle to be explained, but long before their time there were intimations that something dramatic had occurred in the Maya Lowlands.

A Landscape of Ruins

The first Spaniards in Yucatan had no systematic grasp of the Maya past, although they knew that their Indian subjects possessed a rich tradition of oral and written lore that was in some sense historical, and was associated with dates in the sophisticated calendar called the Count of the K'atuns. Landa heard many such stories from his informants, and they were also recorded in the postconquest native documents called the Books of Chilam Balam, penned in Spanish by native scribes of the towns of Chumayel, Mani, and Tizimin.

Featured in these accounts (albeit somewhat confusingly) were the rise and fall of great northern capitals and confederacies centered on Uxmal (the earliest), and later Chichen Itza and Mayapan. Such places, so the legends and histories said, were once ruled by influential families who for a time held sway over far-flung subordinate polities or confederations. Wars, intrigues, invasions, factional jealousies, and other catastrophes eventually brought down these great powers, resulting in the fragmented political landscape that Cortes, Montejo, and other Europeans encountered in the early 16th century. Some of these events, most notably the fall of Mayapan, were said to have occurred not long before the Spaniards arrived. From very early on there was, then, the sense of a Maya past characterized by multiple mini-collapses, a theme to which I will shortly return. For now, the important thing to remember is that the 16th-century Maya themselves conceived their own history, or at least the later segments of it, to be episodic, unstable, and fraught with famines, wars, the failure of leaders, and the migration of peoples.

More durable manifestations of the pre-Spanish Maya past were the thousands of abandoned buildings standing in cornfields or enshrouded by forest. Bishop Landa, who directed the demolition of some of them, remarked that

> If Yucatan were to gain a name and reputation from the multitude, the grandeur, and the beauty of its buildings, as other regions of the Indies have obtained by gold, silver, and riches, its glory would have spread like that of Peru and New Spain. For it is true that in its buildings and the multitude of them it is the most remarkable of all things which up to this day have been discovered in the Indies; for they are so many in number and so many are the parts of the country where they are found, and so well built are they of cut stone in their fashion, that it fills one with astonishment.[1]

Landa and his contemporaries knew that some of these impressive structures, such as the huge temples and palaces falling into disrepair all around them in the Colonial capital of Merida, had been used right up until the Spanish conquest. Others could be associated with various of the earlier polities recorded by Maya scribes. Landa himself left us one of the first drawings of an ancient Maya ruin (Fig. 29) – the great temple, or "Castillo," at Chichen

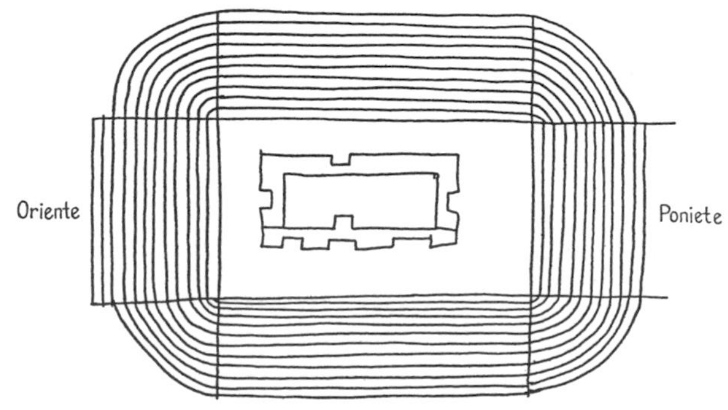

29 *The Spaniards were impressed by the many huge, abandoned Maya buildings they saw in Yucatan. Bishop Landa included this simple plan of the great pyramid at Chichen Itza in his* Relación. *It is one of the earliest European images of Maya architecture.*

Itza – today perhaps the most popular tourist attraction in all of Yucatan, where the shadow of a great serpent is said to be visible descending one of its four stairways each year at the vernal equinox.

Most of the buildings and sites that Landa knew from northern Yucatan long postdated the Classic Maya, but about the same time there materialized tantalizing hints that the impressive architectural tradition he so admired was not confined to the north. In 1576 the Spanish official Diego Garcia de Palacio, traveling on government business along the *camino real*, or royal road, that linked Guatemala with Honduras, took the trouble to visit the ruins of Copan. There, some 640 km (400 miles) southeast of Merida, Palacio recorded a local legend that the city had been founded and built by migrants from Yucatan, a claim that he found plausible because of the similarity of the architecture in both regions.

To account for the number and scale of all these abandoned buildings, Landa surmised

1 that Indian lords built incessantly to keep commoners occupied

2 that the Indians were so devoted to their deities that they compulsively built unusual numbers of religious structures

3 that Indian communities were often moved and so new buildings were frequently erected

4 that earlier Indians were superior in size and strength to their descendants, and so built excessively by comparison.

All these ideas reverberate in various ways in later conceptions of the collapse, namely the notion of oppressive elite demands for labor, the unworldly spiritual devotion of the Maya, and the degeneration of Maya culture from Classic to Postclassic times. Notice that Landa did attribute the ruins to the ancestors of the Maya who lived all around him, anticipating John Lloyd Stephens in this conclusion by 300 years. But neither the histories nor the abandoned buildings suggested to the 16th-century Spaniards any sort of comprehensive "collapse," lacking as they did the concept of "Mayaness" as an inclusive ethnic or cultural label, or the idea of "civilization" itself in our modern sense. Not until Stephens and Catherwood's publications were the abandoned buildings presented to the wider world as remnants of a great, independent New World civilization, plausibly created by the ancestors of the living natives of the Yucatan Peninsula, which had flourished for a time and then suddenly and catastrophically perished.

Of course Stephens and Catherwood had no more inkling of the antiquity of Maya culture than the Spaniards did, nor of the time scale over which this newly discovered civilization had grown and declined (although many, often contradictory stories were told by the Indians). In fact, Stephens's historical acumen most conspicuously deserted him when he speculated that many ruined centers had been occupied right up to the Spanish conquest, and only abandoned under the pressure of the invaders. He even entertained the romantic notion that somewhere, deep in the unexplored forests of the interior, there survived thriving cities where kings still ruled, architects still raised temples and palaces, and scribes still carved inscriptions. As we know, the Itza conformed to this fanciful notion for a time, but they were snuffed out in 1697, long before Stephens's day. There were no more "living ancients" to be found. Fortunately, the Classic Maya themselves left us chronological clues about these issues in the hieroglyphs so accurately recorded by Catherwood and later Maya explorers.

Collapse and the Long Count

Earlier I briefly mentioned the Long Count (sometimes also called the Initial Series) calendar as one of the most impressive intellectual achievements of the ancient Maya and, along with writing itself, the most celebrated element of the Classic Great Tradition. It also provided the first detailed chronological insights concerning the collapse.

Who actually invented this calendar is uncertain because the earliest large monuments with Long Count inscriptions are found outside the Maya Lowlands proper, in places like the Pacific coast of Guatemala and the Gulf Coast of Mexico. Whatever its origins, the Classic Maya perfected the Long Count and used it in the most complex and comprehensive ways. Our modern understanding of the Classic collapse derives heavily from hundreds of Long Count dates, especially those carved or painted on large stone monuments. Because stelae, altars, tombs, and buildings are difficult to move, and so likely to be in or near their original archaeological contexts, dates found on them are particularly useful in working out local or regional chronologies. We must now consider in more detail how this ingenious system of tracking time works.

Conceived most simply, the Long Count is a linear count of days that began, as all such calendars do, at a particular point in time. As it happens, the Maya began their day count on or about 11 August 3114 BC in our terms, long before anything we would call Maya civilization existed.[2] Exactly why Maya priests and scribes chose this particular temporal milestone remains unknown, although some scholars think it represents the day of creation of the most recent great interval of Maya cosmic time (some archaeologists think it originated at Teotihuacan). In any event, the Long Count yields an absolute chronology because each day has its own unique designation, unlike the days in the 16th-century Maya Count of the K'atuns, which recur every 256 years.

Our own Gregorian calendar, of course, is also essentially a count of days beginning at a different culturally significant starting point. But remember that in actual practice we do not simply number days in succession, and neither did the Maya. Not only would dates expressed this way be unwieldy, but they would be divorced from our own experience of shorter and more meaningful cycles, especially those of the sun, moon, stars, planets, and seasons. So instead we lump our own days (the shortest solar cycle) into longer repeating intervals of weeks, months, and years. The longest such cycle that we normally pay much attention to is the century, which of course is no kind of natural cycle at all, but rather reflects the importance of our decimal system of mathematical reckoning. We tend to think of the century as a self-contained numerical cycle in which, after a passage of 99 years, the date "clicks back" to an initial 0 point, as it recently did when AD 1999 shifted to 2000.

We commonly express dates in terms of this 100-year interval, as when we say that an event occurred in '63, or '89, or in the decade of the 90s. These abbreviated numbers are ambiguous, because they recur (remember the recent Y2K computer panic if you don't think this matters). But we also give each century its own distinct sequential number. The new millennium began the 21st century, which is another way of saying that 20 centuries, each consisting of 100 units of 365.24 solar days, had elapsed since our calendar began (ignoring the "correction" of 10 days made when the Julian calendar shifted to the Gregorian calendar in AD 1582). Only when we attach the consecutive year number does each date become an absolute one: the notations 3 January or '89 by themselves are historically confusing because they repeat themselves, but 3 January 1989 is a unique date.

The Maya accomplished much the same thing by using different intervals of time consistent with their vigesimal counting system. In expressing a particular Long Count date the Maya began with the most basic unit, the day (called a *kin*), and then lumped days together into longer periods called *uinals* (20 days), *tuns* (360 days), *k'atuns* (7200 days), and *baktuns* (144,000 days – there are even larger units, but these are the most fundamental ones). Notice that the progression of units here is always by a factor of 20 except for the tun, which is not 400 as expected (20 x 20) but rather 360 (20 x 18), an accommodation Maya mathematicians probably introduced to better fit this unit to the length of the solar year (even so, Long Count reckonings accumulated an error of more than five days each year). The "completions" of various of these periods had great significance to the Maya. Many Classic monuments were dedicated on auspicious days that ended a particular k'atun, or often a shorter five-year period called a *hotun*, and human events were related to these milestones.

Long Count dates consist of a sequence of numbers that expresses these cyclical periods in order. For example, a sequence that runs 9 baktuns, 15 katuns, 6 tuns, 14 uinals, and 6 kins indicates the collective number of days that has elapsed since 11 August 3114 BC; the resulting date happens to correspond to 1 May AD 738 in our own system. According to the conventional notation used by Mayanists, such a date would be written 9.15.6.14.6. What makes the date unique is the beginning number 9, which signals that it falls into the great ninth baktun cycle of the Long Count, just as the first two numbers in 1989 tell to which century the '89 refers.

Because Maya scribes and priests were inveterate intellectual tinkerers, things are not actually as simple as I have presented them. Many Long Count dates are accompanied by other supplementary information, including corresponding dates in various Maya calendrical and astronomical cycles. Also, by the 7th century most Long Count dates were expressed in an abbreviated (Period Ending) form that used a much-reduced number of glyphs. But all these complexities need not concern us here.

By the beginning of the 20th century scholars knew how to read Long Count dates, which provided a chronological framework for the ancient Maya, even though there remained some uncertainty about exactly how to convert them into Gregorian dates (two major competing correlations 260 years apart were hotly debated, and the most likely one determined only in the 1950s and '60s through radiocarbon analysis). Despite the fact that the corpus of Maya dates floated a bit with respect to the Gregorian calendar, it was still internally consistent. By the 1930s and 1940s enough dates had accumulated to demonstrate that almost all of them fell into the great baktun cycles 8 and 9 – that is, between 6 September, AD 41 (the beginning of Baktun 8) and 13 March, AD 830 (the end of Baktun 9), according to the dominant correlation, and the one we now know to be best.

In his grand 1946 opus *The Ancient Maya*, Sylvanus Morley compiled the chart shown in Fig. 30, which revealed how the use of the Long Count changed through time (these data are constantly upgraded and, as we shall see, still central to our conceptions of the collapse). Morley's chart shows that very few "cities" had dates earlier than AD 400. Two hundred years later the

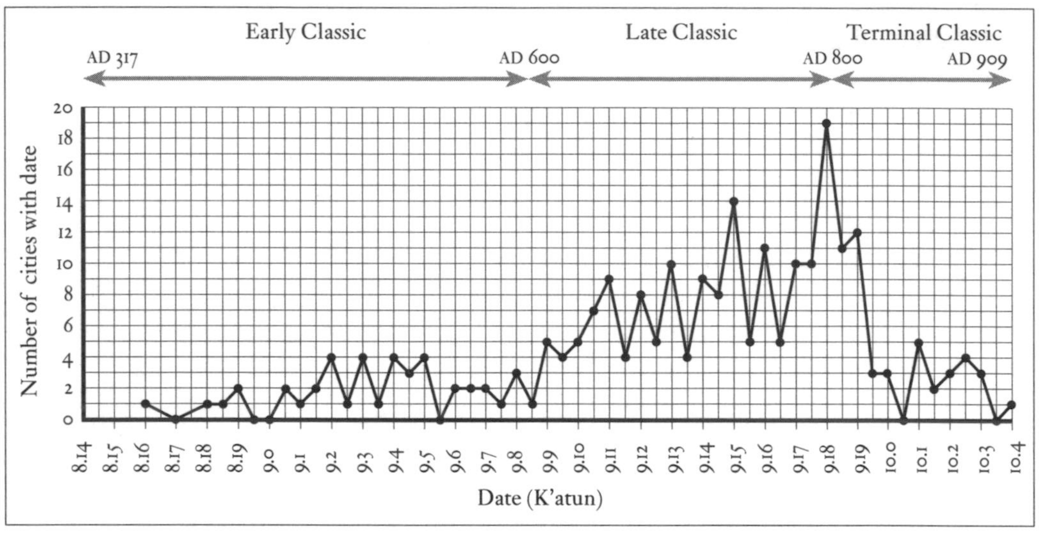

30 *Sylvanus G. Morley compiled this 1946 chart of Long Count dates. At that time it was our principal evidence concerning the chronology of the growth and decline of Classic Maya civilization, and also served to anchor archaeological sequences elsewhere in Mesoamerica in absolute time.*

practice of erecting Long Count monuments began to accelerate, reaching a peak both of frequency and spatial distribution during the three k'atuns between about AD 731 and 790. This interval was consequently believed to encompass the aesthetic and intellectual peak of the Classic Maya. There followed a precipitous drop-off in monument erection, with only a few dates at a handful of centers falling as late as the beginning of Baktun 10.

In 1946 the associated inscriptions could not be deciphered, and most dates seemed to refer only to the endings of calendrically significant periods of time. Morley and other scholars accordingly assumed that monuments were carved with a record of astronomical and ritual activity similar to that found in the surviving Postclassic codices. Fluctuations in Long Count use thus became the principal barometer of the fortunes of Maya civilization, revealing that after several hundred years of slow incubation beginning in Baktun 8, Maya polities experienced a major florescence for two centuries, and then slid abruptly into the abyss of the collapse. Note that the emphasis here is not on a particular Maya center or polity, but assumes instead that there was some kind of larger Classic Maya "system" throughout which stresses and crises were communicated.

Morley's chart was a crude barometer, of course, because it lumped together data from many different centers, and necessarily ignored the many inscriptions that were illegible, as well as the many impressive sites that had no dates at all.[3] It also took into account only one kind of information; at many centers such as Tikal and Altar de Sacrificios we now know that building activity and other signs of elite vigor seem to have slacked off well before the last Long Count inscriptions were made. Kings certainly continued to function at some centers after the last dated monuments were raised, because references to them are found at other sites, often on pots or bones or other non-monumental objects. Nevertheless, the chart did reveal the principal trends of overall growth and decline. Mayanists could finally, it seemed, resolve the issue that had plagued Stephens and Catherwood – when were places such as Copan or Palenque abandoned? According to the Long Count correlation favored by Morley, a crisis seemed to have overwhelmed many centers near the end of the 8th century AD.

Nor was this all they knew. It was pretty clear that the earliest monuments were raised in the Peten region of northern Guatemala, within a radius of 30 km (19 miles) or so of the great center of Tikal and its nearby precocious neighbor, Uaxactun. By AD 790 the "stela cult," as it was sometimes (incorrectly) called, manifested itself over the whole central and southern Maya Lowlands, from Palenque on the northwest to Copan on the southeast, an area of roughly 150,000 sq. km (about 58,000 sq. miles).[4] Because dated stela and altars could be contextually associated with temples, palaces, tombs, ball courts, and other buildings, they provided insights into the gradual development of architectural and artistic styles, and also placed rough chronological limits on the ceramic sequences that archaeologists were beginning to develop for various sites and regions.

Excavations at some centers showed that the largest investments in monumental architecture were made just before Long Count dates ceased, and some building projects seemed to have been abandoned even before they were finished. During this time of crisis local ceramic traditions became impoverished or disappeared altogether, and in some places there were intrusions of "foreign" (i.e., non-local) pottery styles. All these lines of evidence taken together suggested both the rapid collapse of the political structure of Classic Maya society over an enormous area and a huge population decline following closely upon it, often characterized as one of history's greatest demographic catastrophes. According to two early influential Mayanists, Thomas Gann and J. E. S. Thompson, over a period of about a century

> the entire population of all the cities deserted their homes in the south, with the enormous investment which these represented in temples, palaces, monoliths, and private houses, and migrated into the peninsula of Yucatan, where the soil was

> poor, and unsuited for the cultivation of maize, and the water supply almost non-existent, owing to the absence of rivers and lagoons.... It was indeed very much as if the entire population of the towns in the English southern counties were suddenly, for no apparent reason, to migrate to the north of Scotland.[5]

To sum all this up, the perception of the collapse generally shared by most (but not all) archaeologists just before World War II was as follows:

After five centuries of sustained development many Maya ceremonial centers, presided over by priest-theocrats devoted to esoteric astronomical and calendrical rituals, suddenly began to experience a profound crisis. At one "city" after another the compulsive construction of monuments and buildings and the use of Long Count dates ceased, without widespread signs of obvious violence. All this happened over a period of several generations around AD 800 (or possibly 260 years earlier). Although not all centers and regions were afflicted at exactly the same time, the widely shared Great Tradition during the "period of uniformity" ultimately rendered all equally vulnerable to this destructive process. Most of the devoted swidden farmers who had sustained these centers also disappeared within a few decades of their abandonment, although a few squatters still lived among the ruins, depositing their trash in the bat-infested rooms of palaces, moving, defacing, or repositioning some the carved monuments of their ancestors, and making offerings, even as the forest reclaimed the ruins. Refugees from the Classic Maya "Old Empire" of the central and southern Lowlands founded the "New Empire" cities of Postclassic times, located only in the northern half of the Yucatan Peninsula.[6] This scenario, or something very much like it, remains for many people the standard perception of the Classic Maya collapse to this day.

Evidence about the nature of the collapse accumulated before World War II had two major and very obvious problems. First, it derived almost entirely from research at the great Classic regal-ritual centers (then erroneously thought to be vacant ceremonial centers) and so reflected an elite, or more properly theocrat-focused, top-down, perspective about what happened to the Maya. Here we have a good example of making sweeping arguments on the basis of very limited data, a practice that is particularly pernicious, although often unavoidable, among archaeologists. Even in Morley's time, however, some Mayanists recognized this danger. In 1937 the husband-and-wife archaeological team of Oliver and Edith Ricketson, pioneers of some of the first studies of outlying small Maya houses, attacked the abandonment theory based on monument dates, arguing that just because these ceased one could not assume that the whole southern Lowlands was deserted. J. E. S. Thompson, another towering figure in the field, wrote in 1940 that "It is now clear that the interval spanned by inscriptions on monuments bears no relation to the actual occupation of a site."[7] Thompson knew that centers such as Tikal and Uaxactun were occupied in Preclassic times, long before the advent of Long Count dating. More to the point, he also knew that there was plenty of ceramic evidence indicating continued settlement in various regions long after the abandonment of the core complexes of large architecture. As he later sarcastically put it:

> The view has been widely held that when the great Maya ceremonial centers of the Central area ceased to function at the close of the Classic period, that is about AD 900 or shortly thereafter, the whole of the population deserted the region or was wiped out by some unknown catastrophe. It has been further supposed that the great core of the central area embracing most of the great ceremonial centers, misnamed cities, reverted to forest and remained virtually uninhabited for a millennium until awakened from sleep, like some sleeping beauty of the tropics, by the machetes of chewing-gum gatherers and the kisses of archaeological Prince Charmings.[8]

He concluded, quite correctly as we shall see, that "... at the close of the Classic period the Maya peasant did not die, he only faded away. The question is how long and how complete was that demise."

Thompson and the Ricketsons did not object to the idea of the Classic Maya collapse itself. They knew that something dire and dramatic had indeed happened, in accordance with Tainter's "recipe" for the general collapse of civilizations. Clearly there had been a total breakdown of whatever form of central organization the Maya possessed, a corresponding cessation in the most important Great Tradition markers, and ultimately a demographic failure. Instead, they realized that our attempts to explain this decline were methodologically flawed because we lacked a comprehensive grasp of what had happened and over how long a time. Abandonment of whole landscapes at the same time as kings disappeared, for example, would require a different set of explanations than the gradual decline of an outlying population long after the demise of dynastic rule. Archaeologists needed much more information, and of new kinds, before they could be certain about exactly what the pattern of the collapse really was.

The second big problem was that until World War II effective research had been restricted to a handful of centers, most notably Copan, Piedras Negras, and Uaxactun, that together provided our primary windows into this mystery. Little or nothing was known about Tikal, Calakmul, Becan, and scores of others. Given assumptions about the "uniformity" of Maya Late Classic culture, it was easy to assume that one could extrapolate from the few known places to the whole central and southern Lowlands. No one anticipated the enormous variety among centers and regions that Mayanists have since been documenting. There is no one "typical" pattern for the collapse because there is no one "typical" center or region. And we know that there were local or regional disruptions of Maya civilization almost from its inception.

Pre-Classic Puzzles

In my experience, many people think one Maya ruin is much like another. Someone off a cruise ship being squired around the ruins of Chichen Itza often assumes that this great center was contemporary with, say, Tikal, far to the south in the Guatemalan forests, and was abandoned about the same time. The following section on mini-collapses allows us to set straight some of this chronological confusion, and more importantly shows that the course of Maya history was never a smooth one, even in the earliest times.

Imagine that a denizen of 8th-century Tikal, the most powerful of all the Late Classic Maya kingdoms, undertook a journey on foot to the great rival center of Calakmul, located about 100 km (63 miles) to the northwest. After a walk of three days or so along forest paths skirting large swamps, our hypothetical traveler might well have found himself, much like Stephens and Catherwood at Copan 1000 years later, gaping at the sight of many huge, ruined buildings scattered over several square km.

What the Maya called this ancient place is unknown, but since its discovery in 1926 archaeologists have called it El Mirador. Almost inaccessible until recently, El Mirador is arguably the largest center ever built by the ancient Maya. Some of its buildings rise as high as 18 stories, projecting so far above the tree canopy that they look like a line of low hills, a landmark used by aircraft pilots today as a navigation guide. Archaeologists only began to investigate El Mirador systematically in the 1960s, and before that time it was assumed to be a Classic site because of its enormous size.

We now know that El Mirador thrived at the end of the Preclassic period, from about 200 BC to AD 150, or during the end of the 7th and the beginning of the 8th baktuns.[9] A few glyph-like carvings and stela-like monuments are found there, along with fragmentary inscriptions dating to around 200 BC. Unfortunately these glyphs are so far unreadable, and are not associated with dates of any kind. Nevertheless, general conventions of art, monuments, and architecture prefigure those of the Classic Maya Great Tradition, and the inscriptions might be ancestral to later Classic writing. Perhaps this far back in time Classic Ch'olti'an, the prestige language of the later inscriptions, was still a living tongue. However this may be, at El Mirador we enter genuine Maya "prehistory" compared to later Classic centers, but even without names or dates for rulers, we know Mirador must have had very sophisticated social and political organization.

Even more impressive is that El Mirador was not alone in this part of northern Guatemala. Scattered around it over an area of approximately 1100 sq. km (425 sq. miles) in a region of hills and *bajos* called the Mirador Basin, are many other Preclassic centers. Most impressive is Nakbe, situated about 12 km (7.5 miles) to the southeast. There archaeologists have uncovered evidence of modest settlements dating back to 1000 BC or even earlier, and indications of impressive structures and monuments by about 600 BC. Nakbe's greatest buildings, which range up from 30 to 45 m (98–148 ft) high, were erected between about 400 and 200 BC, and Late Preclassic sculptors created some of the earliest Lowland Maya stelae showing gorgeously attired human figures. Nakbe seems to have experienced its major growth somewhat earlier than El Mirador, which later probably eclipsed it as the dominant center.

The whole landscape is richly networked with raised roadways, or sacbes, connecting Mirador, Nakbe, and other early sites. Clearly there was an enormous regional system here in Late Preclassic times that we still barely understand. These precocious developments in the Mirador Basin are important because they show that the foundations of complex Maya society lie much farther back in time than archaeologists believed possible just a few decades ago. For me, in fact, what this Late Preclassic explosion represents is almost as mysterious as what happened to the Maya in the 8th century.

Most significant for us now though, is that Nakbe and Mirador, and perhaps much of the whole basin, seem to have been abandoned by about AD 150–200. We have scant information as yet concerning exactly how or why this regional mini-collapse took place, although a possible fortification wall protecting three sides of El Mirador hints at intensive levels of warfare. Some archaeologists and paleoclimatologists also believe that during the end of the Preclassic there was a drier and warmer interval or outright drought that adversely affected agricultural production, particularly at northern centers. According to the most recent lake sediment analyses, this drought occurred roughly between AD 125 and 210, which seems somewhat late to account for the decline of Nakbe.[10] For whatever reasons, many thousands of Late Preclassic people who originally lived around El Mirador, Nakbe, and some other Preclassic places are thought to have disappeared in a process labeled the

"Preclassic Abandonment" by some archaeologists. Even though we have virtually no settlement information from habitation sites surrounding these centers, the Preclassic Abandonment is often characterized as a great demographic disaster, almost on a par with the collapse proper hundreds of years later. Alternatively, of course, this might have been largely a political collapse, in which most people remained on the landscape (although currently invisible to us) or simply moved away, presumably attaching themselves to burgeoning centers elsewhere.

Not that this abandonment was permanent. Our hypothetical visitor breaking his journey at El Mirador would certainly have found food and lodging, because the site had been reoccupied by Late Classic settlers, who built residences around and atop many of the Preclassic buildings. In a sense they were like the 16th-century citizens of Rome, living amongst the architectural splendors of a more expansive and vigorous culture. We can only guess at what these Maya people thought about the decaying grandeur all about them, and whether, like Stephens and Catherwood at Copan, they drew somber moral lessons from it.

I could cite other examples of this apparent Late Preclassic time of troubles. Impressive centers were also abandoned at Komchen in far away Yucatan (albeit more gradually), and at Cerros in northern Belize. From our perspective these events look like hiccups in the otherwise stately emergence of Classic Maya civilization, but to the lords and farmers who experienced them these mini-collapses, which probably occurred over at least several generations, were undoubtedly very disorienting and disruptive, and plausibly associated with severe mortality and migration.

While the end of the Late Preclassic period brought troubles for many Maya people, it was a time of opportunity and innovation for others. And while continuities with later Classic culture are obvious, some archaeologists and epigraphers see the Late Preclassic/Early Classic divide as the emergence of a new social order. In particular, as epigrapher Simon Martin puts it, "The relationship between kingship and the cosmos was rearticulated, even reconceived."[11] Such a reformulation in kingship might be reflected in the Classic Maya penchant for identifying certain individuals as "founders" of dynasties, even though earlier leaders or distinguished persons are mentioned in the inscriptions. Dangerous as it is to judge from archaeological remains alone, there seems to be a shift from generalized modes of Preclassic authority to a Classic emphasis on individual and highly assertive kings – a syndrome that began in the Maya Lowlands just about the time El Mirador declined, and that finally crystallized in its most extreme form after AD 600.

Whatever caused these Late Preclassic upheavals, they signal severe stresses in Maya society long before the more celebrated "big" collapse of the 8th and 9th centuries.

Troubles at Tikal

Morley's chart of Long Count dates gives us an overview of the Maya Lowlands as a whole, but tells us little about what happened at any particular center or polity. As more and more archaeological evidence accumulates, we know that some of them had extremely disjunctive histories, with intervals of apparent prosperity and power alternating with periods of stagnation, decline, political upheaval, and perhaps even partial abandonment. Our mid-8th-century Tikal traveler, had he been a literate person of historical bent, might have told just such a story about his own kingdom. More recently Peter Harrison has summarized the tale in his book *The Lords of Tikal* (1999).

While not a power on a par with Nakbe or El Mirador, Tikal flourished in Late Preclassic times. During the 1960s, University of Pennsylvania archaeologists dug an enormous trench right through a complicated mass of temples and platforms called the North Acropolis that delimited the north side of Tikal's Great Plaza, and that for centuries had served as the necropolis of early kings. Lurking beneath the architectural accretions of Early and Late Classic times they discovered evidence of monumental Late Preclassic precincts, and buildings of similar age are found elsewhere at Tikal as well.

Perhaps benefiting from the collapse of the mighty powers of the Mirador Basin, Tikal quickly emerged as the most precocious and dynamic capital of Early Classic times. Her first ruler for whom we have any sort of historical documentation is one Yax Ehb' Xook (First Step Shark), credited in later, retrospective inscriptions as the founder of Tikal's dynastic sequence (although other local notables are recorded as preceding him). This founding king probably lived around AD 90, but not until two centuries later was the first Long Count date recorded on Stela 29 in AD 292, inaugurating a sequence of such dates at Tikal spanning 577 years.

Dated stelae and altars shortly thereafter began to appear at other nearby centers. One interpretation of this pattern is that Tikal's royal family spun off cadet branches that founded their own independent or quasi-independent kingdoms. Another is that the "stela cult" proved such a successful adjunct to Maya statecraft that it was avidly adopted by unrelated rulers for their own purposes. In either case, the "package" of Maya Great Tradition elements underwent a great Early Classic florescence under the evident aegis of Tikal.

Much of what we know about Tikal's history derives not only from its own inscriptions, but also from those commissioned at other centers, whose rulers both celebrated their connections with Tikal and their military triumphs over her.

By the 4th century Tikal was firmly under the control of kings of the local Jaguar Claw dynasty. Around AD 350 one of these rulers, nicknamed Great Jaguar Paw (or Jaguar Claw I), built a palace that was carefully enlarged and preserved by his successors. It formed the kernel of Tikal's Central Acropolis, the largest intact royal palace compound, eventually excavated by Peter Harrison in the 1960s (Plate 12). New glyphic interpretations show that a bit later, in AD 378, there was some sort of foreign interference in Tikal's dynastic succession, apparently engendered by the arrival of a great lord from the distant metropolis of Teotihuacan in highland Mexico or one of its other outposts (at this time Tikal was much smaller, both as a center and a polity, than the Late Classic behemoth it became by the 8th century, and much more vulnerable to such outside influences). Despite these intrusions (or perhaps because of them), Tikal continued to thrive, her prestige and influence reaching as far afield as Copan, whose founder Yax K'uk' Mo' had clear Tikal connections in the early 5th century. Inscriptions thereafter began to drop off in frequency at Tikal, and then something very curious occurs: no dated monuments were erected between AD 562 and 692.[12] Nor, according to Harrison, is there much evidence for the incessant construction so common before and after this time.

Archaeologists do not know exactly what to make of this puzzling 130-year interlude. It is not quite a prehistoric time, because ceramic vessels and other small objects in tombs provide short texts, and there are many "outsider" references to Tikal. One of these, carved on Altar 21 at Caracol, about 85 km (53 miles) away to the southeast, indicates that Tikal suffered a serious defeat in a major war in AD 562. Unfortunately the altar is badly eroded, so it is not clear exactly who the victor was. Because of the location of the text, for a long time Caracol seemed to fit this role, but epigraphers Simon Martin and Nikolai Grube now suspect that Calakmul is a more likely possibility. In either case, Caracol was surely part of a mighty coalition dominated by Calakmul, which emerged about this time as the major player in the intense "superpower" wars that engulfed much of the Maya Lowlands in the late 6th and 7th centuries. For a long time Tikal came off a distinct second best in these protracted struggles, so the hiatus in monument dates seems partly occasioned by military defeat and weakness. Although there is no convincing evidence that Tikal was ever sacked in any destructive way, its political and economic power was broken, or at least severely strained. The kings who maintained themselves in this shadowy political twilight were probably required to pay both tribute and obeisance to victors elsewhere. Arlen and Diane Chase, who have worked at Caracol for many years, believe that some of Tikal's people were actually obliged to move to Caracol, which grew mightily after AD 562.

One can imagine the political gloom at Tikal as embarrassed elite factions licked their wounds, bickered over the much-devalued rulership, and incessantly plotted to regain their ancient prestige and privileges. According to some epigraphers, the absence of dated monuments can in part be attributed to systematic destruction caused by internal dissension. At least one Tikal ruler of the time became a refugee: he and his entourage found shelter hundreds of km away at the court of Janaab' Pakal of Palenque, whose own kingdom had also been ravaged by the attacks of Calakmul and its allies around AD 611.

Eventually a champion arose to restore Tikal's fortunes. In AD 682 a new dated monument was finally erected by Jasaw Chan K'awiil, who in that year assumed the lofty title of *kaloomte'* (Plate 13). Obviously a vigorous leader, he commenced some important building projects and then, in the crowning military achievement of his reign, conquered Calakmul in AD 695 and captured its archrival king. Thereafter Calakmul never again raised a monument celebrating military events. This once mighty capital went into a long decline, reminding us that not all Late Classic centers and polities reached their peaks just before the collapse. Jasaw Chan K'awiil lived for almost another 40 years, completing before his death Temples I and II, the most famous buildings at Tikal.

During the 1970s archaeologists thought that the internal crisis documented at Tikal was just the local manifestation of a much more widespread malaise in Classic Maya society. Then-available Long Count dates collectively seemed to suggest a downturn in the fortunes of many centers in the three k'atuns between AD 534 and 593, an interval formally christened the Hiatus, and believed by some to signal another convulsive reorganization of Maya society at the Early Classic-Late Classic transition. Some archaeologists proposed that it was brought about by the collapse of trade relations with Teotihuacan, which declined as a pan-Mesoamerican power about that time, and others noted its correlation with a postulated period of unusual climatic disturbance – increased cold – that was a worldwide phenomena. Some writers have tried to link this climatic shift with a postulated 6th-century volcanic "supereruption" in Java, claimed to have wrought havoc over much of the earth.[13] In 1974 Gordon Willey wrote a famous paper in which he surmised that this Hiatus was a "little collapse," a sort of "rehearsal" for the big collapse of the 8th and 9th centuries.[14]

Research done over the last 25 years, and especially the decoding of the inscriptions, has put to rest this idea of an all-encompassing Lowland decline by revealing how varied the careers of various major centers and polities were, and by filling in some of the apparent gaps at Tikal itself. About AD 628, for example, right in the midle of this supposed hiatus, the Tikal king Animal Skull was buried in a fine tomb beneath a large memorial temple. And Calakmul, Tikal's archenemy and oppressor, in fact thrived during the years of Tikal's political eclipse, along with many other kingdoms including Copan, far away in Honduras.

Nevertheless, the same research has abundantly documented similar episodes of apparent internal discord and inertia at many sites, although these are not well-aligned chronologically. Gaps in the sequences of dated stelae erection at some centers are comparable in length to that at Tikal. To return to Caracol, there are no dated monuments for at least 69 years (and perhaps as much as a century) after AD 702. Elsewhere, as at Palenque, there are shorter but still appreciable intervals when no king seems to be in charge, almost certainly reflecting interregnums caused by dissension over royal succession. As more detail emerges out of the inscriptions, it becomes clear that the course of life ran smooth in very few major Maya polities, especially in Late Classic times when kings were most numerous and most fractious in the southern Lowlands. Nor were northern polities immune from troubles.

Boom and Bust in the Puuc Hills

One of the first great ruins to impress the Spaniards was Uxmal, located about 80 km (50 miles) south of Merida. Of its greatest building (now called the House of the Governor), an early visitor observed in 1586 that

> [it] is of extraordinary sumptuousness and grandeur, and like the others, very fine and beautiful. It has on its front, which faces the east, many figures and bodies of men and of shields and of forms like the eagles which are found on the arms of the Mexicans, as well as of certain characters and letters which the Maya Indians used in old times – all carved with so great dexterity as surely to excite admiration.... The Indians do not know surely who built these buildings nor when.... The truth is that today the place is called Uxmal, and an intelligent old Indian declared ... that, according to what the ancients said, it was known that it was more than nine hundred years since the buildings were built. Very beautiful and strong they must have been in their time, and it is well known from this that many people worked to

build them, as it is clear that the buildings were occupied, and that all about them was a great population, since this is now evident from the remains of many other buildings, which are seen from afar.... [15]

As it turns out the "intelligent old Indian" overestimated the age of the great buildings by several hundred years (but he did came pretty close to the founding date of Uxmal). We now know that the House of the Governor and the other great buildings were abandoned by their traditional Itza lords around AD 1000, although the ruins remained a pilgrimage center well into the 19th century, when Stephens and Catherwood saw offerings made in the still-intact vaulted rooms of its temples and palaces.

Pilgrims and tourists continue to come to Uxmal from afar. On one visit I saw an elderly Japanese gentleman singing a Shinto chant that echoed off the walls of the great four-sided compound called the Nunnery Quadrangle (Plate 26). Just a short distance away a couple of North American tourists had coaxed George, their large German shepherd, to climb the steep stairway to the top of the Pyramid of the Magician (Plate 27). Dogs being what they are, going up was easy, but coming down was another matter. When I left, George was still peering stubbornly down at his owners, 30 m (98 ft) below. To this day I wonder how George ever got off that pyramid.

I have visited Uxmal many times, renting a car in Yucatan's capital, Merida, and then driving south across the scrubby northern plains. I like this journey because it takes me through sleepy colonial towns where traditional Maya houses, with their neatly whitewashed stone walls and thatch roofs, stand amidst household gardens. Seeing them is a reminder of the living reality behind the ruined ancient places that I spend so much of my own time excavating. During the dry season this trip is very hot and dusty, and the countryside is monotonously flat. Then, after about an hour, an escarpment looms up on the horizon. This little chain of hills, which runs for a distance of about 160 km (100 miles) from northwest to southeast, is known as the Sierrita de Ticul. Sometimes more grandiosely called the Puuc "Mountains," it is only about 100 m (328 ft) high, but compared to the level terrain of the north it does seem rather imposing. After an easy ascent one drops down into the Puuc region of Yucatan (Fig. 31), a zone of hummocky limestone hills covered with low, mostly deciduous tropical forest and some grassy savannas. Extending over about 7500 sq. km (4700 sq. miles), this part of Yucatan was almost unpopulated in colonial times and has comparatively few inhabitants even today. During the Late and Terminal Classic, in sharp contrast, this tranquil countryside was packed with Maya farmers and the great centers they supported.

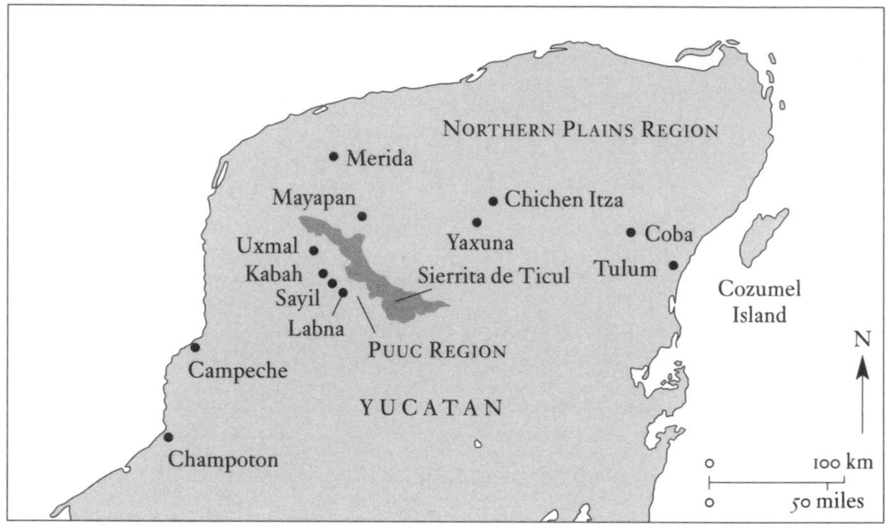

31 *Major sites of northern Yucatan. Uxmal, Sayil, and Labna are in the Puuc zone, while Mayapan and Chichen Itza are on the northern plains. Note how close the big Puuc centers are to one another.*

Like the Mirador Basin, the Puuc region experienced a dramatic ancient boom and bust cycle, leaving behind one of the most impressive landscapes of ruins found anywhere in Mesoamerica. Puuc sites were part of the "New Empire" constellation of polities that Morley and others thought were founded after the collapse in the south. Sayil, Labna, Kabah, and most famous of all, the massive Uxmal, all cluster so close to one another that in 1842 Stephens was able to explore several "cities," as he called them, in only a few days. When these places were occupied and the vegetation cleared away, the monumental buildings of one king would have been visible from those of his neighbors. Now busloads of tourists visit these imposing places each day, wandering about the great buildings that have been heavily reconstructed by the Mexican government. Few of them realize that the remains of thousands of smaller structures and residences, most unmapped and unexcavated, are hidden by the dense, woody undergrowth.

Such abundant signs of ancient settlement are surprising because the Puuc region presents severe challenges to human occupation. On the plus side it gets a reasonable amount of rain – about 1100 mm (43.3 in) annually – and has some of the finest soils in the northern part of the Yucatan Peninsula, capable of growing two crops per year under favorable conditions. On the other hand, the dry season is very long – from about November through April

– and rainfall (along with crop yields) may fluctuate by 30 percent or more from "normal" each year. But by far the greatest obstacle is the lack of surface water. On the flat northern plains of Yucatan the water table is near the surface in most places, and is exposed where the uppermost bedrock has collapsed (producing the steep-sided sinkholes called *cenotes*, from the Maya word *dzonot*) or reached by artificial wells. Cenotes do not exist in the Puuc hill country, and the water table is generally at least 35 m (115 ft) down, and in many places well over 100 m (328 ft). Surface water accumulates in bowl-shaped solution hollows or *aguadas* (natural ponds) during the rains, but these are few and scattered. Most are too small and shallow to serve many people or to hold water permanently throughout the dry season, although some aguadas were modified to make them more useful by the ancient inhabitants.

People who live in the Puuc region accordingly go to extreme lengths to get water. During their explorations Stephens and Catherwood visited a great cave named Xtacumbi Xunan, about 2.5 km (1.6 miles) from the village of Bolonchen. Throughout the wet season the people of Bolonchen got water from nine shallow, natural seeps in the town, but these dried up when the rains ceased. During the dry season all water was obtained from the cave, necessitating a torch-lit descent down ladder-like scaffolds to pools of water hundreds of feet below the surface. There the Indians filled pottery vessels and calabashes, then climbed laboriously back up the ladders and made the long, hot, walk back to their houses. For months Xtacumbi Xunan provided the only water for Bolonchen. And one needs a lot of water. I have never felt so hot anywhere, nor drunk so much, as when visiting Uxmal in April. No wonder that as late as 1979 overall population densities in the Puuc country were barely one or two people per sq. km.[16]

Archaeologists know that a few Maya always lived in this harsh and forbidding territory, but only after about AD 700 was there a major influx of population, apparently from several directions. Fundamental to the success of this colonization effort was a kind of cistern called a *chultun*, a bottle-shaped underground chamber dug into the soft limestone bedrock underlying the harder surface crust. When plastered on their interiors, big cisterns of this kind collected thousands of gallons of water during the rainy season, and served as holding tanks throughout the dry months. Most ancient households had one or several of these tanks, and had their plazas and courtyards laid out to drain rainwater into them. Some refurbished chultunes are still used today.

By AD 750 a vigorous regional variant of Maya culture had blossomed among the dry Puuc hills, its hallmark a distinctive set of architectural features embodied in its fine masonry buildings. Puuc architects and masons created extremely fine wall surfaces veneered with smooth, well-cut limestone blocks (Fig. 32). Their most impressive buildings, which are palace-like structures rather than lofty temples, are decorated, especially on their upper façades, with extremely complicated mosiac designs made by assembling thousands of such blocks, pre-cut to fit the building plan. Designs include deity masks (particularly of the rain god Chaak), human figures, stylized house elements, and much decorative fretwork. Columns, used rarely in southern Classic Maya centers, often define doorways. Puuc builders set their stones in a hard matrix of durable cement, which, along with the comparatively dry conditions of the region, makes for remarkable preservation. Stephens and Catherwood marveled at the wooden lintels still supporting masses of masonry above doorways, and concluded, incorrectly, that most

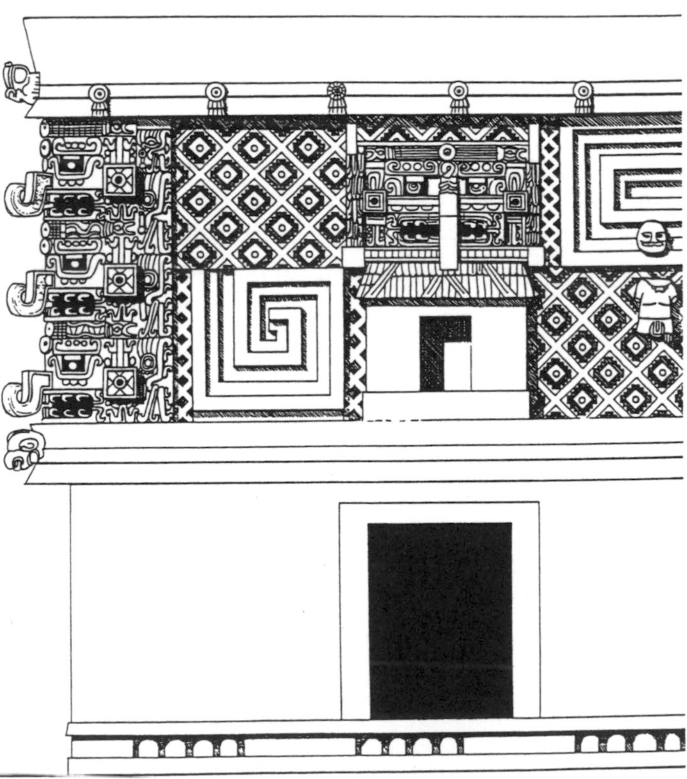

32 *The west building of Uxmal's famous Nunnery Quadrangle exhibits the use of complex mosaic sculpture typical of Puuc architecture. Note the small effigy of a common thatched house above the doorway.*

Puuc buildings had been built very late – perhaps not abandoned until the Spanish conquest.

The eclectic Puuc architectural style was widely admired by people elsewhere in Yucatan, and its distinctive elements were incorporated into buildings at many centers outside the Puuc zone proper, most notably on the northern plains. Nor was this fascination only a prehistoric one. Plaster casts of Puuc façades were displayed at the 1893 World Columbian Exposition in Chicago, where they impressed many architects, among them Frank Lloyd Wright, who borrowed Puuc designs for several of his own buildings.

It is probably no coincidence that the florescence of the Puuc centers occurred mainly between about AD 750 and 950, the very time when the great southern cities were collapsing (remember these dates – they will reappear later). For generations archaeologists have surmised that migrations from the south contributed to the explosive growth of the region, and there are many architectural and other continuities with the Classic heartland, although ceramic traditions are quite different. Unfortunately, because of the inordinate attention paid in the past to clearing and reconstructing large sites to attract tourists, we still lack the kinds of intensive, multi-faceted research for the Puuc region that has been so common since the 1960s farther south, and that can reveal details of cultural processes over time. Nevertheless, some promising starts have been made at Sayil by Jeremy Sabloff, Gair Tourtellot, and their colleagues, and the geographer Nicholas Dunning has completed an ambitious survey of some 725 sq. km (280 sq. miles) around some of the biggest centers.[17] Dunning identified a very complex settlement hierarchy, with six different levels of permanent, nucleated communities. The biggest sites have imposing masonry architecture and are typically spaced only about 6–10 km (3.75–6.25 miles) apart. Some of them are linked by raised ceremonial roads. And more so than most Classic Maya centers to the south, the Puuc capitals tend to have most of their supporting populations clustered closely around them.

Based on their surveys, Dunning and his collaborators conclude that Sayil, the archaeologically best-known of the big Puuc centers, probably had a population around AD 950 of just over 9000 people concentrated in the 4.45 sq. km (1.72 sq. miles) zone immediately around its monumental buildings, and another 8000–9000 living within a few kilometers' walk in any direction. Even more impressively, Dunning calculates that 210,000 people lived in his whole survey area, which works out to an overall density of 290 people per sq. km (751 per sq. mile), comparable to the most optimistic estimates for the earlier Classic Maya heartland to the south. I believe these estimates are too high (although much of the region has particularly good soils), but even so a landscape that was almost vacant in AD 700 had filled in remarkably in just two centuries.

Early on each major Puuc center might have had its own independent dynasty, but by AD 900 or 950 many archaeologists think that most came under the loose hegemony of Uxmal, far and away the granddaddy of them all. The core architectural complexes of Uxmal, which include such celebrated buildings as the House of the Governor, the Nunnery Quadrangle, the House of the Turtles, the Temples of the Dwarf and the Magician, as well as a large ball court, together cover a compact precinct of about one sq. km (0.63 sq. mile) and are all surrounded by a low stone wall. Outside the wall are other structures extending over a much larger area.

Uxmal falls into the penumbra of 16th-century Maya historical memory, which credits its foundation in the 8th century to an individual named Ah Kuy Tok Tutil Xiu. Because of the paucity of hieroglyphic texts at Puuc sites we possess little detailed information about the subsequent dynastic sequence, but fortunately some inscribed monuments were commissioned by a successor of Ah Kuy Tok Tutil Xiu called Lord Chaak, who rose to power between about AD 875 and 900. This king bore the old Classic title of k'ul ajaw and appears to have eventually dominated the political affairs of the whole region after defeating nearby rivals. Following earlier Classic Maya traditions Lord Chaak's parents are recorded in inscriptions, and he himself is shown on a famous stela resplendent in a feathered costume and standing on a jaguar throne, which in turn is supported by naked captives.

Much of what one sees today at Uxmal was refurbished, enlarged, or constructed by Lord Chaak's architects between AD 900 and 925, a time when they probably had access to unprecedented amounts of labor. Their crowning achievement was the most celebrated of all Puuc buildings – the enormous House of the Governor – a combination palace and administrative complex. Ironically, this ambitious statement of royal power in stone seems to have been almost the last one ever completed. Uxmal's latest dated monument – AD 907 – was erected during Lord Chaak's reign.

Details of Puuc chronology are still debated, in large part because the very few inscribed dates from the whole region provide no coherent pattern from which one can intuit either growth or decline. Between about AD 950 and 1000, however, the whole Puuc region seems to have experienced a dramatic political and demographic collapse (some archaeologists would place it slightly later). There is very little evidence for major Postclassic occupation in or around any of the major centers, although a few people using new forms of pottery continued to live in small residences at Uxmal and elsewhere, as they still did in the 16th century, when they placed images in some of the buildings and offerings made to them. If the research done at Sayil and its surrounding survey area is extrapolated to the whole of the Puuc zone, then some hundreds of thousands of people must have died or abandoned the landscape over a very short time. While not a debacle on quite the same scale as the southern Classic Maya collapse that began almost two centuries earlier, it is even more remarkable for its suddenness, and certainly just as dramatic.

From our present vantage point two factors seem to underlie what happened. First, the Puuc polities collectively (and especially after their possible confederation or unification under Uxmal) were one of three great Terminal Classic powers. A second was centered on Coba, in the eastern part of the peninsula, and the third on Chichen Itza on the northern plains. These last two were bitter rivals, often involving other allies and proxies in their wars. Almost certainly the Puuc centers were entangled in these struggles, which have left many archaeological traces. During the 1970s I excavated at three northern sites that were fortified around this time (although in the Puuc zone proper only Uxmal seems to have had fortifications).

Second, if Dunning's reconstructions of population and carrying capacity are reasonably accurate, there were all the makings of a population crisis in the late 10th century, because the whole area was demographically saturated in terms of indigenous agricultural productivity. In a region inherently prone to the risk of insufficient or ill-timed rain, there were just too many people on a landscape that had already been cultivated for 200 years or more. So spectacular is the Puuc boom and bust cycle that I like to think of it in terms of a biological experiment: a few microorganisms are placed in a petrie dish full of nutrients, they multiply wildly as these are consumed, then just as rapidly dwindle in numbers as resources dwindle.

On the human as opposed to bacterial level, of course, a process like this involves enormous political upheaval and also population movement, not just massive mortality. Faced with both military reverses and a deteriorating landscape, many residents of the Puuc zone no doubt attached themselves to more thriving centers on the northern plains, such as Chichen Itza. Distances are not great – Merida is only a three to four day walk away. And remember that something like this happened much earlier when the Mirador Basin was abandoned. In any event, the descendants of the Xiu lords who founded Uxmal eventually reestablished themselves in the north. One of them, as we saw before, was the powerful halach uinic of Mani when the Spaniards arrived in the country. At Mani and their other distant strongholds, though, the Xiu never forgot their ancestral place, and quite possibly made pilgrimages to it in good Mesoamerican fashion.

Chichen Itza and Mayapan

I must end up this section with a few brief words concerning the fates of Chichen Itza and Mayapan, bringing us full circle from the Preclassic mini-collapse to the eve of the Spanish conquest.

While the Puuc centers represented in some ways the last gasp of the old southern Classic tradition, many archaeologists see Chichen Itza, located some 120 km (75 miles) east of Merida, as a new kind of Maya phenomenon (Fig. 33). Although there are some quite early Long Count dates at the site, its main period of growth appears to begin in the mid-9th century, when many of its early structures were built in Puuc style. By AD 900 Chichen Itza's chief rival, Coba, seems to have been in decline, setting the stage for explosive growth that saw the construction of the huge four-sided pyramid called the Castillo (Plate 28), the sprawling Temple of the Warriors, the round astronomical tower called the Caracol, along with the gigantic ball court that dwarfs all others in Mesoamerica. These buildings and many others sprawl over an area of about half a sq. km (0.32 sq. mile) and are linked by a broad northern causeway to the Well of Sacrifice, one of the largest cenotes in Yucatan, from which many treasures of Maya art were dredged around 1900.

Sheer size apart, much of Chichen Itza's architecture is remarkable for sculptural motifs, including skull racks, warrior columns, and depictions of eagles eating human hearts, that are almost identical to those found at Tula, the imposing capital of the Toltecs (immediate predecessors of the Aztecs) in faraway northern Mexico, which, remember, probably represents one of the "Tollans" of Mesoamerican myth. So striking are these similarities (Plate 29) that direct contact of some kind is obvious, and archaeologists have been arguing for generations about just how the two great centers were linked, although there are few signs of the intrusions of Mexican peoples implied by some of the later Maya historical narratives.

Also found at Chichen Itza were highly detailed, panoramic murals (now sadly deteriorated) depicting battlefield scenes in which scores of warriors assault towns and drag away captives (Fig. 34). These are quite unlike the old Classic representations of war, which usually focus on one or several heroic persons – kings and nobles – and their personal exploits. By contrast, the Chichen Itza murals show battlefield panoramas with scores of participants and without much individual emphasis. Nor are there stelae or other monu-

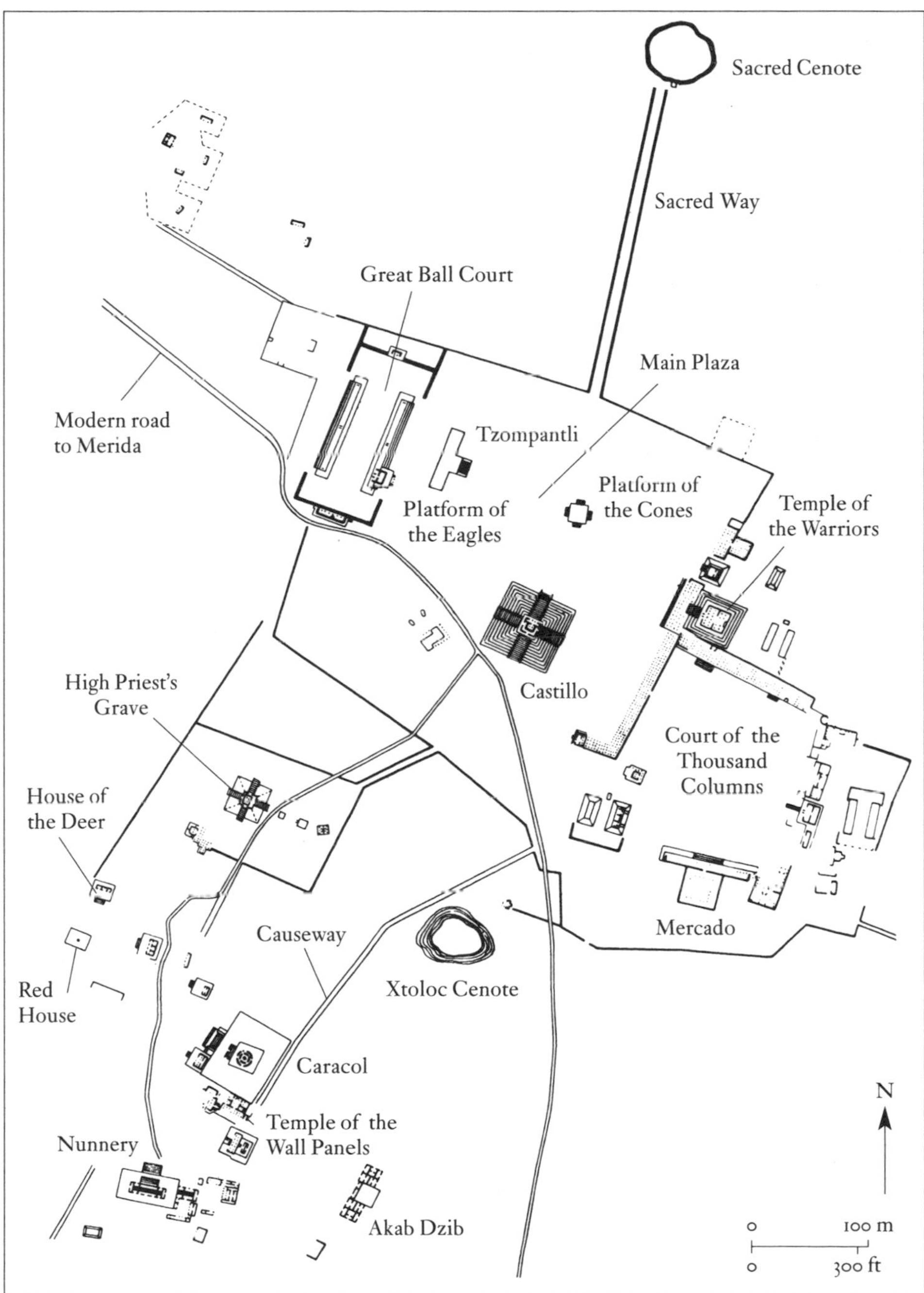

33 *Map of Chichen Itza. This great center dominated northern Yucatan from the 10th to the 13th century, and is a favorite tourist destination today. Among its attractions are Mesoamerica's largest ball court and sculptures that show affinities with highland Mexico.*

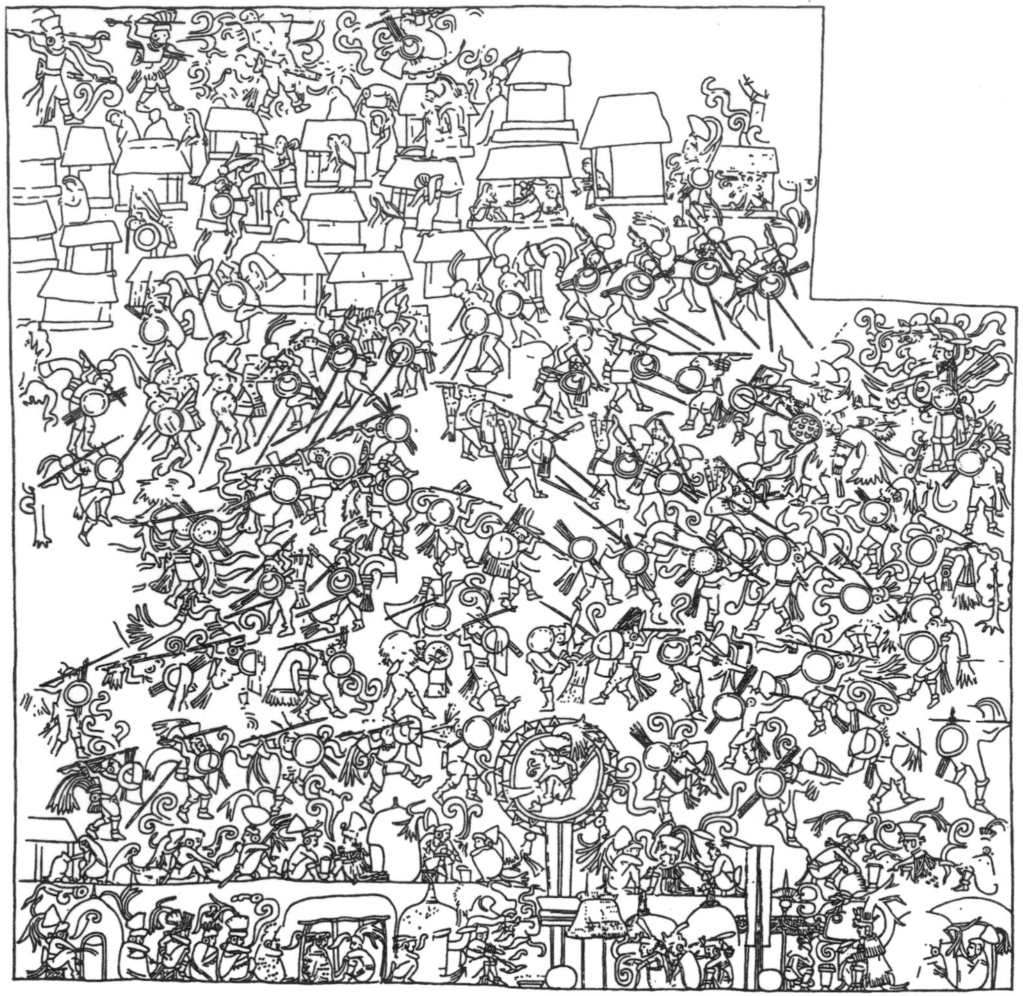

34 *Now-destroyed murals from the Temple of the Jaguars at Chichen Itza show rare panoramic views of Maya military conflicts. They differ markedly from Classic war depictions, which usually focus on individual kings, elite warriors, or prisoners, and seldom give any sense of how a large engagement was fought.*

ments that conspicuously glorify specific kings or a single dynastic line, and as at Uxmal monument dates are few, especially during the major florescence of Chichen Itza in the 10th century. All these things, along with much later native traditions, convince many archaeologists that new patterns of government, in which power was broadly shared, emerged at Chichen Itza.

Inscriptions as well as architecture show probable alliances with the Puuc centers during the 9th century, but after about AD 950 Chichen Itza became the dominant power in the northern peninsula as its rival Coba declined (whereas at Uxmal monument dates are few, and mostly fall before AD 906). By AD 1000, as the Puuc polities collapsed, she emerged as the supreme northern power, not only militarily, but as a mercantile emporium engaged in trading salt, obsidian, turquoise, gold, and other costly materials.

Sometime between around AD 1200 to 1250, according to the native chronicles, Chichen Itza in turn collapsed as a result of internal dissension. Landa heard from his informants that at Chichen Itza

> there once reigned three Lords who were brothers, and who came to that land from the west. And they brought together in these cities a great number of towns and people, and ruled over them for some years with justice and peace ... soon they split into factions, so wanton and licentious in their ways, that the people came so greatly to loath them that they killed them, laid the town waste and themselves dispersed, abandoning the buildings and this beautiful site....[18]

Signs of destruction reinforce these tales; one large structure, the Mercado, had a thatch roof that was apparently deliberately burned.[19] Despite the abrupt downfall of this once-great capital, Maya people long continued to make pilgrimages to the Well of Sacrifice, and a few local lordly residents extracted presents from them, long after the Spanish conquest. As late as 1697 the nobles of Nojpeten, deep in the forests of northern Guatemala, traced their own ancestry back to Itza lords who fled south from Chichen Itza over three centuries before.

Successor to Chichen Itza was Mayapan, located about 48 km (30 miles) south of Merida. There the Cocom family, implicated in the destruction of Chichen Itza, established another confederation in the early-to-mid-13th century. The name Maya that Columbus heard on his last voyage probably derived from Mayapan, and in the early 16th century some natives still called themselves *maya uinic*, or Maya men, in memory of their subordination to this capital.

To western eyes Mayapan is one of the most "urban" looking Maya centers because of the thousands of residential structures that crowd a zone of about 4 sq. km (1.5 sq. miles) entirely surrounded by a low stone wall. Estimates of the population are in the 12,000–15,000 person range, so densities were unusually high. The central precincts are dominated by a small and rather shabby copy of the Castillo at Chichen Itza, around which are arrayed smaller shrines and nobles' residences. Just who lived at Mayapan is unclear, but many of the inhabitants were probably elite people (some perhaps political hostages) from several confederated or subjugated polities who resided there at least part of the year along with their servants and retinues. Visitors to Mayapan today usually find it a distinct disappointment compared to Chichen Itza or Uxmal, and the native chronicles probably much exaggerate its political significance.

What happened to Mayapan is also uncertain. Archaeologists from the Carnegie Institution who worked there in the 1930s discovered that some of the buildings were purposefully destroyed. This squares with historical accounts that attribute the downfall of the site in AD 1441 to the rebellion of resident Xiu lords and their allies against the ruling Cocom lineage, depicted as depraved oppressors who imported Mexican mercenary soldiers from the Gulf Coast to shore up their evil reign. Passages in the books of Chilam Balam also implicate drought and hunger in the demise of Mayapan. We should probably not trust the details of these stories very much, but for whatever reasons, Mayapan presents us with one final case of abrupt abandonment only a few decades before the Spaniards arrived.

Some archaeologists have identified a so-called "Postclassic Abandonment" incident, said to have contemporaneously affected Uxmal and the Puuc region, Chichen Itza, and Mayapan in the mid-15th century.[20] To the extent that these abandonment episodes are chronologically understood (which is poorly; we have a firm date only for the abandonment of Mayapan) – they seem to have happened over a period of as much as 450 years.

We have reviewed a long litany of woes and misfortunes. Apart from providing a useful pretext for making an extensive traverse through Maya culture history, our review reveals that Maya political systems, regional populations, and probably the agricultural infrastructures that supported them both, were often fragile, sometimes vulnerable to situational weakness as at Tikal, sometimes to permanent failure as at El Mirador. Whatever the causes of such instability – war, overpopulation, climatic change – we can now appreciate that over the long run there were many mini-collapses and times of trouble, of which the "big" Classic collapse is only the best-known and most celebrated example. This is one reason why, as I said in the prologue, some of my colleagues don't like to use the word "collapse" to describe what happened in the late 8th and early 9th centuries.

T. Patrick Culbert calls Maya societies "growth systems" that had to keep expanding and changing in order to survive, never attaining any kind of equilibrium.[21] His characterization runs counter to the widespread image of stable and prosperous Maya kingdoms suddenly overwhelmed by catastrophes that they could not control. We will return to this point later, but the mini-collapses and troubles we reviewed certainly support Culbert's point.

Because the Maya – either as separate kingdoms or collectively – weathered so many intervals of apparent turmoil, an important question to bear in mind is "What was different in the 8th and 9th centuries that contributed to a more devastating and permanent collapse?"

We can also now see that the hypothetical tourist introduced at the beginning of this section, who thought of Tikal and Chichen Itza as contemporaries, would be far off the mark. Whatever crisis undermined Chichen Itza and the large polity it dominated occurred almost four centuries after the last dated monument was erected at Tikal – a period of time roughly equivalent to that separating us from the landing of the Pilgrims in Massachusetts, or the death of Queen Elizabeth I of England.

Our survey reveals several other important things that we must remember as we consider the Classic collapse more closely in the following chapters. First, because no monuments were raised for several generations at some centers such as Tikal does not mean that there were no kings and elites still active or that surrounding regions were depopulated, as Thompson and the Ricketsons realized long ago. Second, in the Maya historiographic tradition there is a strong tendency to associate social and political upheaval with the moral failures of leaders, as in the stories about the downfall of Chichen Itza and Mayapan. Third, Maya civilization at all times shows a remarkable capacity to reinvigorate or reinvent itself after its periodic stumbles, maintaining an essential continuity while subtly shifting its modes of organization and the expressions of its Great Tradition elements.[22] Some mini-collapses were parts of larger creative processes in the course of Maya history, as when (as seems likely) Tikal battened on the demise of the Mirador Basin polities, or colonists from the declining southern polities contributed to the growth of the Puuc region.

Closely related to this last point is that Maya people, including both commoners and elites, customarily "voted with their feet," by migrating to distant polities in times of trouble (or opportunity), or moving off to found new ones. I call this strategy to move or to switch political allegiance "flexibility of attachment." An anecdote concerning a recent migration of this kind presents a good example of what probably happened frequently in the past. While I was working in highland Guatemala in 1969, newspapers reported that some 400 farming families from El Salvador, where population densities were extremely high, had gradually traveled all the way to southern Belize, an underpopulated country where political conditions were much better. These migrants had no passports, traveled mostly by foot in small groups for distances of least 250 km (150 miles), and crossed two or three international borders on the way. Just such a process, protracted over a much longer interval, might have brought people from declining Classic centers such as Tikal or Uaxactun to the Puuc country, some 300–350 km (190–220 miles) to the northeast. And remember that according to their own stories the Itza of Nojpeten migrated south to Nojpeten around the time of the fall of Chichen Itza.

Finally, the abrupt demises of El Mirador, Nakbe, Uxmal, and Chichen Itza also reflect, I believe, the essentially non-urban character of Maya centers that we reviewed earlier. Courts of kings and elites were the most powerful forces of social gravity holding such places together, but these were fragile institutions, and when they declined so too did Maya "cities." Centers that have predominantly political and ritual functions are much more easily moved or abandoned than true cities, whose large, dense populations and complex webs of social and economic interdependence with each other and with their hinterlands create considerable geographical and historical inertia.

Patterns of the Collapse: A Current Perspective

To anticipate briefly the more detailed case studies that follow, we can now pose the question "How do our ideas concerning the Classic collapse differ today from those summarized above for the 1940s?" We need allude only briefly to the most important of these changes – the much better grasp of the nature of Classic society. Next in importance, we also have a much sounder understanding of chronology, so let us return to the Long Count dates so fundamental to Morley's conception, and to the crucial archaeological dimension of time.

About ten years ago I gave a series of lectures about the Maya aboard the *Stella Solaris*, a cruise ship plying the Gulf of Mexico. After one talk an elderly passenger approached me and confided that he had a single theory that would explain the extinction of the dinosaurs, the abandonment of the Pueblo cliff-dwellings of the American Southwest, and the Classic Maya collapse. What happened, he said, was that a great meteor had swept down from northwest to southeast, eventually plunging into the sea just off Yucatan. I pointed out that there was a bit of a time problem here, because dinosaurs became extinct about 65 million years ago, the cliff-dwellings were abandoned in the 14th century, and the Classic Maya collapse happened between about AD 770 and 900. Not at all nonplussed by my critique, the gentleman admitted that his theory "needed work," thanked me politely for my opinion, and headed toward the well-stocked ship's bar. The point of this anecdote is

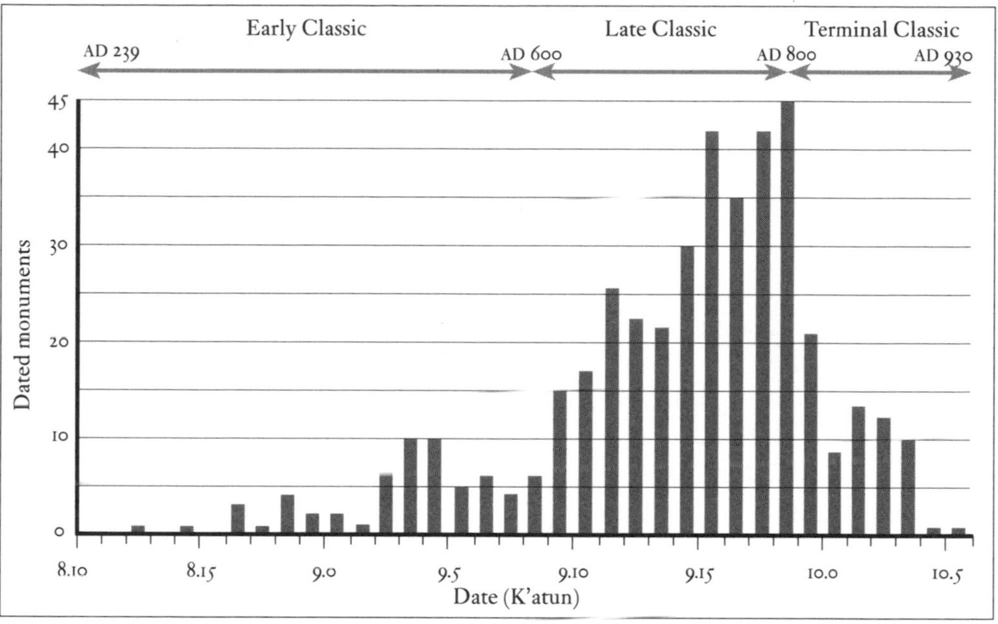

35 *In 1979 Sidrys and Berger devised this chart of dated monuments erected during each k'atun. It tells much the same story as Morley's earlier chart, but by 1979 other kinds of chronological information suggested that Morley's chart provided only a partial view of the collapse.*

that for archaeologists, God is in the dates. If you can't sort things out in time, you have nothing to explain.

In 1979, more than three decades after Morley wrote *The Ancient Maya*, Raymond Sidrys and Rainer Berger assembled all of the then-available Long Count and Period Ending dates for the central and southern Lowlands – some 415 in all from 62 different archaeological sites – as shown in Fig. 35.[23] This is a considerably larger sample than that available to Morley and is arrayed in a slightly different fashion, but a comparison with Morley's chart (Fig. 30) shows that the general patterns are very similar. The newer display has several very early and late dates discovered since the 1940s, but the same peak between roughly AD 731 and 790, and the same abrupt falloff at the end of the 8th century. The earliest monument date shown (in AD 292) is from Tikal, and the last secure one in AD 909 is from Tonina, a major center located at 900 m (2961 ft) above sea level in the highlands of northern Chiapas (one or two problematic dates might be as late as AD 928). Of course, additional dates are continually being discovered (the new monument found in 2000 at Piedras Negras has several) but if a completely current listing were available it would not look much different than the 1979 one. For all practical purposes Maya "history" as represented by Long Count and Period Ending dates took an abrupt downturn around AD 800, and had flickered out entirely by AD 930. Seen through the window of monument dates, the collapse mainly affected the area shown in Fig. 36.

So far the old chronological pattern holds pretty well, particularly the rapid cessation of monument erection. John Lowe calculated that the "death" risk of a particular center (the probability that it would drop out of the stela-erecting tradition) increased considerably after AD 751. Dates of final monuments constitute the standard "events" that contribute to many simulations of the Maya collapse.[24] As Sidrys and Berger put it, "This sudden loss of an established tradition of ruler glorification does favor the demise of the rulers themselves and their entourage."[25] And as their comment reveals, by 1979 archaeologists no longer envisioned the collapse of ceremonial centers and their associated priesthoods, but of rather political capitals and their kings, dynasties, and powerful nobles.

Sidrys and Berger also had something else that Morley did not – a suite of radiocarbon (^{14}C) dates derived from a method of chronological reckoning developed as a spinoff of the Manhattan Project of World War II, that only became widely used by archaeologists in the 1950s. The most important initial contribution of this new and entirely independent kind of dating was confirmation of the superiority of one of the contending correlations between the Long Count and Gregorian calendars (the one Morley championed) and so the 1979 chart is firmly anchored in absolute time as we express it.

When Sidrys and Berger plotted out 126 ^{14}C dates from the central and southern Lowlands and compared them to those on monuments, they saw two interesting things. First, 96 dates that plausibly related to general Maya elite (as opposed to exclusively royal) contexts showed that activity extended, albeit at a reduced rate, until AD 1069, with a few flickers as late as the 14th century. Even more interesting, another set of 30 dates from Maya "commoner" contexts suggested a similar survival of population well beyond the royal collapse of the 8th and 9th centuries. Sidrys and Berger realized that their ^{14}C sample was small (particularly that part relating to commoners) and so might be biased. Nevertheless, they provisionally identified a much more protracted political and demographic collapse process than originally envisioned. Their work thus supported the suspicion of Thompson, the Ricketsons, and others that the prevailing top-down view from the perspective of royal centers and monuments only yielded part of the picture. They urged Maya archaeologists "... to obtain more commoner-associated ^{14}C dates, as these dates should eventually be of great value in resolving the

36 *If we use Long Count dates as our barometer of the Classic Maya collapse, this is the region of the southern Maya Lowlands that was most directly affected. It is approximately the same size as the state of Florida.*

depopulation issue and be more representative of the situation as it really was."[26] As we shall see later, recent research using several kinds of dating techniques shows exactly the kind of "protracted collapse" for some Maya kingdoms that Sidrys and Berger predicted.

There are now far more ^{14}C dates from the Maya Lowlands than monument dates, and another of their contributions has been in charting out the mini-collapses reviewed above. Morley, for example, knew (and apparently cared) little about Preclassic cultures. One wonders what he would have thought about our comparatively recent insights into the abandonment of the Mirador Basin and our much refined understanding of the collapse and depopulation of the Puuc polities. Today we can set the Classic collapse in exactly this wider perspective.

Before leaving the monument dates, I must mention one related study whose results will become relevant later. A few years before Sidrys and Berger published their article, the mathematical anthropologist Edwin Erickson looked at the Long Count dates for another purpose.[27] He was not concerned with finding any particular cause for the Maya collapse, but instead used abstract systems models to discriminate between two general classes of change: those caused by sudden, exogenous factors (e.g., invasion, drastic climatic shifts, introduced epidemic diseases) as opposed to some sort of more gradual, internal, self-limiting process (e.g., population growth, human-induced environmental degradation). He concluded that the latter class of explanation was the more likely.

Perhaps the most fundamental change in perspective is that we no longer "see" the Classic Maya collapse through the restricted lens of a handful of famous centers. Research projects multiplied rapidly beginning in the 1960s as new sources of funding for Maya archaeology became available, and now we possess detailed information concerning dozens of Classic sites and polities. Lurking beneath the general "Mayaness" perceived by earlier generations of archaeologists, even in its Great Tradition elements, is substantial regional variety on all levels.

While working intensively at three centers of the central and southern Lowlands – Becan, Copan, and Piedras Negras – I have been continually struck by the differences among them, from the kinds of pottery elites and commoners used, to the details of their house designs, their architectural techniques, and the symbolism used in their temples, palaces, and ball courts. For example, there are eight "royal" sweat baths known at Piedras Negras and only one at Copan. Human and animal figurines abound in household contexts at Piedras Negras, but are very rarely recovered at Copan. At Becan there are no carved inscriptions, while they are common at Piedras Negras and Copan. Compared to either Becan or Piedras Negras, Copan's inventory of chert tools and weapons is quite simple. Many other examples could be added to this list. Yet all these centers were Maya, all were contemporary with one another, and all participated in the growth and collapse of Classic civilization. Clearly the "folkways" of Maya centers, polities, and regions varied a lot more than we thought a only generation ago.

Not surprisingly, this diversity is also reflected in the local pacing, timing, and character of the collapse – exactly what we should see given the political fragmentation and economic segmentation alluded to in Chapter 5. Tatiana Proskouriakoff, the great artist and art historian, surmised in 1946 that whatever the demographic consequences of the collapse might have been, "... the catastrophically sudden extinction of the arts can be explained only in terms of some widespread and unforeseen disaster that affected most Maya cities soon after AD 800." Even in her day, however, this was more dramatic hyperbole than a statement of fact. Morley's chart reveals a long process rather than a single event, and we now know that some well-established centers stopped raising monuments more than a century before the last ones were set up at Tikal (AD 869) and Tonina (AD 909). Whatever happened did not suddenly eradicate Proskouriakoff's "arts" (presumably inscribed monuments and buildings), but instead played itself out over an interval of time roughly equivalent to that separating us today from the American Civil War.

Many kinds of data, inscriptions aside, now confirm that some centers such as Piedras Negras and La Milpa did collapse rather quickly, in the sense that kings, lords, and most commoners disappeared over a comparatively short interval. At Copan, by contrast, nobles continued to occupy their palaces for as much as two centuries after the kings fell, and their supporting populations dwindled away even more slowly. Lamanai, along with some other centers in Belize, seems to have weathered the crisis without much change. Polities in some regions seem to have gone down in a welter of warfare, while at others internal disruption or environmental deterioration are more clearly implicated as causes. And, of course, many centers and polities developed in unique environmental conditions. Both Copan and Piedras Negras were built near rivers, but their local topography, vegetation, and soils are quite distinctive, and all of these differences affected their fates as well. These examples and others will be discussed in much more detail later, but clearly we can no longer envision a rapid or uniform collapse process, and by extension a simple or single set of causes. And we can also appreciate that the fate of any particular center or polity was bound up with those of others, some nearby, some very distant.

Revealingly, much of our fine-grained appreciation of all this diversity has come from research done outside the great centers themselves, so that we no longer have such a lopsided, top-down picture of what happened. Studies of rural settlements and agro-engineering features such as terraces and raised fields, supplemented by ever-more sophisticated data from geographers, agronomers, soil scientists, and many other specialists, provide a much better grasp of population densities, agricultural production, diet, and environmental change. We now know that the Classic Maya were more numerous than formerly believed, and that there are many signs of ecological deterioration, including severe deforestation and soil erosion.

૯ ૯ ૯

To sum all this up, intimations of crises, abandonments, and population movements were common just prior to the arrival of the Spaniards. Both historical accounts and archaeological data, moreover, reveal many mini-collapses and much social and political discord beginning in Preclassic times. We are principally concerned with only one (albeit the most drastic) of these episodes, the Classic Maya collapse, and here, in a nutshell, is its pattern as we now understand it:

1 Beginning in the late 8th century, royal dynasties disappeared over a huge region of the southern Lowlands. This political debacle happened rapidly at

particular centers, but required more than a century to affect the region as a whole. The process appears to manifest itself slightly earlier on the peripheries of the Classic Maya Lowlands (especially on the northwest); John Lowe, in his 1985 simulation, postulated an "implosion" that progressed inward from the margins toward the old core regions around Tikal in the Peten.

2 Royal courts ceased to function as centers of dynastic power and cultural influence. Monuments were no longer carved, royal buildings were no longer constructed or maintained, and other elements the Classic Maya Great Tradition such as elaborate burials dwindled away, as did the production and exchange of sumptuary goods. The symbolic trappings of Classic kingship in particular disappeared very rapidly.

3 With some notable exceptions, major centers were abandoned without signs of widespread and severe violence or destruction. In many places monuments were subsequently destroyed or defaced, Classic buildings and tombs were robbed, and offerings were made among the ruins, either by local Postclassic peoples or by pilgrims from other areas.

4 At some polities non-royal elites and most or all of the supporting population disappeared at the same time as the kings lost power or very shortly thereafter. Elsewhere Maya nobles survived, as did rural farmers, for centuries. Even in the latter cases, however, few vestiges of the old Classic royal tradition retained much vitality.

5 The process of political disruption began at the time that ruling dynasties were more plentiful than ever before, when court centers were most numerous and imposing, and when overall population reached maximum size and density.

6 However long it took, a region that had supported some millions of people eventually lost most (but by no means all) of its population, leaving behind the all-but-deserted landscape that Cortes and his army later marched across in AD 1524 and 1525.

7 All these changes took place against a Late and Terminal Classic backdrop of environmental deterioration and intense warfare, although each of these differently affected particular centers and regions.

8 The region had not regained any appreciable proportion of its population even as late as 1697, when the Spaniards conquered the Itza of Nojpeten.

Much of this list would not have surprised Morley or his colleagues in the 1940s. Other parts of it, including the nature of the polities that fell apart, our grasp of historical detail, the prevalence of warfare, the size of the populations involved, the many different local expressions of Maya society and of the collapse process, and what we know about the associated ecological and agronomic conditions, would all have astonished them.

Thinking back to Joseph Tainter's list of symptoms of the fall of civilizations (p. 74), we can see that most apply. Loss of kings and (eventually) nobles reduced political centralization, negated whatever managerial roles such leaders might have had, and decreased social differentiation and stratification. As the collapse progressed, those political communities (whatever we might want to call them) that for a time survived certainly were demographically and territorially smaller and more isolated from one another than before. Production and exchange of goods of many kinds were curtailed. Most spectacularly, many of the Great Tradition elements that so fundamentally define civilization anywhere were discarded, and most of the population eventually disappeared.

Two parts of the collapse process stand out as particularly dramatic. First and foremost is the abrupt decline of the Classic Maya institution of kingship. Whatever else it was, the collapse surely involved the failure or rejection of a centuries-old tradition of dynastic rulership, along with its underlying ideological postulates and its most conspicuous and durable symbols. Even where nobles or other leaders survived for a time (as we shall see at Copan) the kings were gone. At any particular center or polity it is this dynastic dimension of the collapse that is most conspicuous and securely dated.

Population decline is equally striking, although by no means as complete or as rapid as sometimes believed. Its long-term effects were obvious to early explorers such as Stephens and Catherwood, because it was the loss of people that produced the landscape of abandoned "cities" that so intrigued them. As opposed to the collapse of kingship, however, just how population decline progressed through time is a very difficult to measure. Whether it took decades or centuries, however, in the long run it ranks as one of the great demographic transformations in history. So complete were its effects that Cortes and his little army almost starved in 1525 while crossing a wilderness that had supported millions of people seven centuries earlier.

While I think that our best strategy to reconstruct the Maya collapse is to focus our archaeological research on particular centers and polities, we must also recognize that in important ways the fates of kingdoms over the entire southern Lowlands were intertwined. The Maya were always politically fragmented, but they did comprise a coherent "system" of civilization, especially in terms of their elite interactions. In some sense the collapse process was thus a "communicable" one, in that the declining fortunes of one center, polity, or region affected the political, ideological, and economic well-being of its neighbors.

One last point about time. In June of 1863 my great-grandfather fought in the battle of Gettysburg in the American Civil War. This date seems very remote to me, yet the Maya collapse required about 130 years to work itself out, equivalent to the amount of time separating me from my ancestor. During this comparatively long period many Maya people probably noticed very little change in their workaday lives from year to year. We must not suppose, however, that this demise was a gradual or uniform process. Instead it was punctuated by recurrent crises, even in the polities that were most durable. Kings and lords were disturbed by tidings of the downfall of ancient dynastic allies and enemies. Refugees appeared on their borders, desperate for land and protection. Harvests failed more frequently, engendering repeated unrest and discontent at home. Rulers and subjects alike probably felt no intimations of ultimate disaster, but certainly they knew in their bones that times were not good, and were getting worse.

As I intimated in the prologue, all this presents a very complicated, messy problem, rather than a nice, neat, sudden, and uniform cultural catastrophe. And even though the "big" collapse seems less puzzling or unique seen in the larger panorama of Maya history, something very dramatic happened beginning in the late 8th century. No wonder that the proposed explanations to which we now turn have been so many and so varied.

– 7 –

EXPLAINING THE COLLAPSE

WHILE I WAS WRITING THIS BOOK people kept asking me if I had a new "theory" about the demise of the Classic Maya. By this they usually meant did I have some specific new or different explanation, or cause, or hypothesis. Most were not referring to theory in the larger scientific sense: a set of very general, testable propositions about the way the world works, or more colloquially, a structure of scientific expectations. Theory on this level has not been prominent in discussions of the collapse, which instead tend to focus on specific proposed causes that operated in limited, culture-historical ways.

In 1931 two pioneering Mayanists, Thomas Gann and J. E. S. Thompson, offered the following explanations for the Classic collapse:

- climatic change
- exhaustion of the soil
- epidemic diseases
- earthquakes
- war (internecine, foreign, or both)
- "national decadence"
- "religious and superstitious causes."[1]

I repeat their list because with just a little rephrasing it is strikingly similar to the explanations still debated by archaeologists today (we could break these down further; one Mayanist claimed recently to have counted over 100 specific "theories, explanations, or hypotheses" – but we will stick to the main categories here). Readers might justifiably jump to the conclusion that 70 years of digging have been pretty futile. Why haven't archaeologists been able to determine that one cause is the correct one? At the very least, why haven't we been able to rule out some of these ideas? One reason is that the collapse was the first big fact we discovered about Maya civilization. Brainstorming about what might have happened was easy, and virtually any proposed explanation seemed plausible in the absence of a good grasp of what the Classic Maya were like and detailed knowledge about what happened to particular centers or populations. And, of course, demonstrating that a proposed explanation is true or not is much more difficult than advancing it in the first place. As we shall see shortly, we can eliminate (or at least demote) some of these suggested causes and substantiate others.

Because the top levels of Maya society – kings, lords, and their associated Great Tradition – were most dramatically and rapidly affected, some explanations relate most specifically to what I call the elite collapse. Ultimately there was a broader total system collapse, for which additional causes must be sought. While both these dimensions eventually affected many centers and polities, it is much easier to detect the disruption of royal and noble activity, and a controversial issue has long been the chronological correlation between political upheaval and broader patterns of demographic decline.

The table below presents a framework of explanations and serves as the basis for this chapter, in which I critically evaluate each one and state my own opinions about its usefulness and plausibility.

Explanations of the Maya Collapse

I ELITE COLLAPSE EXPLANATIONS

- A Peasant revolts
- B Internal warfare
- C Foreign invasion
- D Disruption of trade networks

II TOTAL SYSTEM COLLAPSE EXPLANATIONS

- A Nonecological causes
  - 1 Collapse of trade networks
  - 2 Ideological pathology
- B Ecological causes
  - 1 Catastrophic ecological causes
    - a Earthquakes, hurricanes, and volcanic eruptions
    - b Climatic change (drought)
    - c Epidemic diseases of humans
  - 2 Long-term ecological causes
    - a Degradation of the agricultural landscape through human activity.

This approach is a little like examining each ingredient in a complex recipe on its own terms, instead of focusing on the finished dish. It admittedly oversimplifies things because some explanations were never meant to stand on their own, and others are not mutually exclusive of one another. For example, shortages of good agricultural land might cause warfare over resources, or poor diet make people more susceptible to disease. Nor can we expect today that any "one cause fits all" because Maya centers and polities experienced such distinctive patterns of decline at different times. Remember too the various dimensions of the collapse process. Clearly the abrupt demise of a royal dynastic line requires a different kind of explanation than the more gradual disappearance of a whole regional population. Nevertheless, discussing each putative cause in isolation allows a sharp focus. In fact, some Mayanists, as we shall see, have championed single causes, and have done the rest of us a service by vigorously arguing their positions to their logical limits. In subsequent chapters I show how various explanations fit together and apply (or not) to particular case studies.

Throughout the critique sections I apply a commonsense rule-of-thumb. If what we know about the long course of human history offers no comparable examples of a proposed cause, then I reject it as implausible. In other words, those who advance explanations that are outside documented human experience bear the burden of showing that they uniquely happened to the Maya.

One last thing. Ideas about what happened to the Maya reveal a lot about those who present them. Some people temperamentally prefer one or a few dramatic causes, while others find complicated sets of interacting ones more convincing. Some prefer materialist explanations, others ideological ones. Some envision humans as independent actors who can change history, while others think broad historical change is the result of deeper, more fundamental causes in which individuals are irrelevant. Finally, some invoke extraneous causes beyond human control, thus exculpating the Maya from any complicity in their own fate, while others see the Maya as active agents in their own demise. My own predilections will become increasingly clear, but as we shall see, not all of these are mutually exclusive positions. Even before the political structure of Classic Maya society was well understood it was evident from the cessation of Long Count dates, the abrupt abandonment of building projects, and the defacing and relocation of monuments that something had gone terribly wrong at the top, so we will start with kings and nobles.

Peasant Revolts

The most well-known elite collapse explanation was advanced by J. E. S. Thompson, whose scholarship and personal dynamism dominated Maya archaeology from the 1950s through the early 1970s (the first Maya textbook I ever used in college was his 1954 *Rise and Fall of Maya Civilization* – still in print). Thompson's popular writings almost single-handedly promoted the "vacant ceremonial" and "priest-peasant" models of the Classic Maya. Through his vast influence he also effectively purveyed the idea that Maya elites were overthrown by their ordinary Maya subjects – the peasant rebellion hypothesis.[2]

Just why Thompson thought such rebellions occurred brings us back to the single most obtrusive class of archaeological remains on the Maya landscape – buildings. As one anthropologist remarked,

> it is fair to say that it is the magnitude, number, and artistic elaboration of the monumental structures which have borne the main burden of support for judgments as to the level of sociocultural integration achieved by the "Classical" cultures of Mesoamerica.[3]

Great buildings, in a word, are among the principal hallmarks of civilization anywhere.

Before 1960 many such Classic Mesoamerican cultures, not just the Maya, were thought to be strongly "theocratic" in the sense that they were ruled by priests instead of kings. Impelled by religious zeal, so the logic went, ordinary people worked under the selfless direction of these theocrats to create impressive ceremonial centers. This conception was particularly attractive to Mayanists, and that it is still with us is evident in this more recent characterization:

> The Maya conceived of survival as a collective enterprise in which man, nature, and the gods are all linked through mutually sustaining bonds of reciprocity, ritually forged through sacrifice and communion. This collective enterprise provided the organizing principle of Maya society, incorporating the individual in widening networks of interdependence from extended family through community and state and ultimately the cosmos. The elite directed this enterprise in all its aspects. Above all, they ensured the flow of offerings and benefits between society and the sacred order, and thus the survival of both.[4]

Like most Mayanists of his time, Thompson believed that monumental Maya buildings required enormous investments of human labor. Certainly the Maya seemed to have built incessantly. At Tikal, Copan, and other centers the remains of successive construction episodes were piled one atop another, in layer-cake fashion, and the literature of Thompson's day was filled with references to the "perpetual building," "ceaseless alteration," and "endless enlargement" of temples, ball courts, palaces, and causeways, all using human muscle and without the benefit of metal tools or complex machines.

Moreover, this frenzy of construction seemed to peak during the crucial k'atuns between AD 730 and 790, just when the first manifestations of the collapse were appearing. Thompson reasoned that elite demands for support and labor became increasingly burdensome, undermining the religious devotion and collective enterprise of ordinary Maya people. Eventually long-suffering peasants simply had enough, and they suddenly overthrew their priest-rulers in a series of spontaneous uprisings that broke out at slightly different times from place to place. Just such revolts have been historically common in many parts of the world because peasants, however low in social standing, are not powerless people. Through kinship and other means they form coalitions that can resist unreasonable demands and pursue collective interests.

Given the available archaeological data of the day, the "peasant revolt" hypothesis was attractive because it explained the apparent abrupt collapse of elite activities, particularly the rapid fall-off and frequent defacement of dated monuments, as well as the unfinished buildings found at some centers. Evidence of violence had cropped up by this time, particularly at Piedras Negras, where in the 1930s archaeologists detected the burning of palace buildings and the smashing of an elaborate throne. Internal rebellions also accounted for the wholesale abandonment of ritual centers, presumably built and used under the aegis of the demanding priest-rulers, and why this occurred at different times at different places. On a deeper and more personal level, Thompson greatly admired the character and personality traits of ordinary Maya people, among whom he spent much of his professional life. He depicted them as "... exceptionally honest, good-natured, clean, tidy, and socially inclined" – perfect exemplars of "live and let live."[5] Such people were just the sort to cooperate selflessly under benevolent leadership, but when oppressed they could also be formidable and intransigent enemies, as the Caste War had proved. Thompson himself was an old guard Englishman very conscious of class distinctions, and Marshall Becker has surmised that his anxiety about Communist-inspired class conflict in his own time also helped form his views.

The idea of peasant rebellions long outlived its roots in the "priest-peasant" model. Once it became clear that there were Classic Maya kings, it was widely assumed that monumental construction functioned as a form of political status rivalry, as each tried to impress the others.

Appealing as it is, there are serious problems with Thompson's hypothesis. As he himself realized, peasant revolts could account for only part of what happened to the Maya. Left unresolved was the massive depopulation –

where did all the people go? Relieved of their demanding elites, farmers should have thrived mightily, not declined in numbers. Thompson partly side-stepped this difficulty by denying that the central and southern Maya Lowlands were entirely abandoned at the time of the collapse. While this assertion turns out to be true, he never systematically confronted the fact that most of the Maya in the region did eventually disappear (however gradually) after AD 850–900, musing only that

> It seems possible that when the rulers were no more and the ceremonial centers were reverting to forest, the peasant's relief at being free of that never-ending service to gods and their representatives on earth may not have long endured. It may have been replaced by a loss of purpose, of lack of interest in living and of regret for the past; for with obligations to the ceremonial center and its rulers went privileges and a sense of participation. Pageantry, color, beauty, bustling markets, security against the enmities of the gods and neighboring peoples, and rewards of service had gone; the world had shrunk very much to a village on its own.[6]

The Maya, in short, simply faded away.

An old metaphor about China characterizes its history as the sound of mailed boots going up the stairs, and velvet slippers coming down them. In less flowery terms, one dynasty (sometimes of peasant origins) supplants another. According to Chinese political thought such dynastic cycles were triggered by the moral failures of rulers, which resulted in the withdrawal of the "Mandate of Heaven" and paved the way for reformers. This brings us to something else Thompson never explained. Why did new Maya elites and revitalized political and social institutions fail to reappear after the putative rebellions, as occurred so often in China and other parts of the world under similar circumstances?

Even more damaging to me is the underlying assumption upon which the peasant rebellion hypothesis rests in the first place – that oppressive burdens were placed on the Maya populace. Strangely enough, considering that archaeologists routinely use simple tools and manual labor to take Maya buildings apart (and sometimes to put them back together again), few have ever conducted systematic research to determine what kinds of labor investments were actually involved. In a ground-breaking project my colleague Elliot Abrams did a series of time-motion studies and experiments on construction and sculpture techniques during our work at Copan in 1981. He concluded that Copan's buildings were much less costly in terms of time and labor than previously believed.

One of my students and I later used Abrams's method to model the construction potential of Copan's population, employing one of the site's largest and most celebrated buildings – the Temple of the Hieroglyphic Stairway (Plate 3) – as a standard "currency." Our least intensive scheme of labor mobilization imagined that each Copan peasant family was obliged to provide a single laborer one year out of every ten, and that this person worked only 100 days during the dry season during that year – hardly an oppressive level of demand. Yet our calculations showed that a labor force recruited and deployed this way could have generated the equivalent of 30 such structures during the period AD 750–800 alone. Making allowances for the considerable uncertainties inherent in this sort of simulation, even modest demands on Copan's population over the four centuries of dynastic rule would have resulted in a mass of masonry vastly larger than the existing one.

Many readers will themselves rebel at the counterintuitive proposition that Maya temples and palaces were not particularly "expensive." But this is, after all, an empirical issue. What I know about it convinces me that Maya kings and elites had learned to make grandiose public statements with their buildings, while not incurring much political liability in the process. In doing so they managed to impress not only their own people, but several generations of later Maya archaeologists. Those skeptical of my contention should read the original studies and decide for themselves.[7]

In defense of Thompson, remember that at the time he wrote archaeologists believed that there were far fewer Maya on the landscape than they estimate today, and so less available labor. Furthermore, there might well have been considerable internal discord as various Maya polities collapsed, although for rather different reasons than Thompson imagined. Elite "demand," of course, is a relative concept. What seemed perfectly acceptable to Maya commoners under good economic conditions might have become very burdensome as their well-being deteriorated, just as the same rate of government taxation seems either reasonable or onerous to us today given fluctuating levels of economic prosperity. Note that the peasant rebellion hypothesis also has an ideological implication – the violent uprisings must have been accompanied by a rejection of the political and religious ideology underpinning theocratic rule.[8] We will return to both these points.

Internal War

Pondering the monuments and the (then) unreadable inscriptions of Copan in 1839, John Lloyd Stephens speculated that the Maya, like other ancient civilizations, were afflicted by the blight of war. In stark contrast, a cornerstone of the Classic Maya mystique as it later developed, was the presumed absence of destructive forms of warfare, as these statements by Sylvanus Morley and J. E. S. Thompson show:

> Old Empire [i.e., Classic period] sculpture is conspicuously lacking in the representation of warlike scenes, battles, strife, and violence. True, bound captives are occasionally portrayed, but the groups in which they appear are susceptible of religious, even astronomical interpretation, and warfare as such is almost certainly not indicated.[9]

> I think one can assume fairly constant friction over boundaries sometimes leading to a little fighting, and occasional raids on outlying parts of a neighboring city state to assure a constant supply of sacrificial victims, but I think the evidence is against the assumption of regular warfare on a considerable scale.[10]

Scholars of the time explained away the ubiquity of conflict among the 16th-century Maya as an aberration introduced into Yucatan by Mexican intruders, who disrupted the old peaceful Classic way of life.

Both archaeological research and inscriptions have since demonstrated that war in fact began at least as early as Middle Preclassic times. Thereafter it increased in intensity until by the 7th and 8th centuries it had become an almost pathological condition of Maya society.[11] More fortifications are now known for the Maya Lowlands than in bellicose Central Mexico. Morley's assertion to the contrary, warfare (along with its associated rituals and sacrifices) is perhaps the single most conspicuous theme of Maya art (Plate 22) and texts turn out to have many war-related terms, as listed in the table opposite.[12] The newly discovered Piedras Negras monument shown in Plate 20 is quite typical. In the center of the composition, dressed in a barrel-like costume of quilted cotton armor, stands Ruler 2 of the Piedras Negras dynasty, flanked on either side by his military retainers and kneeling captives. Panel 15, as this sculpture is now called, was raised by Ruler 3 in honor of his father. Singled out among the events of the old king's life were his wars and battles during the 7th century, the details of which are unfortunately lost in the eroded glyphs in the upper right-hand corner of the monument.

By Late Classic times war seems to have become both ideologically and practically a vital component of kingship. Even kings like Copan's Yax Pasaj who fought no known wars took pains to depict themselves in military regalia, and the idea of the king as warrior probably reflects his more fundamental role as queller of cosmic disorder. Because all the existing evidence suggests that war was initiated by kings and nobles and fought in their interests (peasant rebellions apart), I place it in the elite collapse category.

Some Maya Terms for War and its Aftermath

chuk	"to capture" or "to tie up" (or alternatively "to grab" or "to seize" according to Stephen Houston)	the most common glyph
bate'el	"warrior"	
bak, or baak	"prisoner" or "captive"	often used in a possessive form, as "his captive," with numbers specified.
ch'ak	"to chop"	probably referring to sacrifice after war events.
pul	"to burn"	this glyph is often found in connection with captives, and might sometimes also refer to particular places that were burned (deliberate destruction?).
tok' pakal	"flint shield"	a term that somehow refers generally to the essence of war as a royal endeavor, and/or an object used in war-related ceremonies.
hub	"fall," "collapse," or "fail"	as in the failure of a military campaign.
patan	"tribute" or "service/work"	this is a fairly rare term often attached to numbers, and sometimes seems to refer to tribute exacted or being offered after war events.
ikats	"burden" or "load"	sometimes used with expressions for "payment," as possibly in payment of tribute. Sometimes takes the possessed form (yikats).
yubte	"tribute mantle"	a very rare classical Yucatecan glyph identified on a Peten polychrome vessel by Stephen Houston.

By internal war I mean war among the Maya themselves (Classic art almost always depicts enemies with Maya physiognomies). There was never any overall unity among the many Classic polities, each of which had its own distinctive history and political interests. During the 8th century powerful Maya kingdoms and their dense supporting populations were more closely juxtaposed than ever before. Their shared folkways and elite traditions, however, no more prevented conflict than they did among the city-states of ancient Greece or Renaissance Italy.

A few archaeologists attempted to salvage something of the old "peaceful Maya" perspective by insisting that internal conflicts among the Maya were not very destructive or lethal because they were constrained by the commonly understood conventions and values of kings and elites. This argument has become muted as the violence, scale, and frequency of Late Classic warfare become ever more apparent. References to war peak in the 8th century, a time when there is also the greatest regional diversity in ceramic complexes, a good barometer of both political fragmentation and the causes of it. Ironically, this is precisely the period that Morley and others identified as the zenith of the Classic Maya Great Tradition – the so-called "period of uniformity."

Behind the ritual dimensions of war, which are most clearly presented by art and texts, lurk more fundamental motivations – the despoiling of enemy courts, the capture of dynastic regalia, the destruction of royal families, and the extraction of labor and tribute. Many conflicts were carried out for political, military, and strategic advantage, and quite possibly for territorial aggrandizement and capture of resources. According to some archaeologists and epigraphers the frequently occurring but controversial "shell-star" or "earth-star" glyph (Fig. 37) indicates a war event of unusual political or territorial consequence. Destruction episodes are documented at some centers, and one obvious goal was to destroy or capture the shrines and god bundles of enemies, or to otherwise humiliate them. We know that kings were captured and later sacrificed (sometimes after being held for many years), and when this happened there are often signs of political disorder back at the loser's court. Defeated centers and rulers fell under the authority of the victorious king, who apparently could appoint his own sajals as governors. Tribute in the form of cotton

37 *The "earth-star glyph" is still poorly understood, but seems to be associated in some way with major Classic Maya military conflicts.*

mantles, cacao, feathers, and other costly items was exacted from defeated polities, and so, almost certainly, was labor. Kings rewarded successful warriors with prestigious gifts, just as Aztec monarchs did. Hostages seem to have been taken to guarantee good behavior, and celebrated artisans and scribes might have been "captured" and relocated to triumphant capitals as well.

Nor did war consist simply of conflicts between established kingdoms. There were internal struggles over access to the throne, and some elite-led factions used force to break away from their former rulers and form new polities. For example, a dislocated cadet branch of the Tikal dynasty moved far to the west and founded a new capital, Dos Pilas, in AD 671, and later waged war against the parent polity, a story I will tell in greater detail later.

None of this conflict would have surprised Stephens, who possessed a sturdy comparative intuition about how ancient civilizations operated. Certainly the Late and Terminal Classic Maya were far from the peaceful culture envisioned by Morley and Thompson. But what is the significance of all of this for the collapse? Few readers need much convincing that war is extremely destructive. Our own 20th- and 21st-century experience shows that it can bring down states and empires and destroy not only countless lives, but also disrupt larger traditions of culture. Because I think war has been an important process in all ancient civilizations, much of my own career has been spent excavating Maya fortresses and writing about warfare's historical and evolutionary effects in the Maya Lowlands. As a later case study will show, war is certainly implicated in the disintegration of some kingdoms, particularly in the Petexbatun/Usumacinta region.

My enthusiasm for the subject notwithstanding, I doubt the usefulness of war as a general explanation for the collapse. One difficulty is that warfare is not necessarily just a destructive process. I have argued myself that it was one way in which incipient Maya leaders centralized power and authority in Preclassic and Early Classic times, contributing to the emergence of the institution of kingship. Internal upheavals involving factional rivalry probably date back at least as far as the 4th century. Clearly the most obvious effect of such royal and elite struggles is the episodic disruption of dynastic activity at many centers – which is also the most conspicuous feature of the Classic collapse. But remember that several of the mini-collapses reviewed earlier were also associated with war, and we know that great centers and even whole regions waxed and waned according to their military fortunes right up to the Spanish conquest. Defeat at the hands of Caracol probably initiated the hiatus at Tikal, and war is implicated in the much later decline of the Puuc centers. But Tikal recovered its vigor in the 7th century when

Kaloomte' Jasaw Chan K'awiil defeated her enemies, and Chichen Itza grew and prospered even as Uxmal and the other Puuc kingdoms fell.

In short, wars in the Maya Lowlands, as in other parts of the ancient world, produced winners and losers. Anyone wishing to use warfare as a general explanation of the Maya collapse must show why the wars of the 8th and early 9th centuries were so much more frequent and intense than earlier and later ones, and why their effects were so destructive and irreversible, producing only losers, not winners. War in Central Mexico created the dynamic Aztec empire out of a congeries of city-states. Why were its effects so different among the Maya?

A second difficulty is the sporadic evidence for destructive warfare in the archaeological record. Later on we will see that such evidence is pronounced in some regions and centers. Elsewhere it is either entirely lacking, or manifests itself in such minor ways that it is difficult to see how it could by itself account for the permanent dissolution of kingdoms. And, as some Mayanists have pointed out, war can be viewed as a cause of the Classic collapse or the effect of some more fundamental problem (although there is no reason we cannot think of it both ways).

Finally, there is the issue of depopulation – the total system collapse part of the equation. Preindustrial wars the world over were often very lethal for ordinary people, but usually for reasons only indirectly related to combat itself. Crops were seized or burned, disease and famine spread, and trade was disrupted. In regions where wars were violent and prolonged, there must have developed lightly-populated or unused "no man's lands" between competing polities, which reduced agricultural potential and compressed population distribution. Yet one is hard pressed to find any historical examples of regions the size of the central and southern Maya Lowlands that lost millions of people because of preindustrial warfare. And even where local populations were severely affected by conflict in the short run, they usually rebounded quickly. Also, depopulation overall political decline at some centers took centuries to occur (as we shall see later) while dynastic collapse was very sudden. It is difficult to attribute both to the effects of warfare.

Foreign Invasions

This explanation envisions that Maya civilization experienced a crippling external shock, administered militarily by outside forces, and that this shock then generated a cascade of destructive consequences. Given the political geography of Classic Mesoamerica such external pressure would most likely come from the west, where other large and dynamic political systems were to be found. Invasions of "foreigners," usually conceived to be highland Mexicans and/or Mexicanized Maya from the Gulf Coast zone, have been proposed for three periods of Maya history.

Sixteenth-century Maya elites claimed descent from just such foreigners, and Nahuatl words were used in Yucatec Maya speech. This evidence, along with "Toltec" iconography at Chichen Itza, long ago convinced many archaeologists that there was one or more armed intrusions into the northern Maya Lowlands from the west, possibly beginning as early as the 8th century. While we still argue about how to explain the similarities between Chichen Itza and the Toltec capital of Tula, such invasions are now generally discounted – at least on any militarily impressive scale (although the first well-dated "Mexican" Chichen Itza sculpture at AD 998 does fit the Tula chronology). But remember that Teotihuacan considerably influenced the earlier Tikal Maya in the 4th and 5th centuries in the absence of such invasions. None of this, of course, has direct relevance for the Classic collapse; I bring it up only because if there were Postclassic invasions, they certainly did not destroy either northern Maya political institutions or cause depopulation.

We already briefly discussed the second (and earliest well-documented) "Mexican" intrusion – the sudden appearance in AD 378 of Siyaj K'ak' and his supporters, who represent some kind of Teotihuacan-related faction, in the affairs of Tikal, the greatest Early Classic kingdom. Here again there was no profound systemic shock of a destructive kind.

More appropriate for our concerns is a putative invasion that involved the center of Seibal, in the western Maya Lowlands. About AD 800 so-called "foreign" iconographic elements, including images of people with purportedly "non-Classic Maya" physiognomies, appeared on Seibal's carved monuments (Fig. 38). Around the same time new forms of fine-paste pottery also became common at the site. Archaeologists who first detected these influences in the 1960s ascribed them to invaders from the coastal areas of Campeche and Tabasco.

Given 30 more years of research, the Seibal iconography seems less exotic than it once did. We now know that monuments at the end of the Classic period portray a much wider range of personages, and of social and political roles, than they did earlier. Moreover, late monuments in other parts of the Maya Lowlands show distinctive features that probably represent the internal evolution of the sculptural forms, and Seibal's monuments fit comfortably within this range.[13] More important, we can now read Seibal's texts, which are solidly within the Classic Maya tradition of calendrics, rituals, names, and

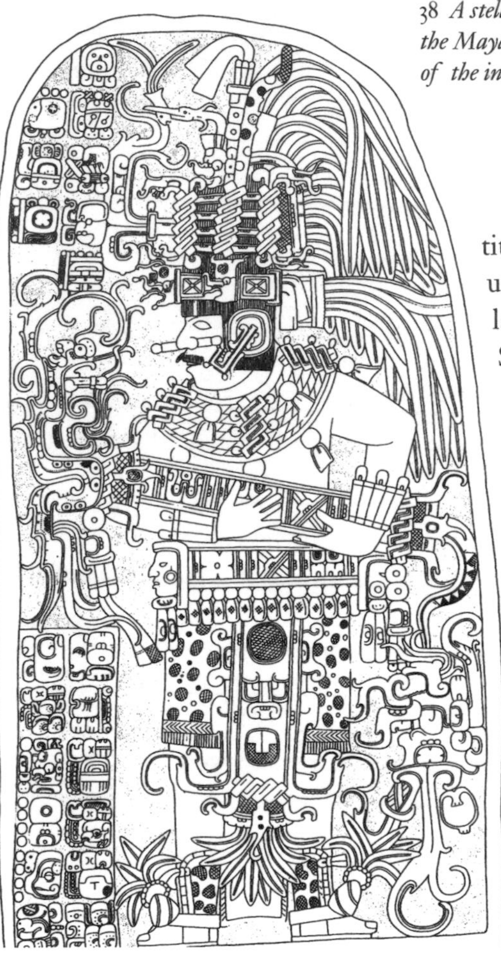

38 *A stela from Seibal, on the western margin of the Maya Lowlands, supposed to show evidence of the intrusions of "foreigners."*

titles. And as we shall see shortly, we understand Seibal's career within the larger Petexbatun region quite well. Some Seibal images and motifs, such as depictions of the wind god, are shared with other distant Mesoamerican cultures, but such representations are quite old in both regions, so they are not necessarily indicative of invasions or migrations. While influences from elsewhere in Mesoamerica, particularly Tabasco, might have been felt at Seibal, similar situations were by no means unusual elsewhere in the Maya Lowlands over many centuries.

Even when the Seibal "invasion" idea was widely accepted, some archaeologists rightly objected that such an historical event had no logical implications for the much more protracted and complex Classic collapse process. No one adequately specified any mechanism whereby such an attack might trigger much more far-reaching destructive consequences. If an invasion like this ever happened at all, it was just as plausibly a symptom, rather than a cause, of the disarray of western Maya kingdoms, and likely to have had mainly local effects. And of course many of the difficulties of the internal war explanation apply as well. If new foreign elites established themselves at Seibal, why did not they, and the regional population, survive? Although we obviously cannot envision the Classic Maya as isolated from wider influences of many kinds that originated elsewhere in Mesoamerica, today few if any Mayanists believe that foreign invasions or intrusions seriously affected Classic polities at the end of the 8th century.

Collapse of Trade Networks

Some of my colleagues believe that Maya kings and elites were participants in an intricate and far-flung network of trade routes that not only operated throughout the Maya Lowlands, but also linked up with a much larger commercial system dominated by the Mexican emporium of Teotihuacan.[14] Teotihuacan was long assumed to have abruptly declined around AD 700–750, triggering a restructuring of economic relations throughout highland Mesoamerica and the Gulf Coast, which in turn contributed to the slightly later Classic Maya collapse. The basic logic of the argument is that Maya kings and elites depended heavily for their authority on the acquisition, display, and redistribution of prestige objects, which attracted and helped bind commoners to their political systems. Because their local economies were not very rich or dynamic, and geared to an increasingly outmoded "theocratic" conception of society, the Maya were excluded from the new post-Teotihuacan commercial order that emphasized more "secular" and "mercantile" patterns of trade. Surrounded by more efficient commercial cartels, Maya kings and nobles lost much of the ceremonial clout essential to their dominance, their hold over their subjects weakened, and commoners increasingly defected to other regions – hence the listing of economic collapse as both an elite and total system explanation.

On the face of it the trade hypothesis looks like an attractive idea. We know that 16th-century Maya lords were heavily engaged in both land and sea commerce, and unquestionably cacao, feathers, shells, precious stones, honey, richly embroidered cotton cloth, and many other precious objects or materials circulated among Classic polities too. There is evidence of some sort of Lowland Maya presence at Teotihuacan itself and, Teotihuacan or Teotihuacan-inspired pottery is found in caches and graves at many Classic centers, as is the distinctive green obsidian imported from the Central Mexican Pachuca source. Architects at Tikal and other sites incorporated Teotihuacan elements into their buildings, and as we have seen, new epigraphic interpretations favor unexpectedly direct Teotihuacan meddling in Maya politics – perhaps even dynastic usurpation. And there seems little doubt that people living in the Basin of Mexico in Classic times conceived of the distant and mysterious tropical lowlands far to the southeast as a treasure house of exotic things.

The trade disruption hypothesis has recently been undermined by a better grasp of Mesoamerican chronology. It now appears that Teotihuacan influence in the Maya Lowlands, commercial or otherwise, was strongest in the 4th and 5th centuries (I think the city reached its apogee as a Mesoamerican power between AD 300 and 400). Moreover, Teotihuacan seems to have lost its political and economic clout earlier than previously believed – about AD 600–650 (some archaeologists think the city was actually abandoned about that time). Classic Maya elites not only survived, but thrived, for another century and more. If in fact Teotihuacan's demise had any serious economic ill effects on the Classic Maya at all, they seem more likely related to the 6th-century "hiatus" than the later collapse. It is even possible that the decline of Teotihuacan opened up new opportunities for Lowland Maya trade. During the 8th century people at Copan and other Classic centers remembered Teotihuacan as a Tollan and celebrated its mystical connection with the founders of their dynasties, but the city itself no longer had any practical effect on their lives.

Teotihuacan aside, the wars of the 8th century might themselves have disrupted important aspects of trade. It remains to be demonstrated, however, that Maya kings or nobles at any time ever managed complex commercial enterprises at all, much less ones essential to the economic well-being of their kingdoms. Chocolate, fancy painted pottery, quetzal feathers, spondylus shells, sting ray spines, and jade often figured in gift-exchanges among prominent people, and no doubt were often moved about in non-commercial ways.[15] And important as all these things were for the construction and display of elite identity, they were not economically vital to the lives of most people in the same ways as food or other basic raw materials were. Several archaeologists long ago correctly argued that long-distance exchange of high-status items is not, strictly speaking, at all necessary to the emergence and maintenance of stratified societies. Hawaiian kings and nobles, for example, managed quite well without it. Few archaeologists have tried to quantify the economic significance of any kind of trade in such exotic items anywhere in Mesoamerica, but those efforts that have been made suggest it was trivial.[16]

Another problem with the long-distance trade hypothesis is that it originated before we had a detailed grasp of the inscriptions, which from our present vantage point are remarkably silent on exchanges of any kind (tribute and gifts aside), much less centrally administered political economies or their (presumably) required bureaucracies.

Ordinary Maya people did routinely consume a few utilitarian materials obtained through trade from distant places. Salt was almost certainly one of these, but leaves few traces in the archaeological record. Flint quarries at Colha in Belize provided large hoe-like implements for farmers in the region, but these were never widely exchanged throughout the Lowlands. Obsidian, a preferred material for cutting tools, was imported from several highland sources and commonly shows up in household excavations. Most families used only a handful of obsidian blades each year, however, so it was not a high-volume trade commodity. Although kings might have had a hand in obsidian procurement and distribution during Classic times, they were not essential to either. Preclassic people used obsidian long before rulers were present, and at Copan farmers continued to do so long after the royal dynasty collapsed. Nor was obsidian a necessity, because in most regions local sources of flint provided an alternative raw material.

Only two commodities make much sense in terms of the trade hypothesis, and the first is food. Food shortages could certainly have caused severe disruption on all social levels, and failure of kings and elites to manage crucial redistribution of food supplies might well have triggered their downfall. But remember that the ancient Maya were so energetically constrained that the movement of cheap, bulk goods essential to the agrarian economy must have been very localized, except where water transport was feasible. Even the Aztecs, with their huge imperial system, did not move maize and beans great distances in large amounts. We have absolutely no evidence that Maya kings and nobles managed the distribution of foodstuffs beyond the boundaries of their own realms (or for that matter within them), except to fund their own households. And even if they did so, the more important question is what kinds of agrarian crises caused local shortfalls in food availability?

I think the real wild card in all trade models is cotton, and perhaps some other fibers. The Maya, like people everywhere, were dependent on the three Fs – food, fiber, and fuel. Fibers were essential for clothing and innumerable other purposes, but we know almost nothing about how or where cotton was produced or how it was moved about.

One thing is certain – the Maya were not ancient "capitalists" whose economies depended on large-scale, administered production and exchange to generate "profits" as we think of them. No archaeologist has ever presented a convincing and detailed explanation of how a proposed disruption of trade could actually destabilize Classic Maya elites, or why such economic disorder might have had major demographic consequences for their subjects. My own argument, as we shall see later, is that it was not the failure to manage well-established patterns of economic exchange that contributed to the collapse, but instead that Maya kings and nobles were unable to adapt to the crises of the 8th and 9th centuries by instituting such exchanges.

We now turn to total system collapse explanations, which broadly speaking break down into the categories of non-ecological and ecological causes. We already dismissed one non-ecological cause, the failure of trade routes. But what about ideological failure?

Ideological Pathology

In the late summer of 1856 the Xhosa, a Bantu-speaking people of southeast Africa, began methodically to kill their cattle, horses, goats, sheep, and fowl. They also consumed or threw away all the grain in their storage bins and stopped preparations to plant new crops. They did all this after listening to the prophecies of a young girl named Nongqawuse, who claimed to have received messages from two dead ancestors a few months earlier near a deep pool in the sacred Gxara river gorge. In her vision, these ancestors directed that all livestock and food should be destroyed, and that new houses, corrals, and grain bins should be built. If these instructions were faithfully carried out, they assured, the world would be reborn. After a great storm and two days of darkness, the earth would disgorge an endless supply of immortal cattle, and the new grain bins would magically fill up. "New people" would appear to defeat the enemies of the Xhosa, and the dead ancestors would live again.

Some Xhosa were skeptical of this prophecy, but once it was accepted by a number of influential chiefs the promise of such profound world renewal proved irresistible to most people. When several auspicious deadlines passed and the ancestors failed to appear, Xhosa believers killed the last remnants of their flocks. After the sun rose and set as usual on 18 February 1857, the final appointed day, the Xhosa finally realized the depth of their collective delusion, but it was too late. Untold thousands of people starved to death. For those who survived, Xhosa culture was broken forever by "... the greatest self-inflicted immolation of a people in all history."[17]

I interject this dramatic story because it shows that under extraordinary circumstances whole societies can virtually will themselves out of existence. The Xhosa demise is an example of what Gann and Thompson meant by "religious and superstitious" causes cited at the beginning of this chapter. Some Mayanists have suggested that a similar ideological pathology contributed to the demise of the Classic Maya. Exactly why brings us back to Maya concepts of time and prophecy.

As we know, during the 16th century the Maya used a cyclical calendar called the Count of the K'atuns. In combination with the 260-day ritual calendar, it produced specific dates that repeated themselves every 256 years. K'atun cycles formed the basis for prophecy by organizing past events into a general, repetitive framework that enabled priests to divine the main outlines of the future. As in astrology, various k'atun shifts were particularly propitious or sinister. The date 8 Ahau was especially associated with a succession of past disasters, and similar (although not identical) calamities were anticipated when 8 Ahau came around again. According to ethnohistorian Ralph Roys "... this belief was so strong as to actually influence the course of history."[18] Evidently Spanish priests (who had their own millennial preconceptions) thought so as well. Knowing of the imminence of an 8 Ahau transition in 1697, they tried to persuade the Itza that their own native prophecies foretold their impending subjugation. Events, as it turned out, almost coincided with this prediction – the Itza capital Nojpeten fell to Ursua's little army just 136 days before the advent of the next 8 Ahau.

Some archaeologists have suggested that the Classic Maya, who used a somewhat different set of calendars, were similarly impressed with the prophetic implications of chronological cycles. Dennis Puleston surmised that periodic historical crises fell into predictable patterns beginning in Classic times, and that Maya belief in regularly repeating disasters partly stimulated them. Scoff as we may at this idea, the recent turn of the millennium of our own calendar shows that many modern people hold somewhat similar views. Puleston thought that the Classic collapse "... was an event fully anticipated by ancient Maya scholars and priests who by means of consultations with their books and prophecies were well aware of their impending doom."[19]

Mesoamericans more generally believed in cycles of creation and destruction that were largely beyond the control of humans. The Aztecs thought they inhabited the 5th world created by their gods, which would eventually be destroyed by earthquakes. A somewhat similar Maya concept is recorded in the 16th-century Quiche Maya book called the *Popol Vuh*, which recounts the creation of three successive previous worlds by the gods, who then destroyed each one because it was in some way defective. Assuming that the *Popol Vuh* preserves elements of much earlier and more widespread beliefs, as most Mayanists do, the Classic Maya quite possibly had an apocalyptic conception of their own end.

To be fair to Puleston and to others who advanced similar ideas, such fatal cultural depression or fatigue was never intended to stand by itself as a cause of the Maya collapse, any more than blind adherence to a faulty prophecy alone precipitated the demise of the Xhosa. In fact, the Xhosa had been under severe military pressure from powerful enemies, including the British, for 75 years. Many of their best lands had been yielded up to foreigners, and the effects of diminution of territory were exacerbated by rapid population growth. On top of all this, a dreaded lung disease was decimating their cattle herds, central both economically and symbolically to Xhosa life. No wonder that they grasped at a prophetic straw, in a kind of revitalistic movement familiar to anthropologists who study societies under extreme stress. Puleston believed that something similar happened to the Classic Maya. They had survived earlier episodes of epistemological crisis, but by the 8th century so many stresses had accumulated that the prophecies proved self-fulfilling.

Our current understanding of the overall pacing of the collapse makes the ideological pathology idea unworkable. There is just too much chronological variability from center to center and region to region for it to be plausible, at least as linked to calendrical dates as Puleston suggested. The political disunity of the Classic Maya also makes it unlikely that such an ideological movement would be uniformly expressed or communicated. And in any case, societies are not collectivities of automatons programmed to conform mindlessly to their own cultural preconceptions, but consist instead of individuals and groups who opportunistically use culture for their own ends. As one hard-headed old Itza chief responded to the Spaniards, why should I obey a prophecy of surrender as long as my spear is still sharp?

Although proposed ideological causes are unconvincing on their own, I agree with Puleston that they might have contributed significantly to the Classic collapse. Later on I give my own ideas about how prophecy and rejection of the ideology of kingship played their parts.

We now turn to ecological causes, by which I mean anything that disrupts human relationships with their sustaining biological environments. Such events may be sudden, catastrophic, and independent of human behavior, or long-term processes to which people themselves contribute.

Earthquakes, Hurricanes, and Volcanic Eruptions

Judging from successful films with titles like *Twister* or *Earthquake*, many people experience a frisson of catastrophic menace as nature reminds us how powerful and capricious she can be. Because of the comparative geological youth of many Mesoamerican landscapes, volcanoes and earthquakes are commonplace (and often co-occur). Hurricanes, as we know, regularly strike the Yucatan Peninsula. Both kinds of catastrophes have two features in common – they are independent of human causation and, at least until very recently, they have been essentially unpredictable. Neither of them can be convincingly linked to the Classic Maya collapse, except possibly through the mechanism of climate change.

The most obvious reason why earthquakes and volcanism are out of the running as local phenomena in the collapse is that neither one much affects the great limestone platform underlying most of the Maya Lowlands, or the people who live on it. To be sure, the modern town of Copan was largely destroyed in 1934 by a major earthquake, and in 1982 I sat on my verandah there watching volcanic dust drift down from the eruption of the El Chichon volcano in the Chiapas highlands, hundreds of km away to the northwest. But Copan was quickly rebuilt, and if anything the dust merely added useful nutrients to the soils of the valley. Damage from earthquakes generally affects comparatively small regions, as do the immediate tectonic effects of volcanoes (intense heat, poisonous gases, heavy ejecta, lava flows, avalanches, and floods). Neither volcanoes or earthquakes are usually very lethal to humans or to crops except on a very local scale. No Classic centers in the Maya Lowlands proper were blanketed by ancient volcanic debris, and there is only incidental evidence of possible earthquake damage (interestingly modern communities, with their dense populations, multi-story buildings, and complex infrastructure of roads, water systems, gas pipelines, etc. are more vulnerable to severe earthquake damage than ancient ones).

Really big volcanic events are another matter. Huge eruptions occasionally eject sufficient quantities of gas into the atmosphere (mainly in the form of sulfur dioxide) so that the resulting aerosol clouds actually change climate for months or even years on hemispheric scales. Chemical signatures of such violent eruptions can be detected in ice cores thousands of miles from the blast. We will return to this putative cause very shortly in the section on drought.

We must look to the Mesoamerican Highlands to assess the effects of tectonic catastrophes, and there we find plenty of examples. Ceren, the little buried Maya town in Salvador we discussed in Chapter 5, was certainly overwhelmed by an eruption around AD 590, but few if any people died, only a few sq. km were blanketed by ash, and eventually the Maya returned. The most destructive recent volcanic event in Mesoamerica – the 1982 eruption of the El Chichon volcano mentioned above – devastated an area of about 155 sq. km (60 sq. miles), destroyed nine villages, and killed about 2000 people.

Much larger regions are often affected in Central Mexico. Around 400 AD much of the southwestern Basin of Mexico was covered by volcanic deposits, effectively destroying what had once been a rich agricultural region. And even as I wrote this chapter, the 18,000-foot-high volcano Popocatepetl (Smoking Mountain) was violently erupting on the eastern horizon of Mexico City. Some 41,000 people, many of whom even today regard the great mountain as a god, were being evacuated by the Mexican army from the downwind regions. Not coincidentally, archaeologists are unearthing whole landscapes, including houses and agricultural fields, that were buried by Preclassic eruptions in the same general area. Ancient people were clearly forced to abandon their crops and homes, and no doubt many died of starvation. Lava flows rendered some of the Cuicuilco landscape permanently uninhabitable, and subsequent erosion and flooding remodeled the topography. Still, only areas of a few hundred sq. km were affected, and there were always refuges nearby to which the population could flee. No widespread political or demographic collapse ensued. In the long run the volcanic deposits weathered into fertile soils and farmers recolonized most devastated landscapes. The ancient Ceren farmers whose houses were buried at the end of the 6th century, in fact, were descendants of people who recolonized the Zapotitan valley after an earlier and more violent volcanic eruption in AD 429. Other highland peoples in Mexico, Guatemala, and Honduras have routinely survived such catastrophes for centuries, and the ancient Maya would probably have adapted just as well, had the necessity arisen.

In 1998 Hurricane Mitch swept through the Copan valley and much of the rest of Honduras, leaving behind a wake of severe destruction. High winds by themselves are seldom very lethal. Most of the immediate threat to humans comes from associated torrential rains, and many Hondurans were drowned by flooding and mudslides. None of these is much of a threat in the Maya Lowlands proper, where surface drainage is rare and the landscape is comparatively flat. More serious is the destruction of crops, because hurricanes often strike during the growing season. Houses can be rebuilt, but loss of next year's food stores and seed supply could certainly devastate local populations. Hurricanes figure prominently in various late Maya histories. They were (and are) especially troublesome along the eastern coast of Yucatan, but Maya communities today recover rapidly from their impact, as no doubt did their Classic ancestors.

One can imagine that unpredictable catastrophic events like these caused a collective psychological panic of "the gods are angry" kind, even in the absence of serious damage. To me such suppositions are fanciful to the point of absurdity. If the El Chichon volcano erupted during Late Classic times (as some volcanologists believe), the inhabitants of nearby Palenque were probably mightily impressed, and maybe frightened out of their wits, but their capacity to grow food was not much affected, their great buildings did not collapse, and they did not abandon their homes as a result. In fact, the escarpment on which Palenque is located, very close to this "dangerous" volcano, was heavily occupied in the centuries just before the Spaniards arrived.

Climatic Change

Like most things, collapse explanations are subject to fashion, and the one most in the limelight today is climatic change, or more specifically, megadrought. This might sound strange because most people associate the Maya with the humid tropics, but in fact much of the Maya lowlands is a seasonal desert in two senses of the word. First, in many regions there is a protracted dry season lasting from four to six months when rainfall is either virtually absent, or at least too sparse and uncertain to grow crops. Second, many sources of surface water shrink or even dry up entirely, so potable water is scarce (remember the laborious dry-season descent into the Xtacumbi Xunan cave made by the villagers of Bolonchen). Given this precarious balance of wet and dry conditions, even a slight shift in the distribution or annual precipitation can have serious consequences. Just how people and their crops are affected partly depends on how much rain falls in a particular region, which can average as little as 440 mm (17 in) in northwestern Yucatan, to 4000 mm (157 in) in parts of the southern Peten of Guatemala. When rains failed seriously in premodern times, Maya people were faced with famine, and on occasion with outright death from thirst.

Drought has always periodically afflicted the Maya, and it exhibits varying degrees of intensity. Even in wet regions such as around Tikal, which averages about 1945 mm (76 in) annually, there are few "normal" years, but instead wide variation around the statistical mean. Sometimes plenty of rain falls, but it arrives a bit late, or there is an unusually dry interval as the crops ripen. In these circumstances the harvest might be sparse, but people can generally tighten their belts and get by. More serious are marked deficiencies in annual rainfall extending over one or several years. Such protracted droughts can cause widespread famine, along with disease and social disruption. Many episodes of hunger, death, and conflict related to droughts of this kind are featured in the various Books of Chilam Balam, and scores of historical droughts are also recorded for northern Yucatan during Colonial and later times. Although exact census figures are unavailable, during the worst of them as many as 30–50 percent of the rural Maya population might have died. So frequent have droughts been, in fact, that they are almost an ordinary, if dangerous and unpredictable, fact of agrarian life. Hazardous though they are, Maya farmers have learned to cope with them, as no doubt did their ancestors. This brings us to the issue of megadrought.

By megadrought I mean periods of severely reduced rainfall that last for decades or even centuries. Instead of short deviations from a "normal" climatic state, such droughts represent long-term shifts in climate that can have very dire results, and against which short-term coping behavior is useless (I list it as a catastrophic ecological cause because it presumably manifested itself very suddenly). Before examining the issue of Maya megadroughts, I must digress briefly about paleoclimates more generally.

Until quite recently climatologists had a rather poor grasp of exactly how global climate works, what causes it to change, or the patterns of those changes over time. To take just one familiar example, today we are all sensitized to the unusual weather generated in the Northern Hemisphere by El Niño events.[20] Just 30 years ago, few people would even have recognized the name of this phenomenon, which then was thought even by climatologists to have strictly local effects along the northwestern coast of South America. Over the last several decades scientists have developed many powerful and sophisticated methods for reconstructing and interpreting details of climatic history, and exactly how the earth's great climate systems operate. Their success is one reason for the current popularity of drought explanations for the Maya collapse. Some of the most spectacular interpretations derive from ice cores extracted from continental glaciers in Greenland since 1989. Preserved in these cores are annually discrete ice and snow layers, much like tree rings, that extend back as far as 110,000 years. Supplemented by independent information from other methods, most notably studies of deep sea sediments, these glacial records have revealed some surprising things. First, all human civilizations and the agricultural systems upon which they depend have evolved during a time of rather unusual climatic stability that began about 11,500 years ago, as the last glacial episode drew to a close. Second, before that time there were wild swings in climate. What we used to think were gradual changes that took place over centuries turn out to have occurred over several decades or even just a few years, and on hemispheric or even worldwide scales. This is an important point, because the onset of the later proposed megadrought that afflicted the Maya might have been quite sudden.

Although it has proved much more difficult to acquire similar longitudinal evidence from tropical regions, paleoclimatologists believe that what happened in the North Atlantic heavily influenced and reflected climate elsewhere. Exactly how these global events affected local or regional climatic conditions is a difficult question that must be investigated by other means, such as discharge rates of rivers, isotopes and sediments recovered from lakes or swamps, macrofossils found in animal burrows and archaeological deposits. Right now what we can see best are the really big swings on the one hand, and comparatively local conditions at the other extreme. Putting these together into a detailed, region-by-region climatic history is the next challenge.

From very early on climate change was implicated in the Maya collapse. Almost a century ago the geographer and environmental determinist Ellsworth Huntington scrutinized tree-ring data from California redwoods. He concluded that although there were many climatic shifts during the course of Maya civilization, the final blow came when conditions turned so hot and moist that stone tools simply could not contend with the burgeoning growth of the tropical forest. Since Huntington's time a huge literature, replete with arguments and counter-arguments, has grown up about this issue – far more than we can possibly review here. Fortunately Richardson Gill has done the job for us in his recent book *The Great Maya Droughts*, which summarizes and interprets an extraordinary wealth of data concerning the workings of the world's atmospheric systems, paleoclimates, historical droughts and famines, volcanic episodes, and much more besides. In particular, he critically evaluates past ideas about how climate change affected the Classic Maya, along with the most recent findings of paleoclimatology.

Following up the work of other archaeologists, principally Vernon Scarborough and his colleagues, Gill believes that water management was an essential role of Maya kings and elites from very early times, and formed a key adjunct to their political economies. Whole landscapes at centers such as Tikal were artificially contoured and plastered in order to channel rainwater into reservoirs that stored sufficient quantities for the long dry season. Maya commoners congregated about these facilities when the rains ceased, and the power and authority of lords battened on their control of water. Then, at the end of the 8th century, an unprecedented climatic disaster occurred.

Succinctly put, Gill's argument is that when temperatures in the Northern Hemisphere are warm, there is increased rainfall in the Maya Lowlands. When cooler temperatures prevail, conditions are dryer and the onset of the rainy season is delayed. While acknowledging the frequency of occasional drought and the resilience of Maya people in the face of it, Gill identifies a series of megadroughts that he correlates with the major minicollapses we reviewed earlier. He calls these the Preclassic Abandonment (around AD 150–200), the Hiatus (AD 530–590), the Classic collapse of the 8th and 9th centuries, and the Postclassic Abandonment (around AD 1450). Building on the earlier ideas of other Mayanists, Gill thinks that the whole course of Maya civilization was thus periodically afflicted with megadroughts caused by larger shifts in worldwide climate, sometimes exacerbated by coincidental volcanic eruptions in Mexico, Guatemala, and elsewhere.

By far the most protracted and destructive of these proposed droughts occurred between AD 800 and 1000. So drastic was this drought (possibly aggravated by an eruption of Popocatepetl around AD 822–823) that, according to Gill, not only did crops fail, but rivers and lakes dried up. Even the sophisticated water collection facilities that had sustained the Maya through previous crises proved inadequate, and natural underground water levels fell so deep that the Maya could not dig down to them using their primitive technology. "The civilization, the cultural tradition including the engineering built up over the centuries, had a fatal vulnerability: its total dependence on consistent rainfall to replenish its reservoirs. When the rains failed, the reservoirs dried up, and the people had no water to drink."[21]

I found Gill's book to be very refreshing, in part because he takes an extreme and controversial position and argues strenuously for it. He avowedly champions one single cause for the Classic collapse, and there is nothing tentative about his conclusion: "... devastation on a scale rarely suffered in world history destroyed Classic Maya civilization beginning about AD 810 as a brutal drought struck the Yucatan Peninsula."[22] This conclusion derives heavily from unique, historical, natural "events," but it is inherently theoretical in the larger scientific sense because it draws our attention to basic ecological problems faced by all organisms – the necessity to extract necessary resources and maintain themselves as individuals and as populations in the face of unpredictable and uncontrollable environmental perturbations. Although Gill insists on one underlying cause, he does not envision the collapse simply in terms of its immediate biological consequences – death by famine and thirst. Disease, war, and internal conflict were also triggered by drought, and people lost faith in the ability of their leaders to manage crucial resources. Still, what happened to the Maya was no fault of their own, but the result of exogenous forces totally beyond their control. It is important to be perfectly clear about this last point: while Gill acknowledges that there were significant stresses in Late Classic Maya society, the collapse would have happened even without them.

The megadrought hypothesis is attractive because it postulates a catastrophe that hit all levels of Maya society at the same time, triggering a total system collapse. Because this catastrophe extended over two centuries, it also helps explain the protracted nature of what happened, and even a certain amount of the selectivity seen in the archaeological record. Gill acknowledges that the drought might have been more severe at some times than others, and affected some regions differently than others (true, but there is a danger here of creating a "chameleon" model that can be used to explain any set of observations). Gill backs up his ideas with masses of information so that readers can make up their own minds about his interpretations, and he knows when to be cautious. Remarking that 85 percent of known droughts in the Maya Lowlands can plausibly be correlated with tropical volcanic eruptions, for example, he properly notes that correlation is not proof. As he also observes, it is an axiom of good science (Occam's Razor) that one should seek the simplest possible answers to complex problems.

I personally find the climatic arguments fascinating for two reasons. Despite the comparative stability of the last 11,500 years, there is no question that the ancient Maya experienced many climatic changes that had significant effects on their lives. I also have long believed that the collapse was triggered by some kind of ecological flaw in the agrarian underpinnings of the Classic economy. That being said, I have strong reservations about the efficacy of megadrought as the cause of the collapse (as well as the earlier crises), to the exclusion of any others.

Part of my skepticism relates to something I noted earlier – the difficulty of inferring local conditions from hemispheric patterns and trends. Most of the climatic data presented by Gill, as well as information on historical droughts and famines, comes from northern Yucatan, for the perfectly understandable reason that no comparable long-term record is available for the sparsely populated Classic Maya core area far to the south. These local data are then linked with the newly understood hemispheric trends to argue the existence of a megadrought that affected the whole Maya Lowlands (as well as other parts of Mesoamerica). Even big droughts do not uniformly affect large regions, and a major problem is that we have insufficient data from the southern Lowlands to confirm extreme, protracted dryness there.

Paleoclimatologists must reconstruct local climatic conditions using indirect lines of evidence that are often equally compatible with other explanations. Say, for example, that fossil pollen is recovered from a dated sediment core, and that in a segment of that core all signs of moisture-sensitive arboreal species disappear and are replaced by grass pollen. Drought might account for this vegetation shift, but so too might extensive deforestation caused by humans. Similarly, both drought and human-induced deforestation might cause severe erosion. Discerning the specific effects of megadroughts on local landscapes is a messy business because disentangling natural from human processes is so difficult.

More damaging is something that has always perplexed Mayanists – the worst effects of the Classic collapse manifested themselves in the humid south, instead of in the much dryer northern half of the peninsula. Not only does the north receive less annual rain, but there are no rivers or large permanent swamps like those of the southern Lowlands, so scattered cenotes and small lakes provided most of the drinking water in the dry season. Soils are thin and stony. About the only ecological advantages the northern Maya possessed were that their land was too flat for soil erosion to be much of a problem, and the water table was not far below the surface. It is on this comparatively inhospitable landscape that the Maya should have been most vulnerable. Yet farmers colonized it very early on, and while the northern centers and polities that subsequently developed were seldom as impressive as their southern counterparts, the northern Maya tradition endured right up to the Spanish conquest. It should be just the other way around if widespread megadrought occurred.

A little exercise using data presented by Gill illustrates the point. The most drastic drought ever actually measured in northern Yucatan occurred in 1902–04. During those three consecutive years the deficits in rainfall were, respectively, 21 percent, 57 percent, and 25 percent. Because northern Yucatan is so dry (averaging only 945.5 mm, or 37.2 in, at Merida) such deficits could be very damaging, in effect depressing rainfall to levels typical of many of the semi-arid western states of the U.S. Now imagine that a similar drought hit the entire Peninsula. If Tikal's mean annual rainfall were reduced by the 1903 proportion, some 860 mm (34 in) of annual precipitation would still fall. Similarly, around Piedras Negras, where the mean rainfall is about 2490 mm (98 in), the 57 percent reduction in rainfall would still amount to about 1070 mm (42 in). Plenty of Maya farmers in northern Yucatan have grown good corn crops on rainfall in this range for centuries.

The point is that detecting drought in a general sense only takes us so far. What really matters is intensity – just how dry did specific local environments become, and how was precipitation distributed throughout the growing season? We currently have no way of making such estimates. But in any case, only an extremely odd megadrought would, over the course of two centuries, destroy the agrarian potential of the south and leave northern Yucatan comparatively unscathed.

Another question is why there are certain puzzling selective effects in the fates of various Maya kingdoms if drought were indeed the culprit. In other words, the archaeological record does not always fit the drought model very well, although Gill labors mightily to make it do so. For one thing, the death-by-thirst dimension that is so conspicuous in his model does not account for why whole populations disappeared in some parts of the Lowlands. Tikal's core population resided about 32 km (20 miles) northeast of the largest lake system on the entire peninsula – the very one around which the Itza lived in 1697. If their elite-managed reservoirs failed, why did the Tikal population not simply move? The nearby ancient center of Yaxah lies on shore of one of these lakes, and along the western margins of the Maya Lowlands major centers such as Yaxchilan and Piedras Negras were right on the Usumacinta river (where elite water-management was never needed), yet all these were abandoned.

To get around these difficulties Gill imagines that even these major lakes and rivers might have entirely dried up, but this is sheer supposition, and to me a real stretch. I was camped on the banks of the Usumacinta at the end of the dry season of 1998, one of the driest years on record, and there was still plenty of water in it. As for the Peten lakes, we presently have very limited knowledge of their historical hydrology. Current evidence suggests slightly higher lake levels today, and also in Preclassic and Early Classic times, than during the Late Classic. Such marginal changes, if linked directly to rainfall, would not create any shortage of water for drinking or for crops.[23]

In fact, Gill uses the surface water argument both ways. Because centers like Piedras Negras were abandoned, the Usumacinta must have dried up. But where population did not abruptly crash, as at Coba, it must be because large permanent lakes were present. Such arguments are not only inconsistent, but also tautological. And as we shall see in some of the following case study chapters, decline within some regions or polities does not fit the hypothesis.

At this point it is useful to look briefly at several recent studies that detected the AD 800–1000 megadrought and how they match the archaeological record.[24] Each was based on a dated sediment core extracted from one of two shallow lakes, Chichancacab and Punta Laguna, in northern Yucatan. Shells of small organisms in these sediments contain specific oxygen isotopes, and changes in isotopic concentrations, as well as other chemical signatures, are used as proxies for temperature/climate variation. On the basis of these geochemical signatures, the paleoclimatologists identified the period from AD 800 to 1050 as "... one of the driest intervals in the last 3500 years." According to the most recent research, intervals of drought are strongly correlated with, and probably caused by, a 208-year cycle of solar energy.[25] Here, Gill believes, is the "smoking gun" that confirms the hypothesis.

When I first read these studies they perplexed me because they do not seem to jibe with important archaeological events. Lake Chichancacab is situated only about 100 km (63 miles) east of the Puuc region. Remember that population started to build up there about AD 750, but the real florescence of the Puuc polities fell squarely during the beginning of the purported drought. Monument dates are too few to establish a sound historical chronology, but some of the most impressive buildings at Uxmal were built around

AD 900–925, and the population of the Puuc region probably peaked around AD 950, right in the middle of the proposed megadrought. How was this possible in a district that only gets about 1100 mm (43.3 in) of rain, when regions to the south that get twice as much were purportedly collapsing from drought?

One retort might be that the Puuc people had ingeniously mastered *chultun* (underground cistern) technology, which enabled individual households to capture and store vast amounts of water despite the drought. But of course the flaw in this argument is that chultunes captured rainwater, and the same rain that drained into them must have also fallen on the agricultural fields that nourished the Puuc population. Where then is the drought?

The Puuc countryside was admittedly abandoned by about AD 1000. But remember that it was succeeded by the greatest northern polity of them all, centered on Chichen Itza. According to Rafael Cobo, who has just finished a multi-year project there, Chichen Itza grew mightily after about AD 950 as its two principal rivals (the Puuc centers and Coba) were eclipsed, and continued as a power for several centuries.[26] Gill surmises that centers such as Chichen Itza survived because, unlike in the southern cities, their populations had better access to water, which was not so deep underground, but of course this again does not explain what watered their crops. And his attempts to get around the Chichen Itza anomaly by radical chronological realignment are extremely labored.

Puzzled by these incompatabilities with the archaeological record, I quizzed a scientific expert over a couple of beers. My colleague at Penn State, Richard Alley, is a noted paleoclimatogist whose book *The Two Mile Time Machine* recounts the fascinating story of the Greenland ice cores, among many other things. Alley believes that although determining the concentrations of oxygen isotopes in lakes like those in northern Yucatan is straightforward, it is far from certain that these are direct proxies for temperature in tropical environments. And even if they were, they might not tell us much about levels of precipitation.

A final problem is the inconsistency and selectivity of the local paleoclimatic yardsticks themselves, which exhibit a kind of mosaic pattern. Well-established lakes in northern Yucatan, including the two from which the sediment cores were taken, show no signs of desiccation despite the presumed drought.[27] Another recent core from the Peten lakes to the south was studied by several of the same scientists who investigated the northern lakes, and is presumably more pertinent to what happened around Tikal. This southern core shows no clear signature of the northern megadrought, and there is considerable difficulty in distinguishing between natural and anthropogenic transformations. A major conclusion of the study, in fact, is that the Maya themselves were responsible for many of the changes detected: "Evidence from lake sediments indicates that the Maya dramatically transformed the local landscape by clearing forests for construction and agriculture."[28]

My own opinion is that the megadrought model, particularly if envisioned as the single knockout blow that destroyed the Maya, has a lot of problems. One of them is overstatement, especially on the part of some of the physical scientists who are not intimately acquainted with the archaeological record. More realistically, what we have right now are apparent correlations between large-scale climatic events, isotopic variation in lakes, and periodic crises in the Maya Lowlands. Until we better understand the local effects of these events, the implications of the isotopic assays, as well as the specific mechanisms by which Terminal Classic kingdoms and politics were affected, identifying megadrought as the cause of the collapse smacks of climatic determinism. And in addition to identifying so many possible correlations between dryness, volcanism, and Maya culture history, we should, like good scientists, ask what kinds of information might falsify the drought argument, which is unclear to me from Gill's presentation.

Right now megadrought is the "hot" explanation for the Classic collapse, and the usual bandwagon effect is in full career among many of my colleagues, although others remain properly suspicious of drought as the triggering mechanism. Generally speaking, the drought explanation seems to be most enthusiastically accepted by natural scientists, and I suspect that they derive a considerable cachet from linking their observations of chemical or astronomical phenomena to the great mystery of the Maya collapse (and how fitting if the great sun-kings were done in by sun-spots). Here is my prediction: wait five years and we will see that drought, mega- or otherwise, has receded into the background as just one more factor in what happened. Skeptical as I am, however, I am receptive to the idea that drought played its part at some times and places, though not necessarily in the ways argued by Gill or the paleoclimatologists. More research will hopefully make things clearer in the near future.

Disease

In 1348 the first wave of the Black Death struck England and killed at least 30 percent of its people. So severe was this demographic disaster that, compounded by the effects of the European Little Ice Age (which arrived at about the same time), the population did not recover its pre-plague levels until as late as 1650. Such dramatic historical epidemics reveal both the destructive power of diseases and the capacity of human populations to rebound from their effects.

At first glance, some sort of virulent disease seems attractive as a potential cause of the Classic collapse. Not only might it explain the putative demographic catastrophe, but it could also account for something equally puzzling – the lack of recovery over the long run. Certain kinds of diseases, we know, can make large regions very dangerous to live in and permanently depress their population levels. One reason why the Puuc zone of Yucatan remained so lightly populated until recently, for example, is that it harbored malaria and yellow fever introduced from the Old World. Effects of a major epidemic are also consistent with the protracted collapse itself. Initial episodes of mortality might have been followed by recurrent, if less severe outbreaks (this is the pattern for the Black Death and many other documented epidemics). Certain diseases like typhus are also closely associated with famines, such as those proposed by the megadrought hypothesis. Even the puzzling north-south discrepancy in the fate of the Maya might relate to some kind of environmental or cultural difference in the etiology of a specific communicable disease.

Nor does damage from disease derive only from its direct effects on human organisms. Many preindustrial economies were based on efficient and intricate use of household labor, with few or no institutional buffers should household production fail. Death or morbidity associated with disease could thus severely disrupt domestic economies, causing other forms of mortality, resource reduction, and social upheaval.

The big problem with this putative cause is that the New World seems to have been a much healthier place than the Old World prior to 1492. Not that populations in Mesoamerica or elsewhere were free of disease. Quite the contrary, they were afflicted by bacillary and amoebic dysentery, pneumonia, yaws, tuberculosis, fevers, bacterial infections (streptococcus, staphylococcus), various kinds of food poisonings (salmonella, etc.), numerous parasitic infestations, and deficiency diseases such as goiter and anemia related to malnutrition.[29] Absent, however, were the big epidemic killers like smallpox, influenza, measles, typhus, typhoid, plague, and cholera, along with malaria and yellow fever, which do their damage more slowly. In fact, some of the best evidence for the long separation of Old and New World populations was their differential susceptibility to infectious diseases upon first contact. Everyone has heard of the massive destruction wrought by diseases introduced by Europeans, to which native populations had no immunity (Fig. 39).

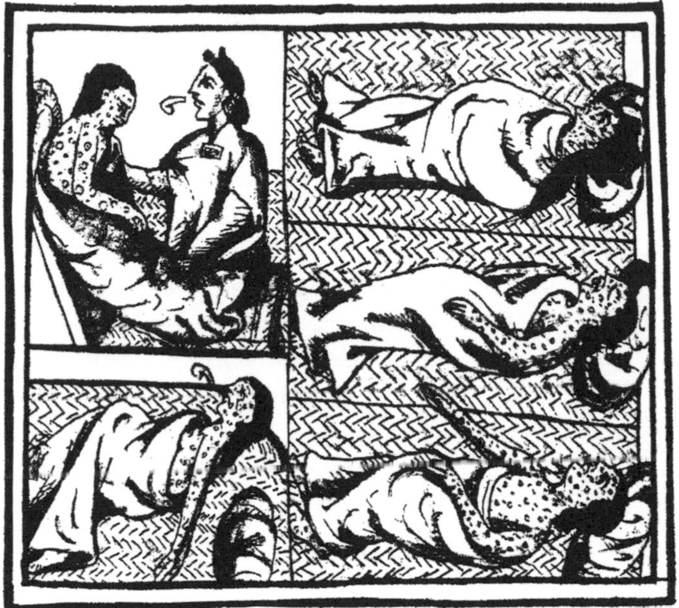

39 *Postconquest drawing of Aztec smallpox victims. The Aztec population had no natural resistance to smallpox, which was introduced by Europeans. Within two to three generations the core Aztec population of the Basin of Mexico was reduced by about 90 percent largely through the effects of this and other foreign diseases.*

Revealingly, no similar transmission apparently went in the other direction, apart (possibly) from venereal syphilis.

Why this curious dichotomy existed has been the subject of many books, most recently Jared Diamond's *Guns, Germs, and Steel.* Diamond points out that virtually all of the microbes responsible for the really deadly Old World diseases had their origins in animals, and particularly in domestic cattle, pigs, and fowl. As we know, New World people developed nothing comparable to the intense interaction between humans and animals characteristic of Eurasia or Africa (nor did native Australians, who were also very susceptible to European diseases). Another difference is that some of the biggest killers, such as measles, are so-called "crowd diseases" that require large, dense concentrations of people to maintain themselves. Not only was the New World generally more lightly populated than the Old, but it also had comparatively few high-density urban centers. Although we tend to think of great epidemics or pandemics as natural disasters, in fact they are intimately related to cultural phenomena such as urbanization and subsistence practices, and other aspects of human ecology.

Our own public health initiatives continually remind us that humans and disease organisms coevolve. Diseases are themselves mutable and cunning, and often adapt quickly to the measures we take against them, so each winter we have to develop new vaccines to combat the latest strain of flu. In fact many communicable diseases that we have historically called by the same name probably took on very distinct forms over time. The "plague" that appeared in 14th-century Europe and recurred for several centuries, for example, might be very different from the plague of today. Accounts of particular historical epidemics sometimes feature strange sets of symptoms that fit no known modern syndromes. And we know from recent tragic experience that terrible new diseases, such as Aids and Ebola, can suddenly appear and ravage large populations, even in the face of modern medical intervention.

Just conceivably one or more lethal New World disease suddenly appeared in the past, ran its course, and then disappeared. For this reason we cannot rule out the possibility (especially if Maya populations were as large and dense as some maintain) that an extremely virulent and totally unknown disease struck the Classic Maya on an epidemic or pandemic scale around the late 8th century. But even if this turns out to be the case, why were the northern Maya not much affected? And why did Maya populations not eventually recover, as did their European counterparts?

Unfortunately, identifying diseases in ancient archaeological populations is problematical, particularly when no soft tissues remain. Lethal diseases that strike swiftly leave no traces on bone or teeth, so only art or historical records might reveal their presence. Even where bones are affected, it is usually unclear exactly which specific disease was responsible. Although we currently lack evidence of any sudden, epidemic disease that might have caused the collapse, the Maya throughout their history, like most tropical populations, carried a heavy endemic disease load. Cultural factors such as increasingly poor diet might have contributed to general debilitation and lowered fertility, and some diseases, such as infant diarrhea and various wormy infections, are closely related to high population density, permanent residence, and intensive agricultural practices such as use of human waste for fertilizer. Such density dependent diseases, of course, would have had their most serious effects in the late 8th century.

According to some early studies of Maya skeletons, elite people were taller than commoners during the Early Classic period, suggesting privileged diets or less stress. As time went on, the stature of people of all ranks was reduced, presumably because of increasingly poorer diets. These patterns are not so obvious today now that we have much better skeletal samples. Nevertheless, paleo-osteologists can often detect the general skeletal signatures of many endemic conditions, some synergistic with malnutrition and other kinds of stresses, that probably increased in frequency as the collapse approached. We will review some of this evidence in the case study section.

Human Degradation of the Agricultural Landscape

I read the other day that the city of Atlanta has grown so huge that it is now generating its own mini-climate. We are all accustomed to stories like this, and have long been conditioned to the idea that humans are active agents in environmental change, usually of deleterious kinds. What most people fail to realize is that this is not a recent phenomenon, linked only to industrial, urban, capitalist economies and worldwide populations in the billions (although admittedly we mess things up faster, and on a far larger scale, than our ancestors). Any archaeologist can point to dozens of ancient examples of human-induced deforestation, erosion, loss of soil fertility, and extinction of native plants and animals (the best recent summary is *Human Impact on Ancient Environments* (2000), by Charles Redman). Read Redman and the other literature on this subject and you will find that the Classic Maya take pride of place among ancient civilizations in terms of this dismal record.

Almost since the beginning of systematic studies of the Maya, anthropogenic destruction of the agricultural landscape has been identified as the prime cause of the Classic collapse. This explanation is the reverse of that favored by Richardson Gill, in that the culprit is not some *deus ex machina* in the form of megadrought; instead, the Maya did it to themselves. Remember that Edwin Erickson came to the conclusion that the collapse was the result of some internal, self-limiting process through his study of the pattern of Long Count dates (p. 211), and this suspicion was widely held long before his time. One early example is the botanist C. W. Cooke, who proposed in the 1930s that the swamps near Tikal were originally deep lakes that had silted up with clay eroded from nearby hillsides as the Maya deforested and cultivated them. Not only did soil disappear, but the resulting shallow swamps became breeding grounds for disease-bearing insects. Another suggestion was that tough-rooted grasses invaded cultivated fields, rendering them difficult to cultivate using hand tools. A bit later, the Ricketsons began to find evidence for unusually dense ancient populations, and concluded that some sort of land use more intensive than the slash-and-burn system ultimately damaged the environment. Morley thought that soil exhaustion and crop failure resulting from milpa agriculture caused the abandonment of the southern "cities" and stimulated a great migration to the north. Although there was not much direct evidence for any of this, such explanations seemed plausible because of general properties of tropical forest ecosystems like that of the Maya Lowlands compared to those of other parts of the world.

Herodotus famously called ancient Egypt the "gift of the Nile" because the annual flooding of that great river rendered its soils so fertile. Other ancient civilizations were not comparably blessed with what ecologists call "natural capital," and the Maya were one of them. In 1954 Betty Meggers published a celebrated article in which she argued that variations in temperature, rainfall, soils, length of growing season, and other conditions encouraged the growth of complex agrarian societies in some regions of the world, and discouraged it in others.[30] Meggers maintained that the environment of the Maya was too fragile and unproductive to give rise to a great civilization (an opinion shared by many geographers of her time), and so the most impressive elements of Classic Maya culture must have been developed elsewhere and then introduced into the tropical Lowlands, where they were doomed to rapid failure.

We now know that Meggers's culture history was wrong. Maya civilization did in fact emerge gradually in southeastern Mesoamerica and endured there for many centuries. Nevertheless, she had a point. Ancient civilizations rarely developed in the humid tropics, except where rice paddy agriculture was used (as in China and southeast Asia), a particularly stable strategy because it mimics the natural ecology of seasonal wetlands. While clearly not as limited as Meggers thought, the Lowland Maya environment does nevertheless pose serious problems for farmers.

Each year beginning in 1997 I made a habit of examining the topsoil right on top of little archaeological sites I was digging around Piedras Negras. In this part of Guatemala there has been virtually no agricultural or other human activity since the region was abandoned about AD 850, so the current topsoil represents the accumulation of more than a millennium. Despite the impressive high forest canopy of mahogany, ramon, ceiba, and sapodilla, the upland soil is unexpectedly thin, generally between 10 and 20 cm (4 and 8 in), and close examination reveals that much of it consists of living roots or recently deposited organic matter in the process of decay. Except in low-lying areas, the limestone bedrock is usually found just a bit deeper. Most temperate environments would develop much deeper soils in the same interval.

When limestone weathers in hot, humid environments like that of the Maya Lowlands, most of it dissipates in the form of liquid (HCO_3) or gas (CO_2), so it takes a lot of rock to make a comparatively small amount of soil. A common rule of thumb is that the ratio is about ten to one – in other words one meter of limestone yields the mineral component of about ten cm of soil, and reducing this amount of bedrock takes a long time. Weathered minerals are supplemented by organic material to produce topsoil through a complex set of input-output processes. Plants are donors of organic detritus, and of course grow best on the deeper, most nutrient-rich soils. They also take up nutrients, and as the biomass of the vegetation matures an equilibrium is eventually achieved.[31] Quite possibly the thin soils I observed around Piedras Negras have reached such a steady state, and the soils there today might be very much like those encountered by the first Preclassic Maya farmers in the region.

This little exercise reveals one of the greatest deficiencies of humid tropical environments – most of the nutrients available for plant growth – about 75 percent – are stored in the living biomass of the vegetation. The rest is in the organic part of the soil, and under warm, humid conditions it is rapidly broken down (essentially metabolized) by "decomposer" organisms including worms, insects, fungi, and bacteria. This breakdown releases important nutrients such as nitrogen. Soils formed under these conditions typically have low nutrient reserves in proportion to those taken up each year by the living vegetation, and they also tend to be very acidic. Because even mature upland topsoils are thin and usually lack large proportions of clay, they also may fail to retain adequate moisture for most kinds of plants, especially during a protracted dry season. Mature arboreal communities maintain the recycling capacity essential to tropical forest ecosystems, and also absorb much of the seasonally torrential rainfall, which otherwise can cause severe erosion on the upland terrain that dominates much of the central and southern Maya Lowlands. Once this natural cycle is broken, as when a field is cut over and burned to grow maize and beans, a series of deleterious effects is unleashed that in the long run can be very destructive, and that results in ever-decreasing yields.

Erosion and leaching of soil nutrients are not the only problems. Weeds grow rapidly, not only crowding out domestic plants, but locking up essential nutrients in their own root systems. Insect pests, whose numbers are drastically cut back during cold seasons in temperate climates, thrive throughout the tropical year and can damage crops severely, as can other plant pathogens, especially if fields are not allowed to lie fallow for long intervals.

One last destructive force deserves mention. During the very dry year of 1998 my tent was pitched right on the Guatemalan bank of the Usumacinta river. On the Mexican side, just a few hundred meters to the west, a fire raged out of control through the forest. "Raged" is perhaps the wrong word though, because this fire did not leap from tree to tree, rapidly engulfing huge areas, as fires do in the western U.S. Instead it was an insidious fire, creeping slowly but steadily along the ground. Every so often it burned out the root system of some forest giant, which then collapsed with a mighty crash, an immense shower of sparks, and a bomb-like explosion. After watching this spectacle for a few days, I realized that the soil was actually burning, leaving only a thin layer of ash over the bedrock. Fires like this show how even short droughts can have disastrous effects, but of course most fires are set by humans, and the more numerous humans are, the more likelihood of runaway fires even during normal dry seasons.

Traditional Maya farmers adapt to these constraints in several ways. They make an effort to plant on the deepest well-drained, high-quality soils they can find, assuming they have a choice in the matter. I indirectly also observed this strategy at Piedras Negras. Since the 9th century the only farmers on the local landscape there were recent guerrillas who carried on a desultory civil war with the Guatemalan army until a peace accord was reached in 1996. Our workmen still find rusting ordinance in caves, and an abandoned guerrilla camp, complete with fortified bunkers, is about an hour's walk south of where we live. These guerrillas supported themselves by growing maize, beans, and other traditional crops, and always made their milpas and banana plantations (which we periodically raid) in the comparatively few zones of low-lying, deep soil. This pattern fascinated me, because they were replicating choices undoubtedly made by their pioneering Maya predecessors thousands of years before. Guerrilla farmers conspicuously avoided the thin and fragile hillside soils that cover most of the steep landscape (and this was not a military tactic – fields on either part of the environment are easily seen from the air).

So long as Maya farmers were comparatively few in number, they could depend on the most productive and stable parts of their landscapes and they could also shift the locations of their fields at frequent intervals as the fertility of old milpas declined. Fires could be carefully controlled, and even if they did escape, the patches of surrounding forest were usually humid enough to resist much damage. Both strategies minimized human-induced damage, maximized yields, and produced good crops with surprising efficiency. In the 1930s ethnographers determined that even in comparatively dry northern Yucatan, a farmer using only hand tools could produce enough food for his family by working about 48 days each year. So-called extensive systems of agriculture such as long-term swidden help preserve the integrity of tropical ecosystems, and humans are not only advantaged by efficient food production but many valuable natural resources are still available, such as timber for construction and firewood, along with animals and birds to supplement the diet. Farmers today who use such shifting cultivation typically do not own rights to land, nor do they want to, because such a pattern would inhibit their mobility and flexibility of choice. Instead, they maintain loose usufruct rights that are acknowledged and mediated by some sort of community council.[32]

When human population density grows beyond a certain limit, this comparatively balanced system of relationships is undermined, and a cycle of destructive changes is potentially triggered because fields are cultivated too frequently. Deforestation becomes widespread, soils cease to be enriched by litter and tree fall, nutrients are leached away, weeds burgeon, along with plant pests and pathogens, erosion denudes hillsides, and fires increasingly destroy the organic "natural capital" of the thin forest soils. Figuring out how the ancient Maya coped with all this is why archaeologists are so interested in how many people made their livings on the landscapes of Late Classic kingdoms. Many archaeologists believe that the Maya found themselves in a kind of ecological trap of their own making. Population growth spiraled out of control and the productive potential of their landscapes degraded as human carrying capacity was reached or exceeded.

That there is plenty of evidence for this conclusion is shown, to take but one example, by data from the central lakes region of the Peten, a landscape particularly well studied by both paleoecologists and archaeologists. Figure 40 illustrates how a whole series of ancient lacustrine and terrestrial processes interacted through time, as reflected in lake sediments recovered in the Tikal region.[33] Deforestation caused soil to erode into the lakes, depositing huge amounts of inorganic sediments that in turn lowered lacustrine productivity. Phosphorous, an essential nutrient of plants which is replaced only slowly in soils, washed into the lakes, one measure of declining soil fertility. Such evidence flies in the face of one dearly-held tenet of the popular "mystique" that we discussed earlier – that the ancient Maya were sophisticated tropical ecologists who lived in some kind of long-term balance with their ecosystem.

Granted that correlations do not necessarily indicate cause-and-effect relationships, it is hard to believe that all these concurrent changes were caused by chance, and are unrelated to human activity. Similar evidence exists for other regions, as we shall see in the case study sections. In the final chapter, we will consider in more detail the convergence of environmental damage and Maya social and cultural practices – the cultural and political ecology of the collapse.

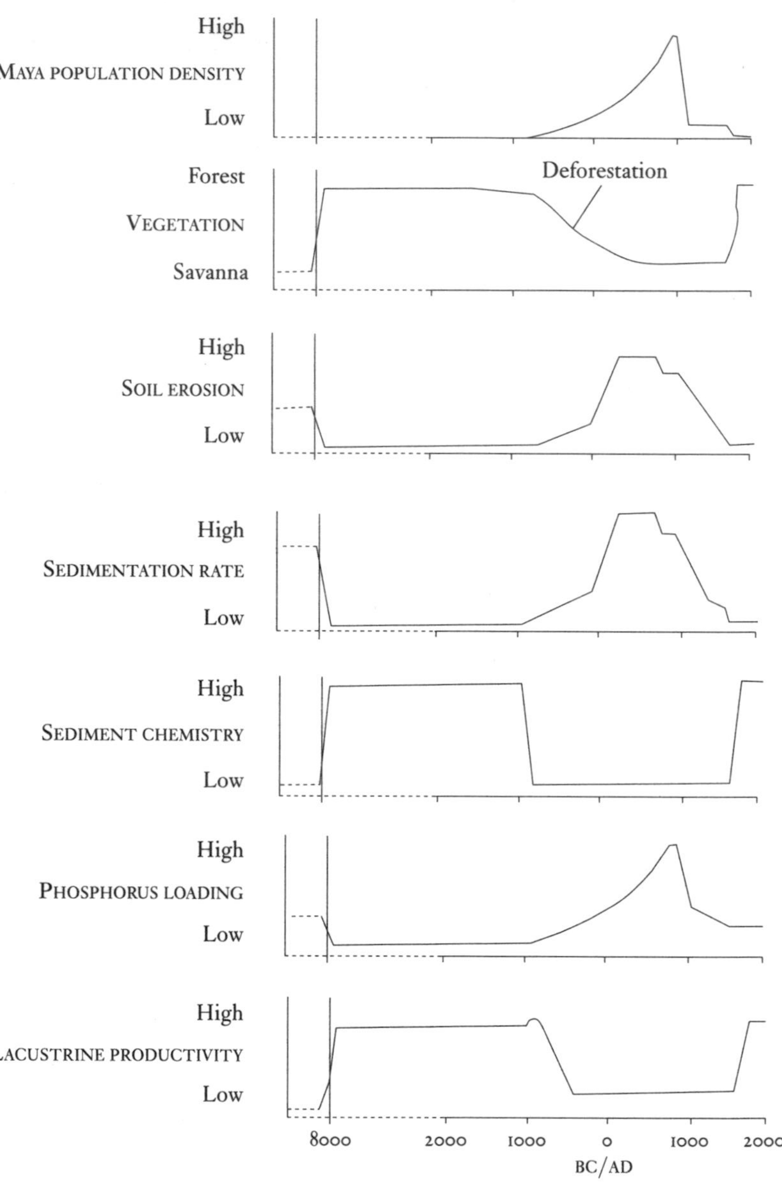

40 *Intensive sampling of lake deposits reveals abundant chemical and sediment signatures of environmental degradation from the Tikal region, Guatemala. Major episodes of erosion and nutrient loss coincide closely with the peak population on the Peten landscape.*

Blaming the Maya collapse on anthropogenic changes in the agricultural ecosystem is attractive because it focuses attention on the all-important energetic foundations of Maya civilization. If this crucial dimension of food energy failed, it is easy to see why a total system collapse might result. Agrarian failure, moreover, could easily trigger war, rebellion, disease, disruption of trade, and ideological fatigue as secondary causes. Deforestation and denudation of soils, if sufficiently extensive, might even cause local climatic change – specifically drought – because the albedo (the proportion of solar radiation reflected by a landscape) is increased. And of course the forest itself is the source, through evapotranspiration, of much of the moisture that is recycled into the atmosphere and falls again as rain. Nor is disruption of the food supply the only problem. Many other crucial materials, such as fuel, materials for house building, and sources of animal protein might have disappeared.

Most Mayanists are convinced that significant problems of these kinds did occur, and contributed heavily to the collapse. There are, however, many dissenters who think that ancient Maya farmers were able to adapt successfully to these stresses by adopting new sorts of staple crops (e.g., manioc, ramon nuts) that had less impact on soils, more intensive forms of agriculture (terraces, drained fields) that were more stable, or by "micromanaging" their environments in nondestructive ways.[34] Some of these innovations (e.g. a largely non-maize diet) seem less likely on the basis of new isotopic studies of skeletons, and others, insofar as they can be detected archaeologically, show unexpected patterns. For example, extensive terrace systems are found around the center of Caracol, but are often lacking elsewhere, as at Tikal or Piedras Negras. Many of the drained fields long ago detected by aerial remote sensing around the edges of swamps have since been shown not to exist, and others are now known to date to the Preclassic, and so have nothing to do with the Late/Terminal Classic population peak. And of course some of the demographic problem goes away if we have been systematically overestimating ancient population densities, as I believe we have. Nevertheless, Maya farmers were clearly very clever people who endured in surprising numbers over long periods of time, and doubtless had skills and strategies that remain unknown to us.

Central to the environmental degradation argument is the idea that Maya populations grew so large that they eventually "overshot" the carrying capacities of their landscapes. Some anthropologists believe that humans in fact keep their numbers in reasonable balance with available resources using conscious and deliberate methods of population control. If this is true, then population size and density become non-issues. George Cowgill, who takes this position, turned the competition idea around by suggesting that Maya population growth was a deliberately-fostered policy on the part of some kingdoms as an adaptation to constant warfare.[35]

Population stress, of course, does not necessarily equate with population growth. Clearly a population might be growing precisely because there were plenty of resources, and a stable or declining one might signal stress. What really matters is the relationship of people to available resources, and this can shift for many reasons other than population change. For example, if drought hit a large, prosperous, but stable population on a landscape like Tikal's, it would both reduce the general carrying capacity and more drastically affect those farmers making a living on thin, and comparatively dry upland soils.

Finally, to return to a point made earlier, we have to admit that the causes of some of the changes we detect are open to argument. Might not the erosion and deforestation evident in Fig. 40 be the product of drought instead of overpopulation? This is a good question. And what made the northern Maya Lowlands resistant to abandonment on the scale of the south? Answers must come from many independent lines of evidence.

❦ ❦ ❦

Identifying the elite and total system classes of explanation makes us face up to a crucial question concerning the Maya collapse: was the elite part of the process in any particular region or polity decoupled from the total system part, and if so, exactly how? Anticipating our upcoming consideration of what happened to Copan, I would introduce still another refinement: did kings and non-royal elites go down at the same time? Clearly these are not easy questions to answer. It is fairly simple to detect and date the cessation of royal activity, both because its archaeological signatures are so obtrusive and because so much work has been focused on regal-ritual centers. Imagine by contrast the problem of determining when hundreds or thousands of outlying households of commoners were abandoned, each one of which has its own distinct occupational history. These little places leave few remains, have no complex architectural stratigraphy, are almost never associated with dates or inscriptions, and for a very long time were ignored by archaeologists who assumed that what happened at the top of Classic society also concurrently happened at the bottom. They are also, of course, essential to resolving the issue of Maya population densities and how these changed through time, which in turn is the key to how much anthropogenic change contributed to the collapse.

It should now be clear that despite the fact that the list of causes we reviewed is so similar to older ones, we are in a much better position to evaluate them. War has become archaeologically much more visible, but more important is our finely textured appreciation of the details of its political and geographical occurrence, thanks to the inscriptions. Similarly, we seem to be on the verge of major breakthroughs in understanding climatic change, and our grasp of settlement patterns and demographic patterns is much more sophisticated than it was 20 or 30 years ago, at least for some important regions.

We can also appreciate how some explanations work better for some regions and polities than others, both because of environmental variation and the specific histories of polities themselves. Nevertheless, although the Maya were never politically centralized, they did comprise a coherent "system" of civilization, especially in terms of their elite interactions. In some sense the collapse process was communicable, in that the declining fortunes of one center, polity, or region affected the political, ideological, and economic well-being of their neighbors.

Examining a list of causes is useful because it focuses our attention on specific issues, but there is another way of conceptualizing what happened to the Maya. Imagine an automobile that has well-engineered individual components, but also serious flaws in overall design that place unusual stresses on essential parts. When the vehicle finally breaks down, we might single out the failure of wheel bearings, crankshafts, or whatever, but the real cause would be the general structure of the automobile's system. As we saw in Chapter 5, ancient Maya society was certainly not "engineered" or "designed" in the same way a machine is, but this logic still applies. John Lowe, in his sophisticated mathematical simulation of the collapse, asserted that the real cause was not disease, or war, or invasion, but instead the nature of the larger Classic Maya sociocultural system itself.[36] Lowe redirected our attention to the general properties of systems, a theoretical perspective called systems theory. Many ancient societies have been plagued with serious stresses of the kinds we have reviewed but have recovered. What was especially unstable about Classic Maya civilization? Might not there have been inherent weaknesses in their larger sociocultural system? Before returning to this question we review several case studies to trace out the variety of what happened to the Classic Maya, and to see how various of our explanations fit the archaeological "facts" as currently understood.

– 8 –

MANY KINGDOMS, MANY FATES

ONE EFFECTIVE WAY TO WRITE a book about the Classic Maya collapse would be to include 20 or 30 chapters, each scrutinizing current information about a specific polity or region. Such an overview would capture the known variation of the collapse process, but it would also be very boring to the non-specialist reader and it is certainly far beyond the scope possible here. And while such broad coverage might tempt us to draw interesting general conclusions, we would be faced with comparing the proverbial apples and oranges. Fairly complete textual histories would be available for some polities, and none at all for others. Some sites would be well excavated, others hardly touched by the spade. At some places we would know a great deal about nobles and kings, but nothing about commoners. For some regions we would have reliable settlement and demographic data, and elsewhere hardly any at all.

In this chapter I instead present thumbnail sketches of five widely separated kingdoms (actually four kingdoms and one large region) that were quite varied in their histories, scales, and local adaptations, and for which various kinds of information are available.[1] After a brief summary of what we know about the growth and maturity of each case example, I review what seems to have happened at the end of the Classic period. These vignettes will show, as I intimated in the preceding chapter, that there is no standard "recipe" for the collapse, either in terms of the specific patterns of decline or the associated causes. A more detailed case example discussing the Copan kingdom follows in Chapter 9.

Fall of a Giant

We have already met Tikal many times in this narrative, and it is only fair to begin our survey with this great kingdom, which has so heavily influenced our opinions about the ancient Maya. Some early Mayanists even thought that Tikal was once the capital of a paramount ruler who presided over all the other "cities." Such claims, along with the unquestioned grandeur of the site, stimulated so much intensive archaeological work at the site that until quite recently archaeologists complained that we had an excessively "Tikal-centric" view about what the Maya in general were like, and of the rise and fall of Classic society (the idea of a pan-Maya hiatus based on dates from Tikal is a case in point). Fortunately we are no longer so reliant on information from this one great center. Nevertheless, because of its ancient origins and location, Tikal is geographically central to the other examples I have chosen, and also has historical connections to some of them, so it is a good place to start.

Tikal is located deep in the lush tropical forests of northern Guatemala, a region of gentle hills and bajos that, along with the Mirador Basin farther north, was the cradle of Lowland Maya civilization. Apparently the main attraction of the immediate locale was abundant and fertile upland soils, because surface water is in short supply despite the almost 2000 mm (78 in) of annual rain. Only 20 km (12.5 miles) to the southwest lies the great chain of Peten lakes. Nojpeten, the Itza capital and last Maya stronghold against the Spaniards, was located near the southwestern end of the largest of these, Lake Peten Itza. Some archaeologists also believe that Tikal dominated a natural east-west trade route across the peninsula.

Half a century ago the Peten was an almost empty landscape except for a few towns around the lakes and some scattered chiclero and logging camps. Local people seem to have always known about Tikal, however, and guided brief Guatemalan expeditions to the site in the 1850s. Beginning in the 1880s a succession of pioneering archaeologists cleared and mapped many of the ruins, drew and photographed the associated monuments, and removed some of them, including a famous set of carved wooden lintels. Still, comparatively little was known about Tikal right up to World War II. Just before his unexpected death in 1948, Sylvanus Morley earmarked the site for a major campaign. Eventually the University of Pennsylvania Tikal Project took up the challenge, and between 1956 and 1970 much of the landscape was accurately mapped, and many structures excavated and restored, so we now have a good understanding of regional settlement and demographic patterns. Over 200 monuments were recorded, repaired, and reset, and many tombs were exposed by the enormous stratigraphic trenches driven into huge architectural complexes. Subsequent research and restoration, especially by Guatemalan government projects, has established Tikal as a major tourist attraction, now surrounded by its own national park. Because so much has already been said about Tikal, I will only briefly summarize the high points of its history leading up to the 8th and 9th centuries, adding a little more detail to what has already been presented.

Although there are traces of early farmers dating back to about 1000 BC, Tikal (whose ancient name was probably Yax Mutal) did not come into its own as a major center until Late Preclassic times. Impressive architecture appeared around 300–400 BC, but nothing on the scale known for El Mirador and Nakbe. Rich burials appeared in the first century AD, and shortly thereafter Tikal began to boom as the major political and cultural beneficiary of the decline of these northern giants. As we already saw, epigraphers have traced its dynastic roots back to a shadowy individual named Yax Ehb' Xook (First Step Shark) who lived about AD 90. There followed a long succession of at least 34 kings, along with two prominent royal women, that endured for 800 years.

From the very beginning of the Classic period Tikal was powerfully influenced by Teotihuacan, the probable origin of Siyaj K'ak', the intruder who disrupted local events in AD 378.[2] Siyaj K'ak' exerted control over nearby Uaxactun (previously an important capital in its own right) and more distant centers in the region, but for some reason never ascended to the Tikal throne himself. Instead, a man with the distinctly Mexican name of Spearthrower Owl (probably the son of a henchman of Siyaj K'ak') was installed as the next king in AD 379, initiating a whole new dynastic line. Later, in the 5th century, Spearthrower Owl's grandson fused Teotihuacan and Maya symbols on his royal monuments, and war texts began to appear. About the same time a system of ditches and earthworks was built along the northern and (probably) the southern peripheries of Tikal's hinterland, linking up with large swamps on the east and west. These apparent fortifications protected a region of 120 sq. km (46.3 sq. miles) that contained the kingdom's core population and agricultural resources.[3] In all likelihood their construction signaled the beginnings of great military struggles that intensified during the next century.

Although there are occasional signs of internal discord, Tikal remained powerful until her fateful military confrontation in AD 592 (apparently with Calakmul and her ally Caracol) that probably resulted in the capture and sacrifice of her king. This defeat ushered in the 130 year "hiatus" (AD 562–692) that we reviewed earlier. But Tikal was neither abandoned nor without kings during this interval, as we know from inscribed small objects and from texts at other centers. Local kings continued to rule, and still sponsored large building projects. Internal politics were probably highly volatile, however, with apparent struggles between rival dynastic lines. Around AD 648 a disaffected group fled to the west, where its leader B'alaj Chan K'awiil founded the kingdom of Dos Pilas (to which we will return shortly). This ruler used Tikal's emblem glyph and remained a claimant to the Tikal rulership, his ambitions supported by his patron, Calakmul, whose kings took every opportunity to meddle in Tikal's dynastic affairs. Shortly thereafter, Tikal's own king seems to have fled as a refugee to distant Palenque under apparent Calakmul pressure, and only later returned to recover his throne.

The energetic Jasaw Chan K'awiil I eventually restored Tikal's preeminence by decisively defeating archenemy Calakmul in AD 695, celebrating this event with ceremonies and symbols harking back to the glory days of Spearthrower Owl. He and his warrior son and successor Yik'in Chan K'awiil continued to harass their old enemy and its allies, and firmly established regional control over nearby territory, especially the lands around Lake Peten Itza. Huge building projects were carried out under the patronage of these two resurgent rulers, who left us the mature architectural landscape we see today, including the most massive of Tikal's grand temples (Plate 15). Quite possibly much of this work was underwritten by labor and other resources drawn from Tikal's newly recovered dependencies.

During the latter years of the 8th century Tikal entered her prime old age. Impressive ceremonial complexes were built to commemorate 20-year k'atun milestones, but there are few inscriptions referring to late rulers. One king nicknamed Dark Sun probably built the last great pyramid (Temple 3) at the beginning of the 9th century, and dedicated other buildings and monuments in AD 810. This seems to be the last gasp of major architectural effort, however, and there follows a 60-year gap in dated monuments, although inscriptions elsewhere refer to continued royal activity. Simon Martin and Nikolai Grube (along with earlier scholars) note that lesser sites in Tikal's traditional political orbit began to set up monuments after AD 859 featuring their own local rulers and appropriating the name Mutal. Apparently Tikal's kings had insufficient power or authority by this time to suppress these assertions of independence.

One final historical flicker occurred in AD 869, when Jasaw Chan K'awiil II placed a monument in Tikal's great Central Plaza. No doubt by appropriating the name of the hero king who defeated Calakmul almost two centuries before, Jasaw Chan K'awiil II hoped to reinvigorate Tikal, but it was not to be. So far as we can tell he was the last of the dynasty. Two nearby centers dedicated monuments in AD 889, and then the whole region lapsed back into prehistory.

Fortunately we have a lot of evidence about the demographic trends that accompany this complicated dynastic history. The 16 sq. km zone immediately around Tikal's monumental precincts has been intensively mapped, as have sites in survey arms extending radially out in the cardinal directions.

Hundreds of large and small sites have been tested by excavations. Analysis of all these data reveals a continuous curve of population growth beginning in Preclassic times, a Late Classic peak, and then a sharp decline. For our purposes the crucial interval is the period AD 700–830, when the Late Classic population grew rapidly. The most comprehensive recent maximal population estimates are as follows:[4]

1 For the 120 sq. km region bounded by the earthworks: population = 62,000 people, for an overall density of 517 people per sq. km (1340 per sq. mile).

2 For a larger region within a 12 km radius of Tikal's monumental core: population = 120,000, for an overall density of 265 people per sq. km (689 per sq. mile).

3 For a region within a 25 km radius of the monumental core which includes nearby subordinate centers: population = 425,000 people, for an overall density of 216 people per sq. km (515 per sq. mile). In particular the area around Lake Peten Itza experienced impressive growth at the very end of the Classic period, possibly fueled by immigration from troubled regions to the west.[5]

These figures are quite extraordinary, all the more so because they do not take into account extensive areas of swamps unsuitable for habitation or cultivation.[6] I believe these estimates are far too high, especially on a landscape that had already been used by farmers for almost 2000 years. It is just possible to imagine that very short fallow intervals or permanent cultivation might have supported, say, 150–200 people per sq. km, but not for long and not without extremely deleterious effects. And, whatever the actual densities might have been, exactly these effects have been documented by paleoecologists, as summarized in Fig. 40. Coinciding with the population peak are deforestation, erosion, and nutrient loss, which appear to trigger a rapid population decline.

Tikal and its immediate rural area seem to have lost most of their population during the interval from AD 830–950, when we see the last glimmers of royal activity. The old central political system apparently broke down quickly. Many rooms in the great buildings were used for a time by squatters, especially in the old royal palace.[7] They blocked up doorways and left behind trash deposits that are a curious mixture of domestic debris and items such as musical instruments that suggest a certain surviving dimension of wealth and ritual activity. Monuments were defaced and in some cases relocated, and looters pillaged ancient burials and caches. After AD 950 Tikal and its immediate environs appear almost deserted, although a few people might have lived in perishable huts scattered among the decaying buildings.

16 K'inich Janaab' Pakal I, whose portrait is shown here, ruled the Palenque kingdom between AD 615 and 683. During his reign Palenque experienced explosive growth, embodied in numerous temples and palaces whose stone sculptures and modeled plaster work are unsurpassed in the Maya Lowlands.

17 (*above*) Palenque's Temple of the Inscriptions was built as a mortuary monument to K'inich Janaab' Pakal I. Deep within the pyramid lies his great tomb chamber and sarcophagus. Discovery of this tomb in 1952 convinced many archaeologists that the Maya were ruled by powerful kings rather than priestly intellectuals.

18 (*left*) This plaster portrait probably depicts Kan B'alam II, who finished the Temple of the Inscriptions and dedicated it to his father K'inich Janaab' Pakal I. During his own reign from AD 684 to 702 royal architects and artists erected many famous buildings and monuments at Palenque.

19 (*opposite, above*) The Palace of the Palenque dynasty attained its final form in the early 8th century, and is distinguished by an unusual tower-like building. Early 19th-century explorers like John Lloyd Stephens slept in its ruined rooms, and correctly interpreted it as the remains of a royal residence.

20 (*opposite, below*) Panel 15 was found at Piedras Negras in 2000. It originally graced the front façade of a high temple, and depicts Ruler 2 dressed as a warrior, flanked by other warriors and captives. Eroded glyphs summarize events of his life. The commemorative monument was commissioned by Ruler 3, his son.

21 Polychrome murals were discovered at the small center of Bonampak in 1946. Military scenes such as this one convinced many Mayanists that the "peaceful Maya" were actually quite warlike. Associated images of processions and rituals provide insights concerning political organization and courtly life during the 8th century.

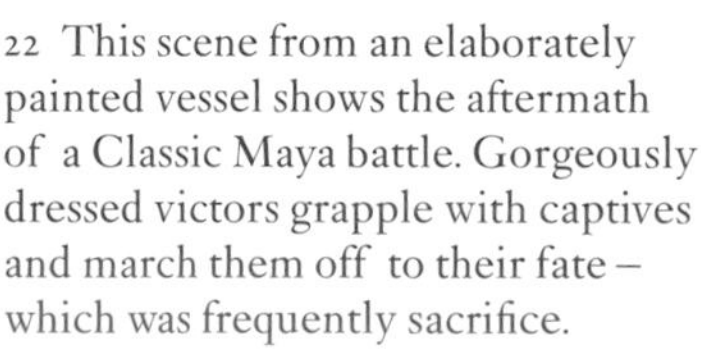

22 This scene from an elaborately painted vessel shows the aftermath of a Classic Maya battle. Gorgeously dressed victors grapple with captives and march them off to their fate – which was frequently sacrifice.

23 Elite Maya people, as in all ancient civilizations, were distinguished from lesser folk not only by their residences, possessions, and tombs, but also by their training and demeanor. Note the extremely elegant gestures depicted on this polychrome vessel.

24 (*top*) Exposed by burning in 1970, the southern sections of Becan's fortifications are clearly visible in this aerial photo. High forest covers most of the site, hiding scores of buildings. This forest has since been heavily cleared for agricultural purposes.

25 (*above*) The author stands on the massive inner earthwork surrounding the center of Becan. Just in front is a wide ditch, originally much deeper. The ditch, parapet, and associated causeways were built about AD 150–250, clear evidence that large-scale warfare afflicted Maya civilization at very early times.

26 (*opposite, above*) Uxmal's great Nunnery Quadrangle, with its complex mosaic sculpture, is a supreme achievement of the Puuc architectural tradition. It was probably the residence of a high-ranking family, and its sculpture symbolically represents basic elements of Maya cosmology.

27 (*opposite, below*) The towering 35-m (115-ft) Temple of the Magician is the highest building at Uxmal, and combines several different architectural styles. Built in several stages, it was probably completed around AD 950–1000, when Uxmal seems to have exercised hegemony over other nearby polities in the Puuc region of Yucatan.

28 An unusual pyramid with four stairways dominates Chichen Itza. Nicknamed the Castillo by early Spanish visitors, it was associated in Maya chronicles with a feathered-serpent god or hero who came from the west. Deep within an earlier phase of the building is a chamber with a jaguar throne.

29 This reclining figure, called a chacmool, sits in front of the great serpent and warrior columns of the Temple of the Warriors at Chichen Itza. Sculptures with this pose are also found at centers such as Tula and Tenochtitlan in highland Mexico, and the similarity of forms suggests Mexican contacts with northern Yucatan.

Other surveys around the nearby eastern lakes show a somewhat different pattern.[8] Don and Prudence Rice detected similarly high Late Classic populations there, but found evidence for continued occupation. After a steep plunge in the early to mid-9th century, the rate of population decline decreased, and even after AD 1200 there were still considerable numbers of people living around several of the lakes. The Rices attribute the long population decline to local demographic processes – an excess of deaths over births. Quite possibly some of the survivors around the lakes represent relocated populations from Tikal's immediate hinterland. If the Itza origin stories are correct, these northerners later moved into a landscape with its own indigenous inhabitants, and their migrations contributed heavily to the region's revival during the 15th–17th centuries. An important lesson from these surveys is that territorial scale of research provides the best information. Conclusions drawn from the region right around Tikal do not necessarily reflect wider patterns, nor does the abandonment of an old dynastic seat mean outlying areas are deserted. We will see shortly how this lesson applies to Copan.

An old saying has it that "happy is the country without history." Even fragmentary surviving texts show that the Tikal polity had plenty of history – bursts of expansion, prosperity, political vigor punctuated by episodes of military defeat, internal discord, and decline. Hidden behind this historical façade were the anonymous acts of countless farmers, who over many generations undermined the agrarian prosperity of the landscape, and impoverished the political economy. At the end the central ruling apparatus seems to have unraveled comparatively slowly, beginning by about AD 810 or even before. There is very little evidence from Tikal itself suggesting the kinds of devastating warfare that afflicted other regions at the end of the Classic period, although the influx of refugees from the western peripheries of the lowlands probably exerted pressure on both a deteriorating landscape and dynasty. Smaller polities formerly under Tikal's sway broke away, but these too failed to survive the end of the 9th century.

Some would argue that all this is consistent with Gill's megadrought, and the failure of the managers of Tikal's essential system of reservoirs that provided drinking water. But there is no sign of serious desiccation of the nearby lakes, where local population still continued to decline after the end of the postulated drought about AD 1200. And clearly there was enough rainfall so that long after Tikal's dynasty fell a population equivalent to 15–20 percent of the Late Classic peak was still able to support itself. In fact, at least until AD 1200 local densities around the lakes were as high as those that supported the complex polities of 16th-century Yucatan. Right now, the most convincing collapse explanation we have for the Tikal kingdom is overpopulation and agrarian failure, with all of their attendant political consequences.

What collapsed was more than just an ordinary Maya kingdom. Tikal had been central to Maya civilization for more than 1000 years, a cradle of kingship, kings and courtly life, and a fount of art, architecture, and many other components of the Classic Great Tradition. During its protracted struggles with the Calakmul confederation it waxed and waned, but even throughout its long hiatus it was still a place latent with cultural and political potency. Then, phoenix-like, it arose once more during the 8th century, and although no longer a preponderant power, it remained an exemplar of Maya civilization. Its subsequent sad decline must have been foreboding to kings and lords trying to patch things together in their own distant polities. And as we shall see shortly, some of them succeeded despite the bad news.

Because Tikal's fortunes are so closely intertwined with that of its great rival Calakmul, it would make another logical second case example at this point. Unfortunately Calakmul is not nearly so well-known as Tikal, so I will say only a few words about it here.[9] Calakmul boasts an unprecedented 117 monuments, but many of these are so heavily eroded that their texts are illegible. Very little is known about its dynastic history before AD 500, but by the mid-6th century the local Kaan (Snake) rulers were already regarded as influential by their neighbors. Probably the most powerful king was Yuknoom the Great, who enjoyed a 50-year-long reign beginning in AD 636. After the defeat of his successor at the hands of Tikal in AD 695, Calakmul's geopolitical power waned, although later kings still erected impressive monuments and temples. A fitful and feeble monument tradition was maintained as late as the first years of the 10th century. So far there have been no regional surveys around Calakmul comparable to those at Tikal or other centers such as Copan, so we know very little concerning the demographic history of the kingdom.

Wars in the West

Our next example focuses not just on one site or polity, but rather on a large segment of the western Maya Lowlands along the middle drainage of the Usumacinta river system. Not only are some of the most celebrated Classic Maya centers located there, but it is also unusually rich in inscriptions and art that provide our most detailed glimpses of the vicissitudes of Classic warfare and political maneuvering. Texts and monuments are found not only at major centers, but at very small ones as well. No other region has contributed so much to the demolition of the old "peaceful Maya" conception. Several major research projects have recently revealed the complex interactions among various Usumacinta kingdoms, reminding us that the collapse cannot be understood from the vantage point of any single polity. Central to our concerns are Dos Pilas, Aguateca, Seibal, Yaxchilan, and Piedras Negras, although dozens of other lesser places are also scattered over the landscape.

One part of our story pivots around Dos Pilas, located between two Usumacinta tributaries, the Pasion and the Salinas rivers.[10] This part of the drainage, called the Petexbatun region (Fig. 41), has many small and medium-sized centers, most located within a half-day walk of one another. Topography is dominated by heavily forested ridges and escarpments interspersed with low-lying wetlands, including the rivers themselves, which in some places widen out to form large lakes. Because annual rainfall is high (2500 mm, or 98 in), much of the area is seasonally flooded. Farmers began to grow maize and other crops on fertile upland soils as early as 3000–4000 years ago, and eventually caused appreciable Preclassic deforestation and erosion. A sizable Late Preclassic community existed at Punta de Chimino, and some archaeologists believe that the impressive earthwork fortifications that defended the Punta de Chimino peninsula were first built at that time. If so, warfare had very deep roots in the region.

Recovery of mature tropical forest during the Early Classic suggests a corresponding population decline, although there was a little local polity with its capital at Tamarindito late in the 6th century, with a real or imagined dynastic line extending back into Preclassic times.[11] Subsequent events reveal a complex and protracted collapse process associated with another period of Late Classic population growth and forest clearance. This bimodal demographic pulse is quite different from the pattern at Tikal.

Dos Pilas itself is a fairly modest center that covers only about .08 sq. km (20 acres). Its early history is obscure, with faint traces of an indigenous dynasty prior to the sudden arrival there in AD 648 of B'alaj Chan K'awiil, a personage we already met at Tikal. Probably the son of a Tikal king, he and his followers seem to have defected from Tikal's political orbit and established a new political base at Dos Pilas, some 70 km (43 miles) to the southwest, imposing themselves (perhaps violently) on the local Tamarindito lords, but also taking wives from prominent local families. What caused this political rupture is still a puzzle, but the first two rulers of the upstart Dos Pilas dynasty continued to use the same emblem glyph used by Tikal's kings. Given the later history of conflict, these Dos Pilas rulers probably regarded themselves as legitimate contenders for rulership of the parent Tikal polity.

41 *Map showing the location of the Dos Pilas region within the Maya Lowlands (inset), and the many centers packed into this small zone of the Usumacinta-Pasion drainage.*

In pursuit of this ambition B'alaj Chan K'awiil became the client of Tikal's implacable enemy, Calakmul, whose forces in AD 657 temporarily drove out the incumbent Tikal ruler Nuun Ujol Chaak. For some reason this defeat did not result in the reinstatement of B'alaj Chan K'awiil, who remained at Dos Pilas. Nor was Tikal rendered harmless. Her forces attacked Dos Pilas in AD 672, forcing B'alaj Chan K'awiil into a five-year exile of his own.

Returned to Dos Pilas after yet another Tikal reverse, B'alaj Chan K'awiil personally made two journeys to visit Calakmul, where he was an honored guest at the enthronement of king Yich'aak K'ak' (Fiery Claw) in AD 686. A monument found in 1990 suggests the much later presence of Calakmul nobles at the Dos Pilas court, so this relationship apparently endured for a very long time. After Calakmul was heavily defeated by Tikal in AD 695, the Dos Pilas rulers seem to have turned their attention to consolidating their own realm. In AD 735 the 3rd king of the dynasty conquered the much older center of Seibal, some 20 km to the northeast. Somehow Seibal's captured king escaped the grisly sacrificial fate that usually followed such defeats, for he took part years later in the royal rituals of his masters. K'awiil Chan Kinich, the 4th of the Dos Pilas dynasty, was an especially active warrior. In AD 745 he captured a lord of Yaxchilan, far to the northwest on the Mexican side of the Usumacinta, and engaged in many other skirmishes about that time.

Then, in AD 761, the Dos Pilas kingdom dramatically collapsed for reasons that are poorly reflected in the surviving texts, initiating a period of even more extreme regional conflict. Defensibility became a prime concern in settlement location, and sometimes palisades were built to enclose little hilltop hamlets and nearby zones of rich soils, particularly in limestone sinkholes. Competition over the best upland agricultural zones was obviously intense. Dos Pilas itself (Fig. 42) was largely or entirely abandoned, and its royal family probably moved to Aguateca, about 10 km (6.25 miles) to the southwest, along with their entourage and other nobles from Tamarindito. Once a minor court center for the Dos Pilas kings, Aguateca was protected by natural chasms and escarpments, and eventually by concentric lines of low palisades quickly built of rough stone and wooden posts (Fig. 44). Back at Dos Pilas, a handful of desperate refugees built a tiny village in the main plaza and surrounded it with crude, concentric walls made with materials scavenged from the old temples and palaces (Fig. 43). So hastily were these walls made that the outer one doesn't even appear to have been finished. Similar fortifications enclose a nearby temple complex.

Simon Martin and Nikolai Grube suggest that larger patterns of geopolitical decline and fragmentation undermined the fortunes of Dos Pilas. Never a large or populous polity, it depended heavily on its patron Calakmul. As Calakmul's power waned, Dos Pilas was increasingly vulnerable to pressure from Tikal and its local proxies. Nearby Petexbatun polities seem to act more independently in the late 8th century, and within a decade of Dos Pilas's abandonment Seibal enthroned a new leader who appropriated the old Mutal title.

Shortly after the turn of the 9th century Aguateca was strongly threatened by some unknown enemy. Its petty ruler (5th of the Dos Pilas line) and his palace entourage cleared out just ahead of the attackers, but Takeshi Inomata's ongoing excavations have uncovered burned elite houses with household objects abandoned right where they were used. The little Dos Pilas community was overwhelmed too, possibly a bit later than Aguateca. Survivors of all this mayhem might well have decamped to the northwest, thus accounting for some of the substantial Early Postclassic population detected by the Rices around the Peten lakes.

But not all was gloom and defeat. Seibal, one of the oldest centers in the

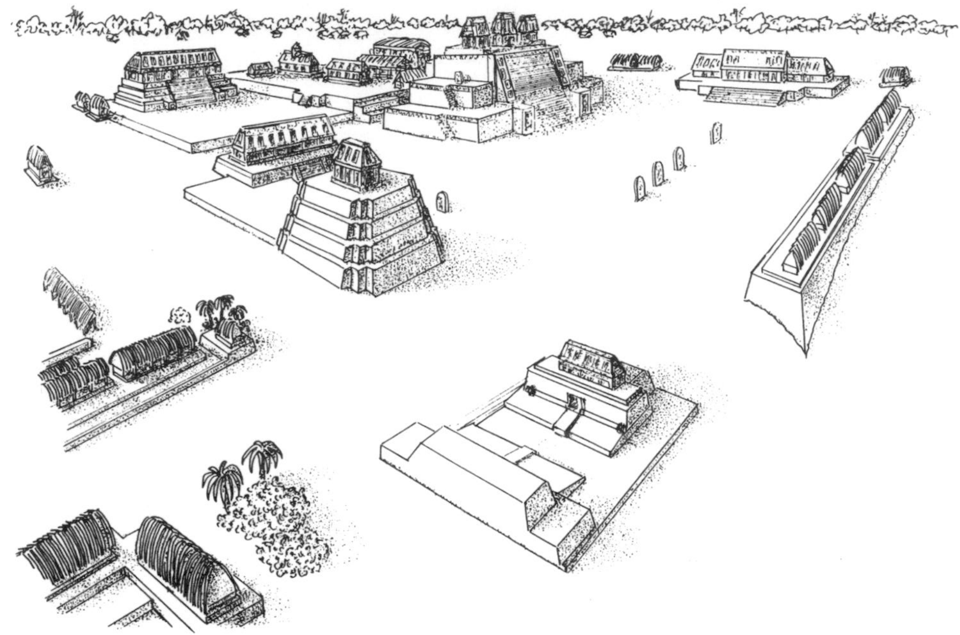

42, 43 *The epicenter of Dos Pilas was undefended when the polity was at the height of its power under its 4th ruler around* AD *750. (Right) After the abrupt collapse of the Dos Pilas polity about* AD *761, the capital was abandoned by its rulers. Maya refugees erected ramshackle walls and palisades around the main buildings and built small houses within the enclosures.*

Petexbatun region, rebounded both architecturally and demographically after about AD 830, perhaps also benefiting from an influx of local refugees. Despite the presence of new forms of pottery and iconographic elements once thought to represent a "Mexicanized Maya" invasion, texts suggest that this new vigor was actually stimulated by intrusive leaders from the site of Ucanal to the east. Seibal prospered to the extent that Tikal's king Jewel K'awiil traveled there to take part in commemorative ceremonies in AD 849. This promising revival, however, did not last for more than a few decades. Although no detailed demographic analysis has yet been presented for the Petexbatun region, population rapidly fell after mid-century by 90 percent or more from its Late Classic peak.

One must bear in mind that most of this political drama played itself out on a landscape of only 3000–4000 sq. km (1860–2480 sq. miles), or about the size of one of the smaller Hawaiian islands. The chief actors in these political games were always, by Tikal or Calakmul standards, petty kings with few subjects. Whatever their lofty ambitions, their reach seems to have been

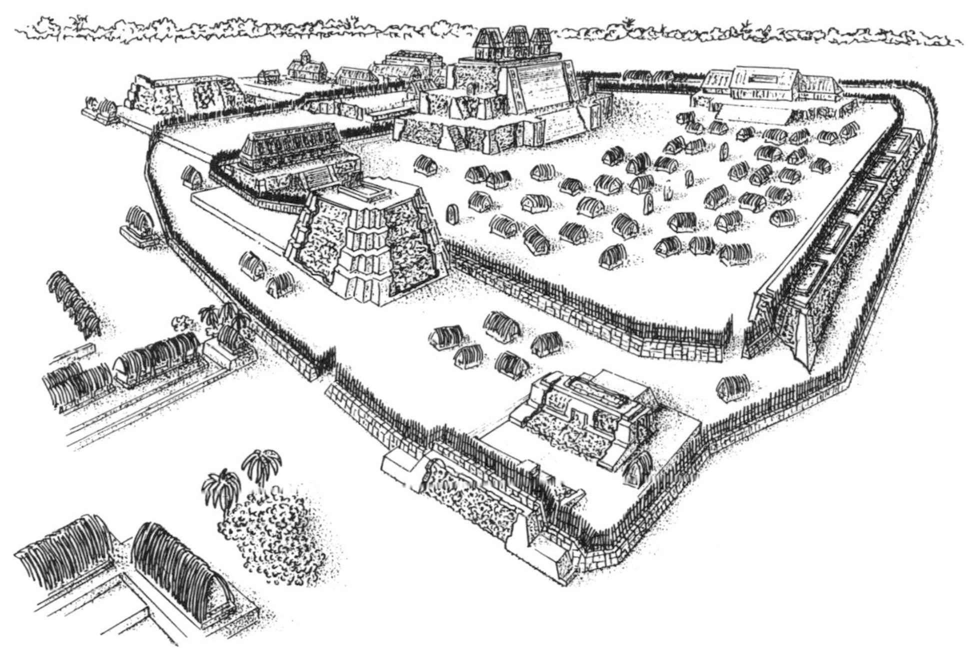

decidedly local, and our general impression is of weak rulers, little central integration of economic activity, and local household management of agrarian resources. One might well think not in terms of the collapse of a stable Dos Pilas kingdom, but rather the inability to create one in the first place.

The Petexbatun region provides a unique view of micropolitics and war that focuses our attention on interpolity relations as barometers of the local collapse.[12] Seen from this perspective, what happened does not conform very well with the proposed megadrought. The Dos Pilas polity was in trouble well before AD 800, and the Seibal revival takes place about 30 years after its supposed start. Nor is a drought clearly indicated in sediment cores extracted from local lakes and aguadas. Many lines of evidence suggest that "... radical ecological, nutritional, or climatological changes cannot be blamed for the cycle of violence and decline that engulfed the area in the mid-8th century."[13] Despite high regional population densities, the Late Classic countryside was not as heavily deforested as that around Tikal. This might reflect a "managed" landscape in which valuable trees were preserved, or the existence of unused buffer zones that functioned as "no man's lands" between contending polities. Terracing on some slopes appears to have slowed or eliminated destructive erosion. Isotopic studies of human bone show that faunal resources contributed significantly to the diet, and so must have remained reasonably abundant, and that late populations in the region were

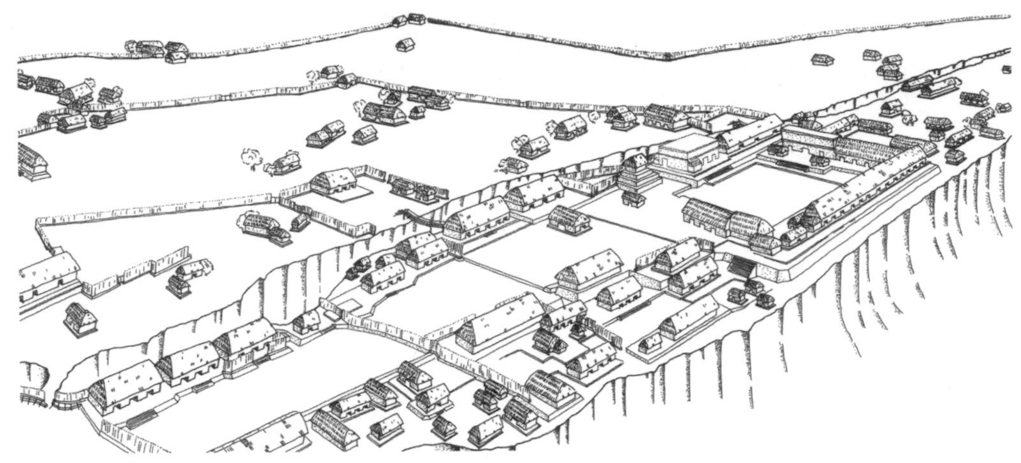

44 *The fortified center of Aguateca, probably the last refuge of the Dos Pilas kings on a landscape consumed by war.*

no less healthy than earlier ones. What does seem certain is that from the 7th century on, much of the agrarian landscape must have been risky to cultivate, a strong social limitation on productivity, and a political stress on farmers.

Downstream from the Petexbatun region, along the Usumacinta proper, lie Piedras Negras and Yaxchilan, respectively on the Guatemalan and Mexican banks of the river. These two centers are within about 40 km (25 miles) of one another, and their abundant inscriptions detail a long history of animosity.[14] Here we also find an unusually complete record of subsidiary lords carrying the sajal title, as well as accounts of royal women. We know very little about Yaxchilan outside its core of large architecture, but archaeologists, myself included, worked intensively at Piedras Negras between 1997 and 2000 during a project directed by Stephen Houston and Hector Escobedo. Although we understand this polity much better now, we still lack settlement surveys comparable to those at Tikal or paleoecological information from sediment cores. Today Piedras Negras is in a protected environmental reserve. Few of the ruins have been restored, and the landscape is covered by mature tropical forest nourished by 2500 mm (98 in) of annual rainfall.

Both of these Usumacinta sites are of respectable size, although by no means comparable to Tikal or Calakmul. The monumental temples, palaces, and royal sweat baths at Piedras Negras are mainly concentrated on and around two sets of steep limestone hills within 300 m (984 ft) of the river, and altogether cover about 0.35–0.40 sq. km (86–99 acres). The southern cluster is the earlier of the two, with architecture going back to Middle and Late Preclassic times. Later rulers shifted the focus of construction to the north, where the imposing mass of the so-called Acropolis dominated the landscape. Much of the smaller residential architecture clustered in the immediate vicinity of these royal buildings, and by Late Classic times also extended out to the northwest and southeast along the solution valleys, escarpments, and hills of this extremely rugged, karstic landscape. Because there are no sizable flood plains along the river, most of the population lived on and cultivated upland zones.

Although our population estimates are still provisional, there seem to have been 3000–5000 people living right in and around the monumental core during the late 8th century, and then a steep drop-off of habitation on the near-periphery within a km or two. The reasons for this pattern, much more nucleated than that found at Tikal, are not yet clear, but it might be an adaptation to interminable conflict.

Yaxchilan is about the same size as Piedras Negras and has been heavily restored by recent Mexican government projects. Situated in an island-like loop in the Usumacinta, most of its major buildings face northeast and extend along a series of low hills and terraces right on the riverbank. Others are perched on higher ground to the west. Unfortunately we have no detailed information concerning its larger settlement patterns or demographic history.

For centuries Piedras Negras and Yaxchilan struggled for supremacy along this stretch of the middle Usumacinta, each abetted by a network of smaller regional dependencies whose subject lords are frequently mentioned in the copious inscriptions. The river here is very swift and has several dangerous rapids. Traveling with the current is easy (if you can traverse the rapids safely) but a powerful motor is required to go upstream. In ancient times it must have been very much a one-way route for heavy dugout canoes propelled only by paddles. Nevertheless, the river was a principal axis of trade and communication uniting the Guatemalan highlands with the coastal plain of Chiapas. Although my concern here is the local fate of Piedras Negras and Yaxchilan, the interests and ambitions of other kingdoms to the west and northwest (Pomona, Tonina, Bonampak, and Palenque) as well as in the Petexbatun region to the southeast (Dos Pilas) all periodically impinged on both centers, which were also caught up in the larger Tikal-Calakmul conflicts. Piedras Negras aside, we know that Yaxchilan fought wars with such powers as Tikal, Calakmul, Palenque, and Dos Pilas, as well as with at least ten smaller centers, several still archaeologically unidentified. Some enemies were not only strategic but traditional ones, as we shall see shortly.

Yokib' ("Entrance") was the ancient Maya name for Piedras Negras, and it possibly refers to an enormous, gaping sinkhole discovered by two of my graduate students in 1998. The local dynasty was attributed extremely ancient origins at a mythical time in 4691 BC, but more realistically, effective rulers at Piedras Negras and its neighboring kingdoms probably extend back no further than the late 3rd or mid-4th centuries AD. The first of seven successive documented Piedras Negras monarchs appears in the mid-5th century, and in an echo of things to come he or some important subordinate (the text is unclear) was captured by the king of Yaxchilan, whose forces inflicted more defeats on the kingdom over the next 50 years.

Fragmentary texts suggest that around the turn of the 6th century the Piedras Negras rulers became client kings of some other power (Calakmul fits the bill best, but the evidence is fragmentary), perhaps to obtain much-needed aid against their enemies. Around AD 514 the 4th king boasts of having turned the tables and captured his Yaxchilan counterpart. Twenty-three years later Yaxchilan recovered sufficiently to capture a Calakmul lord. There follows almost a century of textual silence at Piedras Negras that must reflect some period of political eclipse.[15] Recent excavations have turned up remains of *bajareque* (mud, pole, and thatch) buildings that were destroyed sometime in the mid-5th century. There are textual hints that around this time Piedras Negras was attacked and defeated by Pomona. It seems very probable that about AD 554 much of the site, including its royal palace, was burnt by Pomona enemies and the shadowy Piedras Negras king required to pay tribute to his conquerors.

The 7th century ushered in a new period of prosperity, particularly under Ruler 2, Itsamk'anahk II (AD 639–686), whose biography and battles are summarized on the newly-discovered Panel 15 shown in Plate 20.[16] He continued monumental construction in the northern part of the site, collected tribute from defeated centers, and raised monuments that seem to claim widespread authority over much of the middle Usumacinta region. Nothing is heard from Yaxchilan at this time, so Ruler 2 might have effectively dominated his traditional rival. His successor Yo'nal Ahk II apparently began his long 42-year reign with massive building projects in and around the Acropolis, during the course of which he leveled the old destruction debris and built over it. He seems, however, to have been less influential than his father, perhaps because of encroaching Palenque conquests to the south.

A possibly confused succession eventually elevated Ruler 4 (AD 729–757) to the throne (there is no mention of who his father was). He captured a Yaxchilan lord and was succeeded by two kings about whom we know comparatively little except that they were close contemporaries in age, possibly brothers.

The last king, Ruler 7 (accession AD 781), was probably a third sibling, all offspring of Ruler 4. For the first time the former tradition of father-son succession was violated, and Ruler 7 seems to have assumed power upon the abdication of his predecessor, a kind of event very rarely recorded in royal inscriptions and suggestive of internal trouble. In any event, these last three rulers seldom mention one another. Ruler 7 undertook important new projects, including the construction of an Acropolis palace featuring one of the most famous carved royal monuments, Throne 1, ever found in the Maya Lowlands. Contemporary texts celebrate his conquests, in which he was aided by his noble warriors, and the king especially reveled in settling the 238-year-old score with ancient enemies at Pomona.

All the while, however, Yaxchilan seems to have been politically and militarily outflanking Piedras Negras. In the late 8th century she controlled two centers to the southwest, Lacanha and Bonampak (where her king is portrayed overseeing a local accession in the famous murals). She also had a firm outpost at La Pasadita, close to Piedras on the eastern side of the Usumacinta. Ultimately this maneuvering seems to have paid off, and Yaxchilan had the final (if short-lived) glory of capturing and presumably sacrificing Ruler 7 in AD 808, after a long interval of renewed warfare. Some royal buildings at Piedras Negras were burned and Throne 1 was violently smashed. These events were long ago interpreted as evidence for peasant rebellion, but we can now relate them more plausibly to a long sequence of inter-polity conflict. Perhaps overtaxed by this final struggle, both victor and vanquished lapsed into historical obscurity within a few years. Anonymous squatters used some partly destroyed palace precincts for a time, but Piedras Negras appears to have been completely abandoned by AD 850–900, as do the small residential sites we have excavated on its periphery.

Like the Petexbatun region, the middle Usumacinta kingdoms were convulsed by wars from very early times. Intense conflict among traditional enemies probably profoundly affected the distribution of populations and the economic well-being of centers, and contributed to the final, and apparently abrupt abandonment of Piedras Negras and Yaxchilan. Based on the scanty available data, these kingdoms seem to have been quite small, both territorially and demographically, but future work might change this picture. Regional soils are fertile but thin, and highly prone to erosion on the comparatively steep uplands. While we have as yet no information pointing to massive environmental degradation as around Tikal, I believe that much of the land immediately around the major centers was probably heavily deforested and eroded by the late 8th century.

Becan

If you walked due north from Tikal for about 150 km (90 miles), you would enter a scrubbier, drier region called the Rio Bec/Chenes zone, a name given by archaeologists to its distinctive architectural tradition. Buildings here often combine "temple" and "palace" elements into single structures, and have façades covered with mosaic sculpture in geometric patterns that often depict large masks, and doorways in the form of gaping, fanged mouths. Largest of the Rio Bec/Chenes sites is Becan, one of the most remarkable ancient centers in the entire Maya Lowlands. Within a 45-km (28-mile) radius of Becan are about 50 smaller sites with monumental architecture, so the landscape was densely settled in Late Classic times. Despite their architectural sophistication, Rio Bec sites (Becan included) have very little in the way of inscriptions or representational art. We do not know the name of a single local king or noble, nor have archaeologists found any elaborate royal tombs. Why the Rio Bec/Chenes zone should be so different in these respects from Tikal and the other Classic "heartland" centers farther south remains unknown.

I include Becan as one of my case studies for several reasons. It is located on the northern fringe of the region most affected by the Classic Maya collapse, and thus provides an example less central to events than, say, Tikal. It is also useful to examine a center that is entirely prehistoric in order to remind the reader that many impressive places do not participate equally in the Classic Maya Great Tradition. Finally, a lot of archaeology has been done at Becan since the early 1970s. At that time the whole region was largely uninhabited and covered with dense tropical forest interspersed with low-lying bajos, or swamps. Now it swarms with tourists, who can luxuriate at a Club Med within a few kilometers of where I once lived for months in a thatched hut.

Sometime during the 6th century BC, early colonists settled down on a slightly elevated ridge of limestone bedrock bordered by swamps on the south and west, thereby founding the original core of the Becan settlement. From those modest beginnings Becan developed by the early 8th century AD into several major architectural complexes that include towering pyramids up to 30 m (100 ft) high, a ball court, and range structures with associated tower-like elements, along with a reservoir in the southwestern sector of the site. All these constructions are concentrated in an area of approximately 0.19 sq. km (47 acres), making Becan quite a respectable place in comparison with some other famous Classic Maya centers such as Dos Pilas or Seibal. Although we lack emblem glyphs and other historical information, it seems pretty certain that Becan was the political capital of much of the Rio Bec region, a powerful and influential local polity.[17]

Archaeologists from the Carnegie Institution of Washington who first explored and mapped Becan in 1934 were surprised to find a huge ditch and parapet surrounding that part of the ridge with the monumental precincts (Plate 27). They accordingly called the site Becan, a name derived from a Maya word meaning "ravine or canyon formed by water." Few Mayanists assumed these were fortifications because of the then-prevailing "peaceful Maya" perspective. Others speculated that if indeed the earthworks were fortifications, they must have been built at the very end of the Classic period, and be symptomatic of warfare related to the Classic collapse.

When I began to excavate Becan's earthworks for my doctoral dissertation in 1970, I too thought that a late construction date was most likely. Unexpectedly, the earthworks turned out instead to be one of the largest and earliest fortifications known anywhere in the Maya Lowlands – or indeed in Mesoamerica (Fig. 45). Rapidly built sometime between about AD 150 and 250, they might relate to the troubles at the end of the Preclassic period that disrupted El Mirador and Nakbe or the initial intrusions of Teotihuacan influence that are more obvious at Tikal. Many traces of Late Preclassic features both inside and outside the ditch show that Becan was an important center at the very beginning of the Classic period.

Along with a few previous discoveries, such as the famous Bonampak murals, the Becan fortifications provided some of the first intimations that lethal, large-scale forms of warfare occurred early among the Lowland Maya. We now know that the ditches were never filled with water like the moats that protected medieval European towns and cities, but they still constituted impressive defensive barriers. Becan was not a formal fortress, however, but rather a political capital whose elites continued to build their structures within the defenses for centuries. The earthworks might have been intermit-

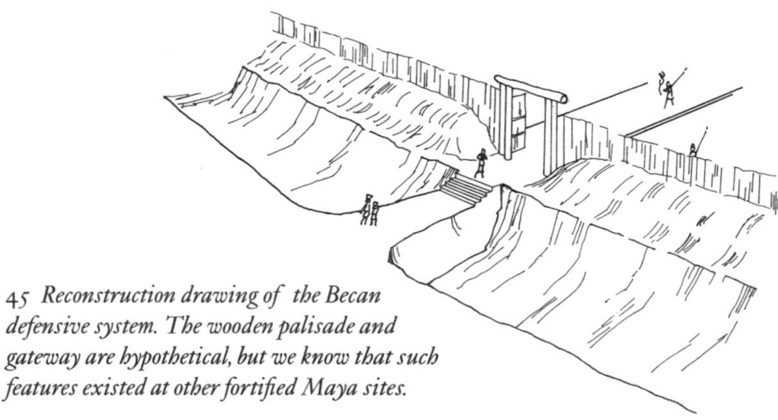

45 *Reconstruction drawing of the Becan defensive system. The wooden palisade and gateway are hypothetical, but we know that such features existed at other fortified Maya sites.*

tently repaired, but in any event they apparently proved both necessary and serviceable long after they were originally constructed. Two of the seven natural bedrock causeways crossing the ditch were cut and repaired sometime between AD 450 and 600. About the same time at least one large building was destroyed, human bones were scattered in refuse, and some outlying elite households were abandoned.

In the mid-5th century there is ceramic evidence of direct or indirect contacts with Central Mexico. Ceramic ties were then strong with the Peten Maya to the south, where Teotihuacan influence and perhaps even Teotihuacan-related rulers appeared a century or so before at Tikal. In all likelihood the local warfare evident at Becan related to larger struggles, and resulted in strong ties to the Peten. As we already saw, by the mid-6th century there is much evidence that various centers were becoming embroiled in the great "superpower" wars dominated by Calakmul and Tikal, located respectively 65 km and 140 km (40 and 87 miles) to the southwest and south of Becan.

Not much of what we know about these great struggles, unfortunately, involves centers in the Rio Bec/Chenes zone. Recently discovered sculptures from Dzibanche, about 60 km (37 miles) northwest of Becan, hint at some sort of northern Calakmul influence as early as the 5th century, but given the general dearth of inscriptions we can only speculate on the military role Becan might have played, and who its allies or enemies might have been. In any event, Becan went on to prosper. Architectural activity peaked during the early Late Classic (AD 600–730), when buildings in the region's distinctive Rio Bec architectural style proliferated at Becan and elsewhere. Interestingly, most of this interval corresponds to the high tide of Calakmul's geopolitical influence in the Lowlands.

Many of Becan's buildings delineate large open courtyards, the most important of which is the East Plaza. Situated on the north side of this courtyard is Structure IV, Becan's most famous building. Completed sometime between AD 730–830, its southern, "public" façade facing the courtyard has the appearance of a temple, but the northern or rear section consists of a series of more private, interconnected, palace-like rooms well equipped with residential features such as large benches and cord-holders (holes in stone walls for cords that tied fabric curtains). Similar dual residential/ceremonial arrangements can be seen elsewhere at Becan and in slightly different forms are typical of much Rio Bec architecture. As the Rio Bec architectural tradition blossomed between AD 600–730, Becan's ceramic connections with the Peten region became weaker and its pottery took on a more distinctive regional character.

During its heyday there was a large regional population, and in the 8th century the polity developed a distinctive pattern of much smaller, but very ornate palace centers distributed over the surrounding landscape. Surveys have revealed many more modest outlying house remains as well. Right around the center itself densities might have reached 300–400 people per sq. km (483–644 per sq. mile). Farther away, on gentle hillsides extending over hundreds of sq. km, the geographer Billy Lee Turner II found the remains of what he interpreted as agricultural terraces interspersed with small house mounds.[18] About 35 km (22 miles) to the east are purported drained fields in large swamps, but these have never been adequately documented.

The first signs of trouble appear after about AD 730. Population seems to decline and become more concentrated in the immediate neighborhood of the fortifications. Curiously, construction of large architecture continues within the earthworks. Then, about AD 830, there are abrupt and massive changes in the local ceramics that suggest an actual invasion of warrior groups from someplace to the northwest. These people brought with them new lithic tools, including distinctive forms of projectile points. Whoever the newcomers were, they blended with the local population and continued to use many of the old palaces and temples, while building no new ones themselves. Most of the agricultural terraces seem to have been abandoned about this time, indicating far fewer farmers using the landscape. Becan's regional population seems to have declined for several hundred years, and after about AD 1200 the only sure signs of human activity were occasional offerings of ritual pottery made near the old ruins.

Becan, it appears, was a troubled polity almost from its inception. Located within the sphere of Calakmul's influence, it was also on or near a probable linguistic boundary between Yucatec speakers to the north and Chol speakers to the south. Influences from both directions ebbed and flowed at various times. Nevertheless, Late Classic population built up to very high levels – certainly high enough to have deforested much of the landscape and caused erosion on hill slopes. Unfortunately we have no sediment cores or other direct measures of such environmental disturbance as we do for the Tikal or Dos Pilas regions (or, as we shall see, for Copan). The implications of Turner's terraces are unclear. They are too low and too far apart to catch and hold much soil on the hillslopes, and might have functioned more as field boundaries. If they are agricultural terraces, they probably would not have provided more food than the original hillside soils, but instead served to stabilize productivity on an already deteriorating landscape – a classic case of putting in more work for the same results.

People might have begun to move away from Becan during the first half of the 8th century, consistent with the idea of agricultural problems. Perhaps this process weakened Becan politically, making it vulnerable to some sort of invasion involving other Maya people a century later. This event seems to have effectively eliminated Becan's old leadership, although many people continued to live in and around the center. Becan's decline, then, appears to begin too early and progressed too gradually to have been caused by a sudden catastrophe like Gill's megadrought. Although warfare is heavily implicated in the regional decline, its effects were probably exacerbated by a damaged landscape.

On the maps of early European mariners the edges of the known world were marked by warnings such as "here be demons." Conceptual maps of the Classic Maya Lowlands today regrettably are often demarked instead by "here there be no inscriptions." The extraordinary success of decipherment has sometimes created such a dependence on them that impressive centers and polities beyond the epigraphic horizon are ignored. Becan is one of these places. Her demise was roughly contemporary with that of Dos Pilas, and if texts were available we could undoubtedly tell a comparably rich story of local lords and kings and battles. Like so many other Classic kingdoms, however, her fate will always be anonymous to us, a reminder that historical accounts, impressive as they are, provide us with only part of the collapse story.

The East

Our final case studies briefly investigate La Milpa and Lamanai, two centers in Belize, an eastern region of the Maya Lowlands that is distinctive in many respects. The north is especially well-watered by several major rivers flowing into the Gulf of Honduras that are navigable along much of their lower courses. Both lacustrine and coastal resources contributed a distinctive dimension to the ancient Maya economy. Moreover, ever since Gordon Willey carried out pioneering settlement surveys in the Belize river valley in the 1950s, we have known that local populations did not always abruptly "crash" at the end of the 8th century as they did around places such as Tikal. Today there are probably more archaeologists per square foot in Belize than in any other country that has Maya ruins, so we know a lot about its culture history.

In 1938 Sir J. E. S. Thompson discovered and named La Milpa, an impressive archaeological site in northern Belize near its border with Guatemala. Two large masses of conjoined temples, palaces, ball courts, and other monumental buildings cover an area of about 0.26 sq. km (64 acres) atop a limestone ridge at an elevation of 190 m (623 ft) above sea level (Fig. 46). Surrounding this epicenter is an extensive residential zone, probably coinciding with the entire regional polity (which has its own emblem glyph), that extends over about 78 sq. km (or a little over half the area delineated by the earthworks and swamps at Tikal). A small segment of these features has recently been mapped by a Boston University project that has worked at La Milpa since 1992 under the direction of Norman Hammond and Gair Tourtellot.[19] Because systematic research at the site began so recently, we presently know much less about it than we do about centers such as Tikal. Nevertheless, the information at hand suggests an extremely interesting pattern of growth and decline.

Like so many other Maya centers, La Milpa has a long history of occupation, but also a very episodic one. Preclassic people lived in a modest settlement in the northern part of the site between about 400 BC and AD 250, and inscribed stelae (along with a royal burial found in 1998) show that there was an Early Classic (AD 250–600) community in the same locale as well, although not much construction dates from that time. Quite possibly Early Classic La Milpa was a dependency of the Rio Azul polity, whose capital is located 20 km (12.5 miles) to the west in Guatemala. Both Tikal and Calakmul are also within 90 km (56 miles), so La Milpa was probably embroiled in the far-flung system of alliances and wars over which they presided. Unfortunately we understand very few details of its history because only one of the 20 stelae at the site has a completely legible text (dedicated in AD 780, it refers to one Ukay, a Late Classic ruler).

All indications suggest that the polity suffered a considerable decline in the 6th and 7th centuries, roughly contemporary with the hiatus at Tikal. Then, as if triggered by Tikal's recovery about AD 695, La Milpa experienced a period of explosive growth, culminating in massive construction projects between AD 750–850. The northern sector of the site was completely remodeled at this time (probably after AD 800), and virtually all of the southern part also dates to the Late and Terminal Classic periods. Much of the effort was expended on a series of southern palaces that involved frequent renovations of throne rooms and their associated polychrome-painted royal benches.

Long survey transects extending out to the east and south have revealed dense residential settlement around the epicenter on a complex topography of hills, ridges and low-lying bajos. In addition to house remains, the surveys recorded many terraces, low walls, and other features suggestive of a heavily "engineered" peripheral landscape, although their functions are still unclear. Some residential units are larger and more impressive than others, and might

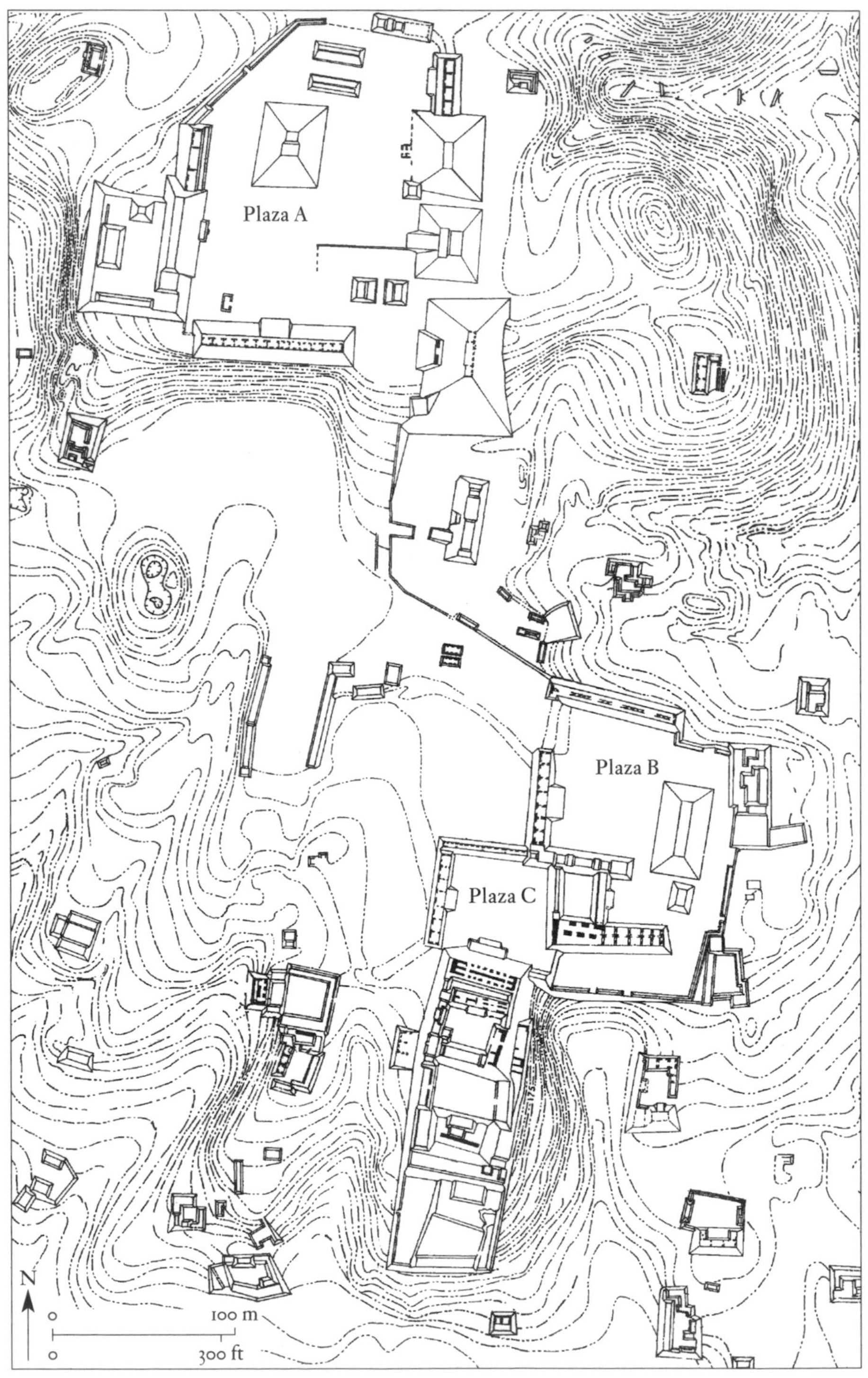
Plaza A
Plaza B
Plaza C
N
0
100 m
0
300 ft

be the foci of neighborhoods. The overall impression is of a dense agricultural population with few or no specialized functions evident for any of the outlying residences. There seems to be a break in outlying settlement distribution about 5 km (3.1 miles) from the main architectural groups, probably representing the limits of La Milpa as an autonomous polity. The provisional population estimate for this zone is 46,000 people, equivalent to a density of 586 people per sq. km (1503 per sq. mile). Notice that this density exceeds even that suggested for the 120 sq. km hinterland around Tikal. Although few details of how these figures were calculated have been published, the procedure seems to have been to assign four inhabitants to each "house" detected in the surveys. Having made many similar calculations myself, I think this method vastly overestimates population, and that more plausible densities are half or less of those suggested. Still, La Milpa obviously had a supporting population around AD 800–850 roughly comparable to that of Copan, a much older and more famous kingdom to which we will turn shortly. More significant for our purposes is that virtually all of this outlying population dates to the period from about AD 700–830.

By AD 800 La Milpa was the largest kingdom in northern Belize, and probably in some ways dominated nearby smaller centers as well. Late in its history four large architectural clusters (one a palace) were built several kilometers away from it in each cardinal direction, producing what Norman Hammond and Gair Tourtellot interpret as a large "cosmogram" on a sacred landscape. In any case, this effort, along with other evidence, suggests strong central control by La Milpa's rulers. Because of the multiple and apparently contemporary palaces and thrones on the central hilltop, they suggest that royal power might have been shared among several factions instead of being focused on a single dynastic line, or that very powerful nobles in addition to the king used such facilities at the site core.

What most concerns us is the abrupt political and demographic career of the La Milpa polity, which is very different from that of our other case studies. From little more than a local village around AD 700, it rapidly grew by AD 800 into a regional kingdom, then was just as suddenly deserted after about AD 830. Many of the largest construction projects took place around AD 800 or later, and some of these were obviously left unfinished at the time of the apparently hurried abandonment. La Milpa, then, is a kind of "flash-in-the-pan"

46 *Plan of La Milpa, Belize. Although extremely impressive in scale, the major structures at this Late Classic Belize center were built and abandoned over a very short time.*

kingdom. Unresolved questions are the origin and identity of the great lords who chose the locale for their capital, and the means by which so many farmers (however we reckon their numbers) quickly colonized the region. Whatever the specific answers might be, this sudden establishment of a thriving kingdom demonstrates how politically mobile and enterprising Maya social groups of all kinds could be, especially in the increasingly troubled times of the 8th century. It also strongly supports the "regal-ritual" or "court" model, because such places are much easier to relocate than true cities. Perhaps the same opportunism and flexibility relates to the abandonment of La Milpa as well.

In any event, there are so far no signs of the violence detected in the Petexbatun sites or at Piedras Negras, and no good data on the paleoenvironmental background. Population was very dense, however, and some hilltop sites have boundary walls, perhaps a sign of competition over land. Terraces suggest attempts to retard erosion, which might have been marked in this hilly country, and even at half the population densities asserted, farmers might have severely degraded the upland soils on this hilly landscape in a century or less. Believers in megadrought might imagine that the whole population decamped for permanent water sources, but this idea is belied by our next case study. In the absence of a historical record, and pending future archaeological discoveries, what we have right now for La Milpa is a very provocative pattern of abandonment, but very little in the way of clues as to why it happened.

Some 40 km (25 miles) east of La Milpa is Lamanai, a sprawling site whose buildings are strung out along a large lagoon of the New river. Archaeologists were first attracted to Lamanai because the ruins of a 16th-century Spanish church were located there, suggestive of late pre-Spanish Maya occupation. Many seasons of research in the 1970s and 1980s bore out this expectation. Its principal investigator, David Pendergast, remarked that "Lamanai has the seemingly unique distinction in the Central Lowlands of having seen a continuous occupation from at least Middle Preclassic times until AD 1675 or later."[20] His conclusion was based heavily on excavation of large ceremonial architecture, with some testing of smaller residential sites. We have very little epigraphic evidence from Lamanai, nor is there settlement pattern data comparable in scope to that from Tikal or La Milpa.

Lamanai was probably first occupied sometime before 300 BC, and ceremonial constructions began at least by that time. One of the largest known Preclassic temples anywhere in the Maya Lowlands outside of the Mirador Basin – 33 m (108 ft) high – was completed about AD 100. In Early Classic times in the 4th to 6th centuries AD the community grew vigorously, and two elaborate tombs of this period were recovered. During the succeeding 7th and 8th centuries Lamanai continued to thrive as the stresses of war and overpopulation built up elsewhere. Then came the crisis. Nearby La Milpa, together with Altun Ha, another imposing center 30 km (19 miles) to the east, both quickly succumbed, but at Lamanai "... the period from AD 850–925 was, in fact, a time of continued vibrance ..." that paved the way for even later developments.[21] Single construction projects at about AD 950–1025 involved volumes of material on the order of 12,000 cubic m (15,720 cubic yds). The only ball court at the site was built about AD 900, and contained a cache of liquid mercury probably imported from Honduras. Pendergast was puzzled by this mercury, because he thought Copan, an obvious Honduran trading partner, was defunct by this time. We shall soon see otherwise.

Other ceremonial activity continued as well. The big Preclassic pyramid, which had been remodeled in the 8th century, continued to be maintained and used for another 350 years. A set of Postclassic structures contained dozens of burials, some accompanied by mortuary offerings of imported copper, pyrite, and sheets of gold, showing that Lamanai was by no means isolated, nor its elites impoverished. Some burials were made as late as the 15th or early 16th century. More than 600 whole or reconstructable ceramic vessels were recovered from contexts spanning the 12th to the early 15th centuries, and huge refuse dumps eventually engulfed some buildings.

Not that all this happened without signs of change or even decline. Strong external ties to the Classic Peten tradition predictably yielded to interaction with northern Yucatan after the 8th century. Some Classic buildings were abandoned and never used again, and small residences were established in former ceremonial precincts. Most Postclassic construction efforts seem more limited than those of earlier times, and the obsidian trade appears to diminish greatly, or even disappear, by the end of the 12th century. What is remarkable is the tenacity of Lamanai's people in the face of appalling news about the failure of one distant (and some not so distant) kingdom after another, and their ability to hold together a surprisingly vigorous polity of their own.

Pendergast thinks one reason they were able to do so was the availability of fish, turtles, and other lagoon foods, and that the river itself permanently linked them to the wider world. Just to the north of Lamanai there are also raised fields in swamps that might have helped stabilize food production as well. But as he says, environment is not everything. We can only guess how Lamanai escaped the worst effects of social chaos, warfare, and breakdown of political alliances and trade routes.

Lamanai is in one sense the exception that proves the rule. So far among our examples it is a unique survivor among well documented failures, and its career reveals less about what happened at the end of the 8th century than what did not happen. It was never sacked by enemies, its sustaining river and lagoon never dried up, its agricultural fields still produced staple crops, and no epidemic disease could have ravaged nearby kingdoms while leaving it untouched.

☾ ☾ ☾

We could consider many more case studies, but these adequately capture the variety I mentioned at the beginning of this chapter. Clearly the southern Lowlands never embraced some monolithic political or cultural entity that was everywhere vulnerable to some sudden disastrous disruption. I hope by now it is obvious that the patterns of collapse or decline are so different from one place to another that no single, simple, cause will ever explain what happened to the Classic Maya in general, although some can be shown to operate powerfully in individual cases. Still, some sort of system of interacting political, social, ideological, and ecological components clearly existed, although we do not understand it as well as we would like. The Classic collapse, in other words, was a communicable phenomenon: what happened to one kingdom or population or local ecosystem affected others in non-random ways.[22] Simply piling up numerous case studies obscures this point. We will return to this theme, but even our own handful of examples shows that it would be difficult to understand the fates of, say, Dos Pilas or Piedras Negras without information about their wider political and military interactions.

It should also be clear how heavily our perspectives are conditioned by the availability of different categories of evidence. We can only guess at how much more sense Lamanai's story would make if it had an epigraphic record comparable to that of Yaxchilan, or what we could say about Piedras Negras if only we had information about ancient environmental changes as we do for the Tikal region. Only for Tikal, in fact, do we have a suitably rich mix of architectural, epigraphic, settlement, and paleoenvironmental information. But there is one more place where the data are arguably even more complete – Copan, which provides us with one final and somewhat unexpected story.

– 9 –

COPAN: THE SLOW DEATH OF A MAYA KINGDOM

AT THE BEGINNING OF THIS BOOK we met Yax Pasaj, the ruler of a celebrated ancient Maya realm perched in the mountains of western Honduras. It is high time we return to this king and see what happened to him, and how his capital was transformed from a bustling, vital place to the overgrown ruin that so impressed Stephens and Catherwood a thousand years later. Copan provides us with a particularly rich case study because more archaeological research has been done there than almost anywhere else in the Maya Lowlands. Early exploration of Copan formed some of our first impressions of the collapse, and many projects carried out there over the last century, and particularly since 1975, have contributed a wealth of insights about the kingdom and its fate. Along with my colleagues and students, I worked at Copan for many years, much of the time on issues related to the demise of the kingdom, so what I recount here is based on first-hand experience. Nowhere, it is fair to say, do we have a comparably detailed picture of what a major Maya kingdom was like at its height, and how it collapsed. This is why Copan is the last of our case studies and deserves a chapter of its own.

Readers who want more documentation should read *Copan: The Rise and Fall of an Ancient Maya Kingdom* (2000), which I wrote with AnnCorinne Freter and Nancy Gonlin, along with the appropriate chapters in Simon Martin and Nikolai Grube's *Chronicle of the Maya Kings and Queens* (2000), and William Fash's *Scribes, Warriors, and Kings* (2001).

The Setting

Imagine that you could hover about 10,000 feet above the Copan valley on a clear day. Looking down, you would first be struck by how rugged the landscape appears – rather like an inert mass of choppy green waves. Each wave represents a hill or a ridge, a few as much as 700 m (2300 ft) high, covered with pine and oak. Fingering up between the hills would be darker green stripes of dense tropical forest adapted to the deeper, more humid soils of little valleys, where streams tumble swiftly during the rainy season. The visual axis of the scene would be a bigger valley about 40 km (25 miles) long running downhill from northeast to southwest. It is defined by the erratic course of a swift little river, seldom more than 30 m (100 ft) wide, that you could see sparkling in the sun. Here and there foothills creep right down to the water's edge, but strung out along the river, like beads on a necklace, are five expanses of flat land (locally called bolsas, or pockets) where the alluvial soil of the valley widens out and is thickly blanketed with tropical forest (Fig. 47). During the dry season these pockets would stand out as islands of deeper green in a much larger sea of brown uplands.

This, at any rate, is what you would have seen had you done your hovering in Stephens and Catherwood's time. Then there would have been few signs of human presence – smoke rising above a couple of little clusters of perishable houses, small plantations of maize and tobacco cut out on the valley floor, a few patches of pasture for cattle, and a network of paths suitable for human feet, and for mules and horses. A thousand years earlier, as we shall see shortly, things were very different.

It is important to realize just how small the drainage basin of the upper Copan river is – only about 500 sq. km (200 sq. miles). Today one can walk from the Guatemalan border on the southeast to the headwaters of the river in about two days. Unlike in the Maya Lowlands proper, most local bedrock consists of ancient volcanic deposits rather than limestone, so only about 15 percent of the region's soils are of high quality, and these are heavily concentrated on the valley floors. All five alluvial zones together have only about

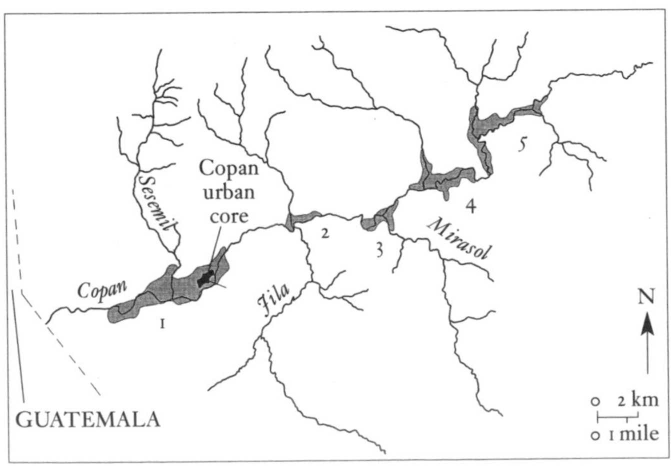

47 *Map of the Copan river valley showing the locations of the five alluvial pockets where most of the ancient and modern human population is located. Note the location of the Copan urban core in the largest of these fertile zones.*

2.5 sq. km (6117 acres) of top-quality land, and most of the inhabitants of the valley at all times have lived on, or close too, this prime agrarian resource. Despite its altitude – the floor of the largest alluvial zone lies at 600 m (1968 ft) above sea level – the landscape falls within the general Lowland Maya range of rainfall and temperature. Most of the traditional Maya crops grow there today.

The Earliest Copanecos

We detect faint traces of people on Copan's landscape as early as 3600 BC, when pulses of charcoal, possibly from the deliberate burning of forest, show up in a sediment core we retrieved from a little intermontane lake in 1989. What appears to be maize pollen is found in levels dating at least back to around 2000 BC, so there were probably part-time farmers cultivating little milpas, and also hunting and gathering in the surrounding hills. Deep soundings of the valley floor and excavations in burial caves have yielded the earliest known ceramics and human skeletons, dating to about 1400 BC. In all likelihood the valley then looked very much like it did in Stephens and Catherwood's time. Exactly who these early inhabitants were in ethnic terms is unclear because Copan lies on or near the southeastern boundary of Mesoamerica. To the east are the broad valleys of central Honduras, where non-Mayan languages were historically spoken, and to the south and west Maya dialects predominate.

So far as we can tell not much happened during Preclassic times. Population remained low – perhaps some hundreds of people, or at most a couple of thousand. Farmers cultivated fields in the choice, humid, deep soil areas, and there was probably a big village or two (now deeply buried) on the largest of the alluvial zones (called the Copan pocket) along with a scattering of farmsteads elsewhere. There are no obvious signs of much social or political complexity, but as early as 900 BC some burials were accompanied by rich offerings of imported jade, and vessels carved with motifs reminiscent of those used by sophisticated Olmec people on the Mexican Gulf Coast.

Kings and Dynastic History

During the first two centuries AD there seem to have been people of consequence at Copan, judging from much later retrospective texts that refer to mysterious early events, especially those featuring the actions of a man named "Foliated Ajaw" during a k'atun ending in AD 159. Then, in AD 426, there occurred an incident of such importance that it was remembered clearly by Yax Pasaj and his contemporaries 400 years later. An individual named Yax K'uk' Mo' took part in an investiture ceremony at some distant place, and then about five months later he and his entourage entered the Copan valley. As we saw, K'inich Yax K'uk' Mo' was much celebrated on the carved monuments of his successors as the founder of the Copan dynasty, and they also accorded him retrospectively with the exalted kaloomte' title. Numerous lines of evidence indicate that Yax K'uk' Mo' had close ties to the much older Tikal royal line, as well as to Teotihuacan. In a sense, his arrival at Copan recapitulated the earlier progress of Siyaj K'ak' to Tikal half a century before in AD 378. In any event, Yax K'uk' Mo' was probably a stranger to the Copan valley who had to assert his authority over an existing (and possibly non-Maya) indigenous polity of some sophistication.[1] Apparently he did this by marrying a local woman of rank, and possibly also through force (one arm of a skeleton thought to be the king's shows signs of injury). Before Yax K'uk' Mo's arrival there is nothing particularly suggestive of Maya culture in the region. Yax K'uk' Mo's reign inaugurated the construction of elaborate buildings, monuments, writing, and all the other features of the elite Maya Great Tradition, with a strong element of Teotihuacan symbolism. Thereafter Copan is firmly in the Maya cultural sphere, no matter what the ethnic or linguistic antecedents of its new king or its original inhabitants might have been.

Nor was Yax K'uk' Mo's importance only local. His own investiture was closely connected with that of the first king of Quirigua, which he apparently supervised. Quirigua is Copan's nearest Classic Maya neighbor polity, about a three-day walk to the north in the valley of the Motagua river. Iconography and rulers' names apparently referring to Copan later occur at the centers of Pulsiha and Nim Li Punit in southern Belize. From the earliest times Copan's kings thus had far-flung relationships on the southeast borderlands. These almost certainly included kinship connections, trade, and more general cultural influence. Whether Copan ever exercised any direct political control over distant polities, however, remains unknown.

Yax K'uk' Mo' established his capital where the Copan Main Group (Fig. 48) now stands – the huge mass of plazas, temples, palaces, and royal monuments that has built up over the history of the dynasty. His own house compound and (probably) burial shrine lie buried deep beneath the East Court. A woman of extremely high rank, in all likelihood his wife, was interred nearby in the most elaborate tomb ever found at Copan, containing over 15,000 objects including mirrors and painted gourds with Teotihuacan motifs.[2]

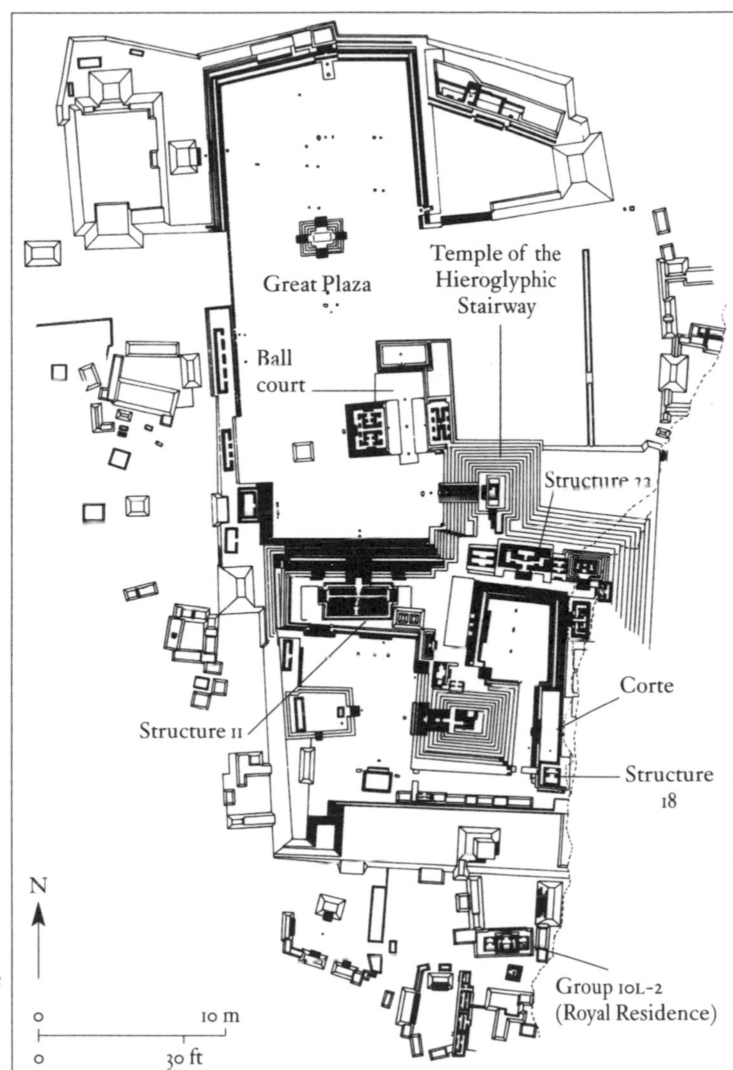

48 *Plan of the Copan Main Group as it looked during the late 8th century, after four centuries of steady growth. The actual residential compound of the last kings is attached to the southern end of this vast conglomeration of buildings.*

The son of the founding pair initiated a vigorous program of construction that continued through the reigns of four poorly-documented successors. Sometime about the beginning of the 6th century, Waterlily Jaguar began an ambitious expansion of the Copan Acropolis. After the intervening short reigns of rulers 8 and 9, Moon Jaguar followed up with his own celebrated constructions, most notably the extraordinary polychrome building called Rosalila, a replica of which can be seen today in Copan's sculpture museum. Butz' Chan's long and prosperous reign followed. The interval between Waterlily Jaguar's accession and Butz' Chan's death is roughly from AD 504 to

628, so there is no 6th-century "hiatus" at Copan, nor any obvious sign of the widespread drought that Richardson Gill and others posit for that time.

Under the next two kings Copan entered the richest phase of its history. Although not a great builder, Smoke Imix raised more monuments than any of his predecessors, particularly a series of seven stelae in AD 652 that appears to delimit the core agricultural zone of the valley. In the same year he participated in some sort of poorly understood event at Quirigua. By living to the ripe age of 83 he achieved the distinction of completing four k'atuns of life, a notable milestone attained by some other rulers such as his near contemporary Janaab' Pakal I at faraway Palenque. Waxaklajuun Ub'aah K'awiil (18 Rabbit), the 13th king, erected many great buildings, including Temple 22, the first phase of the Hieroglyphic Stairway, and the final phase ball court. He also remodeled the Great Plaza and adorned it with ornately carved stelae depicting himself in the guise of various gods, the most famous of all Copan's sculptures (Plate 7).

Some sort of influence was still exercised over the Motagua valley. Waxaklajuun Ub'aah K'awiil apparently presided over the installation of Quirigua's 6th ruler in AD 724, and might have taken part in some sort of military event in the same region. Whatever the nature of these relations, they ended abruptly and violently in AD 738. During an apparent visit to Quirigua, Waxaklajuun Ub'aah K'awiil's god-effigies were seized or defiled, and shortly afterwards he himself was ritually killed. Accounts of this incident are very fragmentary, but it smacks of a political coup on the part of the upstart Quirigua ruler rather than a formal war. We have tantalizing hints of a close connection between some Quirigua personage and Calakmul in AD 736. Though permanently enfeebled by its defeat in AD 695, Calakmul still connived to damage its old enemy, Tikal. Perhaps the Quirigua "incident" of AD 738 reflects such machinations, because Copan seems always to have been loosely in Tikal's camp.

Whatever happened did not directly involve destruction at Copan itself, but it shook the kingdom nonetheless. The 14th king had a short and apparently undistinguished 11-year reign, notable for a long cessation of inscriptions and major construction that continued into the incumbency of his son, K'ak' Yipyaj Chan K'awiil (Smoke Shell). Shaking off the lethargy that afflicted the dynasty, Smoke Shell eventually embarked on an ambitious program of work at the Temple of the Hieroglyphic Stairway (begun decades earlier), which he reconfigured into a vast ancestral monument complete with statues of five predecessors in Teotihuacan warrior garb (Plate 5). Climbing the stairway past these figures, one metaphorically journeyed back to the time of the founder, K'inich Yax K'uk' Mo', whose connections with Teotihuacan (by then probably less a real place than a dimly remembered Tollan) were memorialized in the summit temple. As in most narratives, however, the "historical" information is secondary to the culminating act – the actual dedication of the building and the stairway.

This brings us full circle to Yax Pasaj, who came to the throne as a young boy in AD 763 and who was probably not the son of the 15th king. Despite these disadvantages, he managed to get major projects underway by AD 769, and ultimately left an impressive legacy of buildings, including the final phases of Structure 11, Structure 16, and his own tomb, Structure 18 (for unknown reasons Yax Pasaj abandoned the old Copan tradition of erecting large stelae). He seems to have completed most of his constructions during the first half of his long reign (at least 47 years), one indication that the resurgence of Copan's dynastic fortunes eventually developed internal weaknesses. In AD 776 Yax Pasaj also dedicated Altar Q, the single most succinct expression of dynastic continuity in the Maya Lowlands. In view of subsequent events, Yax Pasaj's insistence on displaying his connection with all previous rulers, and particularly the founder, strikes a strident and insecure note. Sometime after AD 810 (perhaps as late as 820) he finally died, the last of his line, unless we count the shadowy figure (king or pretender?) Ukit Took' whose name is found on an altar that was only partly completed in AD 822.

For many years the cessation of dynastic activity around the beginning of the 9th century seemed to mark both the political and demographic collapse of Copan. As we shall see, this picture has markedly changed as a result of more recent research, but right now a brief overview of Yax Pasaj's kingdom in the late 8th century is necessary.

Copan on the Brink

Yax Pasaj could enjoy a certain amount of complacency as he surveyed his kingdom around AD 785. One measure of a great king was the number of his subjects, and never before had there been so many at Copan. Flanking the looming mass of royal architecture that had accumulated since Yax K'uk' Mo's time were two great residential concentrations, today called the Las Sepulturas and El Bosque residential barrios (Fig. 49). Here, on the flat land of the fertile Copan alluvial pocket, lived as many as 9000–12,000 people, all within 800 m (about 0.5 miles) of Yax Pasaj's own sprawling compound attached to the southern end of the Acropolis (Group 10L-2). This zone has one of the most urban-like concentrations of people in the Maya Lowlands,

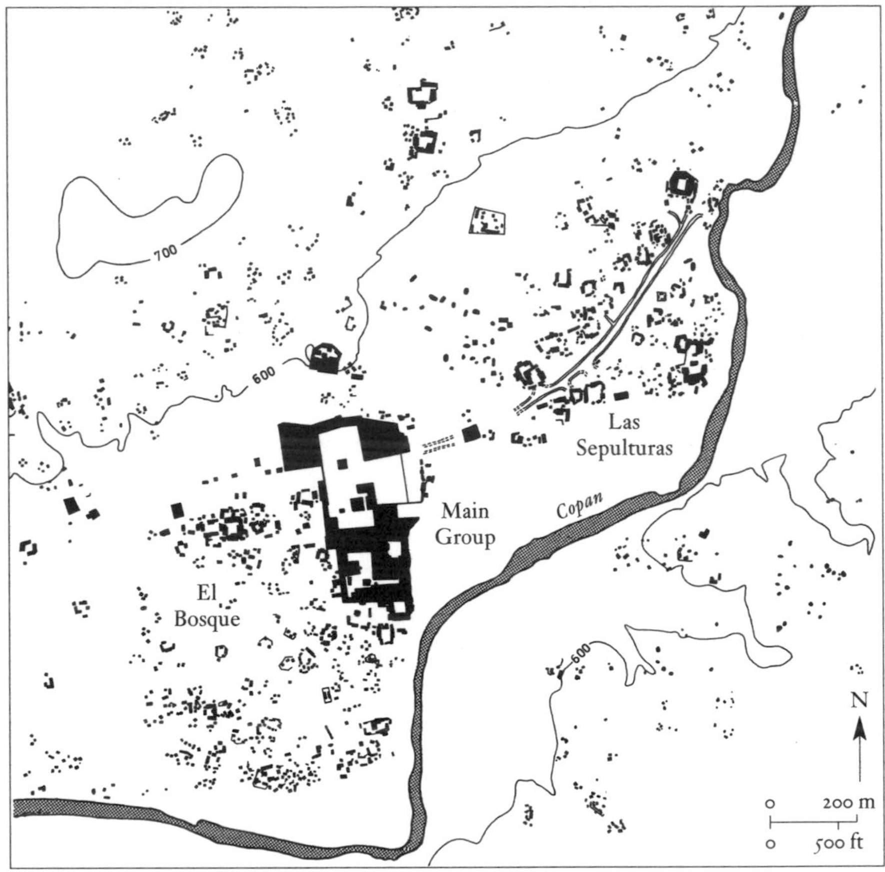

49 *Map of the Copan Main Group and the surrounding "urban core." Copan is unusual among Maya centers for the large concentrations of residences immediately around its regal-ritual epicenter. Although probably urban in population density, the residential enclaves were dominated by elite house compounds and lacked many of the features of cities elsewhere in Mesoamerica, such as Tenochtitlan or Teotihuacan.*

although it is only about one sq. km (0.39 sq. miles) in area, including the Main Group itself.

Stretching away into the surrounding foothills, especially on the north side of the river, was an outer belt of less dense and generally more modest settlement that housed an additional 10,000 people. Still farther out, in the upper river valley and its main tributaries, lived another 5000 people or so. By the end of the 8th century, Yax Pasaj's core realm – the region within about a two day walk – might have had as many as 28,000 inhabitants. Although this seems a pretty modest number by modern standards, it was very respectable for a

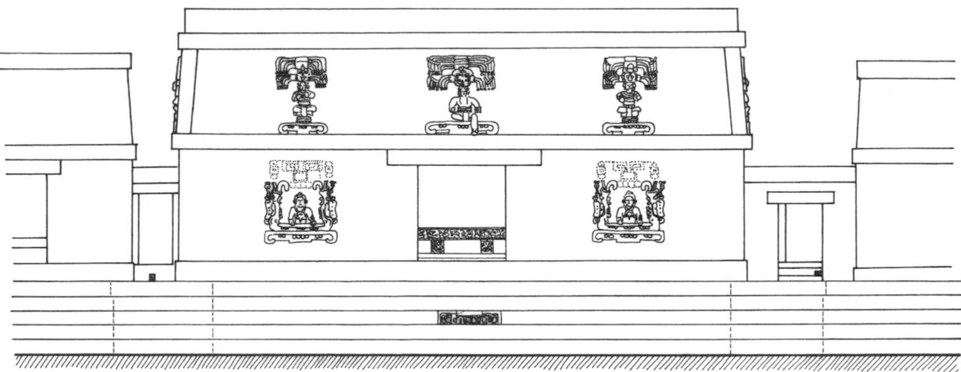

50 *Reconstruction drawing of the front façade of the House of the Bacabs, Copan, Honduras. Note the interior hieroglyphic bench and the complex façade sculpture. This building served important political and ritual functions in the court of the great noble Mak-Chanal late in the 8th century, and might have been his actual residence.*

Classic Maya kingdom, and the inhabitants were pressing seriously on their resource base, as we shall see shortly.

Whether or not Yax Pasaj, like his predecessors, could exercise any authority farther afield in the Motagua valley and southern Belize is unclear. Certainly the Waxaklajuun Ub'aah K'awiil debacle permanently removed Quirigua from any Copan suzerainty that might originally have existed. There are signs, however, that Yax Pasaj was trying to patch things up with old enemies – in fact we last hear of him carrying out some kind of ritual there in AD 810. Imports of jade, shell, flint, obsidian, and pottery still flowed in from other regions on the southeast frontier, including highland Guatemala and the central valleys of Honduras, so Copan was certainly not isolated.

Internally, the kingdom had never been so complicated. Dominating the Las Sepulturas and El Bosque residential enclaves were the impressive households of approximately 20 great noble families, and a few more were scattered in other parts of the valley. Many of these grandees lived in considerable splendor. The greatest of them enjoyed fine masonry houses embellished with sculpture and inscriptions (Fig. 50), around which were arrayed the courtyards and dwellings of their lesser relatives and retainers. Some of them, as we have seen, also possessed elaborate benches or thrones. Such seats of power were associated with rulers elsewhere in Mesoamerica since 1200 BC. More so than elsewhere in the Maya Lowlands, Copan's nobles, at least during Yax Pasaj's time, seem to have had privileged access to these potent political symbols.

Exactly who these nobles were is uncertain. Some of them, like the scribe Mak-Chanal whom we met in Chapter 1, bore exalted titles such as aj k'uhuun that linked them to the royal court. Beyond this, we can surmise that some families were junior branches of the royal line, or hereditary nobility in their own right.[3] Whichever the case, they collectively formed a powerful social stratum. Mak-Chanal's compound probably housed 250–300 people, and by Yax Pasaj's time almost 20 percent of all the people in the kingdom resided in noble households (although not all were nobles). Mak-Chanal's social group was particularly well established and very powerful, while others were more modest in wealth and political connections.

Differences in rank are striking when we compare noble compounds with the tiniest rural commoner houses, but Elliot Abrams's calculations of household construction costs shows a continuum of investment linking the grandest with the most modest ones (Fig. 51). If we exclude royal burials, a similar continuum is apparent in mortuary practices. Using these kinds of evidence at least, it is impossible to segregate the population as a whole into social segments that we can neatly label "elites" and "commoners."

My opinion is that on the eve of the collapse Copan's socio-political organization closely resembled the "house" model we reviewed earlier. In one sense the whole kingdom was the patrimony, or "house" of the royal line, embodied ultimately in Yax Pasaj. But nested within it were the lesser, quasi-independent "houses" of noble families. Great nobles were supported by lesser relatives, clients, or slaves, and thus had their own political constituencies and control over corporate resources. Put another way, the kingdom was horizontally segmented into powerful social groups with considerable scope for independent political action – a kind of organization sometimes called 'heterarchical' by anthropologists because it departs from our usual assumptions about well-established hierarchical arrangements. By the late 8th century the patrimony of the most exalted of these nobles, such as Mak-Chanal, included court positions and titles derived from royal patronage.

Interestingly, the archaeological signs of these great Copan lords are not very obtrusive before about AD 700. Nonroyal elites appear to have really come into their own after the demise of Waxaklajuun Ub'aah K'awiil, when the royal dynasty had lost much credibility. At any rate, during Yax Pasaj's reign they were certainly in a position to assert their own interests against those of the king, and also against each other. Bill and Barbara Fash excavated a possible council house (*popol na*) on the Copan Acropolis dating to the mid-8th century, where, they believe, late kings of the dynasty increasingly had to negotiate decisions there with other magnates. Yax Pasaj probably derived much of his own authority from his relations with these powerful people, and pursued a delicate political balancing act that rewarded allies and marginalized opponents.

In some ways this system is similar to the present one at Copan, and a little visual anecdote might help us to envision how it actually functioned on a day-by-day basis. All the while I was working in the valley we took Sundays off. In those days the town of Copan was a pretty sleepy place without many diversions, so I frequently went to sit in the municipal plaza, an arena of many complex human interactions. Much of the Copan valley is today owned by a few prominent families who maintain impressive houses (the foci of wealthy "houses" in the larger sense of the word) on or near this central square. They also dominate, directly or indirectly, municipal affairs and officials.

I knew, or at least recognized, some of the powerful patriarchs of these families, men who habitually strolled about on a Sunday morning, doing much more, however, than merely stretching their legs. Sometimes they

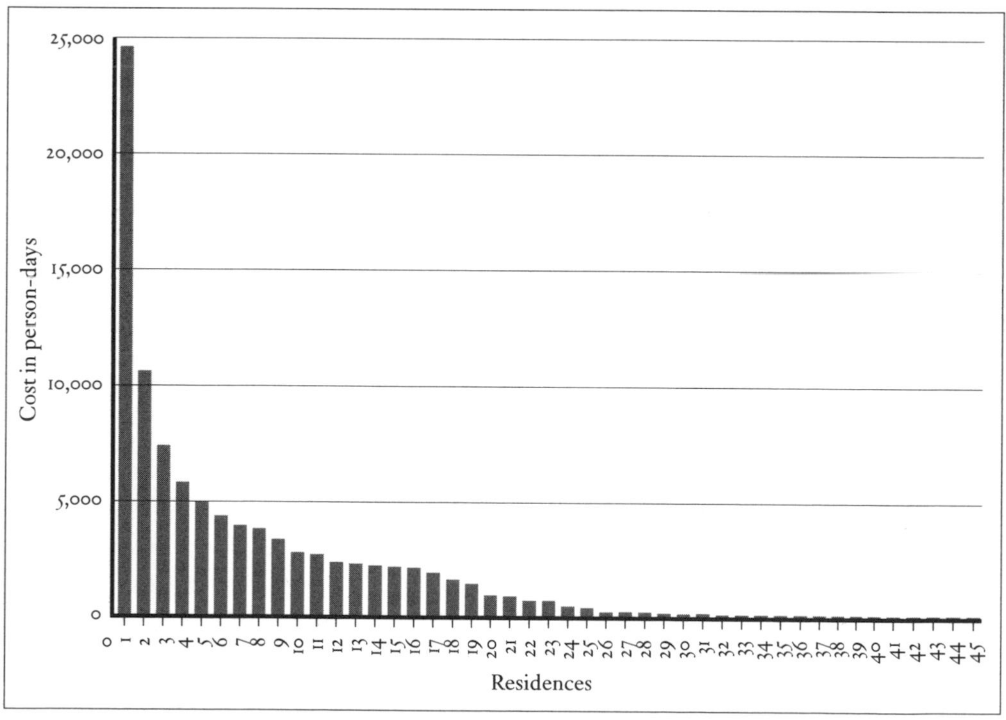

51 Elliot Abrams's calculations of labor inputs required to build a sample of Copan residences. A royal-scale "palace" building is at left, and commoner residences are at the right. Abrams's time-motion studies were instrumental in showing that construction costs were probably far lower than previously imagined.

avoided one another because tensions between their families ran high. More often they conspicuously greeted each other as equals, publicly affirming their positions as big men in the community. Affluent and influential citizens of lesser importance – prosperous farmers, town officials, storekeepers, and the like – took care to greet these grandees politely and respectfully. Sometimes the patriarchs conferred earnestly with men who were obviously their employees, making plans for the next week's work on ranches or tobacco fields. And inevitably they were approached by modest people, supplicants literally tugging their forelocks or twisting their hats in their hands, seeking some sort of minor favor, such as a job or a small loan of money.

The fascinating thing is that a careful observer didn't have to hear a word to intuit the basic meaning of all this social drama, which was acted out with the whole town as an audience and profoundly expressed and reinforced the established political, social, and economic hierarchies. Add a weak royal dynasty, change the backdrop to Copan's Great Plaza, dress the actors in feathers, cotton robes, and loincloths, alter the body language a bit, and I'm convinced you would have seen much the same thing 1200 years ago.

Copan's Common People

Such is the top-down view of Copan in the late 8th century. Beneath it lurks another story, a bottom-up one that is not directly told by monuments, dates, or inscriptions. Its protagonists are the ordinary people who fueled the Copan polity with food and labor. Fortunately we know a lot about them because we have tested or extensively excavated hundreds of the places where they lived. At these modest sites we find the remains of small, perishable houses (Plate 9) and the trash the inhabitants discarded – broken pottery, used-up grinding stones, dulled obsidian blades, and the occasional modest ritual object. Our demographic reconstructions indicate that they comprised at least 80 percent of the whole regional population.

Let's look at things from the perspective of these producer households. As long as land was productive and fertile, Maya producer families at Copan could probably manage their own domestic economies perfectly well. They knew how to acquire and maintain the tools and raw materials they needed. They did not require lords or kings to tell them what to plant or how much, how to recruit and deploy labor, how to negotiate with other farmers, or even how to move and establish new households. Drought or storms sometimes caused bad years for some families, but household surpluses could be stockpiled or exchanged to tide people over situational shortfalls. General productive capacity was not highly varied from one family to the next, nor were there strong social distinctions based on differential access to agrarian capital – land and labor.

As with peasants everywhere, the political economy intervened in their affairs, but the modest food surpluses needed to support a small subgroup of lords and the royal household were easily produced, and labor exactions for building temples or palaces were bearable. All in all, elites were not very demanding or meddlesome, or competitive among themselves. If the great royal projects were inconvenient, their results were undeniably impressive and the rituals focused on them broke the monotony of day-to-day life. People were proud of their rulers, and who knew, anyway – maybe all the royal ceremony and display really did help guarantee the well-being of the world and the prosperity of the kingdom.

Such, at least, were conditions up to the reign of Waxaklajuun Ub'aah K'awiil. As if a portent, his death signaled a downturn in Copan's fortunes, and by Yax Pasaj's time there were ominous rumblings of discontent. Now we are in a position to evaluate what happened next, and how we know it.

The Patterns of the Copan Collapse

As at most great Classic centers, research at Copan tended to progress outward from the royal core. Between 1935 and 1946, with a couple of years off during World War II, many of the great buildings were excavated and restored by archaeologists from the Carnegie Institution of Washington. At that time, of course, these structures were seen as the remains of a ceremonial center. The Carnegie work confirmed the results of Sylvanus G. Morley's earlier studies of Copan's Long Count dates: no more great buildings were erected after about AD 800, although offerings continued to be made among the old monuments. John Longyear, the project ceramist, noted that Copan's latest buildings were well preserved, that the contents of rooms had been largely removed, and that abandonment seemed to have been quiet and orderly.[4] Refuse was later deposited in some of these rooms, and Longyear presciently concluded that people remained living in the valley under local chiefs long after the Main Group was deserted. No one at that time thought of the collapse in terms of kings, dynasties, and royal courts, but the main outlines of what had happened at the top were pretty clear. Although we now have a much more nuanced appreciation of the political breakdown, the Carnegie archaeologists got the basic outlines just about right.

We already saw that the inscriptions (which Longyear and his colleagues could not read) have since revealed the abrupt political collapse of Copan's royal line. Work by Tulane University archaeologists has fleshed out our understanding of this event by identifying the domestic facilities where the last few rulers actually lived – the aforementioned conglomeration of buildings and courtyards called Group 10L-2. Parts of this royal residence were deliberately burned sometime around the mid-9th century. Clearly the demise of the royal tradition was not as peaceful as Longyear imagined. And although it is the most abrupt dimension of the Copan collapse, even the deterioration of dynastic rule might have required two decades or more to play itself out.

But what about lesser nobles and the bulk of the population? Prior to 1975 we had practically no information concerning the larger Copan system. It was widely assumed that the whole central political apparatus of the kingdom disappeared at the same time the kings fell, and that the valley was essentially depopulated by AD 850–900. All of this reinforced the idea of a sudden, dramatic catastrophe. A much more complex picture emerges from several different and independent lines of evidence derived from settlement, environmental, and skeletal data. After summarizing each of these, I will use them to construct a synthetic overview of our current understanding of what happened at Copan.

Population History of the Copan Collapse

Keys to our present understanding of the unraveling of the kingdom emerged from archaeological surveys of much of the valley, and from excavations of household remains, ranging from those of the humblest farmers to the imposing compounds of great nobles like Mak-Chanal. Perhaps the most important result of all this work is our ability to reasonably estimate the regional population history of the Copan polity, thanks to innovative and exacting chronological research done by my colleague AnnCorinne Freter of Ohio University. Based on her obsidian hydration dating of 239 sites of all kinds, we have simulated the rough outlines of demographic change since AD 400.[5] Results are summarized in Fig. 52, which reveals several very interesting things.

On the most general level, there was a single pulse of population growth and decline resembling that of Tikal, but different than that documented around Dos Pilas. Before AD 600 the region had a very small population (although undoubtedly larger than our raw simulation shows because of the difficulty of retrieving early settlement remains). Our informed guess is that there were about 5000 people or so in the valley shortly after Smoke Imix

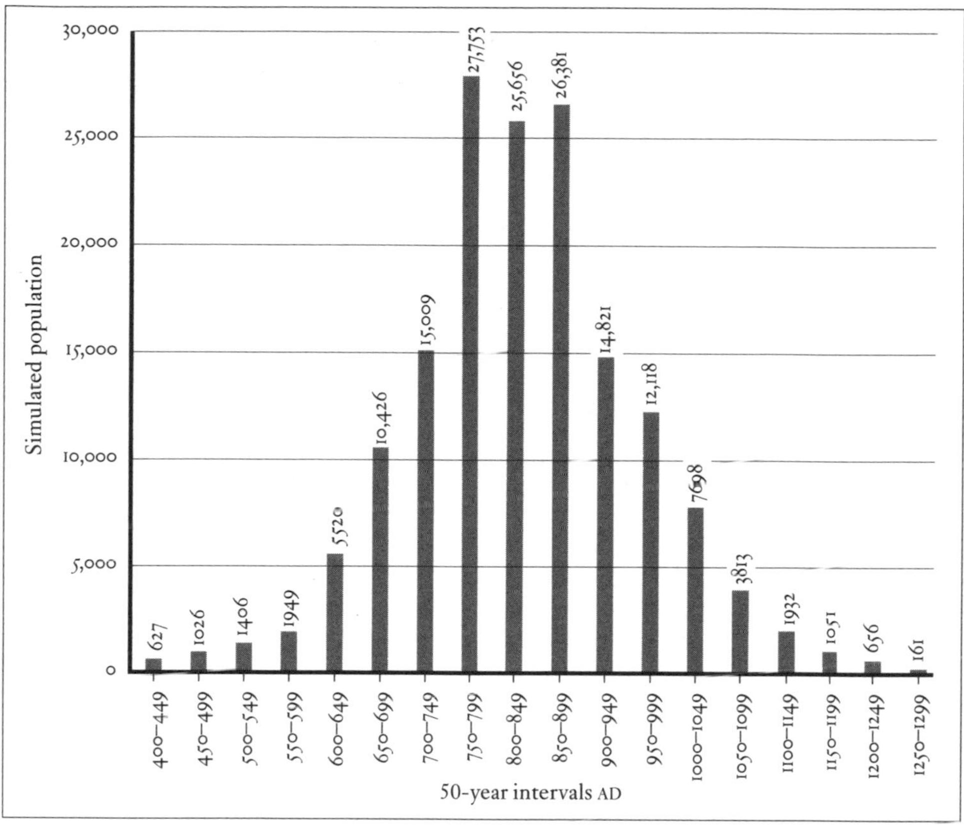

52 Results of the computer simulation of Copan's population history as derived from settlement data. Note the rapid increase in population beginning around AD *600, and the protracted decline after the disappearance of the royal dynasty around* AD *800–822.*

came to power. During his reign the population started to grow rapidly, reaching a peak of just under 28,000 by about AD 750. This represents an overall annual rate of increase of roughly one percent sustained for 150 years, fairly respectable for preindustrial times. Presumably most of it is accounted for by the intrinsic fertility of the local population, but there are signs that Smoke Imix might have tried to attract, or even coerce, outlying farmers into settling closer to the Copan pocket, the agrarian core of his kingdom.

Notice also the shape of the curve, with its single steep rise, peak, and then decline. It closely resembles the kind of "boom and bust" cycle associated with the periodic growth and decline of various wild animal populations. But the peak is not a sharp one. Copan's population hovered in the 26,000–28,000 range for a century or more. Interestingly, the peak population was not rationally distributed with respect to the agrarian landscape of the whole valley, but instead heavily concentrated in the Copan pocket. I believe this pattern reflects not only the high quality of the soils there, plus a desire to live near the royal court, but also elite meddling for political reasons as the kingdom experienced troubles.

Now look at the decline part of the curve. It appears steep, but this impression is somewhat deceiving, in part because the mechanics of the simulation create an artificially abrupt drop between AD 900 and 950. In fact, population at AD 900–950 was minimally 15,000 people. In other words, more than a century after the last king departed at least 54 percent of Copan's regional population still survived. Thereafter the decline continues, closely approximating the rate of growth, but we can still detect traces of human activity as late as AD 1250 in the hydration record. Something not shown in this chart reveals even longer human presence. A radiocarbon date from the skeleton of an infant buried in a little rural site shows that this individual lived sometime between AD 1278 and 1411.[6]

In an earlier summary of the Maya collapse Gordon Willey and Demitri Shimkin remarked that "... indications point to a decline in growth rate throughout the Classic period, largely because of increased mortality."[7] To the contrary, Copan shows an accelerating rate of growth beginning around AD 400 with a peak at about AD 800, a plateau for a century or so, then a protracted decline.

The same household excavations that provided the thousands of dates essential to the population simulation told us some unexpected things about the occupational histories of several elite compounds. Plenty of evidence turned up, for example, that people still lived in and around Mak-Chanal's residence for several generations after Yax Pasaj quit the scene. One might, of course, imagine them as mere squatters in the ruins of abandoned palaces, but fortunately we were able to determine that construction continued at some of these nobles' compounds well into the 10th century.[8]

Even more revealing was a spectacular find made by my colleague Randolph Widmer in 1983. While clearing the rubble of a collapsed masonry building facing one of the smaller courtyards of Mak-Chanal's sprawling complex (Plate 8), Widmer found the intact artifact assemblage of a shell workshop (Fig. 53). Tools, raw materials, and partly-finished objects lay right in their original positions on the bench or floor surfaces, sealed there by the debris of a heavy beam and mortar roof that fell suddenly, perhaps during an earthquake. Whoever was inside managed to escape, but they dropped their implements as they ran out. We were able to date this event to sometime about AD 950–1000. Among the products of the workshop were star-shaped

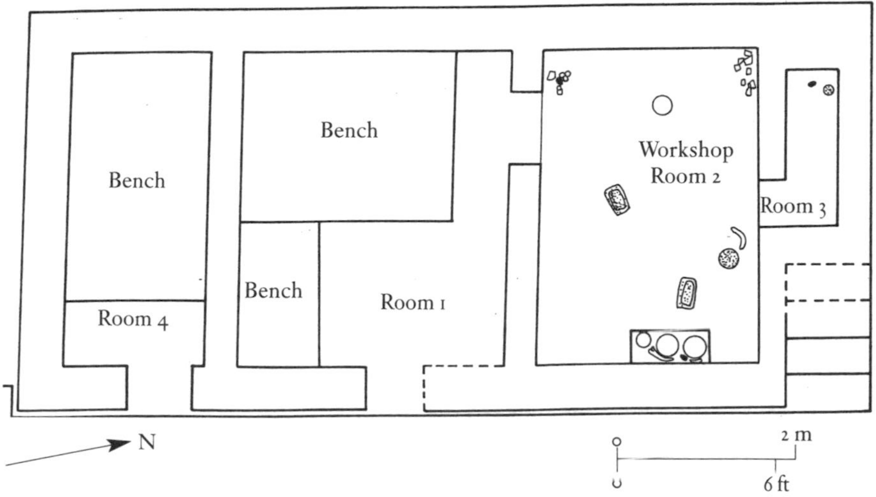

53 *Plan of Structure 110B at Copan, as excavated by Randolph Widmer. A shell workshop was located in Room 2, its contents buried by the sudden collapse of the roof sometime in the 10th century. Among the artifacts preserved on the floor and the small bench were broken ceramic vessels, bone and obsidian tools, stone grinding slabs, worked and unworked shell, and a shell gorget.*

pendants crafted from imported marine shell. Exactly the same kind objects are associated with numerous depictions of Maya gods and nobles, including those figures shown holding up Mak-Chanal's hieroglyphic bench in his house just a few meters away (Plate 6). Artisans attached to the household of some successor to Mak-Chanal obviously still had access to expensive, imported raw materials, and were still crafting objects of the kind consumed by elite people. Perhaps the mercury found by David Pendergast at Lamanai passed through the Copan valley after all, along with shell and other things, at about the same time.

This and similar evidence shows that while many noble houses no doubt disappeared at the time of the dynastic collapse, others such as Mak-Chanal's managed to weather this crisis and still functioned in some privileged capacity for as much as 150–200 years longer. In stark contrast, the old royal precincts seem totally abandoned after about AD 850–900, unless we count a small cluster of houses near its western periphery in the El Bosque residential zone.[9] Ritual deposits, including imported pottery and other materials, were still made around the old stelae and altars until at least AD 1000, consistent with the survival of local elites who remembered their ancestors. Some Mayanists believe that even in decline Copan remained a symbolic Tollan for distant Highland Maya peoples, which might also account for some of the foreign objects ceremonially deposited there.

After AD 1000 people still lived in and around the old crumbling noble residences, but we find no more signs of any conspicuously elite activity, except possibly at one site in the uppermost reaches of the valley.

Environmental Degradation

By AD 750–800 overall population density for the whole Copan river drainage was fairly light – roughly 55 people per sq. km (142 per sq. mile). But of course most of this landscape was unusable or unattractive for growing crops, nor did people distribute themselves evenly on it. Considering only that portion reasonably attractive for habitation and/or agriculture, the effective population density peaked, however briefly, between about 370 and 452 people per sq. km (958 and 1171 per sq. mile). But people were not distributed rationally even with regard to their primary agricultural resources. Instead, about 80 percent of the entire population lived in the Copan pocket in Yax Pasaj's time, where maximal density reached about 935 people per sq. km (2422 per sq. mile). We will return to this puzzling pattern later. Right now what is important is not only that people were so crowded onto a very restricted part of the landscape, but that by AD 800 this zone had already been farmed for centuries. Under the circumstances, we should not be surprised that the environment was showing signs of severe wear and tear.

In July 1989 I found myself standing at the bottom of a narrow trench dug down 2.8 m (9.2 ft) into a sweltering corn field (Fig. 54). I had purposefully excavated here, on the northern fringes of Copan's Las Sepulturas residential zone, to see if I could find traces of severe erosion detected in the area by previous projects. My feet rested on an old Maya floor probably laid down sometime in the late 8th century, and just to my left was an imposing masonry wall, with its footing on the same floor. From the profile of the vertical trench wall in front of me I could read off a story of how this large structure had been buried.

First the Maya had built the floor itself, and then on top of it both a substantial building and a low cobble platform, leaving a little corridor about 0.80 m (2.6 ft) between them. The big building, with its fine stonework and ornate sculpture, was typical of the elite edifices so conspicuous at Las Sepulturas after about AD 700. I had exposed the bottom dozen or so stone courses of what was probably its rear substructure wall, still intact to a height of 2 m (6.56 ft). While the Maya actively used the two buildings, about 0.30–0.40 m (12–16 in) of dark trashy soil, including a lot of potsherds and other debris, accumulated in the little corridor – reflecting the residential messiness so

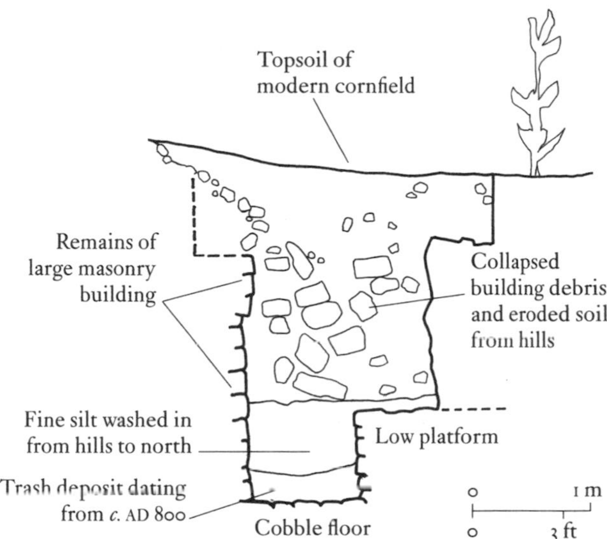

54 *Deep trench showing the effects of hillside erosion in the Copan valley, which largely buried the impressive masonry structure on the left. Much of this erosion probably occurred long after the royal compound and the elite residences of Copan's urban core were abandoned.*

commonly found at such places. Then about 0.60 m (23.6 in) of fine, yellow, silty clay virtually devoid of artifacts were rapidly deposited, filling in the corridor and entirely burying the little cobble platform. The consistency of this soil indicated that it had been quickly washed down from the hill slopes along the nearby northern flank of the valley. Above were thicker deposits of darker silt mixed with collapsed construction material from the building's summit structure, and finally the humus of the modern cornfield. By 1989 the remains of the big building, which originally stood proudly about 7 m (23 ft) high when its superstructure was intact, was so deeply buried by all this erosion that all I could see was a pile of rubble just 1.5 m (4.9 ft) high among the cornstalks.

When did all this occur? We later dated two pieces of discarded obsidian from the trashy soil layer to AD 792 and 819. Because of the error factors associated with these dates we can't be precise, but taken in conjunction with the style of the building itself, the erosion probably began sometime in the mid-to-late 8th century. Even as elite people were raising their imposing houses and shrines at Las Sepulturas, then, it seems that seasonal runoff and flooding from the hillsides was beginning to bury some of them under loads of sediment. Nor is my building the only evidence of such erosion. Many other structures in the area are wholly or partly buried, and anyone walking along the modern road just a couple of hundred meters to the north can see the remains of house floors exposed deep in the vertical road cuts.

Several years before I dug my little trench we had detected evidence of the probable cause of such erosional episodes, preserved as fossil pollen in a sediment core extracted from a swamp in these northern hills by David Rue.[10] Pollen from the lower sections of this core, which extends back only to about AD 1000–1100, showed the presence of grasses associated with agricultural clearing as well as maize. Virtually absent were any signs of the broad-leafed tropical forest that naturally grows on the valley floor or on deep upland soils. Even more surprising was the weak pollen signature of pine, a tree that now covers most hillsides. Apparently much of the landscape was denuded of trees. This pattern is much like that documented for Tikal, but different from that around Dos Pilas. The pollen profile shows that the region did not begin to recover from this severe deforestation until about AD 1250 or a little later. Deforestation is a principal cause of erosion in the humid tropics, especially in regions of pronounced topographic relief like Copan. Rue's pollen evidence independently reinforced our demographic reconstructions – people were still farming in the Copan valley until surprisingly late.

Of course the erosional episodes that buried my elite building had occurred far earlier, and are not directly reflected in Rue's core. But we know that population densities in Late Classic times were much larger than those in AD 1000–1100, and deforestation must have been well advanced by then. Not only were hillsides cleared for farms, but also for construction material and fuel. Elliot Abrams and David Rue have simulated the demand for such materials, and estimate that by AD 800 "... no pine would have been standing for the entire 12 km length of the Copan pocket for a distance of nearly one km away from any zone of settlement on either side of the Copan river."[11]

Interestingly, we have only sparse and highly localized evidence for agricultural terraces and none at all for drained fields. Both kinds of intensive agroengineering are found in other parts of the Maya Lowlands, and had they been applied on a large scale to the landscape its productive capacity might have been stabilized. What probably happened instead was revealed by a complex simulation model.

Because archaeologists cannot directly observe the ancient processes they are interested in, they often create simulations, a common practice among scientists in any field. Both the Copan population reconstruction and the deforestation posited by Abrams and Rue are based on such models. By the early 1990s sufficient data had accumulated so that John Wingard could carry out the most ambitious simulation of ancient agricultural productivity done anywhere in the Maya Lowlands. After analyzing hundreds of soil samples from an area of over 200 sq. km (74 sq. miles), Wingard used a complicated soil analysis program at the Department of Agriculture to simulate the effects of an expanding population on the agrarian resources of the Copan valley between AD 0 and AD 1050.[12] He assumed an initial population of 1000 people and then modeled what happened as their numbers increased and they applied various land-use strategies to the landscape. Central to Wingard's thinking was carrying capacity, a concept disliked by some archaeologists, who think it is too static in the face of the human capacity for innovation. In Wingard's model carrying capacity was in fact treated as a variable and dynamic concept that could be changed (up to a point) by farmers.

Wingard concluded that by the mid-to-late 6th century the regional population, at about 5000 people, had reached the carrying capacity of the best alluvial soils in all parts of the valley if they used a long-cycle swidden system. Farmers on the valley floor then shifted to more intensive forms of cultivation, and the excess population eventually spread to the less productive and more unstable uplands. By AD 800 at least 120 sq. km (46.3 sq. miles) of the most usable lands in the valley had been colonized and deforested, and Wingard predicted a major erosional event during the 8th century. People finally resorted to the most intensive forms of cultivation that their technology and organization allowed. Population peaked between AD 850 and 900 at about 22,000, then began to decline.

Simulations, of course, prove nothing by themselves, and are only as plausible as the components and data fed into them, and how well they agree with other evidence. What is so interesting is the degree of fit between Wingard's conclusions and our own demographic model, which are based on data sets virtually independent of one another. The population figures generated through time by his agricultural model closely approximate our own (the peak population occurs a little later), and Wingard predicts early deforestation and even an erosion event that might be the very one I unearthed in my cornfield trench.

Wingard did not carry his simulation beyond AD 1050, when he estimates there were still about 14,000 people in the region. He informs me that had he done so, however, it would never have predicted complete depopulation. In other words, the model is perfectly consistent not only with our demographic reconstruction, but with the continued farming and deforestation reflected in Rue's pollen samples. Because considerable carrying capacity persisted long after the downturn, Wingard notes that the political collapse of the dynasty was primarily due not only to the drop in agricultural productivity, but also to the associated social disruption.

Revealingly, Wingard's carrying capacity calculations yield a peak population about 20 percent smaller than those we calculated from the settlement data. We deliberately tried to make the latter generate maximal estimates, and I now think that Wingard's figures are the more accurate. If this supposition is correct, Yax Pasaj's subjects numbered in the 18,000–20,000 range, and we should reduce the peak population densities discussed above accordingly. That all these independent lines of evidence agree so well by chance is astronomically improbable. Even more supporting evidence comes from studies of Copan's skeletons.

One of the principal aims of our own household excavations at Copan was the retrieval of a very large skeletal sample. No one knows exactly how many Copan burials have been collected over the last century, but by 1992 the number stood at around 600, and many more have since been found. Most of these, expectedly, come from 8th–9th-century contexts. Analysis of this sample is an extremely arduous task currently being undertaken by several paleo-osteologists, and the final results will not be in for years. Nevertheless, some revealing patterns have already emerged, one of which concerns diet.

David Reed measured stable isotopes of carbon and nitrogen extracted from bone fragments in order to assess the contribution of various categories of food to the ancient Copan diet.[13] The 90 individuals he studied came from both rich and poor households, different parts of the valley, and were of various ages and sexes. Reed's main conclusion was that maize was by far the most important food source, despite the fact that remains of some 42 species of plants have been recovered by Copan archaeologists. He estimates that between 62 and 78 percent of all the calories eaten by the people in his sample came from maize.[14] Other plants such as beans probably made up much of the remainder of the diet, which was notably impoverished in terms of animal protein, in marked contrast to the patterns found on the skeletons in the Petexbatun region. Social status, as implied by the type of site from which the burials were recovered, had remarkably little effect on the adult diet, although adult men seem to have eaten a little more maize than adult women.

Reed's conclusions suggest that signs of nutrition-deficiency diseases might be expected in Copan's skeletons, and confirmation of a heavily maize-based diet makes simulations like Wingard's more plausible. In fact, Wingard's simulation estimate of maize consumption squares very well with Reed's later findings. Some archaeologists have maintained that ancient milpas supported a far wider array of interspersed cultivated plants than modern ones, in which maize predominates. However this might be, these putative other milpa products do not seem to have contributed much to the diet at Copan.

Rebecca Storey and Stephen Whittington have examined hundreds of Copan skeletons to determine paleodemographic patterns and morbidity (ill health or sickness). Reasoning that they would provide a "best-case" scenario, Storey began by studying the remains of 122 subadults (i.e., under the age of 15 years) from Mak-Chanal's great elite compound.[15] She found that 85 percent of these individuals died before the age of five, and larger than expected numbers between the ages of five and nine, suggesting a "high-mortality" population. By examining defects in deciduous tooth enamel, she discovered that a very large proportion of these children had apparently been exposed to periodic stresses related to infection and poor nutrition. Some individuals were even affected in utero or during their first year of life, periods when buffers are commonly provided by the mother's body. Storey concluded that both children and mothers were often in poor condition.

Whittington took a different approach by studying 148 low-status burials from many different sites.[16] Of these, 54 died before reaching the age of 15 (most, in fact, before the age of five). Thirty-two others died in the 16- to 36-year range, and of the remainder only eight survived to age 50. He examined not only teeth, but also bones for signs of lesions or other defects associated with poor diet, infections, and injuries. Individuals of both sexes ate a high carbohydrate diet (men got a little more animal protein), and the young people in his sample, like Storey's, experienced extreme health stresses. Many people who survived to adulthood suffered multiple episodes of infections, and conditions like tuberculosis and pellagra were probably endemic. Anemia due to iron deficiency was also probably common, and would have affected the reproductive capacity of women. Interestingly, neither Whittington nor Storey found much evidence for trauma, such as would be produced by warfare.

Both Storey and Whittington emphasize that these results are difficult to interpret because it is usually impossible to associate a specific disease with marks on bone or teeth. In addition, any "dead" population obviously is in some sense an "unhealthy" subset of the living one from which it is drawn, and hence not representative of it. Even more counterintuitively, one could argue that Storey's skeletons with multiple tooth defects were the healthy ones because such they survived multiple episodes of stress, while skeletons with no such traces represent people who died quickly when first afflicted. Nevertheless, given the larger contexts in which Copan's population lived – one marked by poor diet, high population density, and probably heavy work loads – it seems very likely that if some time machine could magically transport us back to Yax Pasaj's realm, we would observe a population in which life expectancy was short, mortality was high, people were often sick, malnourished, and decrepit-looking, and fertility was beginning to decline.

Linda Schele and David Freidel characterized the Copan collapse this way: "The people simply walked away. Within two centuries of the demise of the last king of Copan, 90 percent of the population was gone. They left a land so ravaged that only in this century have people returned to build the population back to the levels it knew in the time of Yax-Pac...."[17] In fact, almost three centuries after Yax Pasaj's time some 14 percent of the population still remained. Nor did all these people simply "walk away."

Let's think about what you might have experienced had you been an inhabitant of Copan a century or so after Yax Pasaj's dynasty disappeared. The mean annual rate of population loss between AD 900 and AD 1050 works out to about 0.083 percent. Imagine that you were born into a small community of 100 people somewhere in the valley in about AD 950. By the time you attained the impressive age of 50 years, about half of your neighbors would be gone. You would certainly notice the difference, and you might even recognize some of the reasons. Fewer and fewer children were born to replace the old people who died, and every once in a while a family would move away to some distant place. You might find all this discouraging, and even disorienting, but it is hardly catastrophic. Many small rural towns in the United States have in fact experienced population declines just like this over the last couple of generations, albeit for different reasons.

In summary, at Copan there was clearly a phased and extended collapse process, rather than an abrupt, cataclysmic event. First the royal dynasty disappeared, taking with it those parts of the Classic Maya Great Tradition most closely associated with kingship. Some nobles, though perhaps not as powerful and influential as before, preserved other elements of this tradition for another two centuries. Demographic collapse was decoupled from political decline and does not clearly mirror political crises. Population remained near peak levels for about a century after Yax Pasaj's death, and then dwindled away over several hundred years. This is very much the pattern that Sidrys and Berger predicted on the basis of their chronological research in 1979.

In his general "recipe" for the collapse of complex societies we reviewed at the end of Chapter 3, Joseph Tainter emphasizes what one might call processes of diminishment and simplification – less political centralization, less marked social stratification, less top-down management, less economic specialization, and fewer people. This is what happened at Copan. Tainter and others have noted that complex systems rarely fall apart suddenly and completely, but instead break down in steps or stages to those levels that can still maintain effective flows of energy and information. Following this reasoning, Copan's royal dynasty was the most fragile part of the system, the nonroyal lords were somewhat more durable, and the agrarian sector was the sturdiest part of all. Put another way, the Great Tradition elements of Copan were less hardy than the folkways of the mass of the population.

Significant in this regard is that long after kings and lords had disappeared Copan's local farmers still obtained obsidian imported from the Guatemalan highlands. Clearly people moved in and out of the valley, and just as clearly elites were not essential to the exchange of this household commodity. That commoners carried on this aspect of foreign relations, as well as their ordinary farming pursuits, provides convincing proof of the ability of the agrarian sector to function on its own (just as it had, of course, at Copan and everywhere else in the Maya Lowlands long before kings and lords emerged). It is true, however, that in the Copan valley the collapse did not stop at some diminished and simplified, but still sustainable level. Ultimately, no matter how long it took, even the common farmers disappeared from the landscape, except perhaps for remnants so tiny that we can no longer easily detect them.

What Caused the Copan "Collapse"?

Given all this detail we are on a pretty firm footing in our effort to explain what happened to Copan. We can plausibly dismiss volcanoes, hurricanes, and similar sudden and uncontrollable natural catastrophes at the outset, and I will say no more about them. But what about war, invasion, and rebellion?

Although Copan's kings liked to depict themselves in military regalia on dynastic monuments, the inscriptions yield scant evidence of involvement in foreign wars – certainly nothing comparable to the interminable conflicts that embroiled Dos Pilas, Aguateca, Piedras Negras, Yaxchilan, and other polities of the western Maya Lowlands. Even the violent events that are mentioned, such as the demise of Waxaklajuun Ub'aah K'awiil, are ambiguous in character, although they might be distantly related to these larger struggles. And about the turn of the 9th century Yax Pasaj seems to have been reestablishing good relations with Copan's only formidable set of traditional enemies at Quirigua.

Signs of violence are also sparse in the archaeological record. As Longyear noted, most royal buildings showed no signs of the kind of destruction or abrupt abandonment that occurred at Dos Pilas or Aguateca. Of the hundred or so rooms in Mak-Chanal's compound, I saw three that seemed to have been suddenly destroyed or defaced. One of these – Widmer's workshop – collapsed long after kings were gone, probably through "natural" causes. A second building consisted of largely perishable materials and could have burned down in an accidental fire. The one clearly sinister event was the deliberate and apparently ritual defacement by fire of the façade sculpture on Mak-Chanal's house (although the building itself was not destroyed). Most rooms in his compound, though, had been largely cleared of durable artifacts and furnishings, consistent with slow abandonment. This is unfortunate in a way, because the huge numbers of artifacts found in Payson Sheets's little house compounds at Ceren, and by Takeshi Inomata at Aguateca, offer fascinating hints at the much greater archaeological riches we might have found at Mak-Chanal's compound had it been suddenly sacked.

This same pattern of slow abandonment holds for the other elite residences that have been investigated. None of the rural sites we excavated was violently destroyed or swiftly abandoned either, and as we saw Storey and Whittington observed few signs of war-related trauma in Copan's skeletons. Judging from ceramics and other artifacts there was no sudden intrusion of large numbers of "foreigners" into the valley, as at Becan.

While it is thus difficult to make a case for war or invasion as we normally understand them, other kinds of conflict are likely. Parts of the royal residence at Group 10L-2 were burned as the dynasty breathed its last, or just afterwards, and this event smacks of internecine troubles, as does the mutilation of Mak-Chanal's images. My own interpretation is that the last days of Copan were marked by internal dissension and limited violence among the great lords and the royal establishment, and that such conflict contributed to the abruptness of the dynastic collapse. Whether common people were involved in this crisis is unknown, but certainly nothing like Thompson's peasant rebellions occurred at Copan. Those noble houses that survived seem to have lost their authority gradually over many generations.

Although I do not advocate ideological crises as powerful, independent forces in the Classic Maya collapse (or anything else), I do believe they played a contributing role, a subject that I develop more fully in the final chapter. Anticipating this discussion, I think that one factor in the collapse at Copan and elsewhere was the failure of both the institutional and ideological dimensions of a traditional form of kingship. Like their counterparts in ancient Egypt, Sumer, and China, Maya rulers promoted themselves as guarantors of balance and harmony in the cosmos and the well-being of their kingdoms. The Late and Terminal Classic periods were increasingly perturbed by disorder resulting from many causes, and we have no clear evidence that kings, or for that matter their associated officials and nobility, ever took effective and practical managerial action to contend with developing crises. Instead, kings probably responded with time-tested rituals aimed at averting or regulating chaos (which to Maya sensibilities might have seemed just as efficacious). No matter how well these seemed to work in earlier times at Copan, they clearly failed at the end. Crises spawn scapegoats, and I think the Copan royal dynasty became the lightning rod for internal discord, the institution on which lesser elite people, themselves pressured by their kin and clients, could heap blame and vent frustration. Failure of the royal institution was marked most strongly, at Copan and throughout the Lowlands, by the disruption and reorientation of iconographic and literary traditions strongly associated with royalty.

Such a situation would explain many things, including the apparent weakness of Yax Pasaj during the last part of the reign, his abrupt departure, the feeble and unsuccessful attempts to continue the dynastic line, the halt in royal construction and monument carving, and the abandonment of the old royal precincts. It would also explain the continuation for a time of non-royal aspects of the elite Great Tradition. In a word, I think that both dynastic rule and the ideology behind it was ultimately rejected because of its manifest inability to deliver its professed order. Despite the persistence of a large population, no one could revive kingship in anything like its old form because its underlying postulates had been devalued, and its overt symbols were suspect and perhaps even sinister (today we would probably call them "politically incorrect").

Some of my colleagues believe that Copan derived much of its wealth and prestige as a middleman in commerce that connected the Maya Lowlands proper with the highlands of southeastern Mesoamerica and the interior valleys of central Honduras. Disruption of this commerce might consequently have contributed to the collapse. I find this a very dubious proposition. During my own years at Copan I have in fact been struck by how little exotic or foreign material actually shows up in archaeological contexts, and imports from the core of the Maya Lowlands to the northwest are particularly sparse. Most of what we do find is marine shell, jade, fancy pottery, minerals such as cinnabar and pyrite, and other items consumed mainly by elite people. Not only is traffic in these things apparently small, but many of them might have wound up at Copan through other mechanisms than trade, such as exchange of gifts among prominent people. I also think that their importation was intermittent, stimulated by the situational demand for fine materials required for specific events such as royal funerals. Widmer's workshop shows that people continued to work marine shell long after Yax Pasaj's time, so kings were not essential to foreign exchange.

Only one imported material – obsidian – shows up ubiquitously in our excavations. Despite its obtrusiveness, calculations show that it was procured on a small annual scale. Clearly it was a sufficiently "cheap" (though certainly not essential) commodity that everyone had access to it. As noted before, there seems to be no drop-off in its availability after kings (and eventually nobles) disappeared from the scene, so its flow was never in fact disrupted.

No doubt many perishable things that we cannot detect archaeologically were widely exchanged. Perhaps tobacco, for which the valley has been long famous, was an important export essential to the political economy.[18] Even granting such possibilities, no one has made a plausible case for patterns of long-distance commerce so essential to Copan's population that disruption of it produced the effects reviewed above.

Richardson Gill has tried to force Copan's demise into his drought scenario, but the archaeological facts as we know them don't fit well. We certainly have no evidence that the Copan river or its tributaries ever dried up, depriving the local population of drinking water. What fits best is the dynastic collapse around AD 800, just when the megadrought is supposed to have begun. But even here the coincidence is suspect – dynastic stresses apparently started to build up a generation earlier. More revealing is the disjunction between the demographic profile and the megadrought predictions. Population remained near peak levels for at least the first century of the presumed drought interval, and more than half of the people were still there at AD 950. Even elite activity flickered on until about the time the megadrought is supposed to have ended. None of this is consistent with a devastating dry interval.

To be fair to Gill, at first glance the deforestation predicted by Wingard and Abrams, and detected by Rue, along with associated erosion, might be attributed to drought. But remember that our most direct signs of deforestation (in Rue's pollen core) date back only until about AD 1000–1100 and persist until about AD 1250 – two centuries after the megadrought interval is supposed to have ended. Forests elsewhere in the Maya Lowlands were rapidly recovering during this interval, so none of this fits the drought chronology either.

I am perfectly willing to accept that occasional serious and unpredictable deficiencies in rainfall afflicted the Copan valley at the end, just as they no doubt did throughout the long career of the kingdom and as they do today. Their effects were probably much amplified by conditions of dense population, declining crop production, and denuded hillsides. As a contributing cause drought is plausible at Copan, but megadrought as the single knockout blow is not.

Copan's population was not suddenly attacked by some kind of new and devastating epidemic disease to which its people had no immunity. There is no huge population decline coincident with the fall of the dynasty. Patterns of morbidity detected by Storey and Whittington are instead more consistent with endemic and chronic sickness and disability closely related to deteriorating diet and living conditions. These in turn lowered life expectancy and reduced fertility. Admittedly all this would be more convincing if we could compare our current sample of Copan skeletons, which mainly dates after AD 650–700, to some similar sample from much earlier times. Presumably we would see fewer signs of stress early on (there are some hints at this in Whittington's sample, but the numbers are too few to be sure). Still, it is clear that nothing comparable to what struck England in 1348, or that killed so many people in Mesoamerica in the century after Cortes arrived, afflicted the Copan population. I know of no historically documented syndrome of epidemic disease that would create the pattern of decline shown in Fig. 52.

One overarching cause seems clearly implicated in the Copan collapse – too many people on a landscape deteriorating through overuse by humans. This demographic explanation is not only consistent with the evidence for erosion and deforestation, but also with reduced biological well-being, diminished fertility, internal conflict, ideological fatigue, and the dynamics of growth and decline. Envisioning the effects of such ecological deterioration, the famous archaeologist A. V. Kidder remarked over 50 years ago: "Had there taken place a gradual washing away of the soil or the choking of arable land by grasses, their effects should only gradually have been felt and have led to a much longer and slower decadence than seems to have gone on."[19] We now know that Copan declined in just this way – not with a bang, but with a whimper. For whatever reasons, the Copan Maya did not keep their numbers in some effective balance with their resources.

❦ ❦ ❦

Here, in a nutshell, is my dark story of the unraveling of the Copan kingdom. By AD 750 the traditional core territory – the Copan pocket – produced only half the necessary foodstuffs for its residents and was already highly damaged. People had to work harder even on the best lands. Families seeking new fields had to content themselves with the less fertile and stable uplands, and somehow outmaneuver other households for access to them. Annual cropping on the rich valley floor produced the best crops, and long-term claims to these lands intensified, advantaging some farmers at the expense of others, who regarded their wealthier and more secure relatives and neighbors with increasing jealousy. Bad years were more frequent, exacerbated by human-induced deforestation and erosion. Recovery from the occasional drought or hurricane was much more difficult than before. It was harder to produce surpluses, and there was less to share with impoverished relatives and neighbors as productivity declined and household production levels became more invidiously variable. People were sick more often, and fewer babies were born. The very survival of households was more hazardous. Maya farmers, who in good times could manage their own affairs, could not effectively manage internal stresses and conflicts on this level.

As always in times of crisis, there were solutions, and even opportunities for the highly placed and politically savvy. People turned to their prestigious lords to manage problems not resolvable on the household level. Lords increasingly adjudicated the quarrels and squabbles of their lesser relatives and clients, using their influence to guarantee rights to already cultivated lands to some followers, and new lands to others. They probably gathered surpluses where available and redistributed them to buffer fragile household economies.

But alongside such system-serving management lords played out more devious and self-serving games as well. Lesser people increasingly became political clients, dependent on the largess and good will of nobles who were more and more differentiated from them. Lords found themselves each year more effectively in control of the basic agrarian resource – land. They manipulated it, and other things, to promote their own political advantage. Households of these upwardly mobile lords mushroomed in size and elegance; labor, after all, was more abundant than ever, even though the agricultural base deteriorated. Demands for labor or food to support these households weighed much more heavily than in better times on the peasant farmers.

Great families began to perceive that they had common interests opposed to those of lesser people on the one hand, and the royal dynasty on the other. Weakened kings in turn played off one elite faction against another in a complex game of status rivalry, disadvantaging some, while rewarding others with titles and unprecedented opportunities to sport carved benches and façade sculpture. Even as they began to speculatively covet the throne for themselves, some of the greatest lords sought to manipulate rulers through their influence in court politics and hypogamous marriages to royal women.[20]

But these were dangerous games, because lords were caught in the middle. They had responsibilities to their own constituents, on whose support they depended. But no elite managers conceived or initiated innovations, such as terracing, that might have slowed agrarian decline, so well-being deteriorated ever faster as population continued to increase. Still, elites kept their establishments near the royal court to increase their competitive chances, and meddled with the distribution of the commoner population to keep it from effectively colonizing more distant and lightly occupied parts of the valley. Great families had to compete among themselves to retain and augment their privileges and reward their clients. At the end of the 8th century the dynasty fell, perhaps violently, as the scapegoat for all these unresolvable troubles. Some nobles probably went under in this highly fractious political environment, creating dispossessed clients still more tightly bound to surviving elites to whom they had tenuous, if any, kin relationships.

Observing a similar situation of overpopulation, ravaged landscape, and political discord in China in 1931, R. H. Tawney lamented that "There are districts in which the position of the rural population is that of a man standing permanently up to the neck in water, so that even a ripple is sufficient to drown him."[21] By the early 9th century there were many such ripples at Copan, and increasingly frequent crises triggered an irreversible demographic downturn.

Remember my personal wish list of what I would like to know about the ancient Maya? Now it should be clear why I am so concerned with the relations of people to land, and to each other. If more detailed information about these issues were available, we could specify much more exactly what happened at Copan.

Though I am convinced that our general picture of Copan's collapse is pretty accurate, there are two loose ends. Why was the demographic decline, however long it took, ultimately so complete? This is, after all, an alluvial valley where some good soils were always available, and Wingard's simulation does not predict near-total abandonment. Part of the answer might be that people drifted off to other regions where both political and agrarian conditions were better. We have no good archaeological traces of such migrations, but of course they would have involved only a few thousand people, and so would be difficult to detect. More importantly, as the valley recovered after AD 1250, why was effective recolonization so late – not until the last half of the 19th century? I have no answers for either of these questions.

Copan's protracted pattern of decline does present us, however, with an important methodological lesson. We were able to detect it only because we compiled an excellent sample of household remains, and utilized a new dating technique on a large scale. Both obsidian hydration and radiocarbon dates revealed that a general set of household ceramics, formerly believed to disappear around AD 850–900, actually continued in use much longer. Ceramics, so essential to chronological reckoning in most regions of the Maya Lowlands, proved not to be a reliable chronological marker during Copan's late history. I suspect that we have been similarly deceived elsewhere, and that regional population declines were not always so abrupt as we now envision.

What we have reviewed in this chapter is a specifically Copan story, conditioned by the natural, cultural, and historical contingencies of the Copan region. We have already seen that what happened in other parts of the Maya Lowlands is quite different, but I believe that the Copan decline has some relevance for much of the southern Lowlands, as we shall see in the last chapter. To end up, I would like to resurrect a good old reductionist remark from the very dawn of Western historical political commentary. Plato attributes to Socrates the following observation: "No man may consider himself a statesman who does not understand the politics of wheat." In the end, neither society nor the sacred order held against the demands of a growing population, environmental deterioration, inept management, elite status rivalries, and the politics of maize. To paraphrase a more recent politician: "It's the agrarian economy, stupid."

– 10 –

WHAT HAPPENED TO THE CLASSIC MAYA?

WHAT, FINALLY, DO I THINK HAPPENED to the Classic Maya? It should be obvious by now that I am not a proponent of any single cause, such as megadrought or epidemic disease. On the other hand, to simply say that lots of different things afflicted the Maya at the end of the 8th century, as our case studies show, is mere culture-historical obfuscation. To adopt such a view is to admit that the best we can do is just pile up one unique example after another, while never extracting any larger lessons.

Archaeologists who mistrust simple answers for complex phenomena are fond of producing complicated diagrams such as that shown overleaf, summarizing how a whole series of linked causes can affect one another, and ultimately entire ancient populations and cultural systems. Many of my colleagues dislike such diagrams because they seem too general, offering a kind of mix-and-match set of conclusions that can be fitted to any circumstances. To the contrary, I think this is an advantage. One can adapt them to the specific conditions of the Petexbatun region, say, by emphasizing warfare, or to Copan by emphasizing population growth. Another advantage is that such diagrams help us to understand the complex feedback relations that surely existed among many variables, some of which are much more important than others. No "democracy of causes" is implied. To some archaeologists they also seem overly impersonal and mechanistic, dismissive of the real people whose individual decisions and actions shaped what we call history and prehistory. I hope I have shown that Maya archaeology has been enormously enriched by our knowledge of individual kings and lords and what they accomplished, and that Maya commoners were also canny survivors, with rich social lives of their own. Nonetheless, the Maya, like people everywhere, were constrained by their own environments, biological realities, and cultural propensities – including all those summarized in Fig. 55.

Bearing this diagram in mind, my own opinion is that the collapse was fundamentally triggered by three interrelated and dynamic factors, in the

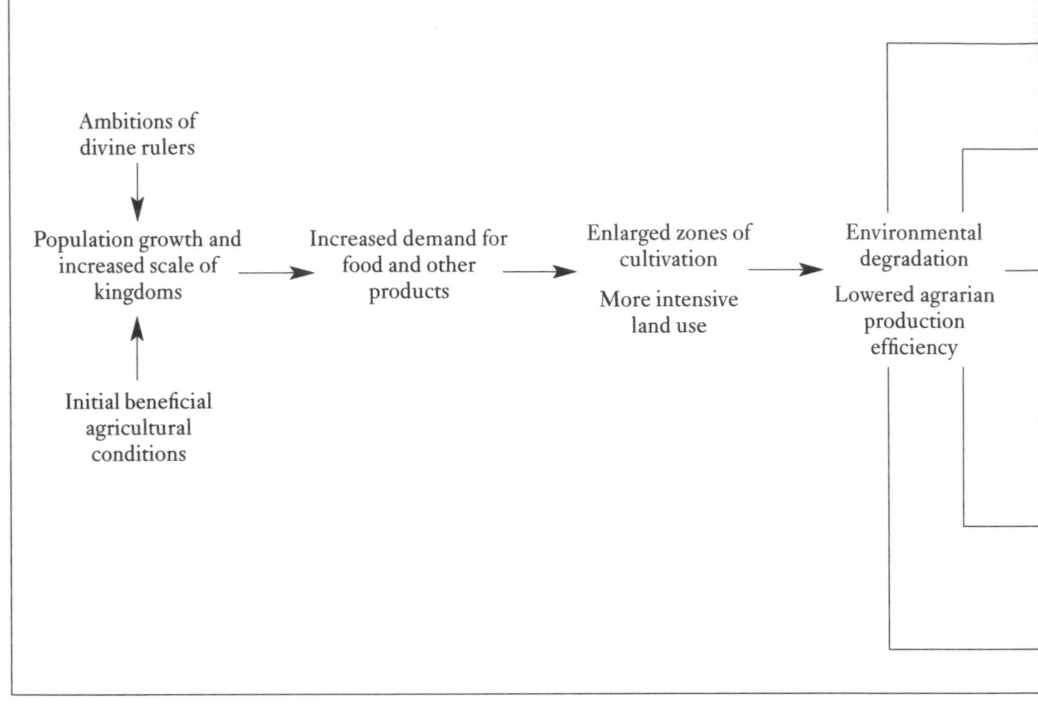

55 Diagram of the systemic relationships that contributed to the Classic Maya collapse. Arrows indicate how one variable increases the effects of another. I purposefully kept this diagram quite simple; other such connections could have been added.

following order of importance: one, a worsening relationship of Maya populations to their agricultural and other resources; two, the destabilizing effects of warfare and competition, and three, the rejection of the ideology and institution of kingship. These in turn created or exacerbated a series of secondary stresses, including increased vulnerability to drought, peasant unrest, and disease. Driving the whole process is the population/resource equation, so my theoretical perspective is basically a Malthusian one.[1]

Resources: Maya Agrarian and Political Ecology

Almost from the beginnings of systematic Maya archaeology there developed a central hypothesis, or more properly a set of strong hunches, that the failure of the ancient agricultural system caused the collapse. Although there were many ideas about exactly what happened, such an explanation seemed to account best for the abandonment of both the "cities" and also whole land-

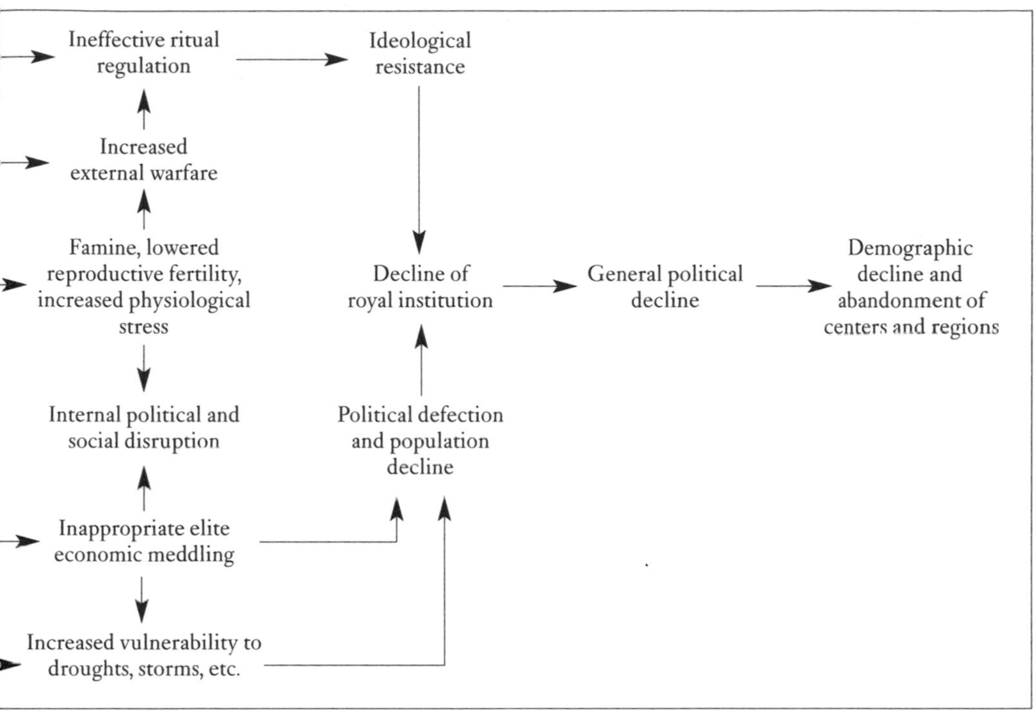

scapes. Food production supported the Maya Great Tradition of art, ritual, monumental architecture, war, and courtly life, just as it did in all other early civilizations. It thus bore roughly the same relationship to the Maya economy as fossil fuels do to our own, so any shortfalls or instabilities could have had extremely disruptive effects. Of all the explanations for the collapse, this one has proved the most durable.

While Maya agriculture could be remarkably productive, it also suffered from strong inherent risks, bottlenecks, and limitations. Some of these constraints, as we already saw, were broadly environmental. Others were cultural, and some were a combination of both. First we need to consider Maya agrarian ecology from the point of view of the common farmers who made up the bulk of the Late Classic population.

Despite the fact that their farming practices were technologically underdeveloped compared to those of Old World civilizations, Maya cultivators enjoyed several advantages, especially where population densities were low and shifting cultivation was still possible. One derived from the very simplicity of their agricultural tasks. Because they could make the modest tools needed to work their fields from locally available materials, Maya farmers did not have to purchase metal implements made by specialists, or buy, rent, and maintain expensive animals to yoke to plows or wagons, like Old World peasants. Necessary agricultural labor could be provided by domestic households, so it was unnecessary to hire farmhands (although illness or death of workers could cause severe problems for the domestic work force). Even capital investments, such as the hillside terraces and drained fields that many archaeologists believe supported vast Classic populations, could be built with domestic labor augmented, when necessary, by the help of neighbors or relatives. In other words, the "overhead" costs of agricultural production were low, and the necessary skills and knowledge were widely available.

Another set of advantages derived from the nature of the principal staple crop – maize. On decent soils watered by adequate rainfall, maize typically produced larger yields per unit of cultivated land – perhaps twice as much – as the Old World small grains such as wheat, barley, or oats grown by medieval European farmers.[2] And because of the way these latter grains were sown, anywhere from 1/6th to 1/3rd of the European annual crop had to be reserved for seed (except where irrigation was used). For maize the ratio of seed input to output was much more favorable, and because there were few domestic animals to feed, virtually all of the harvest could be consumed by humans.

On the other hand there were some severe bottlenecks, one of which was caused by the history of land use itself. By the 8th century many of the most favorable parts of the Maya Lowlands had already been cultivated for hundreds of years. The demographic explosion of Late Classic times took place on local landscapes that were no longer "natural" in any sense of the word, because they had already long been "humanized" (which usually means degraded) by generations of use. Heavy episodes of deforestation and erosion have been documented for several regions as early as Preclassic times, and there is strong evidence that some centers and regions (such as the Mirador Basin and the Petexbatun zone) experienced cycles of growth and abandonment long before the collapse.[3] Even when overall populations were low, early farmers packed into any particular small region could obviously damage their environments severely, as they did around Dos Pilas. Early on mobility seems to have been one of their solutions – people decamped for better lands elsewhere.

Another bottleneck involved technology. Without metal tools, complex machines, and sources of animal energy, Maya farmers could cultivate only very small amounts of land and they also had to schedule their work carefully to the constraints of the seasons. Even where good land was abundant Maya producers could accordingly generate only small per capita surpluses.

Working diligently during a good year, a healthy farmer might cultivate 2–2.5 hectares (5–6.2 acres) which would yield roughly 1000 kg per hectare (890 lbs per acre) of maize.[4] If this land were of sufficient quality it could yield twice as much food – around 2000 kg (4400 lbs) – as his family ate annually, after subtracting that amount reserved for next year's seed stock and lost in storage. In other words, each family, if it had good land and worked hard, might generate enough surplus food to support another family of similar size.

Contrast this situation with that of a peasant cultivating the fertile, naturally-irrigated silt of the Nile valley around 1200 BC. Egyptian farmers produced somewhat more food per unit of land (about 1430 kg per hectare, or 1274 lbs per acre), but their big advantage was the possession of plows and draft animals that greatly reduced the human time and labor required for each unit of land worked. In fact, some records from this period specify that Egyptian farmers were expected to cultivate about 5.5 hectares, which would yield roughly 7865 kg (17,303 lbs) of edible wheat or barley. Allowing again for seed and storage losses, each farmer would wind up with five to six times the amount of food his family needed. Even if some of this grain had to be fed to cattle, surplus production was much greater than in the Maya case.[5] With the superior efficiency of plow agriculture farmers could also afford to put even substandard land into production, which would otherwise be impractical. In effect, more of the landscape became useful with improved tools and energy sources (even if the Maya had possesssed plows and draft animals, they would have been useless on the thin-soiled uplands where many crops were grown).

Despite these differences, my Maya scenario might still seem pretty favorable. But remember that it presupposes optimal conditions – the right amounts of rainfall, no uncontrollable catastrophes, and the availability of good land. Unfortunately these conditions were far from the norm. From the earliest times, as today, Maya farmers were afflicted with periodic droughts, and their cornfields were leveled by hurricanes, eaten by locusts, or infested by plant diseases. No doubt these losses frequently had severe demographic consequences. Preindustrial agrarian people everywhere suffered such Malthusian crises, reminding us that what strongly determines population size is not the level of production during the good years, but rather during the bad ones, and that many crises are not density-dependent and not directly related to population growth or size. Devastating as these catastrophes might be, the Maya seem to have survived them quite well as long as populations were generally low and demands from outside the producing sector were reasonable.

No farmers anywhere, of course, work hard to produce surpluses beyond what they need to eat, plant next year's crop, or otherwise meet their anticipated household needs. On the level of the producer household, one incentive for surplus production is to store food against unpredictable future shortfalls. Because not all years are good years, some provisions must be "banked" for emergency use (domesticated herbivores on the Old World constituted just such a food bank). Maya farmers undoubtedly stored food against such threats, although here they faced a problem. Harvested crops will keep for long periods in hot, dry environments such as Egypt, but not in the humid tropics, where it is difficult to preserve basic staples such as maize and beans for more than a year or so using preindustrial technology.

Another incentive for surplus production is to have a commodity to trade, sell, or barter in markets for things one's own household does not produce, or in order to make a profit. Above and beyond this are the demands of the political economy. Many farmers in all ancient civilizations had to turn over part of their production to landlords because they did not own the land they cultivated, and even the fortunate freeholder everywhere owed taxes to rulers, nobles, or priests. Although market exchange seems to have been very poorly developed among the Lowland Maya during any time in their history, farming families certainly paid taxes or tribute to kings and great lords.

All this excess production, as V. Gordon Childe asserted long ago, is what funds the social, political, and economic complexity of ancient civilizations. The bigger the per capita producer surplus, the greater the potential for such complexity. As I noted earlier, about one to two percent of the U. S. population today grows enough food not only to feed its own citizens, but much of the rest of the world as well. And one reason why Egypt was a far larger and more complex polity than any that ever developed in the Maya Lowlands was its more productive agricultural ecology.

The long-term weakness in the Maya system of human/agrarian relationships was population growth in the absence of significant technological change. Charles Darwin once remarked that rarity is the precondition for extinction. If we substitute "collapse" for "extinction," the opposite was true of the Maya, who at the end of the 8th century were more numerous than ever before. As populations rose and good land became scarce, all across the Maya Lowlands farmers were forced to increase food production on their fragile tropical landscapes. Mayanists agree that this process, called agricultural intensification, was necessary to support the high population densities now evident. What they do not agree about is the variety, scale, and efficacy of the strategies used (remember that intensification was central to Wingard's model of agricultural change at Copan).

One solution was to extend cultivation into substandard land that had previously been avoided – not a good choice, but one no doubt many people often made. More preferable and effective would be the substitution of root crops such as manioc or sweet potatoes for maize, because they produce higher yields per field and make smaller demands on soil nutrients. Sensible as this seems (we know the Maya had these crops), isotopic assays of large skeletal samples from Classic times support the idea of heavy dietary dependence on maize, especially for people living away from the coasts or large rivers (as most Maya did). Another old idea along the same lines was that the Maya shifted to a sophisticated system of silviculture, in which fruits of selected native tree species (especially ramon, or *Brosimum alicastrum*) heavily supplemented or replaced milpa cultivation. Such "tree-farms," it was argued, not only produced large annual yields, but essentially preserved native tropical forest ecosystems. Although the Maya undoubtedly used various orchard products, no widespread silviculture of this kind shows up in the ancient pollen record. It too is inconsistent with the isotope findings, and modern Maya people regard ramon and other semi-cultivated fruits at best as useful dietary adjuncts, and at worst as substandard, starvation foods.

Another alternative was to substitute labor and capital for land. The simplest intensification option involved cultivating fields more frequently, shifting from forest-fallow systems in which land was only used every ten to 20 years or so, to increasingly shorter fallow intervals, and eventually to permanent cultivation. But these shorter cycles required greater inputs of human labor for clearing, hoeing, weeding, and other tasks, and generally resulted in diminishing yields because of nutrient depletion and erosion, as dramatically documented at Copan and around Tikal. Although this strategy might take up the slack for a while, it was ultimately a dead end.

During the 1970s and 1980s archaeologists thought they had finally solved the mystery of how such apparently dense populations of 8th century Maya supported themselves. Application of various kinds of aerial remote sensing technology revealed what appeared to be vast systems of drained fields in swamps and along river margins in several parts of the Maya Lowlands. It was confidently asserted that these cultivated wetlands, along with extensively terraced hillsides, constituted the breadbaskets of a hugely productive and stable agrarian economy. Today the implications of all this agroengineering seem less promising.

Artificial terraces are used in many parts of the world to stem erosion, retain soil moisture and fertility, and thus stabilize productivity, especially when laboriously fertilized or mulched. Various forms of such terraces certainly existed on the hilly uplands that dominate much of the Maya landscape. They are found around Caracol and Becan, among other centers, and are especially numerous in south-central Belize. Diane and Arlen Chase, who have long worked at Caracol, think that terraces there were created by a complex, state-administered economy under whose dictates farmers transformed the whole surrounding landscape into an immense and unusually stable agricultural zone.

My own reading of the potential of terracing is less hopeful. First, terraces have very spotty distributions. None are found around Tikal, and we looked for them in vain for the last several years on the steep terrain around Piedras Negras. Elsewhere, as at Copan, they exist in very small numbers and could scarcely have made much of a difference. Some terraces appear to me to be very restricted soil traps – that is, they locally interrupt the more widespread and destructive process of hillside erosion. Nor is it clear that any terrace soils could be cropped permanently or provide unusually large yields (although of course they are resistant to erosion).[6] Finally, none of the systems thus far described required more skill or labor than available to small farming families, so their implication for centralized administration at Caracol or other kingdoms is dubious.

One last kind of intensification effort involves the actual construction of new land – specifically of drained fields – which are essentially artificial islands built in suitable wet locales. When such features were first found they were enthusiastically (but inappropriately) compared with the extraordinarily productive chinampas that supplied Aztec cities and towns in the early 16th century.[7] While the Maya clearly cultivated wetlands by making drained fields, their overall importance to the Late Classic economy remains uncertain. In some cases the remote sensing evidence simply faded away in the face of surface inspection. Purported drained fields around Dos Pilas, for example, cannot be identified on the ground, and some parts of the landscape originally interpreted from the air as wetlands turn out to be upland topographic features. More surprisingly, close inspection of some celebrated raised field systems in northern Belize reveals them to be Preclassic in date – built and abandoned long before dense populations were present and buried by processes of Classic period upland erosion.[8] Nor, as with terraces, has anyone experimentally examined the productive potential of drained fields (which I suspect pales by comparison with chinampas).

Farmers anywhere are most motivated to make investments of labor and capital in their landscapes when they have secure rights to their fields. While working in the Copan valley we documented many modern examples of deteriorating yields and erosion on cultivated hillsides, and I frequently wondered why farmers did not more often build even small terraces to arrest these problems. Then I realized that most of them owned no land. Many were in fact squatters or clients who could be displaced at the whim of big landowners. Why would they work hard to improve someone else's land? Here might lie one key to the peculiar patchiness of ancient agrarian improvements – varied land holding traditions. This is why knowledge of such patterns is high on my own "wish list" concerning what it is most essential (but probably impossible) to understand about the ancient Maya.

Maya farmers were clearly clever people who developed many strategies to cope with their challenging and unpredictable environments. Recent evidence suggests that not only drained fields, but also other kinds of water management systems were developed by Preclassic communities as local hedges against the risk of drought and production shortfalls. Some of my colleagues almost reflexively associate agricultural intensification with agricultural improvement, in the sense that the landscape is significantly upgraded and unrealized demographic potential is thereby unleashed. Seen from the regional perspective this makes a certain sense, if increased numbers of people is the measure of adaptive success. Because any kind of intensification involves more frequent use of cultivated plots, it solves – at least for a time – the problem of how to support more people on any particular part of the landscape.[9] Maya intensification efforts clearly represent successful short-term adaptation to population pressure, which itself can stimulate more intensive agricultural practices, as the rapidly growing Late Classic populations at polities such as Copan or Tikal attest. On the scale of the producing family, however, each of these steps over the long run results in more input of work for smaller harvests. As the margin between minimal domestic needs and overall productive capacity diminishes, so too does security. This is a hard cycle to break without technological change.

My own position is that much of what we see in the Maya Lowlands is convincing evidence of short-term coping that failed to solve long-term problems. Under the pressure of too many people, I think Maya farmers were increasingly affected by production shortfalls, heavier work loads, and decreased standards of living on a deteriorating environment. And as agricultural resources became scarce, so too did other essential things, such as wood for construction and fuel, thatch for house roofs, and terrestrial animal food sources. Under these conditions the Late Classic Maya system, both locally and regionally, became increasingly vulnerable to even small-scale perturbations that earlier would not have been nearly so damaging.[10]

Now imagine all this from the perspective of Maya kings and lords, which was probably quite different from that of farmers. Historical demographers know that rulers commonly envision large, rapidly growing populations not just as symptoms of wealth, but as wealth itself, or perhaps more accurately political capital – never mind that for the peasant there is increasingly a zero-sum game.[11]

If you are the king, your most basic concern vis-à-vis the agrarian economy is extracting from it each year enough food to feed your family, your retainers, and other non-producers in your kingdom who are dependent on you. You also want additional stockpiles to provide for the feasting so essential to politics and ritual, and perhaps to return to your subjects when they work on your temples, palaces, and other projects (although such open-handedness belies the fact that you collected this food from them in the first place). Because of the high human cost of moving cheap, bulk goods long distances, one thing you cannot do is export food for commercial profit, as Europeans did with their superior transport technology. There is thus not much point in demanding excess production from your subjects for purposes of trade, so in terms of staple foods the political economy is highly localized. Optimally, the staple food energy of a polity should be produced within a walking distance of a day or two from the establishments of its elite (or other) consumers.

Such localized agrarian economies work quite well if the ratio of producers to consumers remains high, and as long as farmers have plenty of productive land near their courtly capitals. But what if this balance changes? Say, for example, the overhead needed to support the elite/consuming sector of society increases because the proportion of nobles and lords grows. One solution is simply to extract more food from each peasant household. But unlike the Egyptian peasant the Maya farmer cannot easily adapt to such demands by cultivating increasingly larger amounts of land (even if they were available) because he is under such constraints of labor and time.

Another solution is to extract the same small surpluses from more people – i.e., to add producing units. Throughout Maya history a preoccupation of rulers must have been to maintain authority over large numbers of farmers living as close to their courts as possible, not only to cultivate the landscape but also to provide construction labor and military capacity. Attracting additional farmers to your polity would have these effects, but this option works only if there is plenty of unused land for them to cultivate. You could gain control of a larger territory and its farmers through warfare or by some other means, but here again you would eventually run up against the transport problem if the new territory is too distant, not to mention stable political administration of these outlying parts of your kingdom.

Nor, putting transport limitations aside, is trade a viable option. Trade in basic staples presupposes differentials of production – farmers in some regions must produce much more food than they or their local elites required. Such differentials are unlikely when farmers have such limited production capacity even in good times, and especially so in the 8th century when local populations were hard-pressed in most places. Moreover, what would you trade with people who produce more or less the same resources you do? Maya kings might be "rich" in jade, shell, feathers, and other exotic things, but whether such items were in any way convertible into staples is unclear.

Ultimately, of course, your farmers are becoming poorer, both because there are more of them in relation to good land, and because this land itself is deteriorating. At this juncture one of the things you might do is take a strong hand in centralized agrarian management by dictating the construction of terraces, extensive drained field systems, or otherwise expanding, or at least stabilizing, productivity. If Classic Maya kings and their officials ever intervened in this way it is not recorded in their inscriptions or art, nor unambiguously evident in the archaeological record. Nor was such intervention part of the ruling style of their better-documented Postclassic successors. My own opinion is that while the rhetoric of Maya rulership celebrated kings as great husbandmen of their people, their efforts never extended to hands-on management of staple agricultural production or resources except for extracting what they needed (with one exception discussed shortly).

Ritual regulation of the supernatural forces that guaranteed agrarian prosperity was probably more the Maya style, but it had no pragmatic effects. That ideology can interfere with competent management of basic resources might strike us as odd, but consider the example of James Watt, U. S. Secretary of the Interior, who in 1981 remarked that we shouldn't worry too much about the environment because the Lord might return at any moment.[12] More perspicacious is the observation of Tip O'Neill, Speaker of the U. S. House of Representatives, that "All politics are local." Despite the obvious interactions of Maya royalty, elites, capitals, and polities, I believe that Maya concern with the political economy at all times was overwhelmingly local and was heavily conditioned by local agrarian conditions. By the 8th century pragmatic fecklessness at the top combined with population pressure from below to create explosive and unresolvable stresses in many parts of the Classic Maya Lowlands.

Warfare and Competition

Compounding all these problems from very early times were warfare and competition, which played themselves out on a tiny political landscape. Remember that the whole Maya Lowlands is roughly the size of Colorado, and that the region most affected by the collapse was much smaller, about the size of Florida. Now imagine Florida packed with scores of independent kingdoms, many with long histories of animosity, and populated by several million people increasingly beset by agricultural crises. That the Late Classic Maya engaged in destructive forms of competition under the circumstances is hardly surprising.

By competition I mean the active demand of two or more organisms for the same limited resources. This is pretty much a straightforward biological definition, but it can be expanded to apply to social and cultural capital as well – for example access to offices, titles, and alliances that bestow prestige, authority, leadership, and political security. These in turn, of course, are keys to control over more fundamental resources such as land, labor, and political power. Although we tend automatically to associate competition with violence, it may occur in much more subtle ways, such as theft, pilfering, or encroachment on the prerogatives of others that are sometimes not even recognized by the participants. And who are the most direct potential competitors for basic resources in a preindustrial agrarian society? People who live close to one another, who make a living in similar ways, and who share the same basic culture. In fact, much of any peoples' culture consists of ideological and behavioral adaptations that limit the inevitable effects of competition.

Long ago I argued that from very early times an important kind of competition in the Maya Lowlands was warfare over agricultural land, and that successful military leadership was one factor in the emergence of strong traditions of kingship.[13] Many of my colleagues disagreed with this assertion, partly because of residual devotion to the "peaceful Maya" perspective. But no matter what caused such conflicts, the evidence for very ancient and destructive forms of warfare has increased exponentially since the 1970s. Today the Maya are widely recognized as having been extremely warlike from very early times right up to the Spanish conquest, with a crescendo of inter-polity violence during the Late Classic period just preceding the collapse. Perhaps equally important was internal factional strife not directly recorded in royal and elite inscriptions. Most leaders are disinclined to raise public monuments recording the messy and sometimes embarrassing details of ursupations, political treachery, or internecine bickering, and this was particularly so for Maya kings, whose royal legitimization was heavily bolstered by claims that they could maintain social and cosmic order.

Warfare against external enemies takes us beyond the local arenas of Maya polities, and makes us confront the wider relationships among Maya centers, kingdoms, and dynasties – what I have referred to several times as the larger Classic Maya "system." Ironically, the most conspicuous element in this system was a divisive one – war. If we use texts as a guide to the interconnections that formed this system, war is among the most frequently mentioned.[14] Other textual expressions of interaction, moreover, such as statements of hierarchy, intermarriage, alliance, or diplomatic exchanges, are all plausibly related to war as well. And one fascinating dimension of conflict stands out in the long and detailed epigraphic record – its apparent unresolvability. Individual polities or alliances were at one moment victorious, then later defeated. Very seldom was a polity or dynasty vanquished so decisively that it did not eventually rebound. Wars were consequently fought between traditional enemies for decades or even centuries as kings sought to redress old insults and ancestral defeats. Elsewhere in the ancient world larger political systems emerged that effectively suppressed such internecine warfare, but for some reason this never happened in the Maya Lowlands. Resulting cycles of unresolved conflict and historical antagonisms accelerated into the late 8th century, when the political landscape was fragmented as never before.

Why did the Maya fight wars? Unfortunately inscriptions do not inform us directly about the reasons. To be sure, most texts have heavy ceremonial overtones, but as David Stuart notes "... deciphered war events are not explicit in emphasizing ritual over more material motivations."[15] Texts and art instead emphasize particular phases of the warfare process such as capture and sacrifice of important enemies, extraction of tribute, rewarding of successful warriors, and desecration of enemy royal regalia. Only when other kinds of archaeological information are available are we able to discern the broader effects of war, and it is increasingly clear that, whatever their ideological and ritual proclivities, Classic Maya rulers and other elites also profited politically and economically from it, at least in the short run. Maya war, in other words, was in large part an extension of politics and economics, just as it has been the world over. Its goals included tribute, territorial gain, strategic advantage, the possession of titles and offices, and the enhanced prestige of leaders.[16]

By Late Classic times, and particularly by the 8th century, the southern Maya Lowlands were packed with kingdoms of different scales. Each possessed a local dynasty with specific origin myths and historical depth, its own network of kinship affiliations, and reputation. Over several preceding centuries royal/elite polygyny, the proliferation of dynasties and their cadet branches, intermarriage among royal and noble families, the high status of elite women, and tendencies toward bilateral descent combined to create a political landscape of almost unimaginable complexity and inherent ambiguities. All this created the conditions for intense status rivalry war among kings and elites, both among and within polities.

By status rivalry war I mean struggles by individuals or factions over the restricted titles, offices, honors, and privileges that were the symbolic correlates of rank, status, and authority. Many of these things were of course valued for non-material reasons, but more importantly they provided access to the most fundamental sources of wealth in any complex agrarian society – rights of disposal over land, and the products and labor of farming households. Such rights in turn structured power relations. Acquiring, maintaining, and augmenting such rights were the fundamental preoccupations of highly ranked individuals and their political supporters. Hereditary rank conferred valued rights, but could be counterbalanced by achievement – most significantly mobilization of followers and use of force for political ends.

War in this milieu became ever more closely associated with royal ideology. Because the rhetorical "style" of Classic Maya rulership focused so heavily on the king's personal ability to suppress discord and chaos, it is easy to appreciate the ideological capital conferred by successful war. Victorious kings derived prestige and renown from military feats and from the subjection, humiliation, and destruction of enemies, who were the personified embodiments of disorder. Victories bolstered rulers' claims to efficacy and legitimacy, and dampened internal opposition. Leaders anywhere must motivate people to follow them, however, especially in such a potentially lethal enterprise as war, and war itself provided the opportunity to do so. Land or other booty could be used to reward military followers outside the network of traditional relationships, thus creating new power factions and strengthening the institution of kingship.

Whatever its causes or motivations, warfare among polities or factions seriously exacerbated the agrarian stresses faced by Maya commoners. At Tikal and Becan, and probably at Piedras Negras and Palenque, war stimulated the heavy concentration of supporting populations close to the main royal centers, which in turn accelerated local agricultural intensification and landscape decline. Extensive buffer zones no doubt separated many kingdoms, further reducing available land. Enemies emerged from these contested and sinister forests to raid fields and food stocks during campaigns, adding to the already numerous risks and shortfalls faced by farmers. Farmers might themselves have been the objects of competition, to be forcibly relocated by victors, or attracted to the more secure territories of victorious kings. The ultimate effects of all this violence are most clearly seen around Dos Pilas, where centers were burned, kings and nobles were uprooted, farmsteads were fortified, and ultimately, the landscape deserted as refugees fled to other regions, where they probably become political pawns in similar, but more distant conflicts.

Lurking beneath all this royal, inter-polity mayhem were other less obvious but equally powerful kinds of competition, and the most fundamental competitors were humble farming families. Although such people had long been able to manage their own affairs effectively, rapidly worsening relationships between farmers and their landscapes created problems not easily resolvable on the producer level. Families had to retain and transmit rights to their all-important fields and other necessary resources even as populations grew. New lands had to be found for the excess population, and households had to devise new productive strategies as their fields yielded less and less. Jealousy and competition became more intense among farmers over increasingly differentiated agricultural landscapes.

Remember that our highly abstract and impersonal assessment of agrarian crisis masks the very dramatic and often stressful choices that ordinary farmers had to make. People did not automatically and without friction choose to work harder for less on marginal as opposed to good land. Farmers did not willingly shift to permanent cultivation, with its higher labor costs and declining yields, if other options remained open. They did not fail to appreciate the increasing productive diversity and risk that advantaged some families and disadvantaged others. And they could not help but find the extremely rapid changes that sometimes occurred over as little as one or two generations extremely disruptive.

It was at this juncture that kings and lords might well have been forced to intervene, possibly at the behest of hard-pressed farmers themselves, in an attempt to manage and ameliorate such stresses. "Resources," after all, are for humans a partly cultural construct, and access to them must be socially mediated. Perhaps elites tried to meddle with the distribution of farmers on the landscape, settle disputes, or redistribute food from those who had it to those who did not. If so, they apparently did none of these things very well, and most plainly never solved the problems of local agricultural shortfalls and environmental decline.

As matters worsened, some strong rulers might have resorted to territorial conquests to acquire basic resources. Although I have repeatedly insisted that movement of bulk staple foods over long distances in Mesoamerica was highly inefficient, remember that under conditions of severe privation or outright famine the value of food rises virtually to infinity. Desperate kings might well have demanded food from distant subordinate polities, rather than the token tributes exacted in earlier times. If such attempts were made, they were not only ineffective in the long run, but also resulted in driving to desperation those distant farmers whose harvests were expropriated, thus contributing to the broader communication of social unrest and agrarian decline.

All this relates to a basic Malthusian process that my demographer colleague Jim Wood calls "variance in well-being." By well-being he means "any aspect of individual health or physical condition that is either positively associated with the probability of childbirth, or negatively associated with the risk of death."[17] Variance becomes greater as populations depend on increasingly marginal subsistence resources. To Wood's concept I would add a sociocultural dimension: some Maya farmers increasingly saw their general household well-being undermined vis-à-vis that of others as they were relegated to more substandard parts of the agricultural landscape, or to more inefficient productive strategies. Even if people are not seriously threatened in biological terms, such perceptions can be extremely disruptive of the social fabric of any society, especially one already characterized by strong social and political divisions.

Something that happened while I was working in the Copan valley illustrates this point. One year there was a pronounced drought and maize yields were clearly in jeopardy toward the end of the growing season. An employee who worked in our laboratory cultivated, along with her husband, some land high in the mountains, which they went to tend on the weekends. One day they arrived to find that someone had stolen all the nearly ripe maize ears. One can scarcely imagine a more antisocial act, and only desperate people would resort to such theft because the chances of being caught are so great. Fortunately the Copan community is now part of the larger national and global economic system, so local droughts and food shortfalls no longer have dire effects. Under similar conditions in ancient times, however, when no such buffers were available, desperate acts like this one were probably very common, particularly in the 8th and early 9th centuries.

No Classic Maya inscriptions at Copan or elsewhere describe such disruption, but some idea of what things might have been like comes from a dramatic Aztec account of a prolonged famine that struck the Basin of Mexico in the mid-15th century:

> This was the time when they bought people; they purchased men for themselves. The merchants were those who had plenty, who prospered; the greedy, the well-fed man, the covetous, the niggardly, the miser, who controlled wealth and family, guardians, the mean, the stingy, the selfish. In the homes of [such men] they crowded, going into bondage, entering house after house – the orphan, the poor, the indigent, the needy, the pauper, the beggar, who were starved and famished; who just went to sleep, just so awoke; who found nothing and got nowhere; who in no place found their rest, relief, or remedy. At this time one sold oneself. One ate oneself; one swallowed oneself. Or else one sold and delivered into bondage his beloved son, his dear child.[18]

During this Mexican crisis people died in huge numbers and fled the jurisdictions of their lords. So enormous was the disaster that the king Motecezuma I began to doubt the validity of his reign. Fortunately the Aztecs recovered, in part through huge state-administered hydraulic projects that created thousands of acres of productive chinampas. No Maya kings were successful at devising similar remedies, if they tried at all. And remember that Landa (p. 99) attributed war, theft, slavery, and social upheaval to the droughts of Yucatan. Further exacerbating such crises is the synergistic relationship among poor diet and heavy disease load on the one hand, and the ability to accomplish strenuous agricultural tasks – in a word, preindustrial farmers under stress lose work capacity just when they need it most.[19]

If we could visit various Late Classic Maya centers on the brink of the collapse, I think we would be struck by the dissonance between courtly elegance and extravagance on the one hand, and the foreboding background of war and declining well-being on the other. As in Mexico, kings and lords tried to carry on as usual even as farmers bickered, starved, sold themselves to the rich and powerful, or deserted their leaders. Nowhere is this better reflected than at Bonampak, where the famous murals were designed to capture an ideal of royal achievement that was never attained in reality. The kingdom fell before the painters ever finished.

The Failure of Kings and Kingship

It is no accident that our first systematic comprehension of the Classic collapse derived from what turned out to be royal monuments. Whatever else it was, all archaeologists agree that the disintegration of Classic society in the 8th and 9th centuries was the failure of a long-standing tradition of kingship and the ideology that supported it. But kingship was very old among the Maya. Why and how was it undermined after centuries of vigor? I believe the answer lies partly in its own ideological precepts, and partly in its synergistic relationship with agrarian failure, war, and competition.

Virtually all cultures have origin stories that posit a "designed" world that operates for the benefit of humans, usually under the aegis of patron deities or other supernatural beings.[20] Behind these stories lies the universal human yearning for order and stability, the conditions that most contribute to our long-term well-being. Yet in real life we all experience disorder of many kinds, which makes us psychologically anxious and thereby stimulates even more instability (think of the behavior of the stock market). Disorder frequently threatened the ancient Maya. Rains sometimes fell sparsely or at the wrong times, winds or locusts destroyed one's crops, and enemies disrupted whole kingdoms. Whether one escaped these catastrophes, in the Maya view, depended heavily on the ritual potency of one's leaders and their relationships to the gods and ancestors.

Bernal Diaz reported that when Cortes asked Motecezuma II to replace the idols in his temples with Christian crosses, the Aztec king demurred, saying that the gods were very good to his people, providing them with health, water, plentiful harvests, and military victories (things had improved since the famines experienced by his namesake two generations earlier). Observance of the proper rituals and sacrifices was essential to such prosperity. Classic Maya rulers would have perfectly understood Motecezuma's world view, which appears to have been very widespread and ancient in Mesoamerica as a whole.

The first Preclassic Maya kings merged their new royal identities with much older shamanistic practices and with ancient assumptions about the nature of the world. Like the Aztecs, they believed that proper attention to the great creator-gods and ancestors ensured human well-being. Emergent royal ideology accordingly emphasized the ruler's responsibility to maintain balance, order, and success in all those aspects of life that affected his people, most importantly food production. Along with other leadership roles, kings appropriated to themselves ritual efficacy that probably had been much more widely shared among members of earlier and simpler Maya communities.

Unknown stresses led to the abandonment of Preclassic royal centers such as El Mirador and Nakbe, but certainly by the 2nd century AD stable dynasties were entrenched at Tikal and elsewhere. Thereafter royal lines proliferated and spread widely, establishing new centers and polities and disseminating the Great Tradition elements of Classic Maya kingship. By the 6th–7th centuries AD the royal institution was reasonably mature in its organizational and ideological features. This process was accompanied, as we have seen, by the rapid growth of regional populations. During the expansive heyday of Classic Maya kingship most rulers most of the time must have been perceived by their subjects as able to deliver the promised order and prosperity. Any particular dynasty might experience occasional setbacks, such as defeat in war, but over the long run most people did pretty well and had reason to accept, or at least tolerate, the authority and pretensions of their kings.

Fundamental to the Classic Maya world view was the idea that collective ills or misfortunes resulted from personal and moral rather than systemic failings, whether the "persons" were gods, ancestors, or semi-divine rulers. In times of trouble, in other words, people did not ask "what is the problem," but rather "who is the problem," much as they did in traditional China. As Stephen Houston pointed out recently, the failure of rulers is a leitmotif of Maya historiography. Inscriptions at Palenque, for instance, characterize its defeat by Calakmul in AD 611 as the time when "the gods got lost, the kings got lost."[21] Much later, the colonial books of Chilam Balam similarly associated chaos, political collapse, and cultural fatigue with weak, debauched, or failed kings and the absence of effective leaders.

Rulers, in a word, were personally culpable for misfortune, and by Late Classic times there was plenty of it to go around. Wars were more frequent and destructive than ever before, and the political landscape was enormously complex and fragmented. I have a hard time imagining how rulership operated under these conditions. How were universalist pretensions to deliver cosmic order reconciled with multiple royal voices stridently crying "I'm the king"? What does it mean for one "divine" king to become subordinated to another? However these ideological paradoxes played themselves out, various kingdoms were increasingly undermined by degradation of their agrarian landscapes and the impoverishment of their farmers.

What happened at the end is most clearly suggested by the evidence from Copan. There the institution of kingship was the first casualty of internal discord, but some noble households managed to survive the royal debacle for a long time. Such extended political collapse is extremely suggestive. Some nobles probably outlasted Copan's kings either because they were not directly related to the royal dynasty, or at least were sufficiently distanced from it to avoid implication in royal failures. As internal upheaval and competition became more pronounced, the most powerful elite houses were able to retain some hold on their kinspeople or clients because their leadership, feeble though it might be, was more critical than before. Moreover, nonroyal elites had long since relinquished to kings most of the order-maintaining ritual responsibilities their ancestors might once have possessed.

I believe that the very process of co-optation by which kings arrogated to themselves moral and ritual authority eventually backfired. Lesser elites were insulated from immediate culpability for disorder. As economic, military, and social conditions deteriorated at Copan and elsewhere, not only commoners, but also elites could point to kings as scapegoats. One can imagine the "don't blame us" assertions of nobles attempting to preserve their own privileges as social order and well-being eroded.

Added to these voices of discontent were probably those of local shamans, diviners, and prophets, whom we know in more recent times traditionally acted as critics of their own leaders and as agents of resistance to the Spanish and the Mexican governments. Abetted, perhaps, by powerful lords, they added a significant chorus of ideological resistance to the old dynastic institutions. While internal violence might sometimes have been part of such resistance, I envision this not as "peasant rebellions," but as factional competition and ideological defection from dynastic traditions. The fate of the Xhosa (Chapter 7) shows that ideological change can well up from the ranks of humble people, and that we should not assume that ideological crises had trivial causes or effects.

Ultimately divine kings at Copan and elsewhere in the Maya Lowlands were unable to deliver order or stability and uphold their pretensions to universality. In the long run, the natural order of things prevailed over a traditional moral order, which was inexorably undermined by the conflicting ambitions of kings and nobles and by the destructive actions of countless anonymous farmers. Always in the past the institution of kingship had weathered the occasional failures of individual rulers or dynasties, but finally it was itself rejected. The conditions of royal time had changed, and the resulting political and ideological vacuum could not be filled by those nobles who clung to power for a time, only eventually to lose their own privileges. David Stuart, referring to widespread political instabilities, says that "In my view, the whole Late Classic sees a single, long-term demise of the institution of southern Lowland Maya rulership."[22] I could not agree more.

Kingship, revealingly, persisted much longer in the northern Maya Lowlands, but in forms very different from the old Classic pattern. Despite continuities in the identities and imagery of gods, Postclassic rulers no longer focused their rituals so intensely on veneration of royal ancestors or claimed exclusive royal patronage of gods and rituals.[23] Very few Postclassic monuments present the royal person in the old ways, and the tradition of portraying kings, nobles, and court scenes on polychrome vessels disappeared. Perhaps most importantly, the Long Count calendar that for centuries had been associated with world order, stability, and divine kingship quickly dropped out of fashion.

None of this, of course, is an argument for the primacy of ideological explanations for the Classic collapse at Copan or anywhere else. Quite the contrary, it is an attempt to show how ideology and prophecy might have been part of a larger series of changes, more fundamentally triggered by demographic pressure, ecological deterioration, war, and internal dissension, that undermined the ruling institution so central to the Classic Maya Great Tradition.

More than a decade ago T. Patrick Culbert concluded that we can make up any scenarios we like about the Classic Maya collapse because of the lack of precise data.[24] His comment was overly pessimistic even then, and scores of field projects and decipherments have since provided much richer information.

Overpopulation, war, competition, and ideological decline are the main ingredients in my own personal "recipe" for the collapse of Classic Maya civilization. It is easy to imagine how these together triggered a whole series of more indirect stresses, such as malnutrition, disease, lowered reproductive fertility, and many kinds of social upheaval. One can adjust this recipe to particular circumstances, stirring in a bigger dollop of war for the western Maya Lowlands, say, and more environmental degradation for Tikal and Copan, while still preserving the larger synergy.

Several times in this book I have asked the question "What was different in the 8th and early 9th centuries?" From one perspective the answer is not much. As they had for hundreds of years, Maya farmers grew the same crops with the same tools, kings and nobles competed for prestige and resources, and great ceremonies were undertaken to assuage the powers of the cosmos. What was different was the scale and complexity of all these things, and their wider contexts. Too many farmers grew too many crops on too much of the landscape. Moving away to find better land was no longer an option for most people. More contending kingdoms existed than ever before, and burgeoning elites squabbled more often over ever-more complex systems of real or imagined entitlements. Rulers demanded labor and food from farmers as they always had, but even modest contributions became oppressive as harvests failed. Everywhere people were more vulnerable to the droughts and other agrarian catastrophes that they had weathered in earlier times. Poor farmers resented richer farmers, and many people defected from their traditional lords. And all the old royal rituals ultimately were powerless to stem this avalanche of misfortune. Life, in short, was increasingly lived on the margins of biological and social well-being, and eventually most of the southern Lowlands slid into the abyss of the collapse.

For those who prefer their Maya mysterious, there is still plenty that we do not know. The biggest remaining puzzle is why the abandoned parts of the Lowland environment remained uncolonized for so long. One possibility is that it took many centuries for the region's tropical soils to recover. Another is that some as yet undetected endemic disease – particularly one that had an established environmental vector – made the region too dangerous for centuries.

David Stuart, the eminent Maya epigrapher, once cogently remarked that the whole Late Classic period was a rehearsal for the collapse. By this he meant that the Maya have fooled us. We see great Late Classic centers such as Tikal or Copan, with their huge buildings, grand palaces, and assertive art and inscriptions as the high tide of Maya civilization. Instead, he suggests, fatal weaknesses lurked behind this glittering façade. The causes of its failure were embodied in its apparent success. Stuart's conclusion has a larger message that we should all think about today.

In many ways modern Maya people are reenacting the demographic processes of the Classic collapse, as reflected in the massive recent deforestation of much of the Maya Lowlands that is visible even from outer space.

Well, there it is. There's the archaeologist's revenge that I threatened at the beginning of this book. "Wait a minute!", I can hear the bleary-eyed reader exclaim just about now. "That's all there is? I asked what happened to all those Maya, and you promised me an answer!" No I didn't. I promised to make the Maya, and what happened to them, less mysterious, and to dispel some of the mystique that has long surrounded this famous ancient civilization and its fate. I've told you what I think, but that isn't the most important thing. What do you think? Don't you now know more about the Maya and what happened to them, and aren't you better able to make up your own mind?

NOTES

Prologue (pages 7–12)
1 Mason 1938.
2 According to some epigraphers it was a lack of cross-cultural perspectives that long impeded the decipherment of Maya inscriptions (Houston, Chinchilla, and Stuart 2001: 153).

Chapter 1 (pages 13–28)
1 Suhler and Freidel 1999: 258.2.
2 David Stuart 2000.
3 Simon Martin informs me of this unpublished interpretation by David Stuart.
4 *Maya Explorer* is the title of Victor Wolfgang von Hagen's 1947 biography of John L. Stephens. My account is taken from this volume as well as Stephens's own travel books.
5 von Hagen 1947: 75–76.
6 Stephens 1949: 78.
7 Stephens 1948: 81.
8 Stephens 1949: 79.
9 Stephens 1949: 80–81.
10 Pasztory 1998: 9–10.
11 Stephens 1949: 80.
12 Stephens 1949: 81.
13 Diego Garcia de Palacio passed through Copan in 1576. He noted the similarity of the ruins there to those he knew from northern Yucatan, but the record of his visit was unknown in 1839. Despite such insights of Palacio, Stephens, and others, it was not until the 1880s that most scholars agreed that the glyphs recorded a Mayan language (see Houston, Chinchilla, and Stuart 2001).
14 Stephens, 1949, vol. 2, 373.
15 Stephens 1949, vol. 2, 374.
16 von Hagen 1947: 166.

Chapter 2 (pages 29–48)
1 See Wilk 1983 for a review of this idea, and particularly for his argument that it is not necessarily bad for science or the public. Some archaeologists also argue that emphasizing the collapse is culturally patronizing because it devalues the Maya and allows us feel superior to them.
2 Interview in the Signs and Symbols segment of the *Out of the Past* video series.
3 Read Becker 1979 to see how this set of ideas emerged and afflicted Maya archaeology.
4 See Dunning 1994.
5 For a fascinating discussion of the folkway concept see Fischer 1989.
6 Different archaeologists prefer slightly varying versions of this scheme. For example, some identify a Protoclassic period between AD 100–250. These quibbles need not concern us, and the chronology used here is pretty standard.
7 For an example of such evidence see John G. Jones 1994.

Chapter 3 (pages 49–75)
1 This account, and those concerning the subsequent voyages, is taken from Sauer 1969, Landa 1941, Diaz 1963, Cortes 1986, Peter Martyr 1912, and Perry and Keith 1984 vols 1–3.
2 Sauer 1969: 128.
3 Peter Martyr 1912: 5.
4 Bernal Diaz 1963: 20-21.
5 Bernal Diaz 1963: 26.
6 It is usually assumed that this sighting refers to Tulum, the famous walled center that is now a major tourist attraction on the east coast of Yucatan.
7 Cortes 1986: 30, 35.
8 Bernal Diaz 1963: 65.
9 Powell 1885.
10 In Cortes's time several kinds of soul faculties were attributed to various classes of living beings. Humans had rational souls (*razón*), so he is here making both a theological and social (or as we would say, evolutionary) observation.
11 Braudel 1994: 4.
12 Jacques Barzun (2000: 74) discerns the beginnings of this idea of progress in the mid-16th century, just after Cortes's time. Interestingly the emergent western "theory" of progress was not initially used to distinguish perjoratively among European and non-European peoples, but rather to ask the question "are we improving" over earlier stages of European history itself.
13 Darwin 1874: 643.
14 Gelb 1963: 12.
15 Duran 1994: 16.
16 Childe 1950.
17 *New York Times* front page, July 12, 2000.
18 Lowe 1985.
19 Tainter 1988: 4.

Chapter 4 (pages 76–110)
1 Sahagun, for example, who left us our most encylopaedic account of the Aztecs and who in many ways sympathized with the Indians,

thought of them this way (Kubler 1991: 54).
2 Beginning about AD 600 copper and eventually bronze were used, but in such small amounts that Mesoamericans were for all practical purposes Stone Age peoples in technological terms.
3 Both Cortes (1986) and Bernal Diaz (1963) left first-hand accounts. Among the many later overviews are Scholes and Roys (1948), and most recently G. D. Jones (1999).
4 The original of this manuscript is lost. A copy made 30 years later was finally found in a Spanish archive in 1863, and so would not have been available to early Mayanists such as Stephens and Catherwood.
5 Other souces include Roys (1943, 1957), Scholes and Roys (1948), Farriss (1984), and Restall 1997, 1998).
6 Landa 1941: 96–97.
7 Morley 1946: 2.
8 Landa 1941: 62–63.
9 Restall 1997, Thompson 1999, and Quezada 1993. All three authors base their work largely on local, indigenous Maya sources, and their interpretations vary slightly from one another. I have tried to produce a reasonable synthesis of their ideas, relying most heavily on Restall.
10 Landa 1978: 40.
11 Roys 1943.
12 See P. Thompson, 1999: 18, Table 1.
13 Landa 1941: 87.
14 Landa 1941: 146–147.
15 Landa 1941: 108.
16 Landa 1941: 111.
17 Landa 1941: 28–29.
18 G. D. Jones 1999: 14–15.
19 J. E. S. Thompson 1966: 29.

Chapter 5 (pages 111–77)
1 Boone 2000: 26.
2 See Coe 1999b for an overview of the history of decipherment.
3 An obscure scholar, the Frenchman Jean Genet, correctly recognized the phonetic nature of the glyphs in the 1930s, and like Stephens asserted that much of their content was historical. Unfortunately his work remained largely ignored or unremarked. Genet also published early allusions to Classic Maya warfare. See Houston, Chinchilla, and Stuart 2001: 282.
4 Morley 1946: 262.
5 Stuart 1999 and Taube 2000.
6 The most recent summary by Martin and Grube (2000) includes the names of 152 kings and four queens just from eleven particularly well-studied centers, and we also know the names of many noble people of lesser rank.
7 Martin and Grube 2000: 140.
8 The most recent or common variants of names, usually phonetic, are listed in bold. Information from Agurcia 1998 and Martin and Grube 2000.
9 Viel 1999.
10 Houston, Escobedo, Terry, Webster, Veni and Emory 2000.
11 Several royal women associated with the Yaxchilan king Itzamnaaj B'alam II seem to have overlapping dates, and provide the strongest direct evidence for polygyny.
12 I believe this event was probably engineered with the connivance of some local Tikal faction. It might have been very similar to the French intervention in Mexican politics in the 1860s, when the ill-fated Emperor Maximillian was installed at the instigation of conservative Mexican factions. Interestingly, just about the time of this Mexican intrusion at Tikal there are signs of internal troubles at Teotihuacan itself (Sugiyama 1998). Quite possibly some dislocated elite faction left that city and reestablished itself in the Maya Lowlands.
13 Mock 1998.
14 Simon Martin 2001: 168–94.
15 Stephen Houston and David Stuart 2001: 54–83
16 Barzun 1999: 106.
17 Sheets 1990.
18 Vogt 1983: 100.
19 For an application of this model to the Classic Maya see Gillespie 2001.
20 Taube 2001.
21 Imagining utopias is a very old tradition in the west, although the word utopia was only invented by Sir Thomas More in the 16th century. Not coincidentally, he was stimulated to write his book of that name partly by reports of New World peoples, who had their own utopian conceptions.
22 These figures come from Berry 1990: 104 and Hobsbawm 1987: 21, respectively.
23 Willey 1956: 780.
24 In Cortes's day "Spanish" cities (there was as yet no Spain as a nation-state) were very small; Madrid, not yet the capital, was a dusty adobe village of 3000 people (Barzun 2000: 91–92).
25 *Moral Community and Settlement Transformation among the Classic Maya*, by Stephen Houston, Hector Escobedo, Mark Child, and Rene Muñoz (n.d.).
26 From Pre-Columbian Art Research Institute Newsletter 31: 12–13, Spring 2000.
27 See Rodenbeck 1999 for a fascinating urban biography of this ancient city.

28 See Inomata and Stephen Houston (eds) 2001.
29 Houston, Robertson, and Stuart 2000.
30 Willey and Shimkin 1973: 473–74.
31 For example, Diane and Arlen Chase (1996) believe that a bureaucratically-administered economy emerged at the Caracol polity.
32 Freidel 1986.
33 Scarborough 1996.
34 D. Jones 2000.
35 Baines and Yoffee 1998.
36 Laporte 2001.
37 Child 1999.
38 Martin and Grube 1995.
39 Chase and Chase 1998.
40 See N. Reed 1964 for a fascinating account of this conflict.
41 From *Morleyana* 1950: 226. By 1921 Morley had become reconciled to the idea of denser populations.
42 Turner 1990.
43 Rice and Culbert 1990: 27.
44 By overall density I mean simply the relationship between population and land area over any large region, disregarding internal variations in population concentrations. Perhaps the highest recent estimate is that of Richard Adams (1999: 146) who thinks that in a surveyed zone of 177 sq. km (69 sq. miles) near the center of Rio Azul, there were 1158 people per sq. km (3000 per sq. mile) around AD 690! Even traditional wet-rice cultivation in south China, one of the most productive peasant agrarian systems used by humans, supported only around 1980 people per sq. mile (Wolf 1966: 29).
45 D. Reed 1998.
46 Turner 1983: 120.
47 Netting 1993.

Chapter 6 (pages 178–216)
1 Landa 1941: 171–72.
2 I say "about" because there is a day or so of indeterminacy depending on exactly how one does the correlation mathematics.
3 It also failed to convey the fact that some centers had a distinct "flash in the pan" pattern of monument use – one or two monuments erected, and then no more – long before the collapse began in the late 8th century.
4 Calculated from map in Sidrys and Berger 1979.
5 Gann and Thompson 1931: 60.
6 Archaeologists in the 1940s knew that the earliest Long Count dates, especially those that preceded the 10th Baktun, were mainly clustered in the great sites of the central and southern Maya Lowlands. This was the geographic heartland of what they called the "Old Empire." There were also a few early dates at northern centers such as Chichen Itza, however, and so the "Old Empire" concept logically included these as well. Although decipherable dates were far fewer in the north, they tended to be late, many of them falling into the 10th Baktun (see Grube 1994). Morley and his colleagues thus envisioned a Maya cultural florescence confined to northern Yucatan after about the mid-10th century, supposedly stimulated in part by refugees from the collapsing southern polities. This they labeled the "New Empire." Despite the use of the term, no archaeologists believed there were Maya empires in anything like the Aztec sense.
7 Thompson 1940: 128.
8 Thompson 1966: 23.
9 Matheny 1986.
10 Hodell, Brenner, Curtis, and Guilderson 2001.
11 Martin and Grube 2000: 17.
12 Harrison (1999) cites AD 557–682 as the period of the hiatus (125 years); Martin and Grube identify the interval as AD 562–692 (130 years). I have used the latter dates here.
13 Keys 2000.
14 Willey 1974.
15 Spinden 1975: 7–8.
16 See Dunning 1994. Until recently, the low population also reflected the presence of malaria and yellow fever, both introduced after the Spanish conquest.
17 For an overview of these and other projects see Prem 1994.
18 Translated by Maudslay, 1889–1902, vol. III, pp. 6–7.
19 Miller 1999: 69.
20 E.g., Gill 2000: 289.
21 T. Patrick Culbert 1988: 77.
22 One of my colleagues has used this propensity to put a positive spin on the collapse: "The Maya decline is a symptom of evolutionary advancement through the innovation of the tribute-based government and the development of the market economy" (Freidel 1986: 430).
23 Sidrys and Berger 1979.
24 Lowe 1985: 205.
25 Sidrys and Berger 1979: 271.
26 Sidrys and Berger 1979: 264.
27 Erickson 1975.

Chapter 7 (pages 217–59)
1 Gann and Thompson 1931.
2 In the 1960s the ethnographer Evon Vogt, who

studied the Highland Maya, championed a slightly different version of Thompson's models. He proposed that the Maya had essentially egalitarian political structure in which individuals rotated through a hierarchy of established civil/religious offices that they periodicallly discharged in central, ceremonial places.
3 Kaplan 1963: 398.
4 Farriss 1984.
5 Thompson, 1954: 131.
6 J.E.S. Thompson 1966: 35.
7 Abrams 1994 and Webster and Kirker 1988.
8 For a model of how the patterning of the collapse might be consistent with internal rebellions, see Hamblin and Pitcher 1980.
9 Morley 1946: 70.
10 Thompson 1954: 81.
11 See Webster 2000 for a review.
12 From David Stuart 1995.
13 See David Stuart 1993 for a critical analysis of this evidence.
14 For example, see Webb 1973 and Jones 1979.
15 By non-commercial I mean circulation based on mechanisms such as gift-giving. For example, we circulate many things by gift-giving at Christmas, but regard such circulation as non-commercial. Production and exchange were distintly non-capitalist (see McAnany 1993).
16 See, for example, Drennan 1984.
17 Mostert 1992: 1187.
18 Roys 1967: 184.
19 Puleston 1976: 1.
20 El Niño is the unusually warm Pacific current that situationally deflects colder water in the eastern Pacific, and is now known to have wide-ranging effects on climate throughout much of the Northern Hemisphere.
21 Gill 2000: 271.
22 Gill 2000: 313.
23 Don Rice, personal communication, Jan. 6, 2001.
24 Hodell et. al 1995; Curtis et al. 1996; Hodell et. al 2001. The exact calendar interval estimated for the drought varies slightly according to method of analysis used, but AD 800–1000 is close enough in round figures.
25 Hodell et al. 2001.
26 Cobo 2001.
27 Curtis et al. 1996: 45.
28 Islebe et al. 1996.
29 de Montellano 1990: 123–124.
30 Meggers 1954.
31 I am grateful to the tropical ecologist John J. Ewel for his advice on soil formation.
32 See for example Reina 1967.
33 From Binford et al. 1987: Figs 5a-b.
34 Fedick 1996. Settlement ecologists know that micro-management often occurs when population density is high. In preindustrial situations such management usually reflects very localized agrarian economies – typical, I believe, of the Late Classic Maya.
35 Cowgill 1979.
36 Lowe 1985.

Chapter 8 (pages 260–94)
1 An invaluable source for much of the dynastic information presented in this chapter is Martin and Grube 2000.
2 This individual might be from Teotihuacan, or alternatively from one of Teotihuacan's "colonies," such as Kaminaljuyu in highland Guatemala or Matacapan on the Mexican Gulf Coast. It is also conceivable that he was a Maya person who made a journey to some Teotihuacan-dominated place to associate himself with their political and ideological authority.
3 Puleston and Calendar 1967.
4 My figures are from the most comprehensive recent overview (Culbert et al. 1990).
5 Don Rice, personal communication, Feb. 2001.
6 The Maya channeled water and cultivated some swamp margins near Tikal's swamps, but there are no signs of extensive drained field systems anything like the Aztec chinampas.
7 Harrison 1999: 192–200.
8 Rice and Rice 1990.
9 For the best recent overview see Martin and Grube 2000: 100–115.
10 Sources for this section include Houston 1993 and Volume 8: 2 (1997) of *Ancient Mesoamerica*, which summarizes much information derived from the Vanderbilt Petexbatun Project, and from many publications by Takeshi Inomata, who has long directed the research at Aguateca.
11 Some of my colleagues believe that a system of earthwork fortifications protecting the nearby peninsula settlement of Punta de Chimino were originally constructed in Late Preclassic times. If so, major conflicts in the region long predate those recorded in the inscriptions.
12 Martin and Grube (2000) note various examples of apparently self-serving manipulations in the corpus of texts of this region.
13 Demarest 1997.
14 The Piedras Negras monuments, many of which were studied and removed by a University of Pennsylvania project in the 1930s,

provided the data for the breakthrough epigraphic research of Tatiana Proskouriakoff (1960).
15 Text gaps like this stimulated the idea of a pan-Maya Lowland hiatus, but they are often a result of poor preservation, as we saw at Tikal. For the interval between AD 540 and 629 there is very little information for Yaxchilan either, but from fragmentary evidence we know that it encompasses the reigns of four kings.
16 Because of the vagaries of textual interpretation and the order of discovery, Ruler 2 is actually the 6th known king.
17 For data summaries see Ball 1977 and Thomas Jr. 1981.
18 Turner II 1983.
19 Hammond, Tourtellot, Donaghey, and Clark 1998. Hammond and Tourtellot also kindly supplied me with some unpublished papers on La Milpa.
20 Pendergast 1986: 226. See also Pendergast 1981.
21 Pendergast 1986: 227.
22 The most sophisticated examination of this systemic dimension is Lowe 1988.

Chapter 9 (pages 295–326)
1 It is also possible that the founder was a native of Copan who, as prospective rulers sometimes did elsewhere in Mesoamerica, journeyed to a distant, prestigious capital such as Tikal to be anointed king, much as Charlemagne traveled to Rome to legitimize his rule.
2 Bell et. al 2000.
3 Viel (1998) thinks that kingship at Copan might have circulated among several ruling lineages. If so, some elite people were not so much "subroyal" in rank as "out of power."
4 Longyear 1952.
5 Freter 1992 and Webster, Sanders, and Van Rossum 1992. The dating method Freter employed is based on the chemical alteration begun when a new surface is created on a piece of obsidian being made into a tool. This method has been extensively corroborated by independent dating methods at Copan, as reported in a forthcoming article: Webster, Freter, and Storey (in press).
6 In radiocarbon parlance, this date (from the University of Arizona AMS Laboratory) reads 655 ± 50 radiocarbon years B.P., or cal. 1 sigma 1288–1393; 2 sigma AD 1278–1411.
7 Willey and Shimkin 1973: 487.
8 Sheehy 1991 and Webster et al. 1998.
9 Manahan 1999.
10 Rue 1987.
11 Abrams and Rue 1988.
12 Wingard 1996.
13 D. Reed 1998.
14 As late as the 18th century in Europe staple grains made up about two-thirds of the caloric intake of ordinary people; see Livi-Bacci 1997: 85.
15 Storey 1992 and 1999.
16 Whittington 1989, 1999.
17 Schele and Freidel 1990: 345.
18 Had Copan's elites sponsored commercial agriculture of some sort on the best lands of the valley floor (where tobacco is grown today) there might of course have been deleterious effects on food production. While reaction to such a stress could have contributed to the fall of kings, it would not have posed any long-term threat.
19 Kidder 1950: 9.
20 A hypogamous marriage is one in which a man marries a woman of higher social status.
21 Tawney 1960: 77.

Chapter 10 (pages 327–48)
1 Malthus (whose ideas are often dismissed, particularly by people who do not read him) emphasized the imbalance between population and resources – basically a population pressure argument, not one specifically tied to population growth. See Thomas Malthus 1970 (original 1796).
2 Here I refer to yields in ancient times, not to those based on modern hybrids.
3 Dunning and Beach 2000.
4 Maya farmers using traditional methods today in Chiapas, Mexico, cultivate just about 2 ha of land per family – very similar to the figures given here for the ancient Maya.
5 The Egyptian figures are from Hassan 1983 and Eyre 1995.
6 This is an empirical issue. Someone should rebuild a couple of old Maya terrace systems, hire local people to plant crops on them for several seasons, and assess the results.
7 The Aztec state subsidized the construction of thousands of acres of chinampas in the late 15th century, and they subsequently provided much of the food supply for the capital, Tenochtitlan, even in Colonial times. Remnants of such systems are favorite tourist attractions in Mexico City, and are often incorrectly envisioned as "floating gardens."
8 Pohl et al. 1996.
9 There are examples of forms of agricultural intensification that result in both increased productivity and sustainability in various parts of the world – wet rice agriculture is perhaps the most successful because it mimics natural

wetland ecosystems.
10 Lowe 1985.
11 Livi-Bacci 1997: 92.
12 *New York Times Book Review*, August 8, 1999
13 Webster 1975, 1977.
14 For a graphic summary see Martin and Grube 2000: 21.
15 Stuart 1995: 314.
16 All these same motives for war characterized the 16th-century Maya as well, even though their populations were much less dense.
17 Wood 1998.
18 Sahagun 1953: 23–24.
19 For a discussion about how poor diet and disease can affect the work capacity of an agrarian population see Fogel 1994.
20 Redman 1999: 16.
21 Houston et al. in press.
22 Stuart 1993: 336.
23 Houston and Stuart 1996.
24 Culbert 1988: 100.

FURTHER READING & BIBLIOGRAPHY

My own book is only the most recent contribution to an immense literature focused specifically on the Maya collapse. John Lowe reviews the timing and nature of the process in his *Dynamics of Apocalypse* (1985). Particularly good general overviews are found in Joseph Tainter's *The Collapse of Complex Societies* (1988), *The Classic Maya Collapse* (1973), edited by T. Patrick Culbert, and *The Collapse of Ancient States and Civilizations* (1988), edited by Norman Yoffee and George Cowgill, although all of these are by now necessarily somewhat out of date. A more recent and very comprehensive overview of the collapse from the perspective of drought and famine is Richardson Gill's *The Great Maya Droughts* (2000). Many more works examine what happened to the Maya in particular sites and regions. These include Peter Harrison's *The Lords of Tikal* (1999), Stephen Houston's *Hieroglyphs and History at Dos Pilas* (1993), and *Copan: The Rise and Fall of an Ancient Maya Kingdom* (2000), which I wrote with AnnCorinne Freter and Nancy Gonlin.

More general books on the Classic Maya include *The Ancient Maya* (1994) by Robert Sharer, *The Maya* (1999) by Michael Coe, *Maya Art and Architecture* (1999) by Mary Ellen Miller, *Precolumbian Population History in the Maya Lowlands* (1990), edited by T. Patrick Culbert and Don Rice, and *Chronicle of the Maya Kings and Queens* (2000), by Simon Martin and Nikolai Grube. Readers specifically interested in the story of how Maya writing was deciphered should read *The Decipherment of Ancient Maya Writing* (2001), edited by Stephen Houston, Oswaldo Chincilla and David Stuart, and Michael Coe's *Breaking the Maya Code* (1999).

For additional information concerning many of the Mesoamerican sites, regions, and cultural practices discussed in this book see *Archaeology of Ancient Mexico and Central America* (2001), edited by Susan Evans and David Webster.

Abrams, Elliot, 1994. *How the Maya Built their World.* Austin: University of Texas Press.

Abrams, Elliot, and David Rue, 1988. The causes and consequences of deforestation among the prehistoric Maya. *Human Ecology* 14: 377–399.

Adams, Richard, 1999. *Rio Azul: An Ancient Maya City.* Norman: University of Oklahoma Press.

Agurcia, Ricardo F., 1998. Copan: art, science, and dynasty. In *Maya*, eds P. Schmidt, M. de la Garza, and E. Nalda, 336–355. New York: Rizzoli.

Alley, Richard B., 2000. *The Two Mile Time Machine.* Princeton: Princeton University Press.

Barzun, Jacques, 2000. *From Dawn to Decadence.* New York: Harper Collins.

Baines, John, and Norman Yoffee, 1998. Order, legitimacy, and wealth in ancient Egypt and Mesopotamia. In *Archaic States*, eds G. M. Feinman and J. Marcus, 199–260. School of American Research, Santa Fe.

Ball, Joseph, 1977. *Ceramics of Becan, Campeche, Mexico.* Middle American Research Institute (Publ. 43). New Orleans: Tulane University.

Becker, Marshall, 1979. Priests, peasants, and ceremonial centers: the intellectual history of a model. In *Maya Archaeology and Ethnohistory*, eds N. Hammond and G. R. Willey, 3–20. Austin: University of Texas Press.

Bell, Ellen E., Robert J. Sharer, David W. Sedat, Marcello A. Canuto, and Lynn A. Grant, 2000. The Margarita tomb at Copan, Honduras: a research update. *Expedition* 42 (3): 21–25.

Berry, J. L., 1990. Urbanization. In *The Earth as Transformed by Human Action*, eds B.L. Turner II, W. C. Clark, R. W. Kates, J. F. Richards, J. T. Mathews, and W. B. Meyer, 103–120. Cambridge: Cambridge University Press.

Binford, Michael, Mark Brenner, Thomas Whitmore, Antonia Higuera-Gundy, and Edward S. Deevey, 1987. Ecosystems, paleoecology, and human disturbance in subtropical and tropical America. *Quaternary Science Reviews* 6: 115–128.

Boone, Elizabeth, 2000. *Stories in Red and Black*. Austin: University of Texas Press.

Braudel, Fernand, 1994. *History of Civilization*. New York: A. Lane.

Brainerd, George, 1954. *The Maya Civilization*. Los Angeles: Los Angeles Southwest Museum.

Chase, Arlen, and Diane Chase, 1996. Organization and composition of Classic Lowland Maya society: the view from Caracol, Belize. In *Eighth Palenque Round Table*, 1993: San Francisco: Pre-Columbian Art Research Institute.

——————, 1998. Late Classic Maya political structure, polity size, and warfare arenas. In *Anatomia de una Civilizacion*, eds A. C. Ruiz, Y. F. Marquinez, J. M. G. Campillo, J. I. Ponce de Leon, A. L. Garcia-Gallo, and L. T. Sanz Castro, L. T., 11–29. Madrid: Sociedad Espanol de Estudios Mayas.

Child, Mark. B., 1999. Classic Maya Warfare and its Sociopolitical Implications. Paper presented at the 1999 Palenque Mesa Redonda, Palenque, Mexico.

Childe, V. Gordon, 1950. The urban revolution. *Town Planning Review* 44: 3–17.

Cobo, Rafael, 2001. El Centro de Yucatan: De area perifericos a la integracion de la comunidad urbana en Chichen Itza. In *Reconstruyendo la Cuidad Maya: El Urbanismo an las Sociedades Antiguas*, eds A. C. Ruiz, M. J. I. Ponce de Leon, and M. C. Martinez, 253–276. Madrid: Sociedad Espanola de Estudios Mayas, Pub. 6.

Coe, Michael, 1999a. *The Maya*. 6th Edition. London & New York: Thames & Hudson.

——————, 1999b. *Breaking the Maya Code*. 2nd Edition. New York: Thames & Hudson.

Cortes, Hernan, 1986. *Letters From Mexico* (edited and translated by Anthony Pagden). New Haven: Yale University Press.

Cowgill, George, 1979. Teotihuacan, internal militaristic competition, and the fall of the Classic Maya (1979). In *Maya Archaeology and Ethnohistory*, eds G. R. Willey and N. Hammond, 51–62. Austin: University of Texas Press.

Culbert, T. Patrick, 1988. Collapse of Classic Maya civilization. In *The Collapse of Ancient States and Civilizations*, eds N. Yoffee and G. Cowgill, 69–101. Tucson: University of Arizona Press.

Culbert, T. Patrick (ed.), 1973. *The Classic Maya Collapse*. Albuquerque: University of New Mexico Press.

Culbert, T. Patrick, Laura J. Kosakowsky, Robert Fry, and William Haviland, 1990. The Population of Tikal, Guatemala. In *Precolumbian Population History of the Maya Lowlands*, eds T. P. Culbert and D. S. Rice, 103–121. Albuquerque: University of New Mexico Press.

Culbert, T. Patrick, and Don. S. Rice (eds), 1990. *Precolumbian Population History in the Maya Lowlands*. Albuquerque: University of New Mexico Press.

Curtis, Jason H., David A. Hodell, and Mark Brenner, 1996. Climate variability on the Yucatan Peninsula (Mexico) during the past 3500 years, and the implications for Maya cultural evolution. *Quaternary Research* 46: 37–47.

Darwin, Charles, 1874. *The Descent of Man*. New York: American Publishers Corporation.

Demarest, Arthur, 1997. The Vanderbilt Petexbatun project. *Ancient Mesoamerica* 8 (2): 217.

de Montellano, Bernard Ortiz, 1990. *Aztec Medicine, Health, and Nutrition*. New Brunswick: Rutgers University Press.

Diamond, Jared, 1999. *Guns, Germs, and Steel: The Fates of Human Societies*. New York: W. W. Norton and Co.

Diaz, Bernal, 1963. *The Conquest of New Spain*. Harmondsworth & Baltimore: Penguin Books.

Drennan, Robert, 1984. Long distance movement of goods in the Mesoamerican Formative and Classic. *American Antiquity* 9 (1): 27–43.

Dunning, Nicholas, 1994. Puuc Ecology and Settlement Patterns. In *Hidden Among the Hills*, ed. H. J. Prem, 1–43. Mockmuhl: Verlag von Flemming.

Dunning, Nicholas, and Timothy Beach, 2000. Stability and instability in prehispanic Maya landscapes. In *Imperfect Balance: Landscape*

Transformations in the Precolumbian Americas, ed. D.L. Lentz, 179–202. New York: Columbia University Press.

Duran, Diego de, 1994. *The History of the Indies of New Spain*. Norman: University of Oklahoma Press.

Erickson, Edwin, 1975. Growth functions and culture history: a perspective on Classic Maya culture history. *Behavioral Science Research* 10: 37–61.

Evans, Susan T., and David Webster, eds, 2001. *Archaeology of Ancient Mexico and Central America*. New York: Garland Publishing.

Eyre, Christopher J., 1995. The agricultural cycle, farming, and water management in the ancient Near East. In *Civilizations of the Ancient Near East* (Vol. 1), ed. J. Sasson, 175–189. New York: Charles Scribner's Sons.

Farriss, Nancy M., 1984. *Maya Society Under Colonial Rule*. Princeton: Princeton University Press.

Fash, William, 1991 and 2001. *Scribes, Warriors, and Kings*. 2nd Edition. London & New York: Thames & Hudson.

Fedick, Scott (ed.), 1996. *The Managed Mosaic*. Salt Lake City: University of Utah Press.

David H. Fischer, 1989. *Albion's Seed*. New York: Oxford University Press.

Fogel, Robert, 1994. The relevance of Malthus for the study of mortality today: long-run influences on health, mortality, labour force participation, and population growth. In *Population, Economic Development, and the Environment*, eds K. Lindahl-Kiessling and H. Landberg, 231–284. London: Oxford University Press.

Freidel, David, 1986. Terminal Classic Lowland Maya: successes, failures, and aftermaths. In *Late Lowland Maya Civilization*, eds J. Sabloff and E. W. Andrews V, 409–432. Albuquerque: University of New Mexico Press.

Freidel, David, and Charles Suhler, 1999. The path of life: toward a functional analysis of ancient Maya architecture. In *Mesoamerican Architecture as Cultural Symbol*, ed. J. K. Kowalski, 250–273. New York: Oxford University Press.

Freter, AnnCorrine, 1992. Chronological research at Copan: methods and implications. *Ancient Mesoamerica* 3: 117–133.

Gann, Thomas, and J. E. S. Thompson, 1931. *The History of the Maya*. New York: Charles Scribner's Sons.

Gelb, I. J., 1963. *A Study of Writing*. Chicago: University of Chicago Press.

Gill, Richardson, 2000. *The Great Maya Droughts*. Albuquerque: University of New Mexico Press.

Gillespie, Susan, 2001. Rethinking ancient Maya social organization: replacing "lineage" with "house." *American Anthropologist* 102 (3): 467–484.

Grube, Nikolai, 1994. Hieroglyphic sources for the history of northwest Yucatan. In *Hidden Among the Hills*, ed. H. J. Prem, 316–348. Mockmuhl: Verlag von Flemming.

Hamblin, R. L., and B. L. Pitcher, 1980. The Classic Maya collapse: testing class conflict hypotheses. *American Antiquity* 45: 246–67.

Hammond, Norman, Tourtellot, G., Donaghey, S., and Clarke, A., 1998. No slow dusk: Maya urban development and decline at La Milpa, Belize. *Antiquity* 72: 831–837.

Harrison, Peter, 1999. *The Lords of Tikal*. London & New York: Thames & Hudson.

Hassan, Fekri, 1983. Population ecology and civilization in ancient Egypt. In *Historical Ecology*, ed. C. L. Crumley, 155–181. Santa Fe: School of American Research.

Hobsbawm, Eric, 1987. *The Age of Empire: 1875–1914*. New York: Pantheon Books.

Hodell, David A., Jason H. Curtis, and Mark Brenner, 1995. Possible role of climate in the collapse of Classic Maya civilization. *Nature* 375: 391–394.

Hodell, David A., Mark Brenner, Jason M. Curtis, and Thomas Guilderson, 2001. Solar forcing of drought frequency in the Maya Lowlands. *Science* 292: 1367–1370.

Houston, Stephen, 1993. *Hieroglyphs and History at Dos Pilas*. Austin: University of Texas Press.

Houston, Stephen, Oswaldo Chinchilla Mazareigos, and David Stuart, 2001. *The Decipherment of Ancient Maya Writing*. Norman: University of Oklahoma Press.

Houston, Stephen, and David Stuart, 1996. Of gods, glyphs, and kings: divinity and rulership among the Classic Maya. *Antiquity* 70: 289–312.

Houston, Stephen, Hector Escobedo, Richard Terry, David Webster, George Veni, and Kitty Emory, 2000. Among the river kings: archaeological research at Piedras Negras, Guatemala, 1999. *Mexicon* 22: 8–17.

Houston, Stephen, John Robertson, and David Stuart, 2000. The language of Classic Maya inscriptions. *Current Anthropology* 41:3: 344–345.

Houston, Stephen and David Stuart, 2001. Peopling the Classic Maya court. In *Royal Courts of the Ancient Maya*, eds Takeshi Inomata and Stephen Houston, 54–83. Boulder: Westview Press.

Houston, Stephen, Hector Escobedo, Mark Child, and Rene Muñoz, n.d. Moral community and settlement transformation among the Classic Maya. In *The Social*

Construction of Ancient Cities, ed. M.L. Smith. Washington: Smithsonian Institution Press.

Houston, Stephen, Hector Escobedo, Mark Child, Charles Golden, and Rene Muñoz, n.d. Cronica de una muerte anunciada: los anos finales de Piedras Negras. In *Simposio Internacional: La Ciudad Antigua: Espacios, Conjuntos e Integración Sociocultura el la Civilización Maya*, Madrid.

Inomata, Takeshi, and Houston, Stephen (eds), 2001. *Royal Courts of the Classic Maya.* Boulder: Westview Press.

Islebe, Gerald A., Henry Hooghiemstra, Mark Brenner, Jason H. Curtis, and David Hodell, 1996. A Holocene vegetation history from Lowland Guatemala. *Holocene* 6 (3): 265–27.

Jones, David, 2000. *An Index of Ancient Egyptian Titles, Epithets, and Phrases of the Old Kingdom* BAR International Series, vols. 1 and 2. Oxford: Archaeopress.

Jones, Christopher, 1979. Tikal as a Trading Center: Why it Rose and Fell. Paper presented at the 43rd International Congress of Americanists, Vancouver.

Jones, Grant D., 1998. *The Conquest of the Last Itza Kingdom.* Stanford: Stanford University Press.

Jones, John G., 1994. Pollen evidence of early settlement and agriculture in Northern Belize. *Palynology* 18: 205–211.

Kaplan, David, 1963. Men, monuments, and political systems. *Southwestern Journal of Anthropology* 19: 397–410.

Keys, David, 2000. *Catastrophe.* New York: Ballantine Books.

Kidder, Alfred V., 1950. Introduction. In *Uaxactun, Guatemala: Excavations of 1931–37*, by A. Ledyard Smith. Carnegie Institution of Washington (Publ. 588). Washington.

Kubler, George, 1991. *Esthetic Recognition of Ancient Amerindian Art.* New Haven: Yale University Press.

Landa, Diego de, 1941. (edited and annotated by Alfred Tozzer). *Relación de las Cosas de Yucatan.* Cambridge: Papers of the Peabody Museum of Archaeology and Ethnology, vol 18, Cambridge: Harvard University.

——————, 1978. *Yucatan Before and After the Conquest* (translated and annotated by William Gates). New York: Dover Publications Inc.

Laporte, Juan Pedro, 2001. Dispersion y estructura de las cuidades del sureste de Peten, Guatemala. In *Reconstruyendo la Cuidad Maya: El Urbanismo an las Sociedades Antiguas*, eds A. C. Ruiz, M. J. I. Ponce de Leon, and M. C. Martinez, 137–162. Madrid: Sociedad Espanola de Estudios Mayas, Pub. 6.

Livi-Bacci, Massimo, 1997. *A Concise History of World Population.* Oxford: Blackwell Pub.

Longyear, John, 1952. *Copan Ceramics: A Study of Southeastern Maya Pottery.* Washington: Carnegie Institution of Washington (Publ. 597).

Lowe, John, 1985. *Dynamics of Apocalypse.* Albuquerque: University of New Mexico Press.

Malthus, Thomas, 1970 (original 1796). *An Essay on the Principal of Population.* New York: Penguin Books.

Manahan, K., 1999. Reexaminando los dias finales de Copan: nuevos datos de la Fase Ejar. In *XIIII Simposio de Investigaciones Arqueologicas en Guatemala*, eds J. P. Laporte, H. L. Escobedo, A. C. de Suasnavar, and B. Arroyo, 1149–1155. Guatemala City: Ministerio de Cultura y Deportes, Instituto de Antropologia e Historia, y Asociacion Tikal.

Martin, Simon, 2001. Court and realm. In *Royal Courts of the Ancient Maya*, eds T. Inomata and S. Houston, 168–194. Boulder: Westview Press.

Martin, Simon, and Nikolai Grube, 1995. Maya Superstates. *Archaeology* 48 (6): 41–46.

——————, 2000. *Chronicle of the Maya Kings and Queens.* London & New York: Thames & Hudson.

Martyr, Peter, 1912. *De Orbo Novo.* New York: G. P. Putnam's Sons.

Mason, J. Alden, 1938. Observations on the present status and problems of Middle American archaeology, part II. *American Antiquity* 3 (4): 300–317.

Matheny, Raymond, 1986. Investigations at El Mirador, Peten, Guatemala. *National Geographic Research* 2: 332–353.

Maudslay, Alfred P., 1974 (orig. 1889–1902). *Biologia Centrali-Americana: Archaeology* vol. V, New York: Milpatron Publishing.

McAnany, Patricia, 1993. The economics of social power and wealth among eighth-century Maya households. In *Lowland Maya Civilization in the Eighth Century AD*, eds J. Sabloff and J. Henderson, 65–90. Washington: Dumbarton Oaks.

Meggers, Betty J., 1954. Environmental limitation on the development of culture. *American Anthropologist* 56: 801–024.

Miller, Mary, 1999. *Maya Art and Architecture.* London & New York: Thames & Hudson.

Mock, Susan. B., 1998. The defaced and the forgotten: decapitation and flaying/mutilation as a termination event at Colha. In *The Sowing and the Dawning*, ed. S.B. Mock, 113–124. Albuquerque: University of New Mexico Press.

Morley, Sylvanus G., 1946. *The Ancient Maya.* Stanford: Stanford University Press.

Mostert, Noël, 1992. *Frontiers*. London: Jonathan Cape.

Netting, Robert, 1993. *Smallholders, Householders: Farm Families and the Ecology of Intensive, Sustainable Agriculture*. Stanford: Stanford University Press.

Parry, John H., and Robert G. Keith (eds), 1984. *New Iberian World* vols. 1–5. New York: Times Books.

Pasztory, Esther, 1998. *Precolumbian Art*. New York: Cambridge University Press.

Pendergast, David, 1981. Lamanai, Belize: summary of excavation results, 1974–1980. *Journal of Field Archaeology* 8: 29–52.

————, 1986. Stability through Change. In *Late Lowland Maya Civilization*, eds Jeremy Sabloff and John Henderson, 223–250. Albuquerque: University of New Mexico Press.

Pohl, M., Kevin Pope, John Jones, J. Jacob, D. Piperno, S. de France, David Lentz, J. Gifford, M. Danforth, and Katherine Josserand, 1996. Early agriculture in the Maya Lowlands. *Latin American Antiquity* 7 (4): 355–372.

Powell, John Wesley, 1885. From savagery to barbarism. *Transactions of the Anthropological Society of Washington* 3: 173–196.

Pre-Columbian Art Research Institute Newsletter 31, Spring 2000.

Prem, Hanns J., 1994. *Hidden Among the Hills*. Verlag von Flemming, Mockmuhl.

Proskouriakoff, Tatiana, 1960. Historical implications of a pattern of dates at Piedras Negras, Guatemala. *American Antiquity* 25 (4) 454–475.

Puleston, Dennis, 1976. An epistemological pathology and the collapse, or why the Maya kept the Short Count. Paper presented at the Second Cambridge Symposium on Recent Research in Mesoamerican Archaeology, Corpus Christi College, Aug. 28–31.

Puleston, Dennis, and D. W. Callender Jr., 1967. Defensive earthworks at Tikal. *Expedition* 9 (3): 40–48.

Quezada, Sergio, 1993. *Pueblos y Caciques Yucatecis, 1550–1580*. Mexico City: El Colegio de Mexico.

Rands, Robert, 1952. *Some Evidences of Warfare in Classic Maya Art*. Ph.D. dissertation, Department of Anthropology, Columbia University. New York.

Redman, Charles, 1999. *Human Impact on Ancient Environment*. Tucson: University of Arizona Press.

Reed, David, 1998. *Ancient Maya Diet at Copan*. Ph.D dissertation, Department of Anthropology, The Pennsylvania State University. University Park.

Reed, Nelson, 1964. *The Caste War of Yucatan*. Stanford: Stanford University Press.

Reina, Ruben, 1967. Milpas and Milperos. *American Anthropologist* 69 (1): 1–20.

Restall, Matthew, 1997. *The Maya World*. Stanford: Stanford University Press.

————, 1998. *Maya Conquistador*. Boston: Beacon Press.

Rice, D. S., and T. Patrick Culbert, 1990. Historical contexts for population reconstruction. In *Precolumbian Population History in the Maya Lowlands*, eds D. S. Rice and T. P. Culbert, 1-27. Albuquerque: University of New Mexico Press.

Rice, Don S., and Prudence M. Rice, 1990. Population size and population change in the central lakes region, Guatemala. In *Precolumbian Population History of the Maya Lowlands*, eds T. Patrick Culbert and Don S. Rice, 123–148. Albuquerque: University of New Mexico Press.

Rodenbeck, Max, 1999. *Cairo*. New York: Alfred Knopf.

Roys, Ralph, 1943. *The Indian Background of Colonial Yucatan*. Washington: Carnegie Institution of Washington (Publ. 548).

————, 1957. *The Political Geography of the Yucatan Maya*. Washington: Carnegie Institution of Washington (Publ. 613).

————, 1967. *The Book of Chilam Balam of Chumayel*. Norman: University of Oklahoma Press.

Rue, David, 1987. Early agriculture and early Postclassic Maya occupation at Copan, Honduras. *Nature* 326: 285–286.

Sabloff, Jeremy, and Gordon R. Willey, 1967. The collapse of Maya civilization in the southern Lowlands: a consideration of history and process. *Southwestern Journal of Anthropology* 23: 311–336.

Sahagun, Bernardino de, 1953 (original 1564), *Florentine Codex*. vol. 7 (Arthur Anderson and Charles Dibble translators). Salt Lake City: University of Utah Press.

Sanders, William T., and David Webster, 1988. The Mesoamerican urban tradition. *American Anthropologist* 90 (3): 521–546.

Sauer, Carl, 1966. *The Early Spanish Main*. Berkeley: University of California Press.

Scarborough, Vernon, 1996. Reservoirs and watersheds in the central Maya Lowlands. In *The Managed Mosaic*, ed. Scott Fedick, 304–314. Salt Lake City: University of Utah Press.

Schele, Linda, and David Freidel, 1990. *A Forest of Kings*. New York: William Morrow and Co.

Scholes, France V., and Ralph Roys, 1948. *The*

Maya Chontal Indians of Acalan-Tixchel. Washington: Carnegie Institution of Washington (Publ. 560).

Schufeldt, Paul, 1950. Reminiscences of a chiclero. In *Morleyana* (no author or editor given), 224–229. Sante Fe: School of American Research and the Museum of New Mexico.

Sharer, Robert, 1994. *The Ancient Maya.* Stanford: Stanford University Press.

Sheehy, James, 1991. Structure and change in a Late Classic Maya domestic group at Copan, Honduras. *Ancient Mesoamerica* 2: 1–19.

Sheets, Payson, 1990. *The Ceren Site.* Fort Worth: Harcourt Brace Janovich.

Sidrys, Raymond, and Rainer Berger, 1979. Lowland Maya radiocarbon dates and the Classic Maya collapse. *Nature* 277: 269–277.

Spinden, Herbert, 1975 (original 1912). *A Study of Maya Art.* New York: Dover Publications.

Stephens, John L., 1969 (original 1841). *Incidents of Travel in Central America, Chiapas, and Yucatan.* New York: Dover Publications.

Stephens, John. L., 1949. *Incidents of Travel in Central America, Chiapas, and Yucatán.* New Brunswick: Rutgers University Press.

Storey, Rebecca, 1992. The children of Copán. *Ancient Mesoamerica* 3 (1): 161–168.

Storey, Rebecca, 1999. Late Classic nutrition and skeletal indicators at Copan, Honduras. In *Reconstructing Ancient Maya Diet*, ed. C. White, 169–182. Salt Lake City: University of Utah Press.

Stuart, David, 1993. Historical inscriptions and the Maya collapse. In *Lowland Maya Civilization in the Eighth Century AD*, eds J. Sabloff and J.S. Henderson, 321–354. Washington: Dumbarton Oaks.

————, 1995. *A Study of Maya Inscriptions*, Ph.D. dissertation, Department of Anthropology, Vanderbilt University. Nashville.

————, 2000. The arrival of strangers. In *Mesoamerica's Classic Heritage: From Teotihuacan to the Aztecs*, eds D. Carrasco, L. Jones, and J. S. Sessions, 465–513. Boulder: University of Colorado Press.

Sugiyama, 1998. Termination programs and prehistoric looting at the Feathered Serpent Pyramid in Teotihuacan, Mexico. In *The Sowing and the Dawning*, ed. S. B. Mock, 147–164. University of New Mexico Press, Albuquerque.

Tainter, Joseph, 1988. *The Collapse of Complex Societies.* New York: Cambridge University Press.

Taube, Karl, 2000. *The Writing System of Teotihuacan.* Washington: Center for Ancient American Studies.

————, 2001. Ancient and Contemporary Conceptions of the Field and Forest. Paper presented at the 21st Symposium in Plant Biology, University of California at Riverside.

Tawney, R. H., 1960. *Land and Labor in China.* Boston: Beacon Press, Boston.

Thomas, Prentice Jr., 1981. *Prehistoric Maya Settlement Patterns at Becan, Campeche, Mexico.* Middle American Research Institute (Publ. 45). New Orleans: Tulane University.

Thompson, J. E. S., 1954. *The Rise and Fall of Maya Civilization.* Norman: University of Oklahoma Press.

————, 1966. The Maya central area at the Spanish Conquest and later: a problem in demography. *Proceedings of the Royal Anthropological Institute of Britain and Ireland*, 97: 23–37.

————, 1977 (original 1940). Archaeological problems of the Lowland Maya. In *The Maya and their Neighbors*, eds C. L. Hay, R. Linton, S. K. Lothrop, H. L Shapiro, and G. C. Vaillant, 117–125. New York, Dover Publications.

Thompson, Phillip, 1999. *Tekanto, a Maya Town in Colonial Yucatan.* Middle American Research Institute (Publ. 67). New Orleans: Tulane University.

Trigger, Bruce, 1993. *Early Civilizations: Ancient Egypt in Context.* Cairo: American University in Cairo Press.

Turner, Billy L. II, 1983. *Once Beneath the Forest.* Boulder: Westview Press.

————, 1990. The central Maya Lowlands: 300 BC to present. In *Hunger in History*, ed. L.F, Newman, 178–211. Oxford: Basil Blackwell.

von Hagen, Victor Wolfgang, 1947. *Maya Explorer.* Norman: University of Oklahoma Press.

Viel, Rene, 1999. The pectorals of altar Q and Structure 11: An interpretation of the political organization at Copán, Honduras. *Latin American Antiquity* 10 (4): 377–399.

Vogt , Evon, 1983. Ancient and contemporary Maya settlement patterns. In *Prehistoric Settlement Patterns: Essays in Honor of Gordon R. Willey*, eds Evon Vogt and Richard Levanthal, 89–114, Albuquerque: University of New Mexico Press.

Webb, Malcomb, 1973. The Peten Maya decline and state formation. In *The Classic Maya Collapse*, ed. T. Patrick Culbert, 367–391. Albuquerque: University of New Mexico Press.

Webster, David, 1975. Warfare and the origin of the state. *American Antiquity* 40:4: 464–471.

————, 1976. *Defensive Earthworks at Becán, Campeche, Mexico: Implications for Maya Warfare.* Middle American Research Institute (Publ. 41). Tulane: New Orleans.

————, 1977. Warfare and the evolution of Maya civilization. In *The Origins of Maya Civilization*, ed. R. E. W. Adams, 335–372. Albuquerque: University of New Mexico Press.

————, 2000. The not so peaceful civilization: A review of Maya war. *Journal of World Prehistory* 14 (1): 65–117.

Webster, David, and Jennifer Kirker, 1995. Too many Maya, too few buildings: investigating construction potential at Copan, Honduras. *Journal of Anthropological Research* 51: 363–387.

Webster, David, Barbara Fash, Randolph Widmer, and Scott Zeleznik, 1998. The Skyband Group: excavations of a Classic Maya elite residential complex at Copan, Honduras. *Journal of Field Archaeology* 25 (3): 319–344.

Webster, David, AnnCorinne Freter, and Nancy Gonlin, 2000. *Copan: The Rise and Fall of an Ancient Maya Kingdom.* Fort Worth: Harcourt Brace.

Webster, David, AnnCorinne Freter, and Rebecca Storey, in press. Dating the Maya collapse at Copan. In *The Maya Terminal Classic Period*, eds D. S. Rice, P. Rice, and A. Demarest. Boulder: Westview Press.

Webster, David, William T. Sanders, and Peter van Rossum, 1992. A simulation of Copán population history and its implications. *Ancient Mesoamerica* 3 (1): 185–197.

Whittington, Stephen, 1989. *Characteristics of Demography and Disease in Low-Status Maya from Classic Period Copán, Honduras.* Ph.D. dissertation, Department of Anthropology, The Pennsylvania State University. University Park.

————, 1999. Caries and antemortem tooth loss at Copan. In *Reconstructing Ancient Maya Diet*, ed. C. White, 157–170. Salt Lake City: University of Utah Press.

Wilk, Richard, 1983. The ancient Maya and the political present. *Journal of Anthropological Research* 41 (3): 307–326.

Willey, Gordon R, 1956. The structure of ancient Mayan society: evidence from the southern Lowlands. *American Anthropologist* 58: 777–782.

————, 1974. The Classic Maya hiatus: a rehearsal for the collapse? In *Mesoamerican Archaeology: New Approaches*, ed. N. Hammond, 417–444. Austin: University of Texas Press.

Willey, Gordon R., and Demitri B. Shimkin, 1973. The Maya collapse: a summary view. In *The Classic Maya Collapse*, ed. T. P. Culbert, 457–502. Albuquerque: University of New Mexico Press.

Wingard, John, 1996. Interactions between demographic processes and soil resources in the Copan Valley, Honduras. In *The Managed Mosaic*, ed. S. Fedick, 207–235. Salt Lake City: University of Utah Press.

Wolf, Eric, 1966. *Peasants.* New York: Prentice Hall Inc.

Wood, James W,. 1998. A theory of preindustrial population dynamics. *Current Anthropology* 391: 99–135.

Yoffee, Norman, and Cowgill, George (eds), 1988. *The Collapse of Ancient States and Civilizations.* Tucson: University of Arizona Press.

ACKNOWLEDGMENTS

I have benefited from the advice of my colleagues Michael Coe, Hector Escobedo, Susan Evans, Norman Hammond, Steve Houston, Heather Hurst, John J. Ewel, Takeshi Inomata, Matthew Restall, Simon Martin, Don Rice, William Sanders, Gair Tourtellot, James Wood, and from the encouragement and expertise of my Thames and Hudson editors and staff. Steve Houston in particular will recognize many nuggets, acknowledged and otherwise, that I mined from our frequent conversations about all things Maya. Simon Martin supplied me with several of the most current glyphic spellings and their possible meanings. Generous support for my own research has come from the National Science Foundation, the National Endowment for the Humanities, the National Oceanic and Atmospheric Association, the National Geographic Society, the Foundation for the Advancement of Mesoamerican Studies Inc., the Annenberg/CPB Corporation, the National Endowment for the Humanities, the Heintz Family Foundation, the Pennsylvania State University, and Brigham Young University.

PICTURE CREDITS

TEXT FIGURES: 1 Reprinted with permission of the Instituto Hondureno de Antropologia e Historia. Original drawing by Ann Dowd. 2 Drawing by Philip Winton. 3 Courtesy of the Copan Archaeological Project Phase 2. Original drawing by Barbara Fash. 4 Courtesy of Hasso Hohmann and Annegrette Vogrin. 5 Courtesy of Hasso Hohmann and Annegrette Vogrin. 6 Map of Piedras Negras, Guatemala, updated by Zachary Nelson from an original 1930s map made by archaeologists at the University of Pennsylvania. Courtesy of Stephen Houston and Hector Escobedo. 7 Copyright Merle Greene Robertson, reproduced with permission. 8 Drawing by Philip Winton. After Fig. 15 in 'Systematic Comparison and Reconstruction,' by Robert Longacre, in *Handbook of Middle American Indians* (1967), vol. 5, Norman McQuown, ed., University of Texas Press, Austin. 9 Courtesy of Stephen Houston, John Robertson, David Stuart, and the University of Chicago Press. Copyright 2000 by The Wenner-Gren Foundation for Anthropological Research. All rights reserved. 10 From D. Charnay, *Les anciens villes du Nouveau Monde* (Paris, 1885), p. 427. 11 Reprinted courtesy of Taylor and Francis, Inc. Modified from J. Parry and R. Keith, eds, *New Iberian World*, vol. 3, Plate 46 (1984). 12 Drawing by Philip Winton. After Fig. 1 in Ralph Roys (1965) 'Lowland Maya Native Society at Spanish Contact,' *Handbook of Middle American Indians* vol. 3:2: 660. 13 From *The New Archaeology and the Ancient Maya.* Copyright 1990 by Jeremy A. Sabloff. Reprinted by permission of Henry Holt and Co., LLC. 14 Adapted from Fig. 5 in *Mayapan, Yucatan, Mexico*, by H. E. D. Pollock, Ralph Roys, T. Proskouriakoff, and A. Ledyard Smith (1966). Carnegie Institution of Washington Pub. 619, Washington, p. 289. 15 Courtesy of Dover Publications Inc. 16 Alfred M. Tozzer, ed., Landa's *Relación de las Cosas de Yucatan: A Translation*, Papers of the Peabody Museum of American Archaeology and Ethnology, Harvard University, vol. 18, 1941. Reprinted courtesy of the Peabody Museum, Harvard University. 17 Adapted from Map 5, p. 17, in Grant D. Jones *The Conquest of the Last Maya Kingdom* (1998). Copyright © 1999 by the Board of Trustees of the Leland Stanford Jr. University. 18 Drawing by David Webster. 19 Courtesy of Takeshi Inomata. Reprinted with the permission of Cambridge University Press. 20 Drawing by David Webster. 21 Courtesy of Heather Hurst. 22–23 Drawing by David Webster. 24 Courtesy of the University of Pennsylvania Museum. 25 Drawing H. Stanley Loten, University of Pennsylvania Museum (neg. number Tikal 98-5-1). 26 Courtesy of Hasso Hohmann and Annegrette Vogrin. 27 John Montgomery. 28 Courtesy of Joyce Marcus and the School of American Research Press. Original drawing by John Klausmeyer. 29 Alfred M. Tozzer, ed., Landa's *Relación de las Cosas de Yucatan: A Translation*, Papers of the Peabody Museum of American Archaeology and Ethnology, Harvard University, vol. 18, 1941. Reprinted courtesy of the Peabody Museum, Harvard University, Fig. 17. 30 Drawing by Philip Winton. After Fig. 1, p. 64, in Sylvanus G. Morley (1946) *The Ancient Maya*, Stanford University Press, Stanford. 31 Drawing by Philip Winton. After a map by David Webster. 32 Courtesy of Labyrinthos Publications, Lancaster, CA. 33 After Morley and Brainerd. 34 Copyright Yale University Press. From George Kubler (1962) *The Art and Architecture of Ancient America.* Penguin Books, Baltimore, Fig. 70, p. 203 (adapted by Kubler from an original drawing by Jean Charlot). 35 Drawing by Philip Winton. After Fig. 2, p. 271, in Raymond Sidrys and Rainer Berger (1979). 'Lowland Maya Radiocarbon Dates and the Classic Maya Collapse.' *Nature* 277:25: 269-277. 36 Drawing by Philip Winton. After Fig. 1, p. 270, in Raymond Sidrys and Rainer Berger (1979). 'Lowland Maya Radiocarbon Dates and the Classic Maya Collapse.' *Nature* 277:25: 269-277. 37 Redrawn by David Webster from an original drawing by David Stuart. 38 Courtesy of Ian Graham. 39 Courtesy of the School of American Research and University of Utah Press. From the Florentine Codex, by Fray Bernardino Sahagun 1975 (vol. 12). Translated and annotated by Arthur J. O. Anderson and Charles Dibble. School of American Research and University of Utah. 40 Courtesy of Don S. Rice. 41 Drawing by Philip Winton. 42–43 *Proyecto Petexbatun*, courtesy of A. A. Demarest. 44 Courtesy of Takeshi Inomata. Reprinted with the permission of Cambridge University Press. 45 Drawing by David Webster. 46 Courtesy of Norman Hammond and Gair Tourtellot. 47 Modified from an original map by AnnCorinne Freter. 48 Modified by Zachary Nelson from an original map provided by Hasso Hohmann and Annegrette Vogrin.

49 Courtesy Copan Archaeological Project, Phase 2. **50** Courtesy of Hasso Hohmann and Annegrette Vogrin. **51** Drawing by Philip Winton. Courtesy of Elliot Abrams. **52** Drawing by Philip Winton. After an original graph by Timothy Murtha from information provided by David Webster. **53** Adapted from an original drawing by Randolph Widmer. **54** Drawing by David Webster. **55** Diagram by David Webster.

PLATES: **1–2** Photos David Drew. **3** Tatiana Proskouriakoff. **4–10** Photos David Webster. **11** Photo Nicholas Hellmuth, courtesy of the Foundation for Latin American Research (FLAAR). **12** Photo David Webster. **13** University of Pennsylvania Museum (neg. number Tikal 74-4-192). **14** University of Pennsylvania Museum (neg. number Tikal 63-4-1536). **15** Photo David Drew. **16** Photo Irmgard Groth-Kimball, © Thames & Hudson Ltd. **17** Photo David Drew. **18** Photo by Linda Schele, © David Schele. **19** Photo David Drew. **20** Photo Stephen Houston. **21** Doug Stern/NGS Image Collection. **22–23** Photos © Justin Kerr. **24** Courtesy of the Middle American Research Institute and the National Geographic Society. Original photograph by Richard Stewart. **25** Courtesy of the Middle American Research Institute. **26–27** Photos Massimo Borchi/White Star. **28** Photo Mary Miller. **29** Photo Jeremy A. Sabloff.

INDEX

Numerals in *italics* refer to text illustration numbers; numerals in **bold** refer to plate numbers